The Political Economy of Health

Lesley Doyal with Imogen Pennell

Pluto Press

Third impression 1983
First published 1979 by Pluto Press Limited,
The Works, 105a Torriano Avenue, London NW5 2RX

ISBN 0 86104 074 0 paperback

Cover illustration: Peter Kennard
Cover design: Marsha Austin

Typeset by Red Lion Setters, London WC1
Printed in Great Britain by
Garden City Press, Letchworth, Herts

Contents

Acknowledgements

There are two people without whose help this book would not have been written at all. Len Doyal kept faith with the project throughout. He gave me confidence to do it in the first place, bullied me into continuing and helped me to finish it, while often doing more than his fair share of domestic labour. Imogen Pennell was initially employed on the project as a research worker at the Polytechnic of North London, but her contribution both to the research and the writing of the book far exceeded what could possibly have been expected. She made a major contribution to the final outcome both in intellectual terms and as a friend.

Throughout the writing, both Imogen and I benefited greatly from the ideas and the support of the Politics of Health Group. We would like to thank in particular the 'Sunday Night Group' - Gill Yudkin, John Yudkin, Angus Nicholl, Mike Joffe, Aubrey Sheiham, Anne Livesey and Tim Lobstein, both for reading and improving the entire manuscript but also for their love and support. Other people who read the manuscript and made valuable suggestions include Geoff Hunt, Ralf Munster, Alex Kay and Richard Kuper, the latter giving continued advice and help even when he must have wondered whether he would ever have a final manuscript to publish! I also need to thank the people who gave me hospitality and looked after me during the worst parts of the writing process - Mike Caddis, Charlotte Weightman, Cathy Waldon, Mike Waldon, and my mother Edna Coates. Madeleine Carter looked after Hannah Lee Doyal so well that not a hint of maternal deprivation could be detected! Jenni Southgate helped in the same and other ways. Julie Phillips and Freddi Cooke typed the final product magnificently while at the same time making their own contribution to improving the final text. My son Daniel Wilsher was an unfailing source of support in every way and I want him to know how much I appreciate it.

Finally, and very sadly, I have to acknowledge the contribution of someone who helped me a great deal, often in ways that she did not even realise. Lin Layram read the manuscript and discussed it with me at a time of great stress in her life. But more fundamentally perhaps, her ceaseless fight against cancer, her struggle to survive, to understand what was happening to her body, and above all her attempts to communicate with and to help others suffering in the same way, were a major source of inspiration. They were a constant reminder that *The Political Economy of Health* was not merely a theoretical exercise but rather about some of the fundamental aspects of people's lives - their health and illness, their suffering and their dying. I am immensely sad that she didn't live to see the book completed but I hope that it will make a contribution towards creating the new society she dreamed of and worked for.

Lesley Doyal
London May 1979

Part One:
Theoretical Foundations

1: Understanding Medicine and Health

It is often said that medicine is going through a period of crisis. The cost of medical care is rising rapidly in both the developed and underdeveloped parts of the world, while the effectiveness of that expenditure is increasingly being questioned. In underdeveloped countries, mortality rates remain extremely high, while in the developed world medicine has made little impact on those diseases which people fear most - cancer and heart disease for example. In the USA - the richest country in the world - even the relatively affluent are now concerned about their ability to pay for medical care, while the poor have always been acutely aware of the gross deficiencies in the medical facilities available to them. In Britain, the chronic underfinancing of the National Health Service (NHS) has been exacerbated by expenditure cuts since the early 1970s and, as a consequence, both the quality and the efficiency of the medical care it provides are becoming matters of major public concern. In many countries in the developed world, women are beginning to criticise the sexist attitudes which they experience as patients, while most health workers are becoming increasingly dissatisfied with their conditions of work and levels of pay.

Interpretations of this crisis vary widely. It is blamed on greedy doctors, on the development of too much medical technology, on the decline in individual initiative which is said to be produced by state intervention, or, conversely, on the failure of particular governments to provide adequate resources to pay for a proper system of medical care. All of these are simplistic interpretations of what is, in reality, a very complex problem, and one which is deeply rooted in the nature of capitalism as an economic and social system. A critical analysis both of the social determinants of health and illness and of the role of medicine in society is now emerging, but is as yet in its early stages. What follows is an attempt to set out some of the major aspects of this newly-developing critical awareness in such a way that it can be used and improved in the struggle to create a healthier society.

Medicine and society: the orthodox view

A close examination of contemporary debates about the current crisis in health care reveals that most of the participants share three central - but problematic - assumptions about medicine and health. First, it is assumed that the determinants of health and illness are predominantly biological, so that patterns of morbidity and mortality have little to do with the social and economic environment in which they occur. As a consequence, the solution to current health problems is seen to lie almost entirely within the framework set down by modern medicine, and broader ideas of social changes are seen as largely irrelevant. Secondly, medicine is assumed to be a science. The way medicine is presented, and society's acceptance of its claim to authority and resources, rest to a considerable extent on its definition of itself as a natural science. Thus, it is assumed that it is possible to separate the doctor from his/her subject matter (the patient) in much the same way as a natural scientist is assumed to be separate from his/her subject matter (the natural world), and medical progress is said to be based on the use of 'scientific method' which supposedly ensures certain and objective knowledge. Hence, it is usually believed that medicine, because it is 'scientific', can produce an unchallengeable and autonomous body of knowledge which is not tainted by wider social and economic considerations. Finally, underlying this common view of health care is a particular view of the relationship between medicine, health and society; namely the belief that scientific medicine provides the only viable means for mediating between people and disease. Medicine is seen as by definition *good* - the only problem being that there is not enough of it to go round, and discussion therefore centres around how this body of scientific knowledge and technical skills can best be dispensed. Even though disagreements will occur over specific questions of resource allocation, there is a common belief that the problem of providing effective health care for all, like the problem of poverty, can ultimately be resolved through the normal processes of parliamentary democracy and pressure group politics. This assumption is, of course, dependent on a broader conception of the nature of capitalism - specifically on a belief in its capacity to solve social problems through economic growth.[1]

This orthodox view of medical care reaches its most sophisticated form in two academic approaches to the study of medicine - social administration and the sociology of medicine. *Social policy* or *social administration* emerged in Britain in the late nineteenth and early twentieth centuries as part of Fabian socialism, and has since developed as an academic discipline in its own right. It is usually distinguished from other approaches on the basis of what has been called its 'problem orientation' and also by its willingness to use insights from any discipline on a relatively ad hoc basis in order to solve particular technical problems. The problems to which the practitioners of social administration address themselves are usually connected with the functioning or malfunctioning of the welfare state - the vast expansion of social policy courses, after the creation of the British welfare state in the 1940s, is a clear reflection of the symbiotic relationship between the two.

> The academic study of social administration mirrors the political ideology of social democracy and welfare; thus the theory of welfare that predominates in British social science is one that reflects almost exactly the ideology behind the setting up of the 'welfare state'.
>
> In many cases the professors of social administration played distinct roles in the actual creation and implementation of social policy itself; creating an organic link between state policy and the study of that policy.[2]

In general, proponents of the social administration approach take the view that there are going to be certain tasks which need to be carried out in advanced industrialised societies ('capitalism' is rarely mentioned) which cannot be left to the market - education for example - and that the state must therefore step in and perform such tasks. Social administrators also accept that there will be certain casualties of the system (e.g. the sick or the unemployed) and that they must be cared for. As a consequence, they see welfare institutions as compensating for the limitations (and sometimes the excesses) of the market mechanism and as basically 'integrative' - holding society together.[3] So far as health care in particular is concerned, the scientific nature of medicine is taken as given, as is its commitment to curing the sick and relieving the sufferings of the incurable. That is to say, the definition of medicine provided by the medical profession is accepted uncritically. The basic mode of analysis is an empirical one, concerned only to a limited extent with the problem of how to minimise environmental threats to health, and to a much greater extent with the problem of how to provide people with more medical care, within the limits of an 'acceptable' level of public expenditure. Thus questions are typically posed in terms such as 'what share of the national cake can go on medical care, and what proportion of *that* should be spent on the old as opposed to the mentally ill?'

This social policy approach can contribute to the development of a more critical understanding of health and medicine, through the statistical data which it generates. Information concerning class differences in health and illness, the differential utilisation of medical facilities by different social groups, and regional and class inequalities in expenditure on medical care are all important in building up a picture of the characteristics of health, illness and medicine under capitalism. However, such data are only of limited value. The fundamental problem with this type of analysis lies in its failure to consider in any depth the nature of medical practice or the broader role of medicine in society. As a result of this failure, it ends up accepting a particular view of society and reinforcing widely-held beliefs about the role of medicine within that society.

While the social administration approach takes the role of the medical care system for granted, the sociology of medicine has traditionally looked more broadly at the social functions of medicine. That is, it has accepted (usually without question) the scientific and curative aspects of medicine, but has looked beyond these to the sociological content of medical practice. Thus, sociologists of medicine have not, in general, been concerned with the practical questions of resource allocation. They have dealt rather with issues

such as the social content of medical situations - doctor/patient interaction for example, or the nature of what they term 'patient-
careers'. Most of this work has been interactionist in its approach.
That is, it has concentrated on the immediate social relationships
between individuals and groups in the medical context. As a result,
sociologists of medicine have paid relatively little attention to the
political and economic structure of the medical care system, or to its
relationship with the wider society.[4] For example, a great deal of
American research in this field has attempted to discover why people
in minority groups (e.g. the poor, the blacks) do not use the services
of doctors more. The answer has usually been sought in the fecklessness of these individuals and their 'culture of poverty' rather than in
the high cost of private medicine or the stigmatising and repressive
characteristics of the charity sector. Analyses of this kind tend inevitably to portray hospitals and doctors' surgeries as though they existed
in a vacuum, with doctors and patients acting out their predeter-
mined roles, unaffected by the material and social world in which
they are living and dying.

The central theoretical formulation which has provided the
basis for much work in the sociology of medicine (especially in the
USA) was developed by Talcott Parsons.[5] Parsons elaborated the
concept of the 'sick role' which both described and prescribed the
appropriate behaviour for an individual who had 'chosen' to be ill.
According to Parsons, people occupying the sick role are not held
responsible for their incapacity and are exempted from their usual
obligations. However, in return, they must *want* to leave the sick role
and get well, and are thus obliged to seek and to comply with
appropriate medical advice. A failure to behave in accordance with
these conditions may result in the removal of the right to be thought
sick. Parsons recognised the potential danger for society in the existence of a sick role (especially in relation to psychiatric illness).[6] It is
one form of deviance which individuals can 'choose' if they do not
wish to fulfil what Parsons would regard as their appropriate role
obligations. He is aware of the possible threat afforded by such
actions - particularly if sick people, relieved of their normal duties,
get together - and therefore emphasises the importance of *controlling* the sick. He sees this control being achieved both through an

emphasis on the duty owed by patients to relatives and friends to get better, and through the maintenance of the authority of doctors over their patients.

Parsons is clearly aware, therefore, of one of the broader functions of medicine - that of social control - and this is an important insight which is a major part of any critical analysis of the real nature and practice of contemporary medicine. However, his own understanding must be located within the context of his broader theoretical position of sociological functionalism.[7] For Parsons, capitalist societies are basically stable and progressive, but he is nevertheless aware that they are likely to produce stresses, strains and frustrations, some of which will be physical and some psychological. However he is less concerned with how these are produced than with how they can be prevented from disrupting the social system. It is here that he sees the sick role as so important, stating approvingly that 'the sick role not only isolates and insulates, it also exposes the deviant to reintegrative forces'.[8] The scientific, curative activities of medicine are therefore accepted, indeed taken for granted, but medicine is given an added function as an agency of socialisation and social control - a function of which Parsons entirely approves.

Thus while the social policy/technical approach has provided empirical data on, for example, class differences in the utilisation of medical care or in sickness rates, it cannot, because of its atheoretical and ahistorical methodology, provide adequate explanations of the creation and sustaining of such differences. Orthodox sociology of medicine, on the other hand, within a functionalist framework, makes certain theoretical statements about the social as opposed to the purely biological role of medicine. But again, it does so ahistorically, and within a theoretical context which accepts the status quo and is hostile to the development of a radical critique of medical science. It is clear then, that because of its commitment to a particular mode of analysis, most orthodox social science does not define the nature of medical knowledge as problematic and pays little attention to wider issues concerning the nature of medical practice in contemporary capitalist society. It is these issues which will be discussed in the final section of this chapter, and which form the basis for the theoretical framework of the rest of the book.

Before turning to these, however, it is necessary to look at another analysis which is represented as a systematic critique of the nature and practice of modern medicine - that presented by Ivan Illich.[9]

Medical nemesis

Illich's analysis of contemporary medicine must be seen as an important advance on those of social policy and the sociology of medicine, in that he is concerned with both the nature and the content of medical practice. He does not simply take medical science and its mode of delivery as given, but attempts a critical evaluation of its real effects on morbidity and mortality. More than this, Illich is concerned with the broader significance of medical practice, and he examines in some detail its effects on individuals' perceptions of themselves and on their potential to control their own lives (and deaths). His analysis centres around three categories of pathology or iatrogenesis (damage caused by the medical system) which he observes in modern industrialised societies. These he calls 'clinical iatrogenesis' (the physical damage caused by doctors in their attempts to cure people), 'social iatrogenesis' (the addiction of people to medical care as a solution to all their problems), and 'structural iatrogenesis' (the destruction of the patient's autonomy, along with the expropriation of her/his responsibility for individual health care).

In describing these aspects of contemporary medicine, Illich is one of a growing body of critics who argue that many modern medical techniques are not just ineffective but often physically harmful.[10] Indeed, he himself takes the view that on balance medicine does more harm than good, and suggests that 'the impact of medicine constitutes one of the most rapidly expanding epidemics of our time'. In his description of the way doctors are increasing their control over people's lives and depriving them of their autonomy in both physical and psychological ways, Illich is again echoing more general critiques of contemporary medicine.[11] The 'medicalisation of life' - the bringing of more and more aspects of daily life into the medical sphere of influence - is a process which has attracted much critical comment in recent years, and the account provided by Illich of social and structural iatrogenesis has been an extremely perceptive and illuminating contribution to that debate. Nevertheless, when Illich begins to discuss solutions to the problems he has described the more fundamental ideas underlying his analysis are revealed and the ultimately unsatisfactory nature of his argument becomes clear.

Before proposing his own solution, Illich documents in some detail the inadequacies of what he calls 'radical' health policies or 'futile political counter-measures'. Consumer control over the medical profession and its activities will, he says, always fail both because the professional monopoly is so strong and also because the worth or value of medical care cannot be assessed in any rational way. He also rejects attempts to obtain a more egalitarian distribution of medical care on the grounds that health is largely determined by factors other than medicine, but more importantly because medicine itself actually damages health.

> Extra therapy of the kind now offered adds to the total negative impact which a poor environment has on the health of the poor. Less access to the present health system would, contrary to popular rhetoric, *benefit* the poor.[12] (emphasis added)

Finally, he rejects a more environmental approach to medicine. He sees this 'engineering for a plastic womb' as potentially leading to an even greater extension of the boundaries of medicine - to what he describes as 'total treatment'. Thus, although Illich clearly recognises the importance of the environmental determinants of ill health, he refuses to accept the legitimacy of 'environmental hygienic engineering' which he sees as just another means for appropriating individual autonomy.[13]

Having rejected all the current proposals for reforming the medical care system, what does Illich himself propose? His solution emerges from his view that it is the medical bureaucracies and industrialised medicine which form the major obstacles to a healthy society. Hence it is modern medicine as such which should be destroyed so that health care could be removed from doctors and reappropriated by the people themselves. For Illich this would necessarily be accompanied by a de-bureaucratisation and de-industrialisation of society in general and he suggests that medicine is particularly strategic in the struggle to move from an industrialised to what he calls an 'autonomous' mode of production.

> . . . since medicine is a sacred cow, its slaughter would have a 'vibration effect' because people who can face suffering and death without need for magicians and mystagogues are free to rebel against other forms of expropriation now practised by teachers, engineers, lawyers, priests and party officials. [14]

There are at least three problems with this analysis.[15] First, Illich's concern to demonstrate the *negative* effects of modern medicine (adverse drug reactions, unnecessary surgery, etc.), while an important antidote to the exaggerated claims of medical science, means that he entirely ignores its positive aspects. Thus, he measures these negative effects against the rate of cure and decides that on balance he would be better off without medicine. In so doing, he is not taking into account the important role of medicine in caring for the sick and in symptom relief. More importantly, rather than attempting any analysis of what is genuinely valuable in technological medicine and what is not, he argues that it should disappear entirely. This wholesale rejection follows from his view that the basic characteristic of the societies which he is discussing is that they are industrial rather than capitalist.

Illich assumes that in any industrialised society, all institutions (including medicine) must be organised on an authoritarian, bureaucratic and hierarchical basis. Hence he sees the only solution as lying in the de-industrialisation of society. He sees all bureaucracies as manipulating individuals for their own advantage and, therefore, demands their removal. Certainly there are problems inherent in bureaucracy as a mode of organisation, but the functioning of bureaucracies basically reflects the nature of the society within which they have been created. Hence, the functions of modern medical organisations and the mode of production of health care are to a very large extent determined outside the health sector. In large part they are a reflection of the need of a capitalist system to sustain a particular set of social and economic relationships within the spheres of production and consumption; and the disappearance of a particular system of medical care would not change this.

Finally, because Illich places all his explanatory emphasis on the fact that modern societies are industrialised, he avoids any examination of the economic and political determinants of particular cases of industrialisation. Hence he gives us no means of distinguishing between capitalist forms of industrialisation and other forms, and makes it difficult to compare processes of industrialisation in the developed and underdeveloped areas of the world. More specifically, he assumes that technological (or industrialised) medicine could only take the form which it has taken in the developed capitalist world, and does not examine the structural tendencies which have pushed it in a particular direction. As a consequence Illich assumes an anti-technology stance, and rejects modern medicine entirely.

Following from the basic tenets of his analysis, Illich emphasises cultural rather than socio-economic change in bringing about the de-industrialisation which he recommends. He talks of regaining autonomy, but this autonomy is discussed in a social and economic vacuum. He believes in individuals *choosing* to change their life-styles and to reject manipulative bureaucracies, but offers little guidance as to how this commitment to change is likely to come about. Nevertheless, certain of his ideas - and his 'life-style' politics in particular - have proved extremely attractive to those who recognise the need for certain changes in medicine (or any other institution) but who reject more radical change in society as a whole. As we shall see, however, there are serious structural obstacles to the achievement of any basic changes in the health sector alone. Moreover, any explanation of the nature of these obstacles is linked theoretically to the nature of capitalism and not just to the process of industrialisation, and it is the reasons behind this which we must now examine.

Towards a marxist analysis

In recent years science and technology have begun to come under critical scrutiny.

> The dominant faith in the automatically progressive character
> of scientific work has diminished in many sectors of society, and

even partly within the scientific community, since the 1960s, giving way to a growing scepticism concerning the liberatory power of science and the very worth of scientific knowledge itself. This situation is related to the pessimism over the possibility of redirecting towards human ends the enormous growth in productive forces that has emerged with the so-called scientific and technological revolution, and to the identification - empirically justifiable - of the roots of this development in the increasing integration of science and technology into the productive structure of mature capitalism.[16]

As a consequence various radical critiques have been developed of the theory and practice of contemporary science and technology. All share a common viewpoint in that they reject the commonsense view of science as neutral and value-free, and ultimately of benefit to all.

Within this radical critique there are however, at least two alternative interpretations of the ultimate potential of science and technology. One rejects scientific rationality and its associated technology entirely, espousing instead, a form of anti-scientific pessimism. The obvious ills of industrialised societies are then blamed on science and technology themselves, rather than on the economic and social forces shaping scientific and technological developments. As we have seen, Illich's views on medicine can be located within this broad perspective. On the other hand, the traditional marxist view distinguishes very clearly between science and ideology. According to this conception, our aim must be to move towards 'natural' and uncontaminated science, even if this can ultimately be realised only under socialism.[17] In recent years however, it has become more widely accepted that a critical understanding of contemporary science (and therefore of medicine as well) must reject both of these positions. Rather, it must attempt a more specific understanding of the links between science as a form of human activity and the particular characteristics of the society within which it is produced. Hence the attempt to move beyond 'the impasse between the anti-scientific pessimism of irrationalism and the naive optimism of abstract rationalism'[18] must involve an understanding of the complex interrelationships between science and society at several different levels.

First, it must be concerned with a detailed analysis of the actual content of the knowledge base of science, including its underlying world views, its substantive theories, their explanatory power and their related technologies. Second, it must analyse the social practice of a given science, examining questions such as who has access to the knowledge base and on what terms; the nature of the division of labour in the production and utilisation of science and technology; how research is funded and on what criteria and how technology is used and in whose interests. Third, it is important to relate both the theory and practice of science more broadly to the social formation within which it is produced. Here it is necessary to look at the direct and indirect role of science and technology in the process of capital accumulation as well as the transformation of scientific knowledge into a commodity. At the same time, it is equally relevant to examine the complex role played by science in generating ideology and in social control. Only through analysis of this kind is it possible to perceive the ways in which the social role of what we call science might be transformed if it were produced within the context of an alternative set of social goals and social and economic relationships. This applies as much to medicine as it does to other areas of science and technology.

It is evident that patterns of health and illness vary greatly between different societies, as do the processes devised for caring for the sick. It is also clear that we can learn a great deal about a particular society or a particular mode of social and economic organisation through examining the patterns of health and illness and the type of medical care that they have characteristically produced. Hence the central theme of this book will be an examination of the specific forms of the social production of health and illness and the social organisation of medical care under capitalism, both in the developed industrial centres and in the underdeveloped parts of the world.

Health, illness and capitalism

The first question we need to consider is the relationship between the biological and the social, between health, illness and society. Most discussions of medical care have, until recently, taken ill health for granted, and have rarely questioned its social or economic origins. While people are now coming increasingly to accept that social and economic factors do have some importance in causing ill health, they argue that this has nothing to do with capitalism. Rather, it is assumed that it is industrialisation itself which tends to destroy health, and hence that there is nothing much we can do about it. Thus, poor health for some is seen as a necessary consequence of economic growth, which is itself assumed to be a desirable goal for everyone. It is certainly possible to argue (probably correctly) that the advantages to be gained from industrial production must always involve, to a greater or lesser extent, the destruction of human and physical resources. Yet the nature and extent of that destruction will reflect the priorities of the society in which the production takes place. Thus if, as we shall argue, it is ultimately profit, rather than a concern to improve overall living standards, which is the most important determinant of economic and social decision-making in capitalist society, this will be reflected in various ways in patterns of health and illness.

While the development of capitalism may have facilitated an improvement in the general health of the population (as measured, for example, in life-expectancy rates), the health needs of the mass of the population continue to come into frequent conflict with the requirements of continued capital accumulation. This produces contradictions which are ultimately reflected in historical changes in patterns of morbidity and mortality. In contrast, while we cannot specify in advance a utopian blueprint for a socialist health policy, we can assume that under socialism profit would no longer be the criterion for making decisions about production or consumption. Very different goods could then be manufactured, possibly using alternative technologies, with labour organised in less damaging ways, and income more equally distributed. While it would be absurd to suggest that all disease would be abolished under socialism, we can assume that a real concern for the health of the population would be reflected in planning and decision making. Thus, through analysing the social production of health and illness in capitalist countries we can learn more about the nature of capitalism itself, as well as becoming aware of what needs to be avoided in future if a 'healthier' society is to be created.

Of course, not all aspects of capitalist development have been equally harmful - a fact which is often forgotten. Indeed, the development of the forces of production made possible by industrial capitalism has formed the basis for a tremendous improvement in average life expectancy for people in the developed world. After the initial period of industrialisation, the level of subsistence rose dramatically, with better food, clothing and housing for the working class, as well as a gradual decline in the length of the working day. All these developments have been important in improving general standards of health - although class differences still remain. However, as we will argue in later chapters, that same process of the development of the forces of production had at least two other dimensions to it. First, it was ultimately dependent on a particular mode of economic and social exploitation of the underdeveloped world, which was damaging to the health of third world populations. Secondly, while it removed certain threats to health in the developed world, the development of industrial capitalism itself created *new* health problems, many of which are only now becoming apparent. Thus the relationship between capitalist development and health has been a contradictory one, as we shall see in what follows.

It is a commonplace of left wing rhetoric that 'capitalism causes disease', but a generalised statement of this kind, uniformly applied to all ill health in all places and at all times has very little theoretical or political content. We are not helped in our attempt to understand the varieties and circumstances of ill health under capitalism by being told that all people in capitalist societies are 'sick'. Enzensberger has rightly criticised this tendency towards empty moralising in his discussion of the predominant marxist response to current ecological debates: it is equally applicable in the case of the social production of ill health.

> It is naturally splendid that anticapitalist sentiments are so widespread, that even glossy magazines cannot avoid them altogether. But it is quite another question how far an analysis deserves to be called marxist, which a priori attributes every conceivable problem to capitalism, and what the political effect of this is. Its commonplace nature renders it harmless.

Capitalism, so frequently denounced becomes a kind of social ether, omnipresent and intangible, a quasi-natural cause of ruin and destruction, the exorcising of which can have a positively neutralising effect. Since the concrete problem in hand - psychosis, lack of nursery schools, dying rivers, air crashes - can without precise analysis of the exact causes be referred to the total situation, the impression is given that any specific intervention here and now is pointless. In the same way, reference to the need for revolution becomes an empty formula, the ideological husk of passivity.[19]

In the light of such comments, it is obviously important that we examine more concretely some of the ways in which the operation of a capitalist system creates contradictions between health and profit.

First, the physical processes of commodity production itself will affect health in a variety of ways. Clearly the imperatives of capital accumulation condition the nature of the labour process, and the need for shiftwork, de-skilling, overtime or the use of dangerous chemicals, will all be reflected in the health or ill health of workers. They may suffer directly, either through industrial injuries and diseases, or in more diffuse ways with stress-related ill health, or psychosomatic problems. Yet commodity production also has more *indirect* effects on health, and the physical effects of the production process extend beyond the workplace itself. Damage to the surrounding environment and pollution of various kinds are often the by-products of industrialised production. Finally, commodity production may damage health through the nature of the commodities themselves. Capitalist production is concerned with exchange values and, as a result, concern about the quality of a product (including its effects on health) will usually arise only in the context of an assessment of its selling potential. If it will sell, then its effects on health are likely to be of little concern to the producer, so that many health-damaging products will continue to be made simply because they are profitable.

But it is also characteristic of capitalist societies that everyone is not equally affected by these illness-producing processes. Class differences in morbidity and mortality are very pronounced. Working-class people die sooner, and generally suffer more ill health than do middle-class people. We therefore need to look at other aspects of capitalist social and economic relations - especially distribution of income and patterns of work and consumption - in order to explain these differences. The most obvious cause of class differences in morbidity and mortality will be the differential health risks of specific occupations. Certain groups of workers (often the lower paid) have more dangerous and unhealthy jobs than others, but these occupational risk factors do not account for all the observed differences in morbidity and mortality. Class differences in infant mortality rates, for example, or the increased rates of morbidity and early mortality among the wives of male manual workers remain unexplained. Some of these differences derive from physical proximity to the production process. Workers 'import' dangers from the workplace into the home, and clearly this will affect working-class families more often. In addition, they are more likely to live near industrial plants and therefore to be more affected by pollution and industrial wastes. But again, this direct or indirect contact with the production process is not enough to explain all class differences in health and illness.

The distribution of ill health in capitalist societies broadly follows the distribution of income. Those with lower incomes tend to have higher rates of morbidity and mortality, for a number of reasons. In a capitalist society income is a major determinant of the standard of housing individuals and families can obtain, of where they live, of their diet, and of their ability to remain warm and well-clothed. All of these factors are significant for health. Moreover, the quality of life (and therefore of health) is increasingly influenced by access to the goods and services provided by the state. Even where these are in principle distributed on a universalistic basis, in practice they are allocated neither equally nor in terms of need. For example, children of unskilled workers are likely to receive an inferior education and therefore to go on to low paid and probably dangerous jobs themselves. Similarly, medical care is not allocated solely on the basis of need. While a more egalitarian allocation of medical resources could not remove inequalities in morbidity and mortality, it is evident that present inequalities in resource allocation serve to reinforce more fundamental class differences in health and illness.

It is, however, in underdeveloped countries that the extremes of ill health and premature death are to be found. Here, the major causes of death are not, as is often assumed, the endemic tropical diseases, but rather infectious diseases and malnutrition. These are not 'natural', but arise in large part from the particular social and economic relationships characteristic of imperialism. The incidence and severity of infectious diseases, for example, are directly related to the misery and squalor of both urban and rural poverty. Similarly, malnutrition does not simply result from too many people and too little food in any particular country. Like urban and rural poverty, it is often a direct result of the exploitative relationship between the metropolitan countries and the underdeveloped world, and the consequent uneven development and allocation of resources.

Ill health cannot, therefore, be attributed simply to capitalism in any crude sense. On the other hand, we cannot make sense of patterns of health and illness outside the context of the mode of production in which they occur. As Eyer and Sterling have said, 'A large component of adult physical pathology and death must be considered neither acts of God nor of our genes, but a measure of the misery caused by our present social and economic organisation.'[20]

The evolution of western scientific medicine

In the developed capitalist world, all aspects of health and illness are seen to fall within the sphere of competence of western scientific medicine. Clearly, both the theory and practice of this medicine are inextricably linked with the society within which it has evolved, and it is these connections which will be examined here.

Most accounts of the development of western medicine reflect the split between theory and practice which has characterised the social scientific approach to medicine. That is, histories of medical thought have been produced in isolation from histories of medical practice. As a consequence, specific theories and discoveries are usually viewed merely as milestones along the path to modern scientific medicine. Karl Figlio has criticised this positivist approach to the history of medicine.

> The concrete record of scientific and medical development
> assumes without question that there are solid facts to discover
> and that the continuous discovery of these facts leads eventu-
> ally to the state of knowledge we have today. But this very
> assumption automatically isolates the endeavour called
> 'scientific' or 'medical' advancement from its social context.
> That is, it neither examines the non-intellectual contingencies
> which mould ideas, nor does it look at the use of scientific or
> medical concepts as cultural, social, religious or ideological
> tools. By their very definition, facts could never carry this kind
> of load. [21]

What follows is an attempt to move away from this positivist
approach, through a brief outline of the development of the theory
and practice of western scientific medicine, placed in its social and
economic context.

It is important to stress, however, that western scientific
medicine represents only one particular medical tradition. While
this is now the dominant mode of mediation between individuals
and ill-health, this has not always been the case. Indeed, it was not
until the twentieth century that most of the population were able to
obtain access to medicine on anything like a regular basis. Hence, in
dealing with the early period of the development of medicine, we are
in fact dealing with something which was relevant to only a minority
of the population. Most healing and care of the sick was undertaken
at this time on an informal or semi-formal basis, often by women. [22]
Their knowledge of healing was based largely on tradition, and
involved the use of empirically-based 'natural' remedies (such as
herbs) as well as religious or supernatural methods - amulets, spells or
prayer for example. The last two centuries have, however, seen the
almost total eclipse of these 'unscientific' methods, and their super-
cession by modern medicine. Healing has become something for
'experts' and it is the development of this medical domination which
will be examined here.

The knowledge base of what we know as western scientific
medicine had its origins in the scientific revolution of the seventeenth century. The natural science which developed during the
Renaissance transformed the Aristotelian view of the world which

had dominated western thought for 1500 years.[23] Increasingly, science was no longer concerned with understanding the essence or teleological purpose of the natural/supernatural world. Rather, the scientist (or natural philosopher as he was called) attempted to discover and explain those regular and recurring sequences of events which could be described and codified in a quantitative and generalisable way. It was believed that this would make possible the utilisation of nature through the making of accurate predictions based on these codified generalisations. In other words, the new science increasingly equated an understanding of the natural world with a capacity to control it - a conception which would come to fruition some two centuries later in the Industrial Revolution. In the case of medicine, the 'new scientists' of the Renaissance began for the first time to map out in detail the internal workings of the human body.[24] Although their activities were limited to this exploration and description, they did provide the basis for the (much later) development of modern technological medicine. These early investigations were largely founded upon a mechanistic view of the nature of men, and of human sickness and health. That is to say, they followed the more general pattern of Renaissance science in analysing living things as sets of mechanical parts - as machines rather than organically integrated wholes. Philosophers like Hobbes and Descartes helped to lay the philosophical and methodological groundwork for this model of human beings. Descartes, for example, argued not only that the human body must be assumed to work in the same way as a machine but also that the mind and the body of a given individual could be separated into two substances - one 'corporeal' or material and the other 'incorporeal' or immaterial.[25] By and large, medicine came to be viewed as concerned only with the former and this mechanistic model remains the basis for medical thought today.[26]

It is important to emphasise that it was this gradual replacement of the Aristotelian paradigm with its belief in the organic unity of living things, which ultimately made possible those aspects of medicine which have been genuinely successful either in preventing or curing disease (e.g. vaccination, antisepsis, anaesthesia or antibiotics) or in providing symptom relief. Indeed, any strategy which merely calls for the abolition of 'mechanistic medicine' must take this point very seriously indeed. At the same time, however, the adoption of a mechanistic paradigm of this kind did limit the nature and boundaries of what is conceived as the medical task. Thus, scientific medicine ultimately became curative, individualistic and interventionist, objectifying patients and denying their status as social beings. Jewson has suggested that we can see scientific medicine as going through three basic stages (which he sees as corresponding to three successive modes of production of medical knowledge) - 'bedside medicine', 'hospital medicine' and 'laboratory medicine'. [27] These stages provide a useful means by which to understand both the development of medical thought and practice and also its relationship to broader social and economic changes.

'Bedside medicine' was dominant in Western Europe from the Middle Ages until the late eighteenth century. It was only available to the relatively wealthy and worked on a patronage system with patients choosing those particular doctors whom they believed could help them the most. [28] During this period, the 'new science' had made almost no impact on medical practice, and the patron/doctor relationship was a very important determinant of the content of medical treatment. What Jewson calls the 'sick man' was still at the centre of medical concern, with the patient being treated as a whole person whose account of his/her symptoms and feelings was of major concern. Medicine was patient centred for two reasons. At a practical level, the doctor had to keep the patient's confidence (and probably liking) or else he was unlikely to be called again. At the more theoretical level, all disease was assumed to be caused by a disturbance in the *balance* of the organism (which included both mind and body). Hence the patient's own account of his/her condition was assumed to be of major diagnostic significance, and all aspects of the patient's life to be of importance in understanding the illness. Although there was much disagreement and controversy over how different bodily processes were to be interpreted, there was a general commitment to the belief that, broadly speaking, disease had one major cause which was related to a disturbance of the total body system. As a result, therapies were usually 'heroic' in their conception since they were intended to bring about a major systemic change.

By the beginning of the nineteenth century, a dramatic change had begun to take place in the medical world view and in medical practice. This was the period of what Jewson has called 'hospital medicine'.[29] The Industrial Revolution and the concomitant process of mass urbanisation had created the unhealthy cities typical of the late eighteenth and early nineteenth centuries. One consequence of this was the establishment throughout Europe of huge hospitals to house the sick.[30] Their creation, and the large number of poor people who entered them, made possible extremely important changes in the nature and content of medical knowledge and in the way medicine was practised. Patients were no longer dominant in the doctor/patient relationship. The doctors themselves were becoming more organised as a profession, and the working-class patients who entered hospitals were inferior in status to the doctors who treated them.[31] As these social relationships changed, the underlying world view of medicine was also being transformed. Patients were no longer individuals with their own particular set of symptoms and problems, but came increasingly to be seen as 'cases' - the disease became more important than the sick person.[32] The continuing Aristotelian flavour which had dominated the theoretical base of individual-centred therapy was not empirically refuted. It simply became irrelevant as the main concern of 'hospital medicine' shifted during this period to diagnosis and classification. It was very important to be able to examine patients and to *decide for them* what they were suffering from, thus assigning them to a particular category, along with other similar cases. Illich has described the significance of this process very well.

> If 'sickness' and 'health' were to lay claim to public resources, then these concepts had to be made operational. Ailments had to be turned into objective diseases. Species had to be clinically defined and verified so that officials could fit them into wards, records, budgets and museums. The object of medical treatment as defined by a new, though submerged, political ideology acquired the status of an entity that existed quite separately from both doctor and patient.[33]

Hospital medicine then, shifted from a belief in disease as a disturbance of the total system to what is called 'localised pathology'.

That is, there was a growing realisation that ill health could be caused by malfunctioning of one particular part of the body. Doctors became concerned to correlate verifiable *external* symptoms (those reported by the patient were of less importance) with those internal malfunctions that they could discover (often on autopsy or after exploratory surgery). As a result, during the early part of the nineteenth century, a variety of instruments were developed to enable the doctor to examine the interior of the patient's body more carefully - the thermometer, the stethoscope, the laryngoscope, and so on. Instead of doctors having to listen to what their social superiors *told* them about their ailments, they were able to probe into the recesses of the bodies of thousands of 'cases' and subject the results they obtained to statistical analysis. It is important to remember however, that this vastly increased sophistication in descriptive anatomy and pathology did not produce a corresponding sophistication in therapy. Very little treatment of any efficacy was available during this period. Indeed, many treatments (particularly surgery) had extremely high fatality rates.[34] Thus the growing social prestige of medicine was in no way matched by its therapeutic effectiveness.

It was during this same period - i.e. the first half of the nineteenth century - that an interest in 'public health' was also developing. Outside the hospitals, the devastating effects of widespread industrialisation and urbanisation were impossible to ignore, and by the 1840s the relationship between disease and urban living and working conditions was becoming widely accepted. It was clear that any significant improvements in health would necessitate a detailed knowledge of the health hazards of the urban environment, and during this period many studies were undertaken of particular urban areas. Investigations of this kind clearly revealed the environmental causes of premature death, as well as the marked differences in morbidity and mortality between social classes, and in Britain, they formed the basis for Victorian public health legislation.[35] But the public health movement was not part of the mainstream of medical development, and only a few of its important activists were doctors. It received few theoretical insights and little practical assistance from medicine proper, since the nature of infection and contagion had not yet been understood on a mechanistic basis, and preventive and environmental strategies were of little interest to most practitioners of curative medicine. Ironically, however, it was due in large part to the success of these preventive health measures that mainstream medicine was able to consolidate its emphasis on cure in the late nineteenth and early twentieth centuries. The major epidemic illnesses of the nineteenth century had been brought under control, and with the development of the germ theory of disease in the late nineteenth century, the emphasis in medical practice swung even more sharply towards the individual 'case'. This was the period of 'laboratory medicine' when doctors were able to probe even deeper into the workings of human bodies, paying less and less attention to the social and economic environment within which these bodies lived their lives.

'Laboratory medicine' was really made possible by the final victory of the mechanistic world view in the latter half of the nineteenth century. The late eighteenth and early nineteenth centuries had seen a struggle in biology and medicine between vitalism (a belief in the inviolability and unity of living organisms) and mechanism (which saw these organisms merely as sets of inter-related parts). By the middle of the nineteenth century, mechanism had become dominant, and experiments and vivisection had replaced comparative anatomy as the basic method for advancing medical knowledge.[36] Doctors were no longer simply *observing* the human body but were emphasising active intervention in human physiological processes. As a result, through its careful use of experimental method, medicine was becoming fully established as a science, on a par with the other natural sciences. In the latter half of the nineteenth century, both histology and physiology were developing extremely rapidly, and the individual cell came increasingly to be seen as the central focus for understanding ill health. Clearly this shift in emphasis produced an even more fragmented definition of the sick person since it saw him/her as made up not just of a set of organs, but of millions of cells. Cell theory and controlled clinical trials did not immediately provide any new therapy, but they did form the basis for twentieth-century developments in clinical medicine. However, at the same time, this form of 'biological reductionism' widened still further the gap between doctor and patient. Most importantly, it reinforced the tendency to view the patient as an object to be manipulated - a trend which has reached its apotheosis in post-war scientific medicine.

How then can we characterise the central concepts of western medicine as it is practised today and what is their broader social significance? Medical definitions of health and illness are particularly important. [37] Clearly there are certain physiological processes (breathing, eating, excretion and so on) which need to be completed if a person is to remain alive, and their successful execution must therefore be included in any definition of health. There are also certain instances (e.g. a broken limb) where there would be little disagreement that the person involved was not healthy in any normally accepted sense of the world. But once we move beyond examples such as these, then health and illness become difficult to define in any absolute way. Yet, the question of how they are defined in a particular society is of the utmost importance.

It is the medical definition, the view of the 'experts', which now forms the basis for the social definition of health and illness throughout the developed world. As we have seen, between the late eighteenth century and the present day, medicine has been characterised by what Jewson calls 'a shift from a person-oriented to an object-oriented cosmology'. Ill health is now defined primarily in terms of the malfunctioning of a mechanical system, and treatment consists of surgical, chemical or even electrical intervention to restore the machine to normal working order. The 'functional' element in the definition of health means that, in practice, health is usually defined as 'fitness' to undertake whatever would be expected of someone in a particular social position. For example, people who are able to carry on with their normal activities are not likely to be regarded as really ill, even though subjectively they may be suffering from depression, anxiety, migraine, insomnia or chronic indigestion. Put another way, health is usually defined - negatively - as the absence of incapacitating and externally verifiable pathology. Anyone not showing signs of such pathology is assumed to be healthy. The defining of health and illness in a functional way is an important example of how a capitalist value system defines people primarily as producers - as forces of production. It is concerned with their 'fitness' in an instrumental sense, rather than with their own hopes, fears, anxieties, pain or suffering. In defining health and illness in this way, the medical model limits people's own expectations of what it is to be healthy and is thus significant in keeping sickness (and also the demand for medical care) under control.

But under capitalism, health is also defined in an individualistic way. It is always individuals who become sick, rather than social economic or environmental factors which cause them to be so. As Evan Stark has commented,

> Disease is understood as a failure in and of the individual, an isolatable 'thing' that attacks the physical machine more or less arbitrarily from 'outside' preventing it from fulfilling its essential 'responsibilities'. Both bourgeois epidemiology and 'medical ecology' ... consider 'society' only as a relatively passive medium through which 'germs' pass en route to the individual. [38]

This emphasis on the individual origin of disease is of considerable social significance, since it effectively obscures the social and economic causes of ill health. The destruction of health is potentially a vitally important political issue, and the medical emphasis on individual causation is one means of defusing this. In recent years the individualism inherent in the scientific medical model has taken a new and more powerful form. As it has become clear that curative medicine is largely ineffective against the 'diseases of affluence', it is now being widely argued that what are referred to as 'way of life' factors - diet, stress, smoking and lack of exercise - are crucial in causing this new 'disease burden'. As a consequence, it is suggested that ill health can be explained in terms of individual moral failings - by blaming the victims for what has happened to them. [39] Contemporary epidemiology has therefore incorporated environmental factors into its understanding of ill health, but it interprets them narrowly and selectively, usually emphasising those aspects which can be seen as the individual's own responsibility. The suggestion that individuals are to blame for their own unhealthy lifestyles means that moral exhortations to be healthier, as well as self-care and self-help are stressed as important future trends in health care. People as individuals must help themselves to stay healthy through changing their *own* lives. Navarro has summarised the obvious appeal of this approach, in the following way,

> . . . it strengthens the basic ethical tenets of bourgeois individu-
> alism, the ethical construct of capitalism where one has to be
> free to do whatever one wants, free to buy and sell, to
> accumulate wealth or to live in poverty, to work or not, to be
> healthy or to be sick. Far from being a threat to the power
> structure, this life-style politics complements and is easily
> co-optable by the controllers of the system, and it leaves the
> economic and political structures of our society unchanged.
> Moreover, the life-style approach to politics serves to channel
> out of existence any conflicting tendencies against those
> structures that may arise in our society. [40]

This functional and individualistic definition of health forms the background against which medicine itself is defined as essentially curative. 'Curing' as the central focus of medical activity is of broad social and economic significance in at least two ways. Most impor-tantly, the expansion of technological curative medicine has pro-vided the basis for an expanding and extremely profitable health care industry. The medical-industrial complex in the USA where the private sector remains predominant, provides the clearest example of the direct role of medicine in the process of capital accumulation. [41] Even in countries like Britain, however, where medical care is organised by the state, it still remains an important source of profit, since equipment and drugs continue to be purchased from the private sector, while state hospitals are built by private contractors. But the medical emphasis on cure is also of wider, though more indirect, economic significance. As we have seen, capitalist production is itself a cause of ill health in a variety of ways. As a consequence, any preventive medicine which was to be substantially effective, would need to interfere with the organisation of the production process itself. Insofar as curative medicine appears to deny or at least to minimise the need for such preventive measures, it serves to protect existing economic interests.

Medical practice and the reproduction of labour power under capitalism

Throughout much of human history, health care has been, in one way or another, an organic part of community life. However, with the decline of feudalism, and the development of capitalism, traditional healers gradually became less important, and health care was increasingly provided on a more formal exchange basis. That is, doctors, midwives, surgeons and apothecaries performed certain services in return for a money payment. This remained the major mode of production of health care until the twentieth century, and within it, doctors gradually consolidated their control over other health workers, so that more informal healing and caring processes were largely superceded.

But medicine is increasingly moving away from this model of the individual entrepreneur. In some countries - notably the USA - the trend towards industrialised, large scale production has still left the provision of medical care mainly in private hands. However, in most advanced capitalist societies, the major responsibility for organising health care now lies with the state. At first sight this might seem anomalous. Why should such a potentially profitable activity have been taken out of private hands? The traditional left-wing solution to this problem has been to argue that socialised medicine was a victory which the working class gained at the expense of the ruling class. Hence, in Britain for example, the NHS is often seen as part of the 'ransom' paid by capital to avoid political and economic disruption. Clearly, all legislation relating to the conditions of the working class is enacted against the background of the struggle between labour and capital, and the relative strength of the working class at any given moment will be an important determinant of the outcome of any struggle to improve conditions. Indeed, the absence of a militant labour movement in the USA must be seen as a major reason for the failure to develop an American state health service. But this is only a part of the picture and to represent the NHS, for example, merely as a working class gain obscures the real contradictions in the nature of state-provided medical care - that it is national-ised rather than fully socialised medicine. Medicine benefits workers, but it benefits capital as well, and as a result, there are few developed societies where medicine has been left as a commodity to be produced on the open market. Why then is medical care of significance to capital as a whole?

If capitalist production is to continue, there must be a renewal of its 'general conditions' as well as a renewal of the means of production.[42] Mechanisms must therefore exist for capitalist societies to reproduce themselves. Two things in particular need to be reproduced - the productive forces and the existing relations of production. That is, there is a need to renew both the 'inputs' of production, and also the sets of beliefs and relationships that hold society together. Included in the forces of production are its material conditions (raw materials, buildings, machines, etc.) and also the labour power of workers. It is the ability of men and women to work which is the most important productive force. The worker sells his/her labour power to the capitalist for a wage, making possible the extraction of surplus value. Moreover that labour power is only made available by the expenditure of labour power in the home and this is often overlooked. Hence, the labour power of both men and women is of vital importance both directly and indirectly for the continuation of capitalist production, and must be continually renewed and regenerated. However it is important not just that the labour force should be physically regenerated, but that it continues to work within a certain set of economic and social relationships. Cynthia Cockburn has summarised the idea of the reproduction of the relations of production in the following terms.

> . . . if capitalism is to survive, each succeeding generation of workers must stay in an appropriate relationship to capital: the *relations* of production must be reproduced. Workers must not step outside the relation of the wage, the relation of property, the relation of authority. So 'reproducing capitalist relations' means reproducing the class system, ownership, above all reproducing a *frame of mind*.[43]

As we shall see, medical care is a highly significant factor in the reproduction of both the forces and the relations of production.

In part, the reproduction of labour power is provided for through the payment of wages to workers, which enables them to feed, clothe and house themselves and their families at a historically and culturally specific level. Marx described this process as follows,

> If the owner of labour power works today, tomorrow he must again be able to repeat the same process in the same conditions as regards health and strength. His means of subsistence must therefore be sufficient to maintain him in a normal state as a working individual. [44]

He assumed that this reproduction of his own labour power would be left to the worker himself to undertake through the normal process of his daily life. [45] However this assumption has been shown to be over-simplified. It has been characteristic of capitalist development during the nineteenth and twentieth centuries, that in most countries the state has taken over responsibility for the *collective* reproduction of labour power through the provision of education, social security and other welfare services. State intervention in the organisation of medical care has been part of this more general process.

Perhaps the most obvious connection between health care and the reproduction of labour power concerns the physical fitness of the worker. As we have seen, the worker under capitalism sells his/her labour power. But all labour power is not of the same quality, and physical fitness can affect the amount of surplus value extracted in a working day. Frequent sickness absence from work may also make it difficult to control the labour process efficiently. It is therefore a matter of some concern both to individual capitalists and to capital as a whole, that the physical health of the labour force should be maintained at a 'satisfactory' level. Clearly this satisfactory level will vary according to the existing supply of labour, the type of technology in use, *and* the expectations which workers have themselves developed about their health. As Kelman has put it,

> At any point in time, functional 'health' is that organismic condition of the population most consistent with, or least disruptive of the process of capital accumulation. [46]

Insofar as medical care can improve standards of health and fitness, it constitutes one element in the physical reproduction of labour power and, as a result, has increasingly been supervised by the state. During the early nineteenth century, for example, the physical health of the British working class was so bad that it interfered with production in a variety of ways. A recognition of this fact was one element in the complex of forces producing the public health legislation of the 1840s, and one effect of these measures was indeed to improve the productivity of labour. Similarly, concerns of this kind have been an important source of pressure for the provision of medical care for urban workers in the underdeveloped world. Yet we cannot assume that medicine will always contribute to the productivity of labour in any direct way. Indeed, there seems to be increasing evidence that in most of the developed world it may not in fact do so. It is true that in cases of acute infection, or a broken limb, modern medical technology can hasten the healing process and cut down the length of time the sufferer must be absent from work, while the use of drugs may enable people to function who would otherwise be incapacitated. However, the major debilitating and chronic diseases of the twentieth century (including psychiatric illness) continue to resist medical efforts to conquer them. Thus rates of sickness absence from work have continued to rise in most advanced capitalist countries, despite the fact that it is the productive and potentially productive groups in the population who receive proportionately more medical resources than the old or the chronically sick. Moreover, changes in the labour process have meant that it is no longer the physically fit worker who is necessarily the most productive. The shift away from certain kinds of unskilled or semi-skilled manual labour, may mean that in many work situations real fitness may be a disadvantage - a fit worker may find it much less easy to tolerate a boring and sedentary job. Historically, it would appear that, except at particular periods, it has been technological changes or a relative scarcity of labour which have been more effective than higher rates of medical expenditure in obtaining increased productivity. Indeed, the present crisis in health care reflects in part a growing recognition that the increasing costs of medicine are not producing a commensurate improvement in labour productivity.

However, as well as being maintained at a reasonable level of physical efficiency, it is also important that the current labour force should reproduce itself by providing the next generation of workers and consumers. It has been characteristic of all societies that controls are placed, to a greater or lesser extent, on the sexual and reproductive activities of women. Sometimes conditions will be such that women are expected to produce *more* children, and sometimes fewer, as Edholm, Harris and Young have pointed out in their critique of the anthropology of human reproduction.

> It seems clear that the growth of human populations is both uneven and fluctuating and is subject to considerable social manipulation and control . . . a central interest of any social group - whether in times of expansion, when presumably increased female fertility is encouraged / enjoined or in times of stability when some proportion of the female population is withdrawn from reproduction - may well be the social appropriation of women and the regulation of their generative powers. [47]

These controls over human reproduction can take a variety of forms. For example they may be external (as in the case of taboos or infanticide) or they may be internal (as when women accept certain ideas about their productive and reproductive roles which then structure their patterns of sexuality and procreation). One of the major social changes taking place in the twentieth century has been the development of more effective means for controlling female fertility through contraception, and to a more limited extent, through new techniques for abortion and sterilisation. These new methods have enabled many women to gain a much greater degree of control over their own fertility than they had in the past, but, at the same time, the medical control of these techniques has given doctors and the state a new means of controlling women's lives. [48]

The question of the relationship between population size and other aspects of economic, political and social policies is a very complex one, which has as yet received little theoretical attention. However we can see that in the developed and underdeveloped areas of the world, the use of medicine in controlling reproduction has been very different. In most underdeveloped countries, an unlimited supply of cheap labour has meant that techniques for controlling fertility have been used in a particularly oppressive way in attempts to keep down population size. [49] Such policies have, of course, been encouraged by the metropolitan countries because of what they perceive to be the political threat of huge and impoverished third world populations. In the developed world however, population policies have been very different. Broadly speaking, with the development from laissez-faire to monopoly capitalism, there has been a shift in the metropolitan countries away from the need for a huge and unskilled labour force towards a more stable and qualitatively superior one, and this is the background against which we can begin to understand changing attitudes towards birth control in the twentieth century. Thus, in the developed world, social policies relating to abortion and contraception have concentrated more on the context of reproduction (keeping it within the nuclear family, for example), and on the quality of the children produced, than on the sheer numbers involved. That is to say, in mature capitalist economies, concern has centred more on the type of people being produced than on the continuous expansion (or reduction) of the supply of labour. It should be clear however, that there are very considerable limitations on the technical capacity of modern medicine either to ensure the fitness of the labour force or to determine its size and quality. Hence it is difficult to explain the very substantial social and economic significance of medicine solely in these terms, and we need to look beyond the accepted boundaries of medicine in order to understand its broader significance as an agency of social control.

It is vital for capitalism that the labour force should be reproduced not just at the level of physical fitness and adequate numbers, but also at an ideological level. This involves the preparation of individuals in a variety of ways for the part they will play in the social division of labour. It also involves the legitimation or justification of the existing mode of social and economic organisation, including the role of the state in society. In advanced capitalist societies, the family, the media, the education system and welfare institutions all play an important part in this process of shaping attitudes and beliefs. Within the broad category of welfare institutions, health care systems function as particularly powerful agencies of socialisation and social control.

First, the *scientific* claims made for medical practice, mean that it must be seen in the light of the more general process by which capitalist societies are legitimated on the strength of their relationship with science and scientific achievements. The availability of high technology medicine and the publicising of individual medical breakthroughs (whatever their real social value) are important window-dressing in maintaining support for the existing system. Second, the mode of production of health care is important in various ways in reproducing both the division of labour, and also more general aspects of bourgeois ideology. The provision of health care involves a set of social relationships which are bureaucratic, hierarchical and authoritarian. For workers in the medical sector, this means that their work situation both reflects and also reinforces the division of labour in the wider society, emphasising the differential allocation of status, power and income on the basis of class, sex, and race. In the case of patients, their unequal relationship with doctors, and their lack of autonomy and power within the system as a whole, mean that the provision of medical care is an ideal mechanism for socialisation and social control. Hence the substantive content of the ideology which informs medical practice, (including for example, a particular form of sexism) can be more powerfully reproduced because of the social relationships involved in its production. The idea that it is only the doctor who can cure, and the belief that one's mind and body can be separated and treated according to the laws of science, both serve to emphasise the loss of individual autonomy and the feelings of powerlessness so common in other areas of social and economic life. People come to believe that they have little control over their own bodies, just as, for example, they have so little control over the conditions in which they spend their working lives. [50]

Finally, it is precisely because health, and therefore medical care, are so vital to every individual that the provision of medical care often comes to represent the benevolent face of an otherwise unequal and divided society. People who are sick are extremely vulnerable, and the ultimate demonstration of concern on the part of the state is to care for its citizens when they are ill, or even to save them from death. As Rodberg and Stevenson have remarked,

> It is important, for the maintenance of the status quo, that the
> members of a society perceive it to be capable of meeting their

basic needs such as provision, when needed, of effective and humane health care. Such a perception can atone for other perceived failings of the system. People may be poor or unemployed, but if there is at least some form of medical care available when they or their children need it, their burdens are easier to bear.[51]

Conclusion

As we have seen, patterns of health and illness are to a considerable extent determined by the existence of a particular mode of social and economic organisation, and under capitalism there is often a contradiction between the pursuit of health and the pursuit of profit. Most attempts to control the social production of ill health would involve an unacceptable degree of interference with the processes of capital accumulation, and, as a result, the emphasis in advanced capitalist societies has been on after-the-event curative medical intervention, rather than broadly-based preventive measures to conserve health.[52] Within this context, the wider significance of health and medical care for both labour and capital has led most capitalist states to organise their own medical provisions. However, it is this dual significance of medical care which lies at the heart of the major contradictions which are inherent in any system of socialised (or rather, nationalised) medicine.

For most people (who cannot afford an alternative) an adequate system of state-provided medical care is one of the pre-conditions of a decent life. The organised working class, as well as other groups of patients and potential patients (women, for example), will therefore struggle for improvements in health care, without increased charges or taxation to pay for it. For some workers, the health sector is also their place of work and they will be pushing for increased wages and better conditions. So far as the state and the ruling class are concerned, nationalised medicine represents part of the cost of the reproduction of labour power. Conflicts will tend to arise, however, when attempts by the state to keep standards of medical care at a 'reasonable' level are opposed by individual capitalists who wish to keep down public expenditure whatever the consequences. At the same time, the organisation of medical care also provides an arena for capital accumulation. Naturally, those sections of capital which are involved in the production of commodities used in the health sector will wish to maximise the level of consumption and the price of their products. This aim may therefore come into conflict with the broader interests of capital as a whole, since the state will attempt to keep down the costs of reproduction by whatever means possible, especially during periods of economic recession. Clearly this may result in decreasing expenditure on specific health-related commodities, thus affecting the profits of firms in the health sector. It may also mean that cutbacks in expenditure will weaken those aspects of health care relating to socialisation and legitimation, just when they are likely to be most important because of the general worsening of social and economic conditions.

As we shall see, health policies and medical care systems in capitalist countries therefore represent the outcome at any particular moment of the struggle between all these conflicting forces. They are not the rational policies of a benevolent state ensuring healthy lives and scientific medicine for all its people, but nor are they the manipulative policies of an all-seeing state controlling every aspect of the daily life of its members.

Questions concerning the social production of health and illness, and issues relating to the organisation of medical care are too often conflated. As Part One has shown, they must be treated as separate but clearly related phenomena, and this division is reflected in the organisation of what follows. The rest of the book is divided into two parts - the first examining the social production of health and illness; the second, the organisation of medical care. Within each section, Britain is used as a case study of an advanced capitalist country while East Africa - part of its former colonial empire - is used to illustrate the relationship between medicine, health and underdevelopment. Naturally, there are problems in any attempt to generalise from particular instances to all capitalist countries. However, it can be argued that in the case of medicine and health, as with other aspects of social and economic life, the similarities between developed countries and between underdeveloped countries within the world capitalist system are much greater than the differences. What follows is therefore put forward as an initial analysis, in the hope that it can form the basis for other, more detailed, studies both of Britain and East Africa and also of other parts of the capitalist world.

Part Two:
The Social Production of Health and Illness

It has been suggested in chapter one that the way health and illness are defined, as well as the material reality of disease and death, will vary according to the social and economic environment in which they occur. This is not to suggest that the physical and chemical laws governing disease mechanisms can simply be abandoned, but rather that they must be seen to operate within a social and economic context which is constantly changing. Thus, the historical development of the capitalist mode of production has had extremely far-reaching effects on health. On the one hand, the development of the productive forces on an unprecedented scale has meant that the standard of living of the entire population in developed capitalist countries has been improved, with a consequent amelioration in standards of physical health. This same process however has simultaneously underdeveloped the health of many third world populations. Moreover, new hazards to health have been created in the developed world by the large-scale economic, social and technological changes which were a necessary part of this development.

Chapters two and three will illustrate these complex processes in more detail. Chapter two examines the impact of capitalist development on patterns of health and illness in Britain, while chapter three looks at the underdeveloped world in general, and the experience of East Africa in particular.

2: Health, Illness and the Development of Capitalism in Britain

The impact of industrial capitalism

Capitalist development ultimately made possible an improvement in standards of physical health as measured by indices such as life expectancy and mortality rates. But this was by no means an immediate effect. The beginnings of capitalist agriculture produced a very significant deterioration in the material conditions of most people in the countryside, while the industrial revolution and the growth of factory production had a similar effect in the cities. As a consequence, the physical health of both agricultural and urban workers, and also of their families, was considerably worsened.

It would be wrong, of course, to suggest that the pre-capitalist and pre-industrial period in Britain was a healthy 'Golden Age'. However, even against a background of extremely high birth and death rates and short average life expectancy, the beginnings of the transition from feudalism to capitalism had savage effects on life (and death) in the countryside.[1] Between the sixteenth and the eighteenth centuries, conditions deteriorated rapidly for those living in rural areas, and enclosures prevented most families from working the land to provide their own food.[2] At the same time, the rationalisation of agriculture led to many workers becoming either underemployed or unemployed, producing widespread poverty and a movement to the towns.

It is important to understand exactly why the development of industrial capitalism should have produced such a rapid deterioration in the living and working conditions of millions of people.[3] The development of factory production meant that workers were deprived of the opportunity to sell their labour on a relatively informal basis in dispersed geographical locations. The newly emerging wage workers were forced to migrate to the cities in order to work - 'encouraged' to do so by the deterioration of conditions in the countryside. As a consequence, towns expanded with enormous speed, and physical conditions soon became extremely unhealthy. In the decade 1821-31 for example, the population of Manchester and Salford rose by 47 per cent, that of Bradford by 78 per cent, and that of West Bromwich by 60 per cent.[4] The standard of most housing was atrocious without clean water and effective sanitation.[5] As E.P. Thompson has put it,

> Certainly the unprecedented rate of population growth and of concentration in industrial areas would have created major problems in any known society, and most of all in a society whose rationale was to be found in profit-seeking and hostility to planning.[6]

The range and reliability of the demographic statistics produced during this period obviously have serious limitations (especially before the founding of the Registrar General's Office in 1837). However, the available evidence indicates that although the average mortality rate *fell* over the nation as a whole between 1780 and about 1810, there was a discernible *increase* after about 1816.[7] This overall increase appears to reflect the significant rise in urban mortality rates which accompanied the early period of industrialisation. William Farr, the most famous of early nineteenth-century statisticians, calculated that the mortality rate in country districts during the period 1831-39 was 18.2 per 1,000, compared with an average rate of 26.2 per 1,000 in urban areas.[8] Moreover, the average rate conceals dramatic variations between different parts of the cities, with many more deaths occurring in working class areas. Studies of urban life during the early part of the nineteenth century pointed out these class differences in health with striking clarity.

> It is precisely among the workers in large-scale industry that we meet with the shortest life expectancy. 'Dr. Lee, Medical Officer of Health for Manchester, stated that the average age of death of the Manchester . . . upper middle class was 38 years, while the average age at death of the labouring class was 17;

while at Liverpool these figures were presented as 35 against 15.
It thus appeared that the well-to-do classes had a lease of life
which was more than double the value of that which fell to the
lot of the less favoured citizens.'[9]

Morbidity statistics - that is statistics showing rates of disease
and disability - are even less reliable than the figures on mortality.
However, to most observers it was clear that the mortality statistics
represented only the tip of an enormous iceberg of ill health. As
Doctor Turner Thackrah of Leeds put it in 1832, 'Not 10 per cent of
the inhabitants of large towns enjoy full health.'[10] It is significant,
then, that one early effect of capitalist development was to sharpen
the differences in mortality and morbidity between different social
groups. Farr himself explained these differences in the following
terms,

> Different classes of the population experience very different
> rates of mortality, and suffer different kinds of diseases. The
> principal causes of these differences, beside the sex, age and
> hereditary organisation, must be sought in three sources -
> exercise in the ordinary occupations of life - the adequate or
> inadequate supply of warmth and of food - and the differential
> degree of exposure to poisonous effluvia and to destructive
> agents.[11]

It is important therefore to look in more detail at the effects of
working conditions on health during the early stages of the Industrial
Revolution. When a new machine first comes into use, its replacement cost is at a maximum. Such machines must therefore be used to
the full if they are to justify their initial cost. This consideration was
of major importance to most employers during the early part of the
nineteenth century, and as a consequence they had a strong incentive
to extend the length of the working day and to employ as many
hands as possible. Moreover, since the need was predominantly for
unskilled labour, of which there was an abundant supply, there
appeared to be little need to conserve labour through any improvement in working conditions. As a result, work was a very unhealthy
activity. Documentary evidence of the period vividly describes the
physical and mental exhaustion resulting from working days of

twelve to sixteen hours hard labour.[12] This was exacerbated by the temperature and humidity of the factories, mines and workshops; by the inadequate arrangements made for meals, and by the unsatisfactory or non-existent sanitary arrangements. Moreover, it is important to remember that the early industrial proletariat was not just a male labour force, but contained men, women and children of all ages. Low wages and the insatiable demand for labour meant that in many areas whole families were employed. Indeed, the labour of women and children was often preferred to male labour because it was cheaper and easier to control, and/or because women and children were assumed to be more dextrous. Under these conditions, women suffered particularly badly. For them, as Engels pointed out,

> Protracted work frequently causes deformities of the pelvis, partly in the shape and abnormal position and development of the hip bones, partly of malformation of the lower portion of the spinal column ... that factory operatives undergo more difficult confinements than other women is testified to by several midwives and accoucheurs, and also that they are more liable to miscarriage. Moreover, they suffer from the general enfeeblement common to all operatives, and, when pregnant, continue to work in the factory up to the hour of delivery, because otherwise they lose their wages, and are made to fear that they may be replaced if they stop away too soon. It frequently happens that women are at work one evening and delivered the next morning, and the case is none too rare of their being delivered in the factory.[13]

Different industries added to the generally debilitating effects of work, through producing their own specific health problems. Chest diseases were especially common among miners and also in the cotton and flax-spinning mills where there were dangerous levels of fibrous dust in the air. Eye diseases and even blindness often occurred among stocking weavers and lacemakers; lead and arsenic poisoning among those making stoneware in the potteries; and consumption among dressmakers and milliners.[14] Even where work did not cause a specific disease, many jobs led to the abnormal development of certain parts of the body at the expense of the rest. Thus flax spinning produced, 'a peculiar deformity of the shoulder, especially a projection of the right shoulder blade, consequent upon the nature of the work'.[15] Similarly, the over-exertion of miners led to,

> the diversion of vitality to the one-sided development of the muscles, so that those especially of the arms, legs and back, of the shoulders and chest, which are chiefly called into activity in pushing and pulling, attain an uncommonly vigorous development while all the rest of the body suffers and is atrophied for want of nourishment.[16]

Finally, all workers, but especially children, were extremely susceptible to accidents in their place of work because of the speed at which they were expected to work, the exhaustion produced by the length of the working day, and the failure of employers to take safety precautions.

Again it was Engels who described the effects of these accidents most graphically,

> The work between the machinery gives rise to multitudes of accidents of a more or less serious nature, which have for the operative the secondary effect of unfitting him for his work more or less completely. The most common accident is the squeezing off of a single joint of a finger, somewhat less common is the loss of the whole finger, half or a whole hand, an arm etc., in the machinery. Lockjaw very often follows, even upon the lesser among these injuries and brings death with it. Besides the deformed persons, a great number of maimed ones may be seen going about in Manchester; this one has lost an arm or a part of one, that one a foot, the third half a leg; it is like living in the midst of an army just returned from a campaign.[17]

This mixture of exhaustion, unhealthy working conditions, damp and insanitary housing, and inadequate nutrition, meant that working-class families became especially susceptible to infectious diseases. A.K. Chalmers pointed this out in his graphic description of working-class areas of Glasgow in the first part of the nineteenth century.

> From 1816, indeed until the early seventies of the last century, the closes and wynds of the city were devastated by recurring epidemics of infectious diseases of several kinds, and of con-

siderable magnitude. Nor did these stand alone; they formed only the high peaks of an elevated tableland of disease, which was capable of maintaining an annual death rate oscillating frequently between 30 and 40 per 1,000 and of rising in occasional years under the influence of epidemic prevalences to 46, as in 1832 during the first cholera epidemic; and 56, as in 1846 when typhus fever alone caused a death rate approaching 14 per 1,000 or only a little lower than the average death rate from *all* causes at the present time.[18]

Among these infectious diseases which killed the poor in such vast numbers, smallpox and cholera are often assumed to have been the most deadly. Smallpox however, had declined in significance after about 1800, with the widespread use of Jenner's new vaccine.[19] Similarly, although cholera had extremely dramatic effects at certain times, (in particular during the epidemics of 1831-32, 1848-49, 1853-54 and 1865-66) its long term significance in the total death rate was not very great.[20] The major causes of death during the nineteenth century were in fact, tuberculosis, 'fever' and childhood diseases. Indeed as Flinn has commented, 'The history of British towns in the first half of the nineteenth century is, to a considerable degree, the history of typhus and consumption.'[21]

Reliable evidence on the incidence of tuberculosis in the early part of the nineteenth century is difficult to obtain, but there is general agreement among historians that it probably accounted for about one third of all deaths.[22] Although tuberculosis claimed middle class as well as working class victims, its incidence was much higher where living conditions were at their worst,[23] so that Dubos and Dubos in *The White Plague* go so far as to describe tuberculosis as, 'the social disease of the nineteenth century, perhaps the first penalty that capitalistic society had to pay for the ruthless exploitation of labour'.[24] Consumption and other respiratory illnesses were often related to particular industrial hazards, but contemporary medical knowledge now indicates that at least two additional factors were probably important in increasing the incidence of tuberculosis. Firstly the standard of nutrition of the potential victim would have been an important element in determining the level of resistance to TB, and underfed families were therefore especially at risk. Secondly

the level of exposure to the tubercle bacillus is also of major significance. Overcrowded conditions at home and at work increased the
extent of such contact, and therefore the likelihood of contracting
the disease.

Those diseases which were almost as deadly as TB in nineteenth
century cities, were for a long period known collectively as 'fevers'.
By the middle of the nineteenth century, however, more effective
diagnosis had made it possible to distinguish them as typhus and
typhoid. Of the two, it was typhus which posed the greatest threat to
the health of the working class. Aptly characterised as 'the poor
man's disease', it was both epidemic and endemic in the poorest
slum areas, and the lack of adequate supplies of clean water was a
particularly important factor in its propagation.

Throughout the nineteenth century, infant mortality remained
very high, hovering around 150 per 1,000 live births. Infant deaths
occurred among all social classes but were much more frequent in
poor areas. Their cause was a matter of heated debate, one of the
most common explanations being that working-class women simply
did not take proper care of their children. Those mothers who went
out to work were, of course, seen as especially blameworthy. Inevitably, many children did suffer when their mothers had to work since
alternative forms of childcare were often extremely unsatisfactory. [25]
Levels of infant mortality, however, are always determined by a wide
range of social and economic factors and there were many aspects of
life in nineteenth-century cities which made it difficult to keep
babies healthy. Young children were rendered especially vulnerable
to infectious diseases by inadequate housing, lack of suitable food,
and the absence of clean water and effective sanitation. As a result,
respiratory and gastro-intestinal infections were a common cause of
illness and death. Children of all ages were particularly susceptible to
the common communicable diseases of childhood, particularly
scarlet fever, whooping cough and diphtheria. These infections were
both more common in their incidence and more severe in their
effects than they are today, and throughout the nineteenth century
scarlet fever remained the main cause of death in childhood. [26]

In general, then, the picture throughout most of the nineteenth
century was one of high mortality rates and high levels of morbidity,

with death and disease unequally distributed between classes and between town and country. As we have seen, these patterns of health and illness were closely related to the social and economic conditions of early industrial capitalism.

From about 1870 onwards, however, a significant change occurred as the adult mortality rate started to fall. For a long time, it was assumed that curative medical intervention had been instrumental in bringing this about, but it is now generally agreed that the falling mortality rate was due mainly to a combination of the effects of public health legislation and an improvement in working-class living standards.[27] Both of these developments must, of course, be understood in relation to the broader changes taking place in the nature of British society over this same period.

The last quarter of the nineteenth century marked the consolidation of British capitalism, with changes in the techniques of production. The widespread use of more complex machines made possible an intensification of the labour process, but required a fitter and more reliable labour force. This was achieved partly through the implementation of public health legislation. Although they were not widely available until the 1870s and 1880s, clean water and effective sanitation and sewage disposal did play an extremely important role in reducing deaths from infectious diseases in the latter part of the nineteenth century.[28] Most importantly, however, the reduction in the prices of raw materials and imported foodstuffs as well as new techniques of production were such that profitability could be maintained at the same time as increasing the surplus which could be made available to the working class in the form of increased wages thereby improving both their standard of living and also their health.

Average real wages began to rise in the 1860s and rose by about 40 per cent between 1862-75. Though they fell briefly in the 1870s, they rose again from the mid 1880s. By 1900 they were one-third above the 1875 level and 89 per cent above the level of 1850.[29] These increased wage levels were reflected in a better standard of living for most sections of the working class, and one of the most important ways in which this improved standard of living was translated into a reduced mortality rate was through an improvement in standards of nutrition.[30] From 1870 onwards, the consumption of meat and fruit in particular rose dramatically - much of it imported cheaply from abroad as overseas trade expanded. Thus the improved standard of living and the amelioration of the material conditions of urban life, which accompanied the general expansion of British capitalism in the latter half of the nineteenth century, were the major factors effecting a reduction in the mortality rate.

During the twentieth century, the adult mortality rate continued to fall, and the infant mortality rate followed the same downward trend after 1914. Naturally, this downward trend was uneven. During the depression, for example, rates of maternal mortality rose and there was a considerable deterioration in health among certain sections of the working class.[31] Nevertheless, by the 1970s, mortality in every age group up to 55 was one-tenth or less of the rate 100 years before, and the infant mortality rate had fallen by 88 per cent during the same period. These figures are very striking and provide powerful support in any attempt to demonstrate the essential rationality and 'benevolence' of contemporary British society. Moreover, despite the crises of the 1970s, it is still commonly assumed that economic growth and the advancement of medical knowledge will allow the progress towards a wealthier and healthier society to continue. It is the validity or otherwise of such assumptions that we must now examine.

Health, illness and British capitalism in the twentieth century

There can be no doubt that capitalist development made possible a dramatic reduction in mortality rates and an increase in life expectancy for the entire British population - a fact which cannot and should not be ignored. Nevertheless, we need to examine the significance of this achievement very carefully. With the disappearance of the obvious causes of death and disease - lack of sanitation, infected water, and grossly overcrowded housing, for example - it is often assumed that ill health is no longer related to environmental factors. It is widely accepted that individuals may produce their own health problems through leading an unhealthy life, but that society itself and the way it is organised can no longer be held responsible. But is this really the case?

To begin with, there are a number of methodological difficulties in any attempt to measure improvements in health through a comparison of national mortality statistics. Of course, the range and accuracy of morbidity and mortality statistics have improved considerably since the industrial revolution, but, even in the 1970s, they still tell us very little about the health of the British population.[32] Mortality statistics are easily available and relatively reliable, but are only of limited value. They tell us what people die of and at what age, and can serve as a significant indicator of the varying material circumstances of different social groups. However, they can give only a very crude indication of the state of health of those people in the population who remain alive. Thus, a falling death rate may not necessarily reflect any overall improvement in basic health, and, conversely, many kinds of chronic ill health (including psychiatric illness) will not be reflected at all in an increasing mortality rate. Figures relating to morbidity are, therefore, more useful than mortality statistics as a guide to health, but at present the range of morbidity statistics provided in Britain is extremely limited. National statistics are not collected on a regular basis and any analysis is forced to rely on statistics collected for other purposes - sickness absence statistics for example, or data on the utilisation of the NHS.[33] All of these sources present their own particular methodological difficulties. The most fundamental problem, however, is that they refer only to those people who are defined as sick or disabled according to medical criteria, or who have actually died. As a result, we are forced to discuss the social distribution of sickness and death rather than being able to assess patterns of health in any more positive sense. It is clear that the absence of death or clinical disease is not in itself synonymous with health, but within the context of the existing techniques of data collection and their underlying philosophy there is no way to solve this conceptual problem. Given these limitations, what do we know about current patterns of health and illness in Britain?

Clearly people live longer now than they used to. In Britain in 1974, life expectancy at birth was approximately 69 years for men and 75 years for women.[34] It is interesting, however, that although the major expansion of scientific medicine and the development of the National Health Service have both occurred during the past 30 years, life expectancy has actually increased very little over this same period. Obviously, people could not be expected to live forever and there are limits to the possible increase in life expectancy. Nevertheless, it is evident that many people are still dying prematurely, and often for reasons which can be related to wider social and economic conditions - an observation confirmed in a recent study by the World Health Organisation.

> A study of mortality trends in the last two decades in the developed regions shows that gains in the expectation of life occurred largely in the 1950s, whereas developments in the 1960s were on the whole disappointing, even though some slowing down was to be expected in view of the good results already achieved . . . For males as well as females there is a noticeable, almost universal reduction in the rate of decline of mortality with a virtual standstill or even setback for males. Evidence is accumulating that in some countries and for some age groups, female mortality may follow the same course. The possibility that environmental hazards in the broadest sense, have set up a barrier towards further improvements cannot be dismissed lightly.[35]

So if life expectancy is not increasing, and in some countries may even be *falling*, what are people dying of - and, most importantly, what are they suffering from?

The new 'disease burden' consists largely of the so-called 'degenerative' diseases, such as cancer, heart disease, arthritis and diabetes, all of which now kill and cripple many more people than they did in the past. In 1975, approximately 26 per cent of deaths in Britain occurred as a result of heart disease, 13 per cent from cerebrovascular disease, 20 per cent as a result of cancer, and 4.5 per cent as a result of chronic bronchitis, emphysema or asthma.[36] In addition, of course, many more people are becoming chronically ill for longer periods in their lives than they did in the past. It is, therefore, vital to make some assessment of the causes of these 'new' illnesses.

It is commonly argued that these diseases are 'residual' and that their increased incidence was only made possible by increases in life expectancy. According to this view, degenerative diseases are an inevitable part of the ageing process. In the past, people did not live long enough to develop cancer or heart disease and hence the fact that people now have longer life-spans, is said to make these diseases appear more common. One obvious consequence of this interpretation is that there is little that can be done to prevent disease of this kind. More plausible however, is the suggestion that to a very considerable extent these diseases are a result of the particular mode of interaction between human beings and the material world which characterises most advanced industrial societies.[37] In other words, it is suggested that these 'new' diseases are environmental in origin - although the term environmental is defined here more broadly than has been customary. So, the longer people live in particular (industrial) conditions, the more likely they are to develop cancer or heart disease, *but* this does not make such diseases an inevitable part of the ageing process.

It has been pointed out in support of this view, that there are certain diseases which are characteristic of advanced industrial societies, and historical and anthropological evidence shows that the incidence of these diseases is very much lower in pre-industrial communities.[38] John Powles has taken this further, seeing two basic changes in the relationship between human beings and nature - first the shift from hunting-gathering to farming (the neolithic revolution) and second the transition from living on the land to living in industrial cities (the Industrial Revolution). Thus there have been three principal types of human ecology, and there appears to be a general trend for the so-called 'degenerative' diseases either to increase with the move from agricultural communities to industrial cities, or to be almost entirely confined to the latter. Powles presents data to demonstrate that arteriosclerosis, diabetes, hypertension, some forms of cancer (especially of the lungs, large bowel and breast), chronic bronchitis, dental caries, duodenal ulcers, appendicitis, diverticulitis and varicose veins occur almost exclusively in advanced industrial societies. He concludes that,

> ... it is insufficient to describe these diseases as degenerative.
> They are more appropriately referred to as diseases of mal-
> adaptation - for whatever their individual causes they may be
> considered as resulting from the fact that man's relation to his
> environment has become removed from that to which he is
> biologically adapted.[39]

This fits well with recent research on the aetiology of cancer and heart disease. For example it is increasingly accepted that at least 80 per cent of cancers are environmental in origin. Philippe Shubik of the US National Cancer Advisory Board has summed up the position succinctly.

> It is a universal opinion that cancer can be attributed to
> environmental factors in the main. I shall not belabour the
> matter of percentages as this seems to serve no useful purpose.
> Cancer is largely a preventable disease.[40]

Similarly, it is now increasingly accepted that the other major cause of death - heart disease - is related to a complex of environmental, and therefore apparently preventable, factors such as smoking, stress, a sedentary life-style, and a diet high in fats and low in fibre.

Powles explains these diseases using the concept of 'mal-adaption' - an idea which does seem to have considerable explanatory value. Thus it can convincingly be argued that over the past 200 years, changes have occurred in the relationship between human beings and the natural world, which have been so rapid and so dramatic as to render *biological* adaptation extremely difficult. Changes in diet for example, have been so profound that evolutionary changes in the human digestive system over such a short period would not be conceivable. Obviously the resulting biological maladaptation can to some extent be compensated for by cultural and scientific measures - in the case of diet for example, constipation due to a reduction in fibre intake can be compensated for by the consumption of laxatives. Indeed, modern curative medicine has itself been described as 'cultural adaptation to biological maladjust-ment', in that it tries (often unsuccessfully) to compensate in a post hoc way, for the ill health resulting from ecological contradictions.

The concept of maladaption as used by Powles is, however,

ultimately limited in that he associates this maladjustment only with the fact that the societies he is describing are *industrialised*. In fact, as we have already seen, societies which are based on industrial production are not necessarily homogeneous. We therefore, have to look beyond industrialisation as a crude category to the various types of industrialised society, in order more fully to understand the forces producing these contradictions between the health of human beings and changes in the material environment. The importance of extending the analysis in this way is made abundantly clear by an examination of the current British statistics relating to class differences in health and illness.[41] While all men and women may have become to some extent maladapted to their material environment, this has not affected everyone equally. That is to say, illness, disability and premature death are not evenly distributed throughout society. Thus it seems clear that it is not merely the industrialised nature of contemporary society, but other aspects of social and economic organisation which structure current patterns of health and illness.

This is illustrated most forcefully by the distribution of deaths among the British population. The standardised mortality ratios* presented in the *Registrar General's Decennial Supplement* show a clear social class gradient in mortality rates (see Diagram one) such that working-class people are always at greater risk of dying *at all ages*.[42] The most dramatic differences are apparent in the rates of perinatal and post-neonatal deaths. In 1970-72, the mortality rate during the first week of life for babies in social class V was just under twice the rate for those in social class I, but by the end of the first year it was four times as great[43] - a fact which illustrates the importance of social and economic conditions in determining who will survive beyond the first year of life. It is significant that these class differentials in mortality show no sign of decreasing - indeed it has been

---

* The standardised mortality ratio is a measure designed to correct for differences in the age structure of the population, so that the actual number of deaths is expressed as a percentage of the number that would be expected if the age structure had remained unchanged from a base year.

Diagram 1. Mortality by social class and age

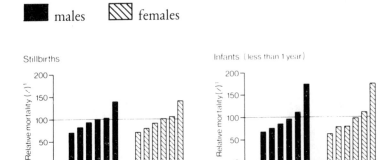

Stillbirths

Infants (less than 1 year)

Children (1-14 years)

Adults (15-64 years)

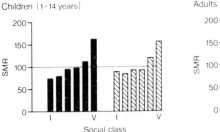

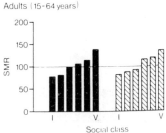

Source: *Occupational Mortality 1970-72*, London, HMSO 1977

argued that the gap actually widened between the 1930s and the early 1960s.[44] These continuing class differences in mortality arise in part from a greater incidence of the 'new' diseases - lung cancer, for example - among social classes IV and V, but they also reflect the continuing death toll from those 'older' diseases such as TB, bronchitis and pneumonia which are traditionally associated with poverty. The striking class gradients evident in deaths from a wide range of causes are illustrated in Diagram two.

Diagram 2. Mortality by social class and cause of death: standardised mortality ratios for men and married women (by husband's occupation) aged 15-64.

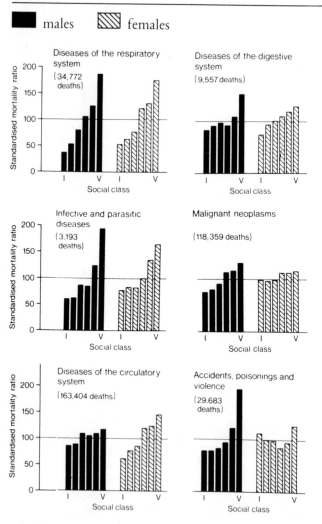

Source: *Occupational Mortality 1970-72*, London, HMSO 1977

These class differences which are so evident in mortality rates are also apparent in the morbidity statistics. Sickness absence data, for example, show that workers in unskilled and semi-skilled jobs are much more likely to be absent from work due to sickness, than those in professional and managerial jobs. Similarly, data from the General Household Survey indicate that semi-skilled and unskilled workers in all age groups report above-average rates of long-standing illness which limits their normal activities. In 1976, for example, men aged 45-64 in professional jobs reported half the rate of chronic sickness reported by unskilled workers and about one quarter of the number of days of acute sickness.[45] (See Table one).

Table 1: Sickness: Men aged 45-64, 1976

	Acute sickness days per year	*Chronic sickness rate per 1000*
Professional	8	185
Employers etc.	14	160
Other non-manual	19	236
Skilled manual	21	270
Semi-skilled	18	294
Unskilled	31	369

Source: *General Household Survey*, London HMSO 1978

These class differentials in morbidity and mortality show the limitations of a generalised concept of maladaptation and provide strong evidence to support the argument that social and economic factors remain extremely important in determining the ways in which people live and die. The precise ways in which this comes about are exceedingly complex but it is evident that any analysis of this kind must begin by redefining the terms of epidemiological enquiry away from an emphasis on the biological towards a recognition of the relevance of the entirety of social and economic life in determining patterns of health and illness. The rest of this chapter wil provide a brief account of some of the relevant variables that need to be taken into account in such an enterprise. It is important, however, to emphasise that while we will, of necessity, be looking largely at *individual* relationships between specific disease agents and ill health, it is the whole complext of elements making up the daily lives of individuals that must be taken into account in explaining the social distribution of health and illness.

Production and the health of workers

The most direct relationship between the process of commodity production and the destruction of health is obviously to be found in industrial accidents and industrial diseases. In these cases, ill health, disability or death are directly produced through the victim being at work. During the twentieth century, technological change and a different attitude towards the conservation of labour power have meant that some industrial diseases have been eliminated, or at least reduced in their incidence. Industrial accidents have also declined from the extremely high rates of the early nineteenth century.[46] But new, and often more serious hazards, have been generated in their place, and work still remains for many an extremely dangerous activity.

Accurate statistics on the number of people who are killed or injured at work, or who contract industrial diseases are difficult to obtain, but the 1972 *Report of the Committee on Safety and Health at Work* (the Robens Report) suggested that,

> Every year something like one thousand people are killed at their work in this country. Every year about half a million suffer injuries in varying degrees of severity. Twenty-three million working days are lost annually on account of industrial injury and disease.[47]

There are cogent reasons however for assuming that these figures seriously underestimate the real numbers involved. This is due (among other things) to the under-reporting of accidents, to the failure of doctors to recognise industrial disease, and to the large number of work-related illnesses which are not classified as such - i.e. are not 'prescribed'. Patrick Kinnersly has argued in *The Hazards of Work* that a realistic assessment of the annual figures for industrial accidents and disease would be about two thousand dying from injuries received at work, one thousand dying from industrial diseases, one million injured or off work with an industrial disease for at least three days, and at least ten million injured and needing first aid.[48] In addition, any such annual reckoning leaves out those disabled and bereaved people left behind by previous years of production, as Kinnersly indicates. In 1975, 203,000 former workers were receiving an industrial disablement pension, while 31,000 widows were in receipt of industrial death benefit.[49]

Whichever set of figures we take, it is clear that industrial accidents are still very common in Britain, affecting at least half a million workers each year. Certain industries have particularly high accident rates (e.g. the mining and construction industries, and the railways). During the year 1975-76, 59 miners were killed at work, 538 were seriously injured, and 52,946 were injured and off work for more than three days,[50] and any miner still has approximately a one in five chance of being injured at work in any particular year.

The incidence of industrial disease is even more difficult to estimate than the number of industrial accidents - the causes are often very complex and the presence of a particular pathological process difficult to identify. Industrial diseases are contracted through the entry into the body of various toxic substances - chemicals, dusts, fumes or gases.[51] The ingestion can be by a variety of routes - lungs, skin or stomach - and the ingested substances can be harmful in several different ways. They can cause direct poisoning (e.g. lead or mercury); an allergic response (e.g. industrial dermatitis); abortions or congenital abnormality (e.g. over-exposure to radiation); or specific diseases such as cancer (lung, skin and bladder cancer are all prescribed diseases *under certain circumstances*). Some of these processes can be illustrated in more detail through looking at the health problems produced by dusts and chemicals.

Dusts have been known to cause serious illness and even death for as long as there have been miners. About thirty thousand miners in Britain still suffer to some degree or other from lung disease. In

1973, 367 deaths were officially declared to be due to pneumoconiosis (although this is likely to be an underestimate), and about seven hundred *new* cases are still being diagnosed by pneumoconiosis panels each year. [52] Dusts of a different kind produce byssinosis, asbestosis, and silicosis. Byssinosis was very common in the textile factories of the nineteenth and early twentieth century, and was produced by the coarse dust and fibres accumulating in factories without adequate ventilation. Improved conditions were assumed to have wiped out the disease by the 1940s, but it has since been 'rediscovered'. Its apparent disappearance illustrates some of the problems involved in isolating industrial diseases from other environmentally-produced ill health. It seems that cases of byssinosis have often been confused with bronchitis, which is commonly found in those manufacturing areas where byssinosis could be expected. Moreover, any respiratory disease such as byssinosis will be aggravated by smoking and by the atmospheric pollution which is common in industrial areas. Therefore, its specific occupational origin may often go unnoticed, particularly where there is such a marked absence of health services in the workplace and when many factory doctors identify with the interests of employers rather than workers. [53]

A very wide range of chemical substances can also be taken into the body while a person is at work. Lead and mercury are still among the most dangerous and since both are being used increasingly frequently, they represent a growing health hazard. In addition, new substances are coming into use all the time, and many of these are receiving very limited toxicity testing. The relative ease with which potentially dangerous chemicals are introduced into the workplace, is a particularly serious problem because many industrial hazards only produce diseases after a long latency period. By the time their pathogenic effects have been realised it is often too late to do anything for the workers who were exposed to them many years earlier. This problem has been highlighted recently by experiences with two chemicals - beta naphthylamine and vinyl chloride monomer.

Beta naphthylamine was widely used in the rubber and cable industries in Britain until 1950, but medical evidence now shows that exposure to it can cause bladder cancer some forty or fifty years later. Vinyl chloride monomer is the major ingredient of PVC and it has now been discovered that exposure to this chemical can eventually cause a very rare form of liver cancer known as angiosarcoma. But it is the 'epidemic' of asbestosis and mesothelioma (cancer of the chest lining) which has occurred during the 1970s which illustrates most vividly the long-term effects of exposure to industrial hazards. Despite the fact that new regulations to control asbestos were introduced in 1969, figures published in the second annual report of the Employment Advisory Service showed an increase in cases of mesothelioma of at least sixty-eight per cent between 1970 and 1976. The latent period for this type of cancer may be anything from five to thirty-five years, and since the worst industrial exposures occurred between 1935 and 1970, the peak incidence still seems some years away. This same problem was examined by the US National Institute of Environmental Health Sciences.[54] Their official report published in 1978 estimated that more than two million American workers will die prematurely of cancer over the next thirty years, because of exposure to asbestos in the course of their jobs. It further argued that as many as fifteen per cent of all cancer cases in the United States are work related, rather than the one to five per cent often quoted.

It is clear that it will often be in the economic interest of employers not to inquire whether their workers are at risk from accident, disease or death. Firms tend to operate on the basis of 'acceptable risks' for a given return on investment but it is often the lives or health of workers which are at stake. It is assumed that in this situation, workers have two basic defenders who are concerned to protect their health - the state and the trade unions. However, it is clear from the incidence of industrial accidents and disease that these safeguards are not operating very effectively in Britain.

Work is generally assumed to create no dangers to health, unless there is clear evidence to the contrary. The health and safety of people at work is, therefore, ultimately dependent on their own awareness of hazards and potential illnesses. However, most medical and legal knowledge is concentrated in the hands of 'experts' and, as a consequence, workers usually have to rely on their unions both to obtain such information, and also to initiate any necessary action.

Despite this, most unions have given low priority to working conditions in general, and to health and safety issues in particular. Thus, an almost exclusive concentration on levels of pay has often detracted from important (possibly life or death) aspects of the physical environment of the workplace. Moreover, when health risks have been identified, unions have tended to demand danger money rather than changes in working conditions. Recently, there has been evidence of growing awareness among unions of the importance of health and safety issues, but much remains to be done. It is clearly difficult, however, for such concerns to be brought to the fore, when attempts to make the workplace safer can so easily be countered with threats of unemployment.

Whatever the priorities of the trade union movement, it is usually assumed that it is, in the final analysis, the responsibility of the state to protect the health of all of its citizens. The history of health and safety legislation, however, shows that this protection has been provided only within certain very narrow limits, and on a fragmented and pragmatic basis. When pressure has been exerted, the state has introduced limited health and safety regulations, and also minimal levels of compensation for those who 'deserve it'.[55] Such legislation has had only a limited effect on employers, and two basic deficiencies are evident in the existing state machinery for dealing with industrial accidents and disease. The first concerns the arrangements for inspection of workplaces and the sanctions that can be imposed on those who endanger the lives of workers; the second concerns the absence of any national industrial health service.

The administrative machinery for enforcing health and safety legislation has always been very cumbersome, and until recently, responsibility was dispersed between several different departments. Following the report of the Robens Committee in 1972, the system was rationalised and improved by the Health and Safety at Work Act, which came into force in 1975. The act did a number of things. It improved the bureaucratic efficiency of the administrative apparatus by setting up a unified health and safety executive. It allowed inspectors to make immediate closures of dangerous premises. It required that all firms with more than five employees should provide them with written statements about the new legislation, and very importantly it required that employees should be appointed as safety representatives. Above all, it extended health and safety provisions to about eight million workers who had not been covered before. Yet the act has very severe limitations, which reflect the underlying philosophy of the Robens Report.

In preparing the way for the act, the Robens Report made its own position very clear.

> Our present system encourages rather too much reliance on state regulation and rather too little on personal responsibility and voluntary self-generating effort. This imbalance must be redressed. A start should be made by reducing the sheer weight of the legislation.[56]

Thus the emphasis in the act was on the rationalisation of the legal situation so that individual workers could look after their own health better, rather than on any strengthening of legal controls. Indeed, the Robens Report effectively depoliticised the whole issue, suggesting that there exists, 'a greater natural identity of interest between ''the two sides'' in relation to safety and health problems than in most other matters'.[57] Moreover, it assumed that the single most important cause of accidents is apathy or carelessness on the part of workers, rather than negligence or lack of concern on the part of employers.[58] The emphasis in the act was, therefore, placed firmly on persuasion and education and the means of enforcing the legislation remained severely restricted. There are still, for example, very few factory inspectors for all the workplaces to be visited, and even when prosecutions do take place, the penalties imposed by magistrates are often derisory - the average fine paid by an employer in 1975 was £75.[59]

The relative ineffectiveness of the health and safety law enforcement machinery, is exacerbated by the lack of a national occupational health service. It has always been a major criticism of the NHS, that it did not include an industrial health service - those industrial health provisions which do exist are organised ·by individual employers. As a consequence, it has been estimated that only about thirty per cent of workers have access to such services.[60] Relatively efficient emergency services are provided by the NHS, so that the lack of an industrial health service is significant not so much in terms of the treatment of accidents but because of the potential role of such a service in the prevention of accidents, and in the identification and prevention of industrial disease.

Industrial health strategies have been developed within the limits set by a capitalist economy and the overall thrust has been towards the adjustment of workers to the pace and the physical conditions of the production process, rather than the reverse. An extremely apt illustration of this is provided by the recent trend towards genetic screening. Since the 1960s, it has been known that a relationship exists between the possession of certain genetic characteristics, and the likelihood of developing particular diseases. As a result, discussions have been going on for some time about the need to identify those workers with a genetic susceptibility to particular industrial chemicals, in order to exclude them from particular jobs. While this may appear on the surface to be a very sensible proposition, it is of course, no substitute for the more desirable alternative of making the workplace safer for *all* workers. There is no evidence to suggest that hypersusceptibility is responsible for any significant proportion of occupational disease, but genetic screening continues to be hailed in many quarters as the way forward for industrial health programmes.

So far we have examined some of the more physical dimensions of industrial ill health, but it is also important to look more broadly at the relationship between health and work. It is now relatively commonplace to suggest that workers are bored and alienated by assembly line work, and that many aspects of the labour process are stressful for both workers *and* managers. The existence of a link between an individual's health in the broadest sense, and the nature of his/her work is increasingly accepted. As yet, very few attempts have been made to look at this relationship in more detail, but it is illuminating to consider patterns of sickness absence in this connection. In Britain, rates of sickness absence have been rising continuously since the early 1960s, and by 1972 the annual number of working days lost through illness had risen to over three hundred and twenty million.[61] This rise is difficult to explain, since during the same period, there was a decline in the number of days lost through those diseases such as TB, pneumonia and stomach and duodenal ulcers, which have traditionally produced a significant volume of sickness absence. However, other causes such as 'sprains and strains', 'nerves, debility and headache' and 'psychoneuroses' have increased. [62] Thus the 'harder', more objectively identifiable causes of sickness absence have been replaced by more subjective psychosomatic ones, and it is the presence of these new ailments which needs to be explained.

It is often suggested that these new illnesses are 'excuses' which workers consciously use because they are lazy, or wish to avoid unpleasant work situations. Increased sickness absence is also said to be a direct consequence of the availability of sickness benefit under the social security system. However, for most workers sickness absence still involves considerable financial loss - only very few (i.e. those with large families and very low wages) are actually better off on sickness benefit than they are at work. Moreover, benefit is payable only *after* the first three days of absence. It seems unlikely then, that conscious and calculated 'malingering' would be a wide-spread phenomenon. An alternative interpretation of the statistics is that for many, work has become not only physically but also psychologically dangerous. Thus the demands of boring, repetitive and deskilled work performed at very high speed, combined with increased rates of over-time and shift work, may well be producing an increasing amount of stress which for many workers is exacerbated by job insecurity. This stress is reflected in an increased incidence of 'psychoneuroses' and of 'nerves, debility and headache' and may also be a precipitating factor in what appear to be more straight-forward physical illnesses.

Any attempt to explain present trends in sickness absence more fully must, therefore, take into account the more qualitative aspects of work and the working environment. It appears, for instance, that the less control workers have over their work, and the less satisfied they are with their job, the greater the number of days that are likely to be lost through sickness absence. [63]

So far, our discussion has concentrated on the situation of waged workers (both male and female). [64] However, the organisation of work in a capitalist society threatens health on an even broader basis. In the first place, employment is not available to everyone who wishes or needs it. As a consequence the experience of unemployment is a source of severe stress for many people, and often undermines their health. [65] Secondly, many women risk their health, both physically and psychologically, in the performance of domestic labour. Women at home have a high accident rate, and the under-capitalised and isolated nature of housework is an important contributory factor in this. In 1971, 6,245 people died in home accidents - 35.3 per cent of whom were men and 64.7 per cent women - while many more were injured. [66] Naturally, none of these figures appear in the industrial accident statistics since domestic labour is not officially counted as work. More importantly perhaps, full-time housewives experience their own version of occupational disease in the form of depressive illness. [67] Obviously there are several factors which could be important in explaining the high rate of psychiatric illness among housewives. Not only is housework unpaid, but the work itself is of low status - it is menial labour. [68] It is hardly surprising that in a society where an individual's value is measured by what they can command on the labour market, anyone doing manual work without pay may have difficulty in maintaining a reasonable level of self-esteem. Moreover, housework is both isolated and extremely repetitive, while the care of young children can be both exhausting and demoralising. Many women respond to these pressures created by the nature of their labour with feelings of depression and anxiety - a widespread if unacknowledged form of occupational ill health. Much research remains to be done in understanding the relationship between work and health, but Marx's classic description of the nature of wage labour remains an important philosophical starting point for such an analysis.

> What constitutes the alienation of labour? First, that the work is external to the worker - that it is not part of his nature; and that consequently he does not fulfill himself in his work, but denies himself, has a feeling of misery rather than well-being, does not develop freely his mental and physical energies, but is physically exhausted and mentally debased. [69]

It is clear then, that the nature and organisation of work under capitalism, threatens the well-being of large numbers of people.

Moreover, it is evident that these effects are not confined to the immediate workplace, but extend outwards to affect the whole spectrum of their daily lives. Far from work being the activity through which men and women realise their potential, it is often both a physically and a psychologically dangerous activity which is undertaken only in order to earn the means of survival.

Production, pollution and health

It is not just workers themselves who are affected by the physical nature of the production process. The hazards of production extend well beyond the workplace, transforming the material environment and contributing to what are often termed 'pollution problems'.

Strictly speaking, pollution is a misnomer as Enzensberger has pointed out.

> This category is misleading in so far as it presupposes a 'clean' world. This has naturally never existed and is moreover ecologically neither conceivable nor desirable. What is actually meant are disequilibriums and dysfunctionings of all kinds in the metabolism between nature and human society occurring as the unintentional side effects of the industrial process. [70]

'Pollution', seen in this light, can either cause subjective discomfort of various kinds, impairing the quality of life, or can be directly involved in the causation of specific disease processes. Here we shall look at three aspects of industrial pollution, and their impact on health. First, the process by which workers themselves (unknowingly) import dangerous material into their own homes; second, the polluting effects of factories on their immediate neighbourhoods; and third, the way in which industrial pollution, combined with the effects of commodities such as leaded petrol, produce more widespread air and water pollution, and affect the total urban environment.

The processes by which workers transport toxic substances into their homes, have begun to be documented in some considerable detail. For instance, a recent independent study in Manchester and Dagenham, showed that children whose fathers were employed by the largest British manufacturer of rechargeable batteries (the Chloride Group) were ingesting traces of lead at home.[71] The levels of lead in these children's blood were much higher than those of other children living in urban areas. Since the levels were higher among the families of Chloride workers than among other children who lived as near to the factories, it was concluded that workers were bringing lead home on their clothes, their shoes and even in their hair. Or again, researchers at Mount Sinai Medical Center in New York have discovered evidence of a higher than normal incidence of cancer of the lung and intestinal tract, of asbestosis and of mesothelioma (all diseases associated with working in an asbestos factory) among the *families* of men who worked in a New Jersey asbestos factory during the 1940s and early 1950s. The *New Scientist* summed up their findings as follows:

> Last year Selikoff's group started to look at the families of Paterson Asbestos workers, who received slight exposure to fibres brought back by the wage earners in their hair and clothing. To date, the team has X-rayed 210 people and the results are disturbing indeed. Almost 40 per cent of the subjects were found to possess abnormalities in their lungs, of the type common to asbestos workers. Even more alarming is the fact that some of the abnormalities have shown up in the lungs of subjects whose asbestos industry kin spent no more than a few days at the Paterson plant.
>
> The problem is not restricted to lung abnormalities. Recent months have seen three cases of mesothelioma among the asbestos workers' families who were indirectly exposed to the mineral fibres, and Selikoff fears an increase in such cases in years to come.[72]

But workers also bring home the dangers of the workplace in an even more insidious way. This occurs because certain substances commonly used in industrial processes have the capacity to affect the human reproductive system. Through altering chromosomal material, exposure to these substances can cause damage to unborn (and possibly even unconceived) children. It has long been known that both radiation and lead can produce this type of effect and evidence is now accumulating that at sufficiently high levels of exposure, lead can produce significant alterations in the number, structure and motility of sperm. But even more frighteningly, these effects may not be immediately apparent. A recent study by Fabio and Dam Thuy examined the occupation of the father at the time of birth, for a number of Canadian children suffering from malignant disease.[73] It was found that an excessively large proportion of the fathers were employed in hydrocarbon related occupations, including motor vehicle mechanics, machinists, miners and painters. As the authors of the study point out, much more research is needed to explain these striking results. They could be caused either by the child's contact with substances brought into the home by the father, or by the direct effect on sperm production of some hydrocarbon contained in petrol and oil - i.e. a genetically transmitted effect. At present, however, very little attention is paid to more indirect health hazards of this kind, and only women are prevented from working in certain jobs known to involve this type of risk.[74]

Workers then, transport dangerous substances from their work into their homes. In addition, the wider community is also exposed to industrial pollution through the spreading of industrial wastes into the surrounding neighbourhood either in the air or in water. Those cases of pollution which receive the most attention are the sudden and dramatic ones - the disaster which occurred at Seveso in 1976 for instance, when dioxin, one of the most toxic substances known, was released over a large area of suburban Milan. Dreadful as such disasters are, they should not be allowed to detract attention from the disease, discomfort and even death caused by more continuous and often invisible pollution of urban environments. In recent years some of the more extreme examples of such pollution have come from Japan - the mercury poisoning of Minamata Bay in the 1950s, for example, and the recent discovery of widespread chromium pollution in Tokyo. Similar incidents have occurred in Britain. It is now clear that the 'epidemic' of asbestosis in the Yorkshire village of Hebden Bridge first reported in the mid 1970s, is not confined to workers or even to workers and their families but extends to the whole community.[75] Asbestos fibres from the local factory had polluted the whole area, and, in the process of just going about their daily lives, people were breathing in enough fibres to produce asbestosis. One of the most striking studies of local pollution of this kind has recently been produced by the National Cancer Institute in the USA.[76] It has long been known that copper, lead and zinc smelting can all produce an excess rate of lung cancer among workers. This study demonstrated that the risk involves not just workers in the smelting plant but the whole local community. An examination of lung cancer rates in different countries concluded that average mortality rates from lung cancer among male and female whites in the USA from 1950-69 were significantly higher in counties with copper, lead or zinc smelting and refining industries. In these 36 counties, the mean increase in lung cancer mortality (corrected for demographic influences) was 17 per cent for males and 15 per cent for female. This increased rate was assumed to be due to community arsenical poisoning.

Finally, there is what could be called general rather than local pollution - that is, the more diffuse atmospheric pollution typical of urban areas. The precise combination of factors producing this pollution varies geographically. In most areas in Britain, it is caused by the accumulation of irritant gases such as sulphur dioxide combined with atmospheric suspensions of tars and resins, and with matter such as cotton or asbestos fibres. Complex processes, many of them industrial in origin, combine to produce this characteristic urban pollution which has been implicated in the production of ill health in a variety of ways. It can, for example, be responsible for irritation of the eyes and of the bronchial passages, as well as for increased susceptibility to infection, particularly in children and old people. More seriously, atmospheric pollution, especially in industrial areas, is one element in the production of chronic bronchitis and emphysema.

Another hazard arises from the high concentration of atmospheric lead (most of it from leaded petrol) particularly for children living near roads with heavy traffic. In such circumstances, atmospheric lead becomes attached to sticky food (such as sweets) and to children's hands, and recent studies have shown that it is quite possible for a child to consume almost ten times its tolerable daily lead intake in ten contaminated sweets.[77] Severe lead poisoning causes serious damage to the central nervous system and is relatively easy to detect. Slightly increased lead levels, on the other hand, cause apparently minor symptoms such as constipation, tiredness, headaches or colic, and in such cases lead is unlikely to be identified as the real cause.

The rapid increase in potentially toxic substances coming into daily use poses the problem of what should be regarded as a 'normal' level of any given substance in the body. So-called 'safe levels' vary at different times and between different countries, providing an illustration of how supposedly scientific decisions are affected by wider social and economic considerations. The concept of threshhold limit values (TLVs) is used to determine what dose of a given substance is safe for an individual - i.e. what level should not be exceeded - and a concern to minimise interference with production is often clearly in evidence when 'safe levels' are being set. Although TLVs appear very precise and scientific, they are by and large, very crude measures, often based on inadequate knowledge, especially of the subclinical effects of the substance in question. Moreover, they are usually applied without differentiation, to individuals with very varied levels of tolerance. In the case of industrial workers, for example the TLV will be applied uniformly, even though workers with different roles in the production process will have very different 'tidal flows' of toxic material through their bodies. Similarly, in the case of atmospheric pollution, separate TLVs are not calculated for women, for children, or for those with respiratory illness. [78] Finally, TLVs are calculated separately for each potential pollutant, or for the same pollutant from different sources, so that the cumulative and synergistic (interacting) effects of different substances are not taken into account.

People, therefore, continue to be polluted in a variety of ways as a consequence of industrialised commodity production - probably to a degree that we are not yet even aware of. Moreover, that pollution is most severe for those who come into closest contact with the production process in both their living and working lives. Problems of this kind can often appear to be accidental or to be a natural and unavoidable consequence of the use of industrial technology. In fact, they represent the inevitable outcome of a situation where extremely powerful techniques for controlling the natural world have been developed within the context of a social and economic system which ensures that these techniques are used primarily for private rather than public gain and that most individuals are unable to protect themselves from these widespread threats to their health.[79]

Consumption, health and illness

We have examined the health risks inherent in many aspects of the actual process of commodity production, showing that they play an important part in creating class differences in morbidity and mortality. But it is also true that many of the goods produced are in themselves dangerous to health. Commodities are being produced for sale and consumed at an ever-increasing rate, and a great many of these products are not 'useful' according to any commonsense definition of the term. More than this, they may actually damage the health of consumers. This section will concentrate on case studies of the production and consumption of two of these potentially dangerous commodities - tobacco and certain food.

Cancer causes approximately twenty per cent of deaths in Britain every year. Of these, approximately forty per cent in men and eleven per cent in women are a result of cancer of the lung (and the rate of lung cancer in women is increasing very rapidly).[80] The relationship between carcinoma of the lung and cigarette smoking has now been clearly established, and smoking has also been implicated in the causation of a range of other diseases - heart disease and bronchitis in particular.[81] According to the Royal College of Physicians, 'Cigarette smoking is now as important a cause of death as were the great epidemic diseases such as typhoid, cholera and TB that affected previous generations in this country'.[82]

Estimates vary as to exactly how many deaths are caused by cigarette smoking. George Godber, (then chief medical officer to the DHSS) estimated in 1970 that nearly one hundred thousand people died prematurely in Britain *each year* as a result of smoking (more than all the civilian casualties in Britain in the second world war).[83] In addition, of course, smoking greatly increases levels of morbidity. It is difficult to calculate exactly how much illness is due to smoking, but tobacco-related ill health has been estimated to cause the annual loss of as many as fifty million working days, and clearly produces much incapacity and suffering in those affected.[84] The health-damaging effects of smoking extend beyond smokers themselves to their children (both born and unborn). Besides producing on average, smaller babies, mothers who smoke greatly increase the chance of their pregnancies ending in spontaneous abortion, still-birth or neonatal death.[85]

In 1976, 42 per cent of the adult population were cigarette smokers - 46 per cent of men and 38 per cent of women.[86] Working-class smokers are becoming an increasingly large proportion of the total, so that in 1975, only 29 per cent of men in social class I were smokers, compared with 57 per cent in social class V.[87] Between 1958-75 smoking by people in social class I fell by 53 per cent for men and by 15 per cent for women; in social class V there was an increase of 9 per cent in men and a staggering 63 per cent in women. Not surprisingly, there is therefore a very much higher incidence of the diseases associated with smoking - especially lung cancer - in social classes III, IV, and particularly V.

The official explanation of the continuation of such a dangerous habit on a mass scale, is that smokers are too weak to stop and hence have only themselves to blame for anything that may happen to them. This is a convenient, but naively simple explanation. Thus, while it is now widely accepted that the present 'epidemic' of lung cancer is caused by smoking, the social pressures which are crucial in creating and maintaining the 'need' for cigarettes have been ignored, or greatly underestimated. In fact, we can only understand the use of nicotine as a dependence-producing drug, within the context of the prevailing social climate which encourages smoking much more strongly than it discourages it.

The enormous advertising and promotion effort of the tobacco companies defines smoking as a desirable and prestigious activity, which supposedly conveys sexual attractiveness, social status, virility, maturity and so on. It is difficult to obtain precise figures on the size of the advertising budget of the tobacco companies, but reliable estimates suggest that in Britain alone they spend well over one million pounds *each week* on persuading people to smoke.[88] Research on the link between smoking and ill health has made it clear that this advertising and promotion represents a threat to the life of every actual or potential smoker. However the tobacco companies are in the business of selling cigarettes and so will wish to encourage a continued and deadly dependence on them. Their response to the evidence concerning the health risks of smoking has been to cast doubts on the medical evidence itself, while at the same time agreeing to certain limitations on advertising, to putting warnings on cigarette packets, and to searching for a 'safer' cigarette. They are committed though to maintaining and, if possible, extending the smoking habit itself. Profits depend on it.

Given the clear interests of the tobacco industry, it apparently falls to the state to regulate the activities of the industry in the public interest. But the relationship between the state and the tobacco industry is a complex one. In 1960 10 per cent of all government revenue came from taxes on the sale of tobacco. Although this figure had fallen to less than five per cent by 1975, it still represented a very considerable sum - approximately one thousand, five hundred million pounds. [89] Hence any reduction in tobacco sales would mean a substantial cut in government tax revenue, *unless* the rate of taxation were considerably increased. [90] It would be possible to shift the basis of taxation, so that the equivalent amount of tax could be raised in another way, but there would be difficulties in finding another politically acceptable source of tax revenue. In any case, the economic significance which smoking has for the state is not based only on the amount of tax revenue obtained from tobacco. This revenue must be set against the costs to the economy and to public funds, of the diseases and deaths caused by smoking. The calculations involved here are very complex but it has been estimated that smoking costs the NHS as much as £300,000 every day. On the other hand, the cost to the state of social security payments is actually *reduced* in certain respects by the present pattern of lung cancer deaths. For instance, the *New Scientist* recently reported that,

> As a grisly analysis undertaken by the Department of Health three years ago showed, a reduction in cigarette smoking would eventually cost the country more than was gained - not only would there be loss of revenue from taxation but also the additional 'burden' of having to pay out pensions to the people who had given up smoking before it killed them. [91]

Moreover, there are even wider economic and political issues involved in the control of smoking which cannot be measured by a simple cost-benefit approach. One estimate has suggested for example that a 25 per cent drop in cigarette sales would lead to the loss of 5,000 jobs in Birmingham and Nottingham. [92] Similarly the financially precarious newspaper industry earned £11.5 million from cigarette advertising in 1974 (which explains some of the virulent editorial opposition to curbs on tobacco firms) and many sports are dependent on the sponsorship of cigarette manufacturers. [93] Factors such as these obviously militate against any significant curtailment by the state of the activities of cigarette manufacturers, thus reinforcing the powerful lobbying coming from the tobacco industry itself.

As a consequence of these various pressures, attempts by the state to control smoking have been very limited. They have concentrated mainly on attempting to change individual habits through health education, rather than directly controlling the industry. Moreover, the resources made available to do this have been very limited. In 1975, for example, less than one million pounds was spent on publicising the dangers of smoking, compared with the estimated fifty to seventy million pounds spent by the tobacco industry on persuading people to smoke. [94] Thus the continuing loss of life and health through smoking reflect, on the one hand the induced dependence of smokers on cigarettes and their importance as a source of relief from the pressures and tensions of daily life and on the other hand, the importance of cigarettes to the tobacco industry as the source of all their profits.

The case of food - our second illustration of the health risks inherent in particular commodities - is of course very different from that of tobacco. Food of some sort is essential to survival, whereas people do not *need* cigarettes in the same sense. However, food is also produced for profit, and the transformation of food into a commodity has had profound effects on what is produced, how it is produced and how it is distributed. As a result of the mechanisation and concentration of food production, 'we eat a more highly processed diet, and are further removed from the agricultural sources of our dietary items than at any other time in history'. [95] Indeed, as

Harry Rothman and David Radford have pointed out, we now eat 'the diet of industrial-capitalist man', and this diet would be unimaginable without the social and economic changes associated with the rise of industrial capitalism. [96]

The staple diet for most urban families in the early nineteenth century seems to have been white bread and tea, and most of the food consumed was of a very inferior quality. John Burnett has described the widespread adulteration of food in the early nineteenth century.

> As soon as there emerged a consuming public, distinct and separated from the producers of food, opportunities for organised commercial fraud arose. Cheaper and nutritionally inferior substitutes might be used to replace the proper constituents of a food, essential ingredients might be removed, or foreign substances added to impart fictitious flavour, appearance or strength. [97]

As a consequence, generalised malnutrition or undernourishment were common during the Industrial Revolution in both urban and rural areas and many people were actually poisoned by dangerous substances in food they had no alternative but to consume.

However, in the latter half of the nineteenth century, working-class diets began to improve. By about 1850, food adulteration had become such a major problem in the cities that laws were passed to control it (although, of course, it is often argued that new technological forms of adulteration have now replaced these older methods). More importantly, the consolidation of British capitalism made possible an improvement in both the quantity and the quality of food available for working-class consumption. Overseas expansion meant that a cheaper and wider range of food became available for the home market, while new techniques of storage (canning and freezing, for example) and new methods of transportation (especially railways) facilitated the creation of a mass market for this broadening range of foodstuffs. As a consequence of these developments, the early extremes of mass malnutrition gradually disappeared, and have not returned. Hence, one outcome of the industrial revolution and of capitalist expansion has been the capacity to provide an appealing and varied diet for the majority of people in the metropolitan countries.

But despite the disappearance of widespread malnutrition, food did not become equally distributed among the population as a whole. John Boyd Orr in his 1930s study, *Food, Health and Income*, accepted that the average consumption of food had increased since the beginning of the century, but showed how unequally it was still distributed.[98] He divided the population into six income groups and then assessed the diet of each. Only the two most prosperous groups could afford an entirely adequate diet - all the others had a diet that was unsatisfactory in some respect or another. The diet of the most deprived group (consisting of four and a half million people) was *entirely* deficient, requiring additional proteins, fats, calories, mineral salts and vitamins to bring it up to even a minimum standard. In the poorest group the average consumption of milk (including tinned milk) was 1.8 pints per week - less than one-third of the 5.8 pints consumed by the richest group. The poorest group spent less than one-eighth of what the wealthiest spent on fruit and consumed on average only one-third as many eggs as the richest.[99]

However inadequate diets are not just a thing of the past. Rising food prices in a period of stagnation and unemployment, have made it increasingly difficult for many people to feed themselves adequately. In 1976, for example, the National Food Survey showed that the energy content, the iron and the vitamin D_1 contained in food eaten at home by families with at least four children had fallen below the total intake recommended by the Department of Health and Social Security.[100] It also showed the very considerable differences which continue to exist in the quality of diet of rich and poor. (See Table two.)

Overall, those who are richer tend to eat more fruit, vegetables (except potatoes), meat (except tinned meat and sausages), milk and cheese, while the poorer eat more bread, potatoes and sugar. These differences in diet are important, not just because they reflect the access of the wealthy to preferred foods, but because they represent social class differences in nutritional status and, as we shall see, may well constitute a significant element in explaining some of the social class differences in morbidity and mortality.[102]

Table 2: Food Consumption by Income Group in 1977
          Ounces per person per week

| | Income group | | | |
	A	B	C	D
White bread	18.0	25.0	28.0	31.0
Brown bread (incl. wholemeal)	4.9	3.4	2.8	3.3
Sugar	9.3	11.0	13.0	15.0
Potatoes	29.0	39.0	49.0	52.0
Fruit	33.0	24.0	20.0	17.0

Source: *Household Food Consumption and Expenditure*,
London, HMSO 1978

Over the past 150 years, dietary patterns in most industrialised countries have changed in three very important ways, and Britain provides a typical example. First, there has been an increase in the consumption of refined carbohydrates, especially sugar. Between 1860 and 1960, the average annual consumption of sugar in Britain approximately doubled.[103] By 1960, it had risen to 120 lb per head, although it then declined slightly to 95 lb per head by 1977.[104] At present, sugar provides approximately one-fifth of the calories in the average British diet. Second, fat consumption is estimated to have risen by about fifty per cent between 1860 and 1960,[105] so that a total of 41 per cent of food energy is now derived from fats.[106] Finally, it has been estimated that between 1880 and 1960 there was a 90 per cent *decline* in the volume of fibre in British diets.[107] During the nineteenth century, the introduction of steel roller milling made possible the mass consumption of white bread. As a consequence, the poor lost a large proportion of the fibre in their diet, as well as about one third of their vitamin B_1 intake, and up to half of their daily iron.[108] This loss of fibre was exaggerated by the decline in the consumption of cereals, and especially after the second world war, by a decline in the consumption of fresh vegetables. As Table two shows, both the increase in sugar and the decline in fibre have affected working-class diets disproportionately.

The expansion and concentration of the food industry in the post-war period, has meant a continuation and even an acceleration of these general trends. It was in the 1930s that well known food manufacturers such as Unilever and Tate & Lyle, first began to play a significant part in providing food for the British population on a mass basis. This trend has continued and since the second world war, food production has increasingly been taken over by huge, often multi-national companies such as the Imperial Group, British American Tobacco, Allied Bakeries, Spillers and Ranks Hovis McDougall. This has led to the use of the term 'agri-business' to describe the present-day pattern of food production, processing and distribution.[109] Farming has been made less and less labour intensive through the expanding use of agri-chemicals - chemical fertilisers, insecticides, herbicides and fungicide are all very widely used. This has meant increased profits for the chemical industry, and also a loss of jobs on the land, while so far as consumers are concerned, it has meant that a variety of incidental additives are likely to contaminate the final food product. More importantly perhaps, the increasing concentration of food production in the post-war period has meant a dramatic increase in food processing. If a particular item is to be marketed all over the country, then it must be easily transportable and storable. It must also be an identical product wherever it is purchased. As a consequence, food is processed and packaged so that it is relatively impervious to travel, has a reasonably long shelf life, and does not vary in quality or taste. This often means the addition of artificial flavourings and preservatives - some of which may represent a health risk if consumed in large quantities.[110] There is, however, more behind food processing than the attempt to create a homogeneous and longer-lasting product.

There is an ultimate physiological limit to food consumption - any individual can eat only a certain amount in a given period of time. However, if the food industry is to maintain its profit margins, then it must continuously expand sales. For food manufacturers, the answer to this problem has been to persuade people to buy new food products which are often low in nutritional value and may well be harmful to health. 'Needs' are therefore created for specific flavours and textures and a vast number of additives (currently said to be between two thousand five hundred and three thousand) are put into food to colour, flavour, preserve, thicken, emulsify and so on.[111] Thus, people are persuaded to buy food which is increasingly created in a factory rather than grown on a farm. This pressure towards the increased consumption of highly processed and even 'junk' food (especially by children) has reinforced existing dietary trends, as people increase their consumption of food which is high in sugar and fat and low in vitamins, minerals, protein and fibre. But what effect have these changing dietary patterns had on the social distribution of health and disease?

It is generally accepted that an adequate diet containing all the necessary nutrients *in the right proportions* is a necessary pre-requisite of good health. Thus a poor diet - one low in vitamins for example - will increase individuals' susceptibility to disease through reducing the effectiveness of their immunological system. More specifically, although there is still much debate about the relationship between dietary factors and particular disease processes, most of the so-called 'diseases of affluence' are now being linked in one way or another with diet. In the case of coronary heart disease, for example, it is now generally agreed that the level of consumption of saturated fats must be regarded as *one* significant contributary factor.[112] With cancer, on the other hand, the main dietary hypothesis to have emerged in recent years has been the suggested connection between the decline in the amount of dietary fibre consumed in industrialised societies, and the increase in intestinal cancer in those societies.[113] Epidemiological studies have shown that one of the main differences between pre-industrial and modern diets is the amount of vegetable fibre they contain. As a consequence, the time taken for the faeces to pass through the colon is much longer in 'advanced' countries than, for example, in rural African communities. It has been cogently argued that this delay increases the incidence of large bowel cancer, as well as a range of other diseases only found in the developed world, including piles, varicose veins, appendicitis and diverticular disease. Finally, it is evident that excessive consumption of sugar is implicated in a range of disease processes, including diabetes and dental decay.[114] But, above all, the intake of too many sugary foods plays an important part in producing widespread obesity, which is itself a serious threat to health.

Most people in the developed capitalist world now have enough to eat, but the balance and quality of their diet has produced a new kind of malnutrition - obesity. Too much food (often of the wrong kind), rather than too little, now constitutes a major health problem. People are encouraged to consume more food than they need, particularly starchy and sugary food high in calories. Processed foods in particular encourage overconsumption because of their lack of bulk. Moreover, the predominantly urban and sedentary nature of much contemporary life makes this diet increasingly inappropriate and dangerous. Formal measurements of obesity are difficult to make because of variations in individual build, but surveys in London general practices have estimated that about fifty-six per cent of women and fifty-two per cent of men over the age of forty are at least fifteen per cent above their ideal weight.[115] Again, there are very marked class differences in the incidence of obesity, with working-class women being particularly prone to excessive weight gain.[116] Obesity constitutes a very serious threat to health, as Lock and Smith have pointed out.

> Overall, the mortality of men 10 per cent or more overweight is one-fifth higher than average; the corresponding increases for men 20 per cent and 30 per cent overweight are about one-fifth and two-fifths. In women the risks are slightly less: 9 per cent, 20 per cent and 30 per cent respectively. These increased risks are associated particularly with deaths from diabetes (130 per cent excess mortality in men) and from vascular disease (30 per cent excess for coronary disease and 50 per cent for vascular disease of the central nervous system in men).[117]

A recognition of the relationship between obesity in childhood and in adult life, has been one of the factors behind the recent concern about patterns of infant feeding and their relationship to health. In the post-war period in particular there has been a very dramatic trend away from breast-feeding. In 1946, nearly fifty per cent of babies were still breast-fed at three months, but by the 1970s the figure had fallen to about six per cent.[118] The reasons for this trend are clearly complex, but it has been encouraged by the advertising and promotional activities of the baby milk and baby food manufacturers who have consistently suggested that their products are as good as, if not superior to, mother's milk. They also imply that the earlier babies start to eat solid food the better for their health. However, recent research has thrown very considerable doubt on both these claims, through showing that breast-fed babies gain undoubted advantages over babies fed with modified cows milk.[119] On the one hand, they are actually protected from gastro-enteritis and certain other infections, while also avoiding the risk of bacterial contamination which is always a possibility with bottle feeding. Bottle-fed children, on the other hand, may occasionally experience chemical disturbances because of the high levels of phosphate, sodium and protein in modified cows milk. They seem to be more likely to suffer from sudden unexpected 'cot death', and are certainly more prone to obesity than breast-fed babies. Manufactured food for older babies has also been criticised, and it is now being argued that campaigns to persuade mothers to give solid food to babies as early as possible has been a major contributory factor in childhood obesity.

The feeding of babies has therefore become an extremely profitable enterprise. Mothers milk (which is free) has been replaced by an expensive commodity - manufactured milk - and the majority of mothers of young babies have become captive consumers. Moreover it seems that these costly substitutes, while being extremely useful under certain circumstances, are less healthy than breast milk for the majority of babies.[120]

There is now a growing awareness of the health-damaging nature of much modern food and for many people in the developed world, food is becoming a political issue.[121] Not surprisingly, most food manufacturers either ignore criticisms of their products altogether, or respond by trying to persuade consumers that these criticisms are unfounded. The bread industry exemplifies both these strategies very clearly. Recent research has criticised the nutritional content of most bread, pointing out that bread manufacturers remove many of the essential parts of the wheat, replacing them with additives which are not as nutritionally accessible and cannot replace the lost fibre content.[122] Evidence is unequivocal that wholemeal bread is more nutritionally satisfactory than white bread, yet, rather than producing more wholemeal bread, the bread industry has organised expensive advertising campaigns to persuade consumers of the desirability of the white sliced loaf. The reasons for their resistance to nutritional criticism are clearly economic and relate to three basic considerations.

First, the bran which is milled out of bread, thereby depleting its fibre content, is resold as animal food, and provides a profitable by-product. Secondly, bread factories are at present geared to the production of white bread made from wheat imported from the USA, and any alterations to these plants would be expensive. Finally, wholemeal bread is much more filling. Therefore it seems likely that if only wholemeal bread were available, less of it would be consumed and the total bread market would decline. As a consequence, the bread industry continues to concentrate on the production of the pre-packed sliced white loaf, irrespective of its nutritional value.

This is not to say of course, that the bread industry does not produce wholemeal bread - clearly it does. However this is defined as a luxury, is more expensive than the ordinary white loaf, and is mainly produced by small independent bakers. This provision of an alternative 'health food', in addition to the nutritionally suspect commodity, represents an alternative strategy which many manufacturers have developed in response to the increasing recognition of the deficiencies of modern food. During the last few years, the 'health food' industry has expanded dramatically, providing (at a price) food which has not been subject to the usual commercial processing - wholemeal bread, brown rice, pure honey and so on. In addition, manufacturers have marketed a wide range of 'natural health products', often not natural at all, aimed at the health conscious, (though not necessarily well-informed) consumer, and designed to compensate for deficiencies in 'normal' food. For example, the recognition of the importance of fibre in the diet, has meant a dramatic increase in the production of cereals and laxatives containing bran.[123] The food and drug industries have utilised the fibre debate to increase their profits, so that bran is now manipulated and packaged into a sophisticated and relatively expensive commodity. Similarly, an increasing awareness of the lack of micronutrients in much of our food has resulted in a quite disproportionate consumption of dietary supplements (such as vitamins or 'tonics') which are often of very limited effectiveness. Finally, the problem of widespread obesity has produced a huge market for slimming products - in Britain the slimming industry now reports a turnover in excess of sixty-five million pounds per year. This new market in 'health' extends far beyond food and associated products, into elixirs, beauty products of all kinds, and a variety of home remedies.[124] 'Health' has become one more commodity which manufacturers can sell, while continuing to produce those health-damaging products which were often instrumental in producing the original ill health.

Most governments in the developed world have now come to accept (if sometimes rather slowly) the significance of dietary patterns for health and illness. However apart from attempting to prevent the use of clearly toxic substances in food processing, they have placed very few constraints on the food producers. Rather, official policy has concentrated on the use of moral exhortation and some degree of re-education in order to persuade people to adopt a healthier diet.[125] This clearly parallels the official approach to smoking - little direct interference in production, coupled with limited attempts to alter patterns of consumption.

As Rothman and Radford have pointed out,

> Within our economic system, food production has a twofold function: to satisfy both the human need to eat, and the capitalist need for profit. To a far greater extent than was the case in previous historical periods, what food is grown and how it is grown, and what food is processed and how it is processed, depend on the criterion of profit as well as on biological and psychological criteria. From this state of affairs, one may observe that nutritional science contains a socially critical potential, in so far as it is able to highlight contradictions between nutritional needs and economic expediency.[126]

Thus government policies with regard to food (or any other potentially dangerous commodity) are constrained by a range of economic and social interests which are often in direct conflict with wider health needs.[127]

Stress as a source of ill health

We have so far been concerned largely with the more material aspects of life under capitalism, and have emphasised the physical causes of health and illness. But health and illness cannot be defined in purely physical terms - no rigid distinction can be made between mind and body, between psyche and soma. Hence we also need to take into account the psychological effects of a particular kind of social and economic environment on health and well-being. The most obvious way to do this is to consider the social production of mental illness.

Any attempt to assess the real incidence of psychiatric illness in Britain today faces very serious difficulties. Even assuming that we accept that there is such a thing as psychiatric illness (and there are many who would not), it is extremely difficult to estimate the extent, the nature or the causes of such 'illness' from the official statistics. [128] Nevertheless, what we do know is that there has been a rapid rise in recent years in the number of people seeking psychiatric help. About one woman in eight and one man in twelve can expect to enter a psychiatric hospital at some time in their lives, while approximately fifty per cent of NHS expenditure is now used to provide psychiatric care of one kind or another. [129] Thus, it could be said that Britain, like most other developed countries, has experienced an 'epidemic' of psychiatric illness during the post-war period.

It is an almost inescapable conclusion that this sharp rise in the number of people seeking medical help for psychological problems is somehow related to what are loosely called the 'stresses and strains of modern life'. Moreover, the social distribution of different types of mental illness between the sexes and between classes does strongly suggest that, in most instances, illness of this kind must be linked to aspects of social and economic organisation, rather than solely to individual genetics or 'innate predispositions'. [130] That is to say, there appear to be certain aspects of life in developed capitalist societies - in this case Britain - that are potentially damaging to psychological as well as physical health, although few studies have yet looked in detail at precisely what these relationships might be.

However, we cannot look at the psychological impact of the social environment only through the production of mental illness -

mind and body cannot be separated in this artificial way. It is evident that emotions and feelings are also important in the creation of health problems which at first glance appear to be almost entirely physical in their origins. There is a commonplace acceptance, as we have seen, that stress at work may often play a part in damaging an individual's health - although this is more often applied to an airline pilot or a 'coronary-prone executive' than it is to a manual worker struggling to support his or her family. Thus it is increasingly accepted that stress of various kinds can affect physical health - a belief that has been given support by a wide range of epidemiological studies.[131] It is important, therefore, to be clear about the precise role that stress can be said to play in the causation of ill health. The effects of stress do not seem to be direct. Rather, the experience of stress seems to increase a person's susceptibility to other disease agents, and hence increases the overall likelihood of their becoming ill. How this comes about is complex, but it must be understood, at least initially, in terms of the physiological processes associated with stress.

When someone experiences stress, the immediate cause - the 'stressor' - may be either physical or psychological. In either case, it has certain physiological correlates, notably a process of arousal which causes an increase in heart-rate and blood pressure, changes in the distribution of blood around the body and the release of glucose, fatty acids and large amounts of adrenalin into the blood stream. It seems that frequent experiences of this kind are potentially destructive to health, not because they produce specific stress-related diseases (as is often assumed), but rather because they will tend to predispose the individual concerned to ill health *of all kinds* - both physical and psychological.

The idea of stress as a variable in the creation of ill health is obviously an extremely important one, since, potentially at least, it brings wider aspects of the social and economic environment into epidemiological thinking. It is for this reason that stress has become a central concept in recent attempts to develop a 'historical materialist epidemiology'.[132] Arguments of this kind start from the assumption that for a variety of reasons a capitalist mode of organisation will entail large numbers of people leading particularly stressful lives.

One of the central tasks of epidemiology it is argued, should therefore be to explore the significance of this fact in explaining the current 'disease burden'. Following this pattern, Joseph Eyer, for example, has suggested that we can divide these sources of stress under capitalism into two categories: those which derive from external controls over the labour force; and those which relate to internal controls.[133] In the case of the former, he is concerned with phenomena such as the mobility and fast turnover of labour, unemployment and job insecurity, and the increasing division of labour which is accompanied by a rapid pace of work. In the case of internal controls he is concerned among other things, with the consequences of the fact that people are socialised into being individualistic, competitive and concerned only with the acquisition of material possessions. Eyer's argument is that these forms of stress are inherent in capitalism as we know it, and he explains much of the current pattern of morbidity and mortality in terms of the differential experience of such stress within the population. Thus he suggests that class differences in sickness and death, the disparity between urban and rural death-rates, the variations in mortality rates during the business cycle, and the increased rates of morbidity and mortality that accompany industrialisation and urbanisation can all be understood in relation to what he calls the 'accumulation of stress-induced bodily insults'. It is likely that in his analysis Eyer underestimates some of the more directly physical determinants of ill health, and it is certainly true that much work remains to be done in relating particular sorts of stress to specific patterns of morbidity and mortality. Nevertheless, this growing emphasis on the notion of stress is clearly very important in the development of a critical epidemiology. The well-being of any person is related not just to the absence of physical injury or disease, but to their own experience as a human being living in a particular natural and social environment. An examination of specific types of stress - or their absence - as well as a general exploration of the effects on health of the more subjective and phenomenological aspects of life must, therefore, be a central element in any attempt to understand health and illness under capitalism (or any other economic and social system).

3: Health, Illness and Underdevelopment

Few attempts have been made to examine the relationship between health and economic underdevelopment, and the burden of ill health which exists in most third world countries is usually attributed either to 'tropical' diseases or to food shortages produced by the 'population explosion'. Thus the extremely high rates of death and disease which characterise underdevelopment tend to be seen as the inevitable consequence of 'natural' climatic and demographic conditions. Somewhat perversely, however, population growth is simultaneously cited as evidence of a dramatic improvement in third world health which is widely credited to the introduction of western medicine. Such a view has two serious defects. First, it mystifies the role of scientific medicine and exaggerates its potential for solving health problems. Second, and perhaps more important, it obscures the role of imperialism itself in the creation of ill health in the underdeveloped countries of the world. In contrast to the experience of the metropolitan countries, the prevalence of most diseases in the third world is, in fact, as great - if not greater - than a century ago and it is this which requires explanation.

The underdevelopment of health in the third world

It is important to stress at the outset some of the difficulties entailed in obtaining reliable data on health patterns in the third world. In the first place, there are tremendous practical problems involved in collecting accurate and complete information of the most basic kind in countries lacking a developed administrative infrastructure. For this reason, there is usually a serious underestimation of the prevalence of disease, a large number of deaths go unrecorded, and their causes remain unidentified.[1] Most importantly, the available statistics are drawn overwhelmingly from the more prosperous areas, while remote rural areas are greatly under-represented. Secondly, the standard international indices of health and medical care are even more crude and conceptually inadequate when applied to the third world, than they are in relation to industrialised societies. For example, the statistics are usually presented as aggregates, concealing vast differences between rich and poor, and between urban and rural areas. Moreover, it is characteristic for city limits to be defined so narrowly that their squalid shantytowns can be excluded from the data altogether.[2] Health statistics are also especially vulnerable to bureaucratic manipulation because of their political and economic implications. Thus efforts to attract foreign investment and to promote tourism clearly encourage the concealment of unfavourable health data.[3] Furthermore, the very terms in which the statistics are formulated tend to obscure both the nature of disease in a living population and the means by which it might be eradicated. The availability of clean water for instance is a more relevant criterion of health in a third world population than the number of hospital beds provided. It is evident, however, that in order to make any assessment at all of the health situation in the third world, we must of necessity use whatever information is available, despite its limitations. It is therefore important to bear in mind that it almost certainly represents a serious underestimation of the real health problems.[4]

The major diseases in third world countries fall into two basic categories: infectious diseases, and those directly associated with malnutrition. Between them, they are responsible for the bulk of all mortality, particularly deaths in children under the age of five which account for at least half of all deaths.[5] Over fifty per cent of all childhood mortality can be attributed to nutritional deficiencies. Viewed on an international scale,

> It may be approximately estimated that 10 million of the children under five years of age in the developing countries are suffering from severe malnutrition, 80 million from moderate malnutrition and 120 million from less obvious, milder forms of malnutrition. In total therefore, about half of all the

children in the developing world may be inadequately nourished.[6]

Although malnutrition can be a primary cause of death - especially among the very young - it more often produces chronic ill health and debility. It also lowers resistance to infectious diseases, and considerably increases their severity once they have been contracted. A recent Latin American study established that almost ten per cent of childhood deaths were due to measles, and that in 60 per cent of these cases malnutrition was a contributory cause.[7] Chronic malnutrition in third world countries is often exacerbated by parasitic diseases which may cause so much damage to the intestinal walls that sufferers are unable to absorb the little food they actually manage to consume.[8]

Specific dietary deficiencies cause a great deal of chronic disease in underdeveloped countries. Lack of vitamin A causes many thousands of people in the third world to go blind. In India, for example, some fifteen thousand children under five go blind each year as a result of this deficiency.[9] Illnesses such as beri-beri, pellagra and scurvy are also the result of particular dietary imbalances. However, none of these specific problems, serious as they are, should obscure the fact that malnutrition in the third world today is primarily due to a general lack of basic sustenance. People simply do not get enough food ever to be healthy.[10] Hence it would be more accurate to describe the problem as one of *under*-nutrition, rather than malnutrition. One of the clearest indicators of this is the stunting of physical growth in young children, which is virtually impossible to compensate for later, even under the best conditions. The effects are then perpetuated through succeeding generations, since mothers, themselves stunted by childhood malnutrition and deprived of adequate food during pregnancy, tend to give birth to underweight babies. Under these circumstances the risk of both infant and maternal mortality is greatly increased.[11] Moreover, in some countries there has been a discernible decline in average body size in the course of this century, reflecting the worsening diet of recent generations. Inadequate nutrition before birth and in the earliest years of life is also thought to endanger neurological and intellectual development.[12]

Clearly the only effective solution to these problems of death and disease, caused by malnutrition, would be the provision of a food supply adequate to the needs of the whole population within each third world country. However, some five hundred million people in the world are already thought to have insufficient food to sustain a basic level of health,[13] and the World Health Organisation (WHO) expects the situation to worsen in years to come.

> Owing to rapid deterioration in the food and nutrition status of a vast segment of world population, there has been a reversal of the trend towards nutritional improvement in the developing countries associated with a general decline in the quality of life, the consequence of which will have to be faced by the health services of the affected countries.[14]

The other major category of disease found in third world countries can broadly be described as infectious. In standard medical literature this category is often subdivided according to the site of the infection itself (e.g. gastro-intestinal infections or respiratory infections). Alternatively, infectious diseases can be analysed according to their method of biological transmission (e.g. faecally-related diseases, air-borne diseases and vector-borne disease). This latter classification is preferable and will be used here, since it allows the identification of the environmental factors which generate these infections and suggests the potential means for preventing them.

The best known *faecally-related diseases* are probably polio, typhoid and cholera, but in underdeveloped countries the most common are the intestinal parasitic and infectious diarrhoeal diseases (including enteritis and dysentery). These diseases are a major cause of death in much of the third world as well as causing chronic and debilitating disease.[15] Millions of people are continuously exposed to parasites such as hookworm, and possibly one quarter of the entire world population is thought to be infected by roundworms.[16] All of these diseases are a direct consequence of insanitary conditions and contaminated water. The vast majority of third world populations still live in rural areas where fewer than fifteen per cent of the inhabitants have access to clean water supplies.[17] Moreover, although amenities such as sewerage and clean water supplies are concentrated in the towns they generally benefit only limited groups, while the characteristic proliferation of unplanned, overcrowded shantytowns often produces an even greater threat to hygiene than life in the countryside.

Air-borne diseases prevalent in the third world include tuberculosis, diphtheria, whooping cough, meningitis, influenza, measles and chickenpox. At least fifty million people are thought to suffer from tuberculosis alone.[18] The spread of such diseases is greatly facilitated by the overcrowded and inadequate living conditions so commonly found in the expanding urban areas of underdeveloped countries.

Vector-borne diseases are caused by organisms which are transmitted to human beings by disease vectors such as mosquitoes (malaria), water snails (schistosomiasis) or tsetse flies (sleeping sickness). Many of the so-called tropical diseases fall into this category. For example, some two hundred million people throughout the world now suffer from malaria. After the age of twelve months, almost every child in tropical Africa has the disease and each year approximately one million African children die of it.[19] Despite the fact that malaria eradication has been a cornerstone of WHO policy for over twenty years, it is actually having a resurgence in areas where it was once assumed to have been controlled.[20] Other vector-borne diseases, too, are on the increase. Recent estimates of the incidence of schistosomiasis (sometimes known as bilharzia) indicate that two hundred and fifty million people are now affected and that numbers are rising.[21] In many areas, African sleeping sickness (trypanosomiasis) is also becoming more prevalent, while river blindness (onchocerciasis) now affects more than half the inhabitants of the African savannas, and in some areas is responsible for blindness in twenty per cent or more of the adult population.[22]

Contrary to common belief, these diseases of underdevelopment are not necessarily bound up with tropical conditions in the geographic or climatic sense. Cholera, plague, leprosy, smallpox, typhoid, TB and many intestinal parasites have all thrived in western Europe in the past. Indeed, there is a striking similarity between disease patterns in underdeveloped countries today and the experience of the industrialised capitalist countries in the nineteenth century. In the third world, infant mortality rates, child wastage rates (deaths before 15 years), life expectancy and the incidence of major communicable diseases all show a clear parallel with nineteenth century Britain.[23] Yet these diseases now associated with underdevelopment have long since disappeared in the metropolitan countries,

> not because they were driven out by marvellous discoveries of medicine, they faded away before the general amelioration of our state of living as a result of improvements in sanitation - improvements in housing, draining, refuse disposal - in education and elevation of the standard of living for the generality of the people.[24]

In the underdeveloped world however, such changes are not occurring. As we shall see, both the extent of contemporary health problems and also the evident failure to combat them, must be seen not as a 'natural' and unavoidable part of life in the third world, but as a consequence of a particular form of capitalist expansion.

The early effects of colonialist expansion

One of the most immediately visible effects of imperialism has been the spread of infectious disease. Throughout history the extension of world trade and travel has involved not just economic and cultural contact, but also the dissemination of new infections - the Romans and the Moguls for example, are known to have spread major epidemics in Europe and Asia. However, the extent and intensity of worldwide communications initiated by mercantile capitalism was unprecedented. From the sixteenth century onwards, European expansion unleashed a series of catastrophic epidemics in every corner of the globe. The literature of the Spanish Conquest includes numerous accounts of the decimation of the indigenous Indian populations of the West Indies and Central and South America by smallpox, measles and typhus. All accounts maintain that these diseases were unknown before the coming of the Spaniards and many indicate that the ravages of smallpox were instrumental to the success of the Conquest.[25] A similar range of diseases was brought to North America by the English a century later.[26] However, the most continuous diffusion of disease, spanning some four hundred years, was generated by the slave trade. Not only did the trade cause excessively high mortality among its direct victims, but many diseases, including yellow fever, leprosy, hookworm and yaws, were carried from West Africa to the Americas in the process.[27]

There is nothing mysterious about why Europeans left so much death and disease in their tracks. Centuries of war, conquest and migration in Europe had created a relatively large pool of infectious organisms, and the growth of commerce and urbanisation continued this process. Exposure to a particular pathogen over time does tend both to increase human resistance and to lessen the severity of the illness concerned. However, most of the societies which suffered as a result of European expansion had adapted to a smaller number of quite different pathogens; and levels of health which could be maintained in relative geographical isolation, were often completely undermined by the opening up of communications.

The intention here is not to apportion moral blame, but to make clear the objective significance of this process in the particular context of capitalist development. Although the spread of infection was often unintentional, it clearly reinforced the genocidal policies carried out in many white settler territories, as well as weakening resistance to imperialist domination elsewhere. Epidemics also helped to destroy the economic and social foundations of indigenous communities and the resulting disintegration and impoverishment greatly facilitated the establishment of colonial hegemony.

The health of indigenous populations has also been seriously affected by the wars which accompanied imperialist expansion. We can see this very clearly if we look at the experience of East Africa during the late nineteenth and early twentieth centuries, when it was torn by resistance struggles and also by the fighting between rival imperialist powers. From the 1880s onwards, East Africa became a focus for Anglo-German commercial rivalry, with the two governments staking claims on behalf of their respective imperial trading companies. Britain acquired Zanzibar, Kenya and Uganda, while Germany secured Tanganyika (known as German East Africa until 1920). In the case of Tanganyika in particular, early military intervention was required to deal with a growing resistance struggle.[28] The persistence of this opposition was extraordinary in the face of the notorious brutality of the German military campaigns. As in more recent guerrilla wars the invaders sought to crush the population at large and to destroy its means of subsistence. The most concerted Tanganyikan uprising culminated in the Maji Maji wars between 1905-07. Villages were burnt and harvests destroyed, famine swept the countryside and some seventy-five thousand Africans died as a result. But it is important also to identify the more long term consequences of these campaigns and their impact on the life and health of the Tanganyikan people. The destruction was such that the Southern Province, where the major resistance occurred, remains sparsely populated to this day.[29] More generally the repeated devastation of farmland over a thirty-year period had enduring structural consequences. It not only undermined the economies of some of Tanganyika's major peoples, but crucially reduced the capacity of the countryside to feed the remaining population. Thus much of the malnutrition and disease which came to characterise rural Tanganyika in the twentieth century was in a very real sense a product of early colonial repression.[30]

By 1914, some thirty years of colonial domination had seen a marked deterioration in the economic and physical health of a large part of the East African population, and the first world war was to add greatly to this catalogue of disaster. Both Britain and Germany relied heavily on African manpower in the inter-imperialist campaigns. The Kenyan administration, for example, conscripted the greater part of the able-bodied male population, although at least half of all conscripts were rejected as unfit.[31] They were used mainly as beasts of burden to carry supplies and heavy equipment on their backs whilst negotiating difficult terrain for an average of fifteen miles per day. On some occasions they had to conduct entire marches up to their armpits in water. Physical exhaustion and injury were compounded by dysentery, respiratory diseases and lack of nourishment, and throughout their ordeal they were plagued by mosquitoes and tsetse flies.[32] The carriers received no medical attention and many thousands died along the way. Dr J.C.Wilson, medical officer in Kenya, was one of several who recorded the details.

> The appalling mortality among the African porters who accom-
> panied the fighting troops and maintained the lines of com-
> munication was a feature of the campaign outstanding in its
> grim tragedy. An early and unforgivable mistake was made
> when it was proposed to maintain the corps in the field on a
> ration of nothing but mealie meal. [33]

Among Africans, ten times as many casualties were caused by disease
as by enemy action. Nor did civilians escape. The populations of
Kenya, Uganda and Tanganyika experienced even more severe food
shortages as the agricultural labour force was depleted. Moreover,
throughout the war, the opposing armies sustained themselves by
raiding African fields and foodstores. The people of Tanganyika
fared worst since their territory was the major battleground for over
four years. The destruction and requisitioning of crops and the dis-
location of local trade led to prolonged economic difficulties, and
serious famine remained a major problem after the war had ended. [34]
In addition, porters lucky enough to return to their villages took a
range of new infections home with them, and illnesses such as
malaria and influenza became rife among a highly susceptible rural
population. [35]

However, despite their severity, the importation of new diseases
and the effects of war were not the only reasons for the deterioration
in health which accompanied the expansion of colonialism. More
important in the long term was the establishment of the colonial
system itself with the destruction of indigenous modes of production
and cultural patterns, and their replacement by new forms of social
and economic organisation. This is not to imply that Africa was once
an idyllic, antiseptic world. Historical and epidemiological evidence
does, however, suggest that most pre-colonial African civilisations
were successfully adapted both socially and physiologically to their
particular natural environments. [36] In such societies, fluctuations in
levels of health would be largely a function of the continuity of food
production, which would itself be closely dependent on uncontroll-
able variables such as climatic conditions. Under these circumstances, it is no surprise that early European travellers in East and
Central Africa (as in other parts of the world) reported very favour-
ably on the physical well-being of many of the societies they

encountered. Given these conditions the East African population is thought to have grown steadily during the nineteenth century. Kuczynski has shown, however, that between 1895-1920 the population was decreasing and in Tanganyika it did not begin to rise again until after 1925.[37] It is against this background that we must understand the impact of colonialism on health.

The establishment of the colonial economy

The formal establishment of colonialism as an economic and social system in the early part of the twentieth century involved the deliberate transformation of the socio-economic organisation of the colonial territories to meet the needs of the 'mother country'. Dominant European ideology maintained that the role of a colonial empire was to assist and complement the development of the metropolitan economies, and that in so doing, the colonies would themselves become 'civilised'.[38] The first important task for colonial policy makers was therefore to identify the most useful resources which a given territory might supply. In the case of East Africa, it was evident that the absence of major mineral deposits meant that the area had to be exploited primarily for its agricultural potential and this was done in a variety of ways. In Kenya, for example, where the intention was to encourage white immigration, settler-planters came to dominate agriculture. Cash crop production in Uganda, however, was carried out almost entirely by independent peasant producers. This was also true of Tanganyika, although there was in addition a significant foreign-owned plantation sector.

The fundamental assumption was that every British colony should be economically self-supporting. Government funds were therefore restricted to meagre grants-in-aid which were only intended to cover the initial costs of territorial occupation and the establishment of colonial hegemony.[39] Most colonies therefore began to impose taxes on the African population at the earliest opportunity (in Tanganyika it was from 1897 and in Kenya from 1899). Taxation was used to finance the infrastructure required for new modes of production but it was, in addition, a deliberate instrument of colonial labour policy. Attempts to develop cash crop production and also to create essential facilities, such as railways, were severely hampered by difficulties in recruiting labour. The imposition of taxes, however, compelled large numbers of Africans either to leave their villages in search of paid employment or to grow cash crops in order to pay their taxes. This veiled compulsion was reinforced where necessary by more overt forms of coercion, as in the compulsory drafting of labour for such things as the building of roads and railways. [40]

This colonial system was designed to facilitate the production of the agricultural commodities most in demand on world markets and to guarantee British manufacturers a dependable source of raw materials as well as cheap tropical foodstuffs and beverages for the domestic market. The significance of these exports was eloquently described by the Royal Institute of International Affairs in 1932.

> Two generations ago the banana was a luxury; oranges were a seasonal fruit only; the use of tobacco was for the rich alone, and cocoa unknown. Today, bananas, oranges all the year around, tea, coffee and cocoa figure in the humblest domestic budget in North America and Great Britain. Forty years ago, butter, olive oil, beef fat and lard were practically the only edible fats available in western Europe; today the oil from cottonseed, groundnuts, sesame, palm kernels, the coconut, soybean, etc., provide margarine, cooking and salad oils... soap, candles and lubricating oils... Man and beast are fed increasingly from tropical countries. [41]

It should be clear from what has been said earlier that the contribution of imported consumer crops to the health of the British population has been mixed. For instance, the benefits of citrus fruits would today have to be seen in conjunction with the harmful effects of tobacco and sugar. On the other hand, the conversion of luxuries into items of mass consumption gave instant gratification, and the significance of colonial food policy, as a material and ideological symbol of improving living standards, is usually greatly underrated. Despite the savage wage cuts of the 1930s 'the great Depression caused a relatively small cut in *average* consumption (though it slowed down the rate of growth), mainly because the fall in the price of imported foodstuffs helped to keep up living standards in the worst years of slump'.[42] However the effects of these policies on the nutritional status and general health of the *colonial* population were almost universally disastrous.

Food production and malnutrition

In order to appreciate the effects of European imperialism on African standards of nutrition, it is necessary first to say something about the nature of the pre-capitalist economy. The popular stereotype of pre-colonial Africa is one of 'primitive homogeneity' with family subsistence production carried on in small, non-hierarchical communities. However as Cliffe and others have pointed out, such a mode of production was by no means typical, and only a minority of East African societies were dependent on such a system.[43] Indeed, Kjekshus regards the very term 'subsistence production' as a misnomer, and his research makes it clear that indigenous agricultural systems in pre-colonial Tanganyika were highly productive. A wide variety of crops were produced, capable in most cases of providing a well-balanced diet. The development of exchange, food storage techniques, and the traditional 'beer party' indicate that there was normally a surplus in the economy.[44] There is therefore good reason to question the colonial premise that widespread food shortages had always been a problem. Such a view was evidently a backward projection based on the experience of the recurrent famines which marked colonial rule.[45] Of course there had always been the threat of random disaster, of drought or of locusts and there is no doubt that life in pre-colonial African societies was often hard. However the rural misery of the colonial epoch was something qualitively new.[46]

There is always a close relationship between economic and physical health, so that the ability of a population to maintain a given standard of health is always directly related to its capacity to maintain and control the material means of production. Colonial expansion in bringing about the destruction of the vital social and ecological relationships which enabled people to feed themselves, also destroyed the health of local populations on an unprecedented scale.

The history of the disease known as sleeping sickness provides a very clear illustration of how traditional methods of control over nature were often disrupted (intentionally or unwittingly) by the consolidation of colonialism. Sleeping sickness is caused by organisms (trypanosomes) which are transmitted by the tsetse fly. It is invariably fatal to livestock and can also cause high rates of human mortality. Today vast areas of East Africa are entirely devoid of cattle due to the incursion of the tsetse fly, yet there is conclusive evidence that in the nineteenth century Africans kept large herds very successfully in these same areas.[47] Thus the 'tsetse problem' is a recent one in East Africa and widespread sleeping sickness is another health problem dating from the onset of colonialism.

Most accounts suggest that sleeping sickness was first introduced to Uganda from West Africa by Stanley's relief expedition for Emin Pasha in 1887. When the disease appeared in Tanganyika in about 1904, it was thought to have been transmitted by migrant labourers infected while working in colonial enterprises in Uganda. It is probable, however, that this emphasis on the diffusion of sleeping sickness by human agents is misplaced. Sleeping sickness was rather, as John Ford argues, an endemic condition of long standing over which Africans had historically come to establish effective control.[48] This was achieved through the systematic application of their knowledge of both the tsetse fly and its habitat. For example, the tsetse were known to thrive in dense bush inhabited by an abundance of wild animals. Thus African pastoralists not only avoided infested areas, but employed a wide range of preventive measures such as bush clearing and game control. It appears therefore that the emergence of sleeping sickness as a major problem in the twentieth century was precipitated by new socio-economic conditions which undermined these traditional methods of controlling the physical environment. The most important factors were the human depopulation and the elimination of grazing stock which occurred from the 1890s onwards as a result of colonial wars, famine and disease. As Kjekshus explains,

> In a short period of time they led to the collapse of the man-controlled ecological system of the nineteenth century. With fewer people to till the fields and fewer cattle and goats to graze the ground and keep the bush at bay, and with imperial laws

prohibiting grass burning and hunting, nature was quick to commence its recovery. The managed culture became overgrown by shrubs and trees. Wild animals, recovering from the rinderpest, soon moved in to establish grazing grounds in old cultivations. In their wake the tsetse fly spread to put vast domains of land beyond the reach of economic activity. [49]

There is little doubt that colonial policy towards the disease contributed to the problem it was designed to solve. The British, for example, ordered the mass evacuation of Africans from the advancing tsetse fly belts and their resettlement in new 'concentrations'. [50] This actually reduced the total amount of land in productive use and left depopulated zones to be swallowed up by bush, wild animals and the tsetse fly. Thus, while colonial policy succeeded in lowering the incidence of sleeping sickness in certain districts, it simultaneously created the conditions for its propagation elsewhere. By 1913 approximately one-third of Tanganyika was plagued by tsetse flies, by 1937 this had increased to two-thirds and by 1948 it was fully three-quarters of the land surface. [51] This contributed greatly to the breakdown of local economic systems and also led to a chronic shortage of animal protein and, for many, a permanently impoverished diet. [52]

However the most important single factor undermining existing methods of food production probably stemmed from the economic requirements of the colonial system for profitable agricultural exports. John Iliffe has examined in some detail the impact of colonial policy on the structure of the economy of what is now Tanzania. By the end of the 1930s, three distinct types of regional formation could be identified and each of these was characterised by its particular functional role in the colonial economy. [53] First there were the areas established for sisal plantations and the cultivation of cash crops such as cotton, coffee and tobacco. Surrounding these were the areas which had to supply the crops needed to feed the colonial labour force. The remaining regions were not directly drawn into production, but were designated as reservoirs of migrant labour. While the establishment of this pattern of regional specialisation corresponded to the requirements of a colonial economy, it systematically undermined existing economic structures and hence had far-reaching effects on the economic and physical health of affected populations. Fertile land was increasingly absorbed into cash crop production, thus reducing the availability of land on which food could be grown for local consumption. At the same time, there was a considerable narrowing of the range of food produced. [54] As population size increased and agricultural expansion was ruled out, fallow periods were reduced, soil exhaustion and erosion occurred and yields declined. [55] Thus cultivation methods of proven efficiency under pre-colonial conditions were largely undermined by their subordination to the requirements of the colonial export economy.

The development of cash cropping and the introduction of new techniques to facilitate it, received active economic and technical support from the British administration. In Tanganyika, agricultural research facilities were set up to improve the production of cash crops such as sisal, cotton, coffee and tea. No such research was undertaken on the cereals and pulses which formed the basis of African diets, and there was no encouragement of technical innovation in the subsistence sector. [56] That is to say, peasant production was still required to supplement the needs of migrants and cash crop producers, and to support them during sickness, unemployment and old age. It also had to support the families of workers since no allowance was made for them in the payment of wages. Indeed this informal support from the subsistence sector provided the objective basis for cheap labour in the colonies. [57] As a result, the introduction of cash cropping and the development of a migrant labour system combined to cause a substantial reduction in the quality of diets in both cash and subsistence crop areas.

Even colonial regulations designed to prevent famine actually tended to depress the nutritional quality of African diets. Whereas the periodic threat of famine had previously resulted from the vicissitudes of climate or other natural disasters, by the 1930s imperialist economic policy had made it a more permanent feature of African life. To meet this contingency, colonial regulations required the compulsory cultivation of particular foods such as maize and cassava. These hardy crops are known to have been effective in allaying starvation in difficult years but their nutritional value was substantially lower than that of the traditional crops such as sorghum and millet which they came to replace. So although government policies could mitigate temporary food shortages, there is evidence of widespread general malnutrition, indicating that the switch to cassava may have resulted in survivors living at lower levels of health.[58]

The deterioration of health under the migrant labour system

A hundred years ago measles and tuberculosis were almost unknown in Africa and yet in the early years of this century they became firmly established, and remain two of the principal causes of death in Africa south of the Sahara.[59] This was in part because the migrant labour system brought many rural Africans into direct contact with Europeans, and in part because of the unhealthy living and working conditions it imposed on the labour force. Moreover, these new diseases had far-reaching effects on the population as a whole, resulting mainly from the transitory nature of colonial employment. That is, the structure of the labour system created not only the environmental conditions in which disease proliferates but also the ideal mechanisms for its widespread dissemination beyond the immediate labour areas.

There is little doubt that for the vast majority of Africans, participation in wage labour meant a marked deterioration in living standards. Whereas the early industrialisation of Britain took place in the wake of long term rural impoverishment, in East Africa rural decline was more a consequence of proletarianisation than a factor contributing to it. This is why coercion played such a central role in the creation of an African labour force. Men usually had to make long, perilous journeys to the labour areas, where large numbers of them were then crowded into settlements directly servicing the plantation, mine or railway on which they were employed. Under these circumstances, it is both difficult and misleading to try to distinguish the direct hazards of the work process from other health problems. Compound life was in itself an occupational hazard, and this is graphically illustrated in van Onselen's historical account of the life of African mineworkers in Southern Rhodesia.[60] He shows that even in the mines (among the most dangerous of workplaces) by far the greatest killers were diseases such as dysentery, scurvy and pneumonia, which were directly attributable to the bad diet and appalling living conditions experienced by all migrant workers.[61]

It has already been noted that colonial labour depended for much of its subsistence on non-capitalist peasant agriculture. In practice this meant either that workers were paid wages too low to cover basic food costs, or were given rations too meagre to provide adequate nourishment. Employers favoured cheap bulky diets which were usually short in nutrients and therefore induced various deficiency diseases.[62] It was also common for managers to cut costs by obtaining staples of such poor quality that they tended to precipitate intestinal illness.[63] On purely economic grounds these practices would appear to have been absurd since they undermined productivity. Administrative attempts to rationalise the system were not however very successful. Most colonial employers were extremely reluctant to 'invest' in their workers and knew only too well that labourers could be forced to supplement their rations by alternative means. Indeed, it was acknowledged that the health of African workers depended to a large extent on the proximity of peasant farming, which could provide an important additional source of food.[64]

Migrant workers again fared very badly as regards general living conditions. In both the labour compounds and the expanding urban areas, accommodation tended to be structurally inadequate, damp, insanitary and chronically overcrowded.[65] Combined with malnutrition and long hours of arduous work, these conditions encouraged the spread of many communicable diseases. As in nineteenth century Britain, common infections included tuberculosis, measles, whooping cough, typhoid and gastro-enteritis. In Britain, this critical phase was relatively short lived, but in East Africa, as in most countries of the third world, the serious health problems initiated under the migrant labour system have persisted until the present day.

The obvious threat to labour productivity posed by ill health might have been expected to spur improvements in the physical environment of workers. During the colonial period however other solutions were available to meet the problem of high morbidity and mortality. In the case of diseases such as TB, for example, it was common practice among employers to despatch sick workers home to their villages, and to replenish the labour force with new migrants.[66] Thus, despite the serious labour shortage which existed until the depression of the 1930s, employers relied on a high turnover rate among their workers in order to reduce the effects of illness on productivity. This system made possible the maximum use of able-bodied migrants drawn from the peasant economy, while throwing the burden of providing for the sick and disabled back onto that same sector. Consequently, employers could afford to destroy the health of their workers as long as production by a structurally impermanent labour force remained economically viable.

The more specific problems of work-induced morbidity and mortality - industrial disease - must also be looked at. Work in the asbestos mines of Southern and Central Africa, for example, carried the risk of extremely serious illnesses such as asbestosis, lung cancer and mesothelioma. The dangers to which these miners were exposed can readily be appreciated.

> On the asbestos mines child labour was used to separate the mineral fibre from the rock matrix in which the mineral occurred. As early as 1910 it was reported that several mines used considerable numbers of children, and at least one mine was entirely staffed by child labour.[67]

While the British government originally issued (admittedly feeble) regulations for asbestos plants in the UK in 1932, it was almost twenty years before a health inspector first visited the South African mines which produced asbestos. This visit not only revealed that children were still at work in the mines but that several under the age of twelve already exhibited symptoms of asbestosis.[68]

Mining is certainly an inherently dangerous occupation and safety was not a serious concern for the lucrative imperial mining industries; but deaths due to accidents were relatively few compared with the vast numbers who died from disease. When accidents did occur, however, they were often a consequence of the structure of the labour process itself. For example, irrespective of official regulations, many mines continued to operate shifts of such length as to jeopardise safety. In addition, tough piecework systems tied not only wages but even daily food rations to productivity levels. Miners were thus put under great pressure to take risks, many of which inevitably proved fatal.[69]

The migrant labour system affected Africans' lives in many fundamental ways. Whatever the miseries of industrialisation in Britain, it was usually possible for workers to keep their families together, but this has not been the case in most third world countries. In Tanganyika, for example, male workers were typically recruited from designated labour supply areas great distances from the centres of economic activity. This entailed prolonged family separations which had serious physical and psychological repercussions for all concerned. The populations of African towns 'recruited by migration' were characterised by a heavy preponderance of men living in intolerably insecure and depressing conditions and lacking the benefits of family life or other customary supports. The misery of the material, social and environmental deprivation caused by this fragmented existence took various forms, among them a high incidence of alcoholism and 'mental disorder' and widespread resort to prostitution. These were then taken by European observers as confirmation of the inherent fecklessness and depravity of 'the native', although as we shall see, the colonial system was in fact, instrumental in creating the very social problems it so harshly condemned.

In most African societies, the brewing of beer had been carried out within 'traditional' modes of production long before the imposition of the colonial system. Beer drinking was literally a celebration of the economic surplus, and the consumption of alcohol was regulated by custom. From the colonial period onwards, however, the social character of drinking began to change. Among migrant labourers the reasons for taking to drink turned on the alleviation of personal suffering and alienation, particularly in the absence of alternative diversions. Moreover, their consumption of alcohol had become totally divorced from the kind of production in which they were now engaged. For both these reasons the inbuilt constraints which had formerly controlled drinking tended to disappear. Although employers might have been expected to impose their own constraints, in many cases they actually encouraged beer drinking. In the first place, it had long been recognised that beer drinking improved the overall health of the workers by making good some of the basic deficiencies in their diet.[70] In particular, the vitamin content of African beer was important in reducing the incidence of scurvy. Thus workers were encouraged to meet the costs of improving their health through buying beer. This absolved employers from the need to provide fresh vegetables while simultaneously reinforcing other advantages of a plentiful beer supply which were related mainly to questions of social control.[71]

While heavy drinking was obviously socially disruptive and detrimental to labour productivity, the availability of alcohol provided an outlet for boredom and frustration which might otherwise have exploded in more coherent forms. Even the dependence which beer drinking fostered had positive consequences for employers. For example, as they became concerned to retain as many able-bodied workers as possible, they came to see the presence of local brewing as a useful mechanism for stabilising the workforce. Similarly, by absorbing a worker's wages, alcohol tied him more firmly to the capitalist mode. Sometimes the connivance of imperialist interests in promoting excessive drinking was even more directly economic. In the mining areas of South Africa for instance, white farming interests were anxious to put their grain surpluses to profitable use in the distilleries, and this strategy depended on greatly raising the level of alcohol consumption among blacks.[72] Hobsbawm has described mass alcoholism as 'an almost invariable companion of headlong and uncontrolled industrialisation'.[73] In the case of underdeveloped countries, it began to emerge first through the capitalist organisation of primary production, while the prolonged and continuing crisis of industrialisation in the third world has tended to aggravate problems of this kind without generating the economic and social capacity to begin to overcome them.

In a similar way, venereal disease became - and still remains - a major health problem in many parts of the third world where it was previously unknown.[74] It is hardly surprising that the disruption of the economic and personal foundations of family life led to the disintegration of long-established marital and sexual patterns.[75] In this context, the growth of prostitution represented one form of adaptation to the intolerable strains faced by men and women alike.

In the case of male migrants, the absence of their wives was compounded by the fact that their new environment was almost exclusively masculine. This unequal sex ratio made it difficult for men to establish stable sexual liaisons with women, and encouraged prostitution. For the women involved, prostitution was usually a matter of sheer economic necessity. As van Onselen makes clear, the *role* of prostitute is no less a product of imperialist development than the demand created for it.

> Basically, prostitutes - just like male African labour - were a product of the process of proletarianisation. Once the redistributive economy of the traditional society was undermined it offered little security to the young, the old, the powerless or those without kin, and when the standard of living in rural areas dropped, women who were not part of a family production unit were increasingly vulnerable. Those who lost their access to land were forced into the urban areas to seek cash and fend for themselves.[76]

The structure of the colonial economy made it virtually impossible for women to sell their labour, and in order to survive, most were compelled to live off the low wages of male workers. Often this involved either formal or informal prostitution.

The prevalence of prostitution clearly had serious consequences for the health of both men and women, and venereal diseases spread easily under the migrant labour system. The resulting morbidity among male workers often provided a major focus for the concern of employers about African health. Yet despite the contempt colonialists expressed for the 'evils' of prostitution, underlying attitudes were more ambiguous. In the first place, sexual needs clearly required an outlet and female prostitution was considered preferable to other alternatives. Where white women were present, black prostitutes were regarded as protecting them from rape. More generally, employers and administrators saw prostitution as a means of attracting and retaining male workers. Finally, they recognised the importance of prostitutes as surrogate wives who prepared meals and cared for the physical well-being of male workers, which in turn improved the men's performance as workers.[77]

It is also important however to consider not just the problems of physical ill health but also the psychological distress caused by the colonial system. Clearly mental stress and disorder are difficult to prove or to quantify empirically and such an exercise may in any case be of dubious value when applied to people in such extreme social conditions. As John Berger has said of the situation in contemporary Europe,

> it is absurd to consider the health of migrant workers as though they were healthy or sick like others. Their function, the conditions of their presence . . . are incompatible with the norms of preventive and clinical medicine. The norms do not apply to them.[78]

Despite their conceptual limitations, psychiatric categories have been applied to the inhabitants of third world countries. The results invariably show an increased rate of psychiatric disorder among the urban population[79] - a fact which is hardly surprising given the nature of the migrant labour system, and the stress caused by frequent unemployment and severe physical and social deprivation.[80] Moreover, external domination, with its specific racial connotations, seems to produce additional levels of psycho-social injury. This can be characterised as what Fanon has called the 'systematic negation of the other'.

> The defensive attitudes created by this violent bringing together of the colonised man and the colonial system form themselves into a structure which then reveals the colonised personality . . . In the period of colonisation when it is not contested by armed resistance, when the sum total of harmful nervous stimuli overstep a certain threshold, the defensive attitudes of the natives give way and they then find themselves crowding the mental hospitals. There is thus during this calm period of successful colonisation a regular and important mental pathology which is the direct product of oppression.[81]

Empirical evidence of such illness has come from recent studies in South Africa, where current experiences under apartheid are in many ways comparable to the social and economic relations formerly imposed in most colonial territories.[82] These problems were, however, of little interest to the colonial authorities unless they posed a threat to social order and, to meet this contingency, mental institutions and prisons became early features of colonial 'development'. Nevertheless, any threat to the colonisers themselves was greatly reduced by the fact that it was characteristic of 'successful' colonisation that when anger and hostility surfaced, its victims were generally black neighbours in the immediate vicinity rather than the oppressors themselves.[83]

Most accounts tend to focus on male workers, but any assessment of the effects of the migrant labour system on the rural population must also consider the increased pressures it placed on the women who stayed behind. Despite the fact that women have traditionally been the main agricultural producers in many African societies,[84] subsistence economies have been dependent on the contribution of the whole family. As men were increasingly drawn into the migrant labour system, the oppression of women, who had to take over all the tasks involved in food production was greatly intensified.[85] In Tanganyika for instance, where men had customarily undertaken tree and bush clearance to prepare new farming land, their removal from the labour process tended to prolong the cultivation period on established plots, hence reducing the fertility of the soil. Lack of land and the sheer burden of their labour also induced women to substitute higher yielding crops such as cassava for their more nutritious and palatable staples. Consequently there was a steady erosion of the dietary standards of women and children.[86] This brought particular problems for women. As in many underdeveloped countries, the small and abnormally shaped pelvis associated with malnutrition made childbirth an increasingly prolonged and dangerous ordeal.[87] In addition, the spread of venereal disease began to cause a growing incidence of pelvic inflammatory disease among women in the rural areas, bringing with it both infertility and the danger of an ectopic pregnancy.[88] Increased economic hardship and the disintegration of personal and social relationships under the migrant labour system is also known to have produced distinctly new forms of mental disturbance among rural women in many areas.[89] On the basis of health data from Tanganyika, Turshen concluded that, 'the emiseration of the population in labour supply areas was reflected in persistent high rates of maternal, infant and child mortality, in widespread malnutrition and in high levels of morbidity'.[90]

Without in any way romanticising traditional conditions of life, it has been observed that the squalor of the expanding urban areas was in stark contrast to the cleanliness of the rural villages. However, for a variety of reasons, the combined effects of cash cropping and migrating labour gradually reduced the capacity of the rural areas to fend off disease. Thus, a report published in 1932 pointed out that, 'many hygienic native customs which were most valuable in preventing the spread of disease, are disintegrating under the spread of civilisation'.[91] In communities where cash cropping encroached, and in the 'native reserves' and sleeping sickness concentrations to which many Africans were confined, pressure on land caused village sites to become increasingly restricted and unhealthy.[92] Similarly, the imposition of the hut tax encouraged overcrowded living conditions, and led to the abandoning of long established practices such as the isolation of the sick.[93] In some cases colonial policy explicitly prohibited indigenous methods of controlling disease as part of the campaign to obliterate traditional religion.[94] Most destructive of all, was the way in which workers, travelling from the labour areas back to their villages, opened up much of the countryside to new diseases such as tuberculosis and VD. Whether or not these migrants survived their diseases, the diseases invariably survived *them*, often spreading rapidly among an increasingly susceptible population.[95]

Thus, it is clear that in the case of health and illness, as with other aspects of social and economic life, the effects of imperialism went far beyond the immediate capitalist sector. Though the degree of integration into the external economy varied from region to region, over the decades it transformed the social and material life of the mass of the people, creating characteristic patterns of disease, disability and death.

Malnutrition and monopoly capitalism

During the post-war period, most former colonial territories have gained their independence. As Arrighi and Saul have commented,

> The winning of formal independence in Africa must be seen in
> relation to the process of the internationalisation of centre-
> periphery relations. It is in fact evident that the complex of
> international capitalism, particularly when seen to be increas-
> ingly skewed in an American direction, had little reason to be
> hostile to the process. Formal decolonisation had, in fact, the
> virtue of liberalizing economic access to the erstwhile
> colonies.[96]

The gradual transformation of the world economic system
which has accompanied formal political independence, has in fact
initiated a new phase of economic domination by the developed
capitalist countries. We must therefore examine in more detail the
social and economic structure of what is often called neo-colonialism,
particularly its implications for the material conditions and the
health of third world populations.

The period immediately following the second world war gave
short-lived credence to imperialist claims to be laying the foundations for economic take-off. Massive increases in the demand for raw
materials and foodstuffs brought a concomitant rise in world prices
which was further accelerated during the Korean War. Orthodox
economists predicted that a new era of increased agricultural productivity would stimulate export-led industrialisation in the underdeveloped world, but by the late 1950s many primary producers had
already begun to experience a deterioration in their trading position.
A relatively small number of multinational companies were increasingly able to dominate world production and markets in all the major
agricultural commodities, largely because of the tremendous growth
in their productive capacity. At the same time, industrial developments in the capitalist centres began to lessen metropolitan
dependence on agricultural raw materials. Cheap synthetic fibres,
for instance, reduced the demand for natural fibres such as cotton
and sisal, while exports of tropical foodstuffs and beverages also
flagged. In East Africa, the prices of the four major exports (sisal,
cotton, coffee and tea) have all shown a marked downward trend
since the 1950s. The 1960s and 1970s have seen not only a continuing
deterioration of terms of trade for third world countries, but also a
decline in their total share of world trade.

Although some degree of industrialisation has occurred in the third world during the post-war period, most marxists have challenged the idea that it can lead to self-generating economic development. Cardoso, for example, has pointed out that as the developed capitalist states have progressively lessened their dependence on primary products imported from their former colonies, they have tended to transfer their investment *away* from these countries to other industrialised countries. He has described this process as the 'marginalisation' of the third world within international economic development.[97] Two major strategies have been employed. In the first place there has been a gradual development of 'import-substitution' policies designed to minimise potential competition either from other foreign concerns or from local industry. At the same time, the subsidiaries thus created perform various functions designed to enhance the overall profitability of the parent corporation.

The other main strategy behind industrial involvement in underdeveloped countries has been the creation of 'export platforms'. Here, multinational companies take advantage of low labour costs and negligible trade union organisation to organise third world production geared almost entirely to their existing metropolitan markets. The persistent need for capital to reduce the cost of labour power has therefore prompted the introduction of particular kinds of manufacturing industry in many parts of the third world, although the extent of industrial development varies greatly between countries. However, despite political independence and some degree of industrialisation, most underdeveloped countries remain extremely dependent on the developed world both economically and in a broader social and cultural sense.

As we shall see, the health problems created under colonialism by malnutrition and the migrant labour system remain extremely severe even today. Moreover a new range of health problems has been added by the increasing rate of urbanisation and by the spread of industrial production and western patterns of consumption. In the post-colonial period, malnutrition continues on a massive scale. Decades of agricultural and nutritional depletion are now packaged for the popular imagination of the west into a 'food crisis' of the

1970s. The most usual explanation of the crisis is a Malthusian one - population in the third world is seen to be increasing at a much faster rate than agricultural production hence there is too little food to go round. But anthropological studies have shown that under normal circumstances, a population increase is likely to lead to the adoption of more intensive systems of agriculture and to an increase in total output. This means that, 'the population within a given area can double several times without having to face either starvation or lack of employment opportunities in agriculture'.[98]

In the case of the third world today, it is the structural obstacles to this expansion of food production (as well as to its more equal distribution) that need to be explained. The most obvious obstacle that could be encountered here would be a limited supply of land, but in fact, most third world countries have lower population densities than many of the developed countries.[99] Hence, as we shall argue in what follows, it is more plausible to suggest that it is the relations of dependence generated by the present system of economic production that ultimately underlie the inability of most third world countries to provide an adequate diet for the mass of their people. According to Gail Omvedt,

> The issue is not one of limits of land, but of the limits of a social organisation that fails to generate investment in agriculture leading to growth . . . Any analysis of the problem of food dependency in third world countries must focus not on the patterns of *consumption*, but on the much more basic and determining factor of *production* . . . [100]

Further, as the Transnational Institute has pointed out,

> . . . population could decline and production increase, but if the great majority of the population lacked the purchasing power to pay for its food the only result would be that the minority will continue to live in luxury, while the great masses of the people live in misery, as the case of Brazil demonstrates today.[101]

While population growth may present many problems, it is not in itself the major cause of famine and undernutrition in third world countries. Indeed, any suggestion that population control can solve the problem of malnutrition must contend with the fact that it is precisely those whose means of subsistence is most threatened who are induced to have more children, particularly as their livelihood is usually dependent on family labour and infant mortality is high. Geoffrey Barraclough has put this point most succinctly.

> ... every reputable demographer knows that the only histori- cally proven way of reducing population growth is to improve living standards, beginning with adequate feeding and that it is the hungry, indigent and despondent who have large families. No one is going to practice birth control if he expects five out of six of his children to die of starvation before the age of three.[102]

In direct contrast to the situation in most third world coun- tries, basic food production in the industrialised west has become increasingly capital intensive during the past fifty years. Nowhere is this more apparent than in the USA. Here the early application of highly mechanised techniques favoured the growth of agricultural monopolies, as well as the creation of a grain surplus and as a conse- quence, increasing productivity was gradually transformed into chronic overproduction. But instead of allowing agricultural prices to fall according to the logic of market forces, the crisis facing farming interests was diffused by the timely intervention of the state. In fact the interventionist policies first adopted by the American govern- ment during the depression have been crucial to the viability of US agriculture ever since.[103] The usual policy has been to subsidise American farmers to *abandon* cereal production on millions of acres of their land. Any surplus that then remains is usually bought up and stockpiled by the government. These stockpiles have served to reinforce the uncompetitive nature of third world cereal production since the declining capacity of underdeveloped countries to meet their own food needs has provided an ideal opportunity for offload- ing the American surplus, both on a commercial basis and in the form of aid.

> The American economy in its present form is absolutely
> dependent on agricultural exports. Not steel, nor transistor
> radios, nor even old armaments, but wheat, corn, rice and soya
> beans are the major product it has to sell the world.[104]

As a result most third world countries have now become net
importers of food, undermining indigenous agriculture still further,
while simultaneously increasing their economic and political
dependence on the west.

The export of food on favourable credit terms became a
convenient and increasingly important part of the US foreign aid
programme throughout the fifties and sixties. Food aid has clearly
been a means of exerting considerable commercial pressure on
underdeveloped countries through transactions of an apparently
humanitarian nature. It has therefore been important in maintaining the general dominance of the US economy and also in securing
international conditions favourable to the profitability of metropolitan agribusiness.[105] However, in the early 1970s, the foundations of
US agricultural policy began to change and prices began to fluctuate
wildly. Between 1970-73 agricultural export prices doubled, and as
attempts were made to stabilise the US economy, several countries
which had in the past come to rely on the US food programme were
suddenly forced to buy American wheat on commercial terms.[106] As
de Janvry explains,

> Promotion of commercial exports, in particular through
> devaluations of the dollar, has become the key to restoring the
> balance of payments and strengthening the dollar. The explicit
> policy is 'food for cash'. And shipments under Food for Peace
> dropped from 14 million tons of grains in 1965 to 1 million
> tons in 1974 (Public Law 480 Title 1) precisely when major
> famines struck in the Sahel and Bangladesh.[107]

Thus food aid has had the effect of creating a dependency on
imported food. Since this aid was discontinued for economic reasons
at a time when need for it was greatest, extremely poor countries were
forced to pay commercial prices which they could not afford, and
starving people were kept short of food.[108]

The United States has not, of course, been alone in adopting food policies of this kind. The European Common Agricultural Policy resolves the contradictions of its own anarchic system of food production in a similar manner. In the EEC, however, food itself rather than land is taken off the market in order to maintain artificially high prices. Thus Europeans have to pay above world market prices, while vast food surpluses accumulate in the form of beef or butter 'mountains'. As is well known, these reserves have on occasions been sold off to selected groups such as EEC pensioners or consumers in the Soviet Union. Other surpluses, such as skimmed milk have been off-loaded in third world countries through the Food and Agriculture Organisation (FAO) World Food Programme. As in the American case, a pragmatic solution to the problems of over-production is simultaneously credited with meeting European food aid obligations[109] - a strategy which is not only politically expedient, but also ideologically acceptable.

It is important, however, that we consider not just the role of governments, but also the activities of 'agribusiness' as these affect underdeveloped countries in general, and standards of nutrition and health in particular. As Emma Rothschild has pointed out,

> US agriculture is very far from any ideal of competitive enterprises . . . The five large corporations that sell and ship almost all the grain exported by the USA (and many other countries) operate under conditions of notable confidentiality, license and oligopoly.[110]

Among British companies, too, the degree of concentration in the food industry is renowned. Many of them owe their very existence to colonial cash crop production, and their profitability has remained heavily dependent on third world agriculture ever since. During the post-war period their monopoly position has been greatly strengthened through mergers, which have enabled them to diversify their food interests. More importantly perhaps, food corporations have achieved a remarkable degree of vertical integration which made formal colonial ties increasingly irrelevant to their operations. A recent advertisement produced by Tate and Lyle illustrates the scope of the economic interests of one such company.

> Tate and Lyle's interests in foods and foodstuffs are worldwide, embracing starch, glucose, molasses, malt, beans, seeds, pulses, tea and coffee as well as sugar. And the company's service with these commodities is wide ranging - it covers shipping, storage, processing, refining and distribution. Tate and Lyle Ltd is therefore a vital link between primary products and end users.[111]

Vertical integration of this kind creates an almost impenetrable system of external domination of third world economies. It also gives the food industry the flexibility to intervene in food production and distribution at various stages in order to regulate output and transfer profits. The mechanisms by which such aims are achieved have enormous significance for the global allocation of food resources and for nutritional standards in third world countries. We shall therefore examine one such mechanism in more detail - the 'upward conversion' of grains into meat.

Upward conversion is the means by which high quality cereals are diverted from human consumption to feed livestock, which are then sold as meat in the industrialised countries. This would obviously be a very inefficient way of producing food if the object of food production was the alleviation of hunger.

> Meat is notoriously the most wasteful of all foodstuffs, requiring an input of four to seven pounds of cattle feed for every pound of meat produced, and the consequence is that over sixty per cent of US grain output - or something like one hundred and forty million tons a year - is consumed entirely by cattle, sheep, pigs and poultry.
>
> We have only to recall that the total world shortfall of cereals in 1972-73 amounted to no more than sixty million tons to see the significance of this in relation to what Kissinger has called 'the desperate struggle for sustenance'. According to one calculation, the livestock population of the United States alone (leaving out dogs and cats) consumes enough food material to feed 1.3 billion people.[112]

In fact, it is largely because of the success of meat promotion, that the industrialised countries - with approximately thirty per cent of the world's population - account for about fifty-four per cent of the global consumption of cereals.[113] In the USA, for example, per capita beef consumption more than doubled between 1940-72, and other industrialised countries have shown even greater increases over the same period.[114] This trend is usually assumed to be the logical outcome of some innate human predeliction for meat and is rarely seen as a factor in the world food crisis.

The tremendous increase in the quantity of staple foods exported to the third world in the post-war period has not lessened the problem of malnutrition for a number of reasons. First, although food aid and the commercial export of food have greatly expanded since the war, the actual volume involved has been insignificant in relation to the needs of growing third world populations - aid in particular has never met more than a small proportion of the food needs of most underdeveloped countries. Second, the amount of such aid fell steadily during the 1970s. Until then approximately fifty per cent of food exports to the third world took the form of aid, but less than fifteen per cent of food now falls into this category.[115] In addition, although commercially imported food is usually cheap relative to that produced locally, it is nevertheless expensive in absolute terms for countries with a low GNP and limited foreign exchange reserves.

There is another sense in which food imports to third world countries may be of very little value in alleviating malnutrition. This is related not to the amount of food involved, but rather to its distribution among the population. In fact, food aid characteristically benefits the urban élites and often exacerbates the existing unequal distribution of resources within underdeveloped countries. This sometimes stems directly from government policy as an expression of specific class interests. It had recently been suggested, for instance, that in Bangladesh in 1976 as much as ninety per cent of food aid went to the middle classes and state employees through the 'ration system'. As little as five per cent seems to have gone to the urban poor and the rural poor received almost nothing at all.[116] Similarly, when imported food is put on sale on the open market, poor people often cannot afford to buy it. It was even reported from India in 1977 that an unusually large amount of wheat and rice was available as a result of good harvests but had to be stockpiled because some two-fifths of the population had insufficient income to pay for it.[117]

Even when the poor are able to obtain imported food it may sometimes do them more harm than good. A particularly striking instance of this is the export of baby milk to the third world. This has been freely distributed as aid in underdeveloped countries, but has done more to aid the assiduous efforts of multinational companies to promote bottle feeding, than to alleviate malnutrition. Not only does such aid foster dependence on expensive manufactured food, but the shift to bottle feeding itself has contributed to a phenomenon which has been called 'commerciogenic malnutrition'.[118] Jelliffe and Jelliffe have described this in some detail.

> All major infant food firms, especially the large international concerns, have continually carried out advertising and promotional campaigns in competition with each other in less-developed countries since world war two. Without any doubt whatsoever, they have been one of the major factors responsible for the present decline in breast feeding in areas where bottle feeding is neither economically nor hygienically feasible. They have therefore also been responsible in considerable measure for the present rise in such regions in the prevalence of marasmus and diarrheal disease in infants, resulting in high mortality, costly and prolonged treatment and considerable risk of permanent brain damage.[119]

The main disadvantages of bottle feeding stem from the nutritional inferiority of cows' milk, coupled with the possibility of infection being introduced in the preparation of artificial foods. Both these problems are clearly much more serious under third world conditions. The poorer general nutritional levels are, the more significant is the superiority of human milk over cows' milk. Moreover, once breast feeding is abandoned, a mother is forced to go on buying powdered milk and this necessitates a recurrent outlay of money whatever her economic circumstances. Poverty also induces many mothers to over dilute the milk, and as a result bottle fed babies often suffer malnutrition which could have been avoided by breast feeding. These infants are also at a greater risk of contracting infectious diseases, because feeds often have to be prepared with unsafe water in insanitary conditions.

At an ideological level the distribution of milk as aid to the poor carries particular force as a charitable act. This stems largely from the special importance attributed to high protein foods in western countries. After kwashiorkor was first ascribed to protein deficiency in the 1930s, medical - and hence lay - opinion came to view malnutrition in terms of a 'protein crisis'. Expensive food policies based on this assumption have been adopted at national and international level throughout the postwar period. Only since about 1972 has expert opinion accepted that the real problem is not lack of protein, but lack of food.[120]

Given the evident failure of present food policies to solve the problem of under-nutrition in the third world, what alternative strategies are proposed? One argument stresses the need for increased food aid and food exports from the metropolitan countries, but as we have already seen such a strategy would be unlikely to improve the situation.

> To give priority to stepping up the export surplus of the United States and other advanced countries could only perpetuate the dependence of the underdeveloped upon the industrial world and ensure that the poor countries will remain, as at present, beggars at the rich man's table.[121]

The potentially more realistic alternative of increasing agricultural productivity in the third world countries themselves has also received much international attention. So far, however, attempts to improve third world agriculture have been extremely limited, and have often had undesirable consequences for the agricultural population. The failure of such strategies usually stems from the fact that they see 'technology' rather than broader social and economic change as the key to increased productivity. The limitations of technical solutions of this kind are exemplified in the failure of the so-called Green Revolution which was initiated in several third world countries during the 1960s. It represented a response by certain US foundations and international experts to the anxiety being generated in the west by increasing famine, rural poverty and urban migration in the third world. The intention was to increase food production in third world countries through the introduction of high yielding varieties of seeds (HYV's) which necessitated the intensive use of fertilisers. In its early stages the Green Revolution was hailed as a miraculous innovation by observers with widely differing political views. However, it is now generally accepted that it has failed to achieve either self-sufficiency for underdeveloped countries, or even an increase in the amount of food available to those who need it.[122] It is therefore important to understand why it failed.

The main reason clearly lies in the fact that the Green Revolution proclaimed the possibility of a technical solution to what are in fact socio-economic problems. As a result, it actually intensified structural inequalities through reinforcing existing class divisions in the countryside. The major obstacle was the pre-existing material poverty of most of the peasants under the grossly inequitable systems of land ownership which characterised most of the areas involved in the scheme. The Green Revolution meant a new reliance on technology and this necessitated substantial investment for which only the landowners or richer peasants could obtain credit. The industrialisation of food production therefore resulted in a concentration of capital and increased profits for the few and an increased rate of rural unemployment and urban migration for the masses. Moreover, the benefits of any increase in output were rarely available to those in need. Indeed, existing nutritional standards among the rural poor have been threatened by the fact that the research on which the Green Revolution was based, was narrowly focussed on cereal crops. The greater relative yields of cereals then made nutritious pulses such as peas, beans and lentils unprofitable to grow and many third world farmers were induced to switch from vegetable to cereal production. In India, for example, per capita pulse consumption dropped by 27 per cent between 1964-69.[123]

Finally, it is important to stress that the Green Revolution fostered even greater dependence on the industrialised countries, because it was based on scientific agriculture developed by multinational corporations, promoted by US foundations and government agencies, and transferred to the third world by means of World Bank loans.[124] Expensive technological inputs such as fertilisers have to be imported on a continuing basis, on terms dictated by the multinational companies which supply them. The Green Revolution has therefore not only failed to solve the problem of hunger in the third world, it has actually increased the economic dependence of the countries involved and reinforced the material poverty which in itself produces malnutrition.

Migration, urbanisation and neo-colonialism

Aidan Southall has observed that, 'slum living has been conferred upon Africa by the colonial experience . . . developing in African cities most of the characteristic social evils of the poorer areas of western cities during the industrialisation period'.[125] The difference is that in the third world, this situation has been endlessly prolonged because the industrial transformation is neither constant nor assured. Nevertheless large scale migration to the towns continues, encouraged by the widespread failure of peripheral agriculture. The commercialisation of peasant farming and the individualisation of land rights have sharpened class divisions in the countryside, reducing the size of some family plots so that they can no longer provide subsistence. Others have been thrown off the land altogether. The level of economic development in the cities, however, is no more able to generate adequate employment than the agricultural sector. As a consequence the unhealthy character of contemporary urban life is similar to that of the colonial period. Indeed, the increasing rate of urban expansion since the war has meant that if anything the living conditions of many town dwellers have worsened.

The migrant labour system and all that it entails in the way of social disintegration and disease, still continues in Africa, as in most of the third world. As Arrighi has commented, 'The main failure of the labour migration system in colonial times was that it did not create the conditions that would have made it obsolete.[126] Moreover, these migrant workers have now been joined by a large number of occasional or unemployed workers who live with their families in urban areas and are entirely dependent on the capitalist sector for their subsistence. Conditions have improved for certain groups in the population, notably the skilled working class and state employees who, in addition to obtaining regular wages, often benefit from various public provisions. On the whole, however, the limited improvements that have been made over the years in housing and sanitation have been more than offset by the massive influx of people to the urban areas.[127] The unhealthy quality of life in most third world cities is at its most extreme in the shanty towns - the 'spontaneous settlements' which have grown up around the major towns in many underdeveloped countries in the postwar period. Here there is an almost total lack of basic services such as water, electricity, sewage and refuse disposal. Housing is both scarce and notoriously inadequate, reflecting the tremendous rate of expansion of the shanty towns which is estimated to be as high as twelve per cent a year in some countries.[128]

Under these conditions, infectious diseases remain the major health problem in third world cities. Recent studies by the World Health Organisation have suggested that over two-thirds of town dwellers in underdeveloped countries have a water supply which is either contaminated or insufficient to meet minimal health needs. The WHO has also predicted that by 1980 there will be some five hundred million people without a safe water supply *in the towns alone*.[129] The crucial importance of clean water supplies in determining the incidence of a wide range of infectious diseases has been shown by David Bradley who suggests that 17 out of the 25 main water-related diseases commonly found in third world countries, could be reduced by 50-100 per cent simply through the provision of ample, safe water.[130] The potential benefit of clean water supplies, however, is lost without an effective means of waste disposal and since the development of sewerage systems in most third world countries lags far behind even that of piped water, the scale of the problem is vast. The WHO assessment is that at present only 28 per cent of the urban population of underdeveloped countries have water-borne sewerage and that 29 per cent have no sanitation whatsoever. They also estimate that the population without sewage disposal will double in the next ten years.[131] It is almost inevitable, therefore, that faecally-related diseases will become an increasingly serious problem. Cholera for example, first appeared in West Africa in 1970; it has already become endemic in many parts of the continent.[132]

It is important to view this tremendous burden of infectious disease against the background of the nutritional deficiencies that have already been described. In the towns, moreover, new forms of malnutrition are developing which are directly related to the export of western commodities and patterns of consumption to the under-developed world. Thus simple lack of food is not the only problem. Entry into the cash economy and the need to purchase food as a commodity invariably entails the consumption of more refined foods. Even basic grains are sold in highly refined forms in the urban areas. Both nutrients and fibre are therefore lost, whereas they are retained by the traditional methods of preparation used in country areas.[133] This is particularly important since lack of access to a variety of traditional vegetables forces urban dwellers to substitute refined starches, reducing their intake of vitamins, proteins and minerals. Excessive starch consumption is consequently a noticeable feature of urban diets in the third world, and the resulting imbalance can produce deficiency diseases such as pellagra, or kwashiorkor in children.[134]

In most underdeveloped countries, an increased income does not necessarily imply better nutrition, particularly at the lower end of the scale. In fact, as income rises, the consumption of refined carbo-hydrates normally rises too.[135] A growing proportion of the urban diet in most underdeveloped countries consists of items such as white bread, polished rice, refined sugar, soft drinks, snacks, sweets and 'tonics'. In contrast to the prestige which attaches to such foods, nutritious traditional foods such as green leaves, small animals and insects have increasingly been rejected.[136] The marketing monopoly of the international food industry ensures that there is every induce-ment to turn to processed foods, especially those with a high sugar content. Together with the intensive promotion of western patterns of food consumption, this increasingly shapes the dietary habits (and disease patterns) of those so poor that food is virtually the only consumer good they can afford.

Similar pressures favour the rapid growth in cigarette sales observed in most underdeveloped countries today. At present smoking is largely confined to wage-earning males in the towns, but its potential rate of increase now offers much more scope to manufacturers than the industrialised countries. Since tobacco is a major cash crop, many governments favour its expanded production. Moreover, the absence of safeguards and counter-information allows cigarettes to be sold with a much higher tar content in under-developed countries than in the west.[137]

We can see then, that in the postwar period urban life in much of the third world has the same health-threatening character as it had in the colonial era. Lack of a satisfactory physical infrastructure (houses, water, sewerage and so on) is reinforced by the inadequacy of food supplies, thus swelling the burden of infectious disease, while new patterns of consumption introduce the so-called diseases of affluence as well. All these problems have been greatly exacerbated by the growing rate of migration to the towns. For some migrants, the social pressures of urban life have been alleviated by the presence of their families, but this has simultaneously increased the economic pressures on them, while submitting the families themselves to the new stresses of slum conditions. Finally, although industrialisation has created employment for a small proportion of urban settlers, it has done so at the cost of increasing pollution in general, and occupational health hazards in particular. It is the impact of factors such as these that we will examine in the final section.

Technology, 'development' and disease

Although they remain 'underdeveloped', all third world countries have experienced the effects of advanced technology and modernisation in the postwar period. In addition to the industrialisation of agriculture already examined, industrial production has expanded rapidly in certain third world countries, while most of them have experienced western technology in the implementation of infrastructural projects. All of these developments have had significant effects on the health of third world populations.

As indicated earlier, the neo-colonial phase has seen the selective transfer of industrial production to the third world, largely in order to utilise its flexible and cheap labour supply. Additional factors are now beginning to encourage investment in more capital intensive production in third world countries. Foremost among the industries attracted to the third world are those involving particular health and safety hazards, either to workers or to the population at large.

Advanced capitalist countries are increasingly introducing controls on dangerous or polluting industrial processes. Whatever their limitations it is often now more economical for firms simply to transfer plant to somewhere more congenial, and this is likely to be an underdeveloped country lacking protective legislation.[138] Given the economic aspirations of most third world states, even the most hazardous industries are often welcomed. A Brazilian economic minister recently remarked that if environmental pollution was the cost of providing work and food for the Brazilian population, his country could not have enough of it![139] This approach was endorsed by a recent UN report which suggested that environmental controls in the metropolitan countries are a spur to third world industrialisation and are therefore 'in keeping with the desire to achieve a new economic order'.[140]

Dangerous industries are therefore being exported to third world countries, taking ill health with them. Yet, as Elling has pointed out, the effects of occupational health hazards in particular are likely to be even more serious in the third world than they have been in the advanced capitalist countries.

> The poorer nutritional levels of workers associated with higher rates of debilitating disease, the absence of union organisation, the lack of official awareness of, concern for, and action in relation to pollution and occupational health hazards, the newness of workers to the industrial environment, the lack of industrial health services and personnel, and still other conditions relating to the underdeveloped countries themselves are all factors leading to the hypothesis that occupational health hazards resulting from industrialisation will be at least as great and probably greater in the underdeveloped countries than has been the case in developed countries.[141]

There is increasing evidence of serious ill health resulting not only from urban industrial processes, but also from new hazards whose potential effects extend far beyond the industrial centres. Among the most serious of these are modern agricultural pesticides, many of which have been banned in the metropolitan countries but are nevertheless exported to the third world.

> Over fifty per cent of all US pesticide exports in 1975 went to Africa, Asia and Latin America. That pesticide misuse in developing countries constitutes a rising health hazard is widely acknowledged. The technology of pesticides crosses borders and cultures much more quickly than the social and legislative superstructure essential to its proper control.[142]

Irrespective of their degree of industrialisation, most third world countries have felt the effects of modern technology through the creation of major civil engineering schemes. Yet as with many of the trappings of modernisation, the potential contribution of these projects to genuine economic development is often negligible: the costs, however, are not. The building of dams and the creation of man-made lakes in third world countries forces the compulsory resettlement of the inhabitants, often destroying their means of subsistence.[143] Fertile lowlands may be flooded and the local people forced to cultivate less productive land elsewhere. When the Kariba dam was built, for instance, the Tonga people were displaced and subsequently faced severe malnutrition. This arose in part from the failure of their traditional crops in a new habitat, and in part from the inability to supplement their diet with the fish and rodents previously available to them.[144]

Hydro-electric schemes tend also to produce ideal new breeding grounds for disease vectors. The WHO reports for example, that the international incidence of schistosomiasis is growing as a direct result of the increasing number of man-made lakes.[145] In regions of the world where river blindness is endemic (notably west Africa and parts of Central America) it, too, can be exacerbated by the construction of dams. The turbulent water near the sluice gates creates excellent breeding grounds for the simulium fly which transmits the disease.[146] Irrigation schemes also produce new health hazards, creating conditions favourable to the breeding either of malaria-carrying mosquitoes or the schistosome-carrying snails.

Clearly irrigation schemes and energy supplies are fundamental requirements for any kind of economic development. Yet it is wrong to assume that the health hazards described above are the regrettable but inevitable cost of economic progress. In fact, it is quite possible to design such schemes with health considerations in mind.[147] However, despite the fact that adequate water supplies are so essential for health, the manner of their provision - if indeed they are provided at all - is determined largely by the requirements of international capital.[148] Indeed, so long as vital resources such as food and water remain commodities appropriated in the name of economic growth, they will be systematically denied to the vast majority of people in the third world whose health and development depends upon them.

The diseases of underdevelopment, and the high mortality rates which accompany them, are not somehow a natural, and therefore inevitable aspect of life in the third world. Rather, they are a direct consequence of the wretched material conditions imposed on most inhabitants of third world countries. While certain elements of medical technology are of undoubted value in dealing with some of these diseases, modern medicine cannot provide any real solution to the health problems of the third world while social and economic conditions remain unchanged. Nor can a solution be sought simply by looking to an improved standard of living produced by 'development' within the current international order, for as we shall see, the historical form of capitalist expansion in the third world has not only systematically undermined the health of the population, but has also created obstacles to the realisation of effective health policies.

Part Three:
The Social Production of Medical Care

In capitalist societies, despite the obvious importance of social and economic factors in the causation of ill health, the characteristic response to health problems has not been prevention, but an almost total reliance on after-the-event medical intervention of a curative kind. Part three examines the implications of this in more detail. Chapters four, five and six look at the social production of medical care in the developed world, using the British National Health Service as a case study of state-financed health care, while chapter seven examines the significance of the export of western medicine to the underdeveloped countries of the world.

4: Public Health, Medicine and the Development of British Capitalism

The 'condition of the working class' was a topic of considerable concern in Britain throughout the nineteenth century. The ill health of much of the urban proletariat posed an immediate threat of infection to the inhabitants of the wealthier parts of towns, while at the same time epitomising the danger of the slums as a breeding ground for a wide range of social problems. More fundamentally perhaps, in the latter part of the century, chronic ill health appeared to present a serious obstacle to economic and military expansion. To many members of the ruling class, the very future of the race seemed to be threatened by the excessive breeding of a weakly and degenerated working class. Attempts by the expanding central and local state apparatus to solve these problems were concentrated on public health measures - the control of disease through the provision of clean water, sewage disposal and some slum clearance. These developments, crucial in raising general levels of health, had little to do with emergent medical science. Curative medicine was still very limited both in its availability and its effectiveness, and, as pointed out in chapter two, it is now widely accepted that it played little or no part in the reduction of the national mortality rate which began in the 1870s. Despite its therapeutic ineffectiveness, the development of medical science was nevertheless of tremendous social significance throughout the Victorian period. The nineteenth century saw a shift from religion to science as the dominant framework used to define and to explain the nature of the existing social order. Medicine and biology were of crucial importance here, providing the basic concepts through which the class and sexual divisions of Victorian society were expressed and ultimately justified.

Early public health measures and the development of industrial capitalism

The 1848 Public Health Act represented one of the earliest moves towards state control of the lives of individuals in what was still a predominantly laissez-faire society. Orthodox interpretations of this 'sanitary revolution' have often explained it simply in terms of increasing humanitarianism or increasing 'rationality' in society.[1] Such explanations emphasise the role of individuals associated with particular reforms - Shaftesbury in the protection of women and children working in the mines, or Chadwick and Simon in the field of public health. Any adequate analysis must, however, begin not with 'great men' but with an account of the forces that were shaping state policy in Britain during the early stages of industrialisation.

During the late eighteenth and early nineteenth century, a cease-less drive to expand production was supported by a laissez-faire economic theory which stressed the importance of a self-regulating free market necessitating only minimal state interference. A com-mitment to individualism also characterised the social and political philosophy of the period. Benthamite utilitarianism had gradually replaced the paternalism of previous centuries, forming an impor-tant part of the ideological framework within which industrial capitalism developed.[2] The utilitarians believed firmly in the capitalist system, in unhindered competition, in a free labour market and in a minimum of state interference in social and economic affairs. However, neither the economic nor the physical conditions of the early nineteenth century could be characterised as free and unhindered, in part because of the vested interests of the old landed aristocracy, but in particular because of the destructive consequences of early urbanisation and industrialisation on material life in the cities. Hence utilitarianism accepted the necessity for strong central-ised control *under certain circumstances*, in order to leave the way clear for individual initiative.

Political developments in the early nineteenth century laid the foundations for state regulation of this kind. The 1832 Reform Act enfranchised the urban middle class, thus consolidating the political power of the rising bourgeoisie. As a result, the state with its newly emerging bureaucratic and legal structure began to play an increasingly important role in the creation of the conditions necessary for the further development of capitalist production. This was reflected in early public health legislation, as well as in the major social policy of the nineteenth century - the Poor Law. Before 1834, poor relief had been administered by local parishes on the basis of legislation enacted during the Elizabethan period.[3] However, during the late eighteenth and early nineteenth centuries a series of circumstances combined to increase the cost of poor relief. The 1834 Poor Law Amendment Act was intended to reduce this cost by centralising the administrative system - parishes were to be grouped into unions. But, above all, by making the conditions for the receipt of relief so undesirable that no one would apply unless they were in the direst poverty, it was designed to strengthen and foster the discipline of the labour market. The Poor Law Commissioners summed up their philosophy concerning the recipient of poor relief as follows:

> The first and most essential of all conditions, a principle which we find universally admitted, even by those whose practice is at variance with it, is that his situation on the whole shall not be made really or apparently so eligible as the situation of the independent labourer of the lowest class.[4]

Under such conditions it was assumed that people would survive outside the workhouse if this were at all possible. This would have the effect of reducing the cost of poor relief, while at the same time maximising the supply of cheap labour. As Bentley Gilbert has noted, 'The goal of the Poor Law Amendment Act had been to force the individual workman to place himself at the disposal of the British productive system.'[5] These same concerns - to save money while simultaneously maximising the supply of labour - were also extremely important in the Public Health movement in the 1830s and 1840s.

The aim of the 1848 Public Health Act was to combat infectious diseases by defining a narrow range of sanitary services which local authorities could adopt if they so chose. It provided for the creation of a General Board of Health, as well as boards at local level, which could appoint medical officers of health. The intention was to persuade towns to provide clean water supplies and effective refuse and sewage disposal. At the most commonsense level, it was fear of infectious disease in general and - after the epidemics of the 1830s and 1840s - of cholera in particular, which motivated middle-class support for public health legislation. Cholera was no respecter of the social status of individuals. It attacked the poor and the respectable middle class indiscriminately.[6] Thus, for the middle class in Victorian cities, public health reform was an important form of self defence against contagion spreading outwards from the slums.

This bourgeois self-defence is an explanation which is often seized upon by historians, but it cannot by itself account for the 1848 act. Many enquiries during the early nineteenth century - in particular Chadwick's immense investigation published in 1842 as *The Sanitary Conditions of the Labouring Population of Great Britain*[7] - had illustrated the close relationship between poverty and disease; a connection which was stressed in contemporary debates on the public health question. Emphasis was placed, not on the fact that poverty caused ill health but rather on the belief that disease produced poverty among its victims, and therefore added to the escalating cost of poor relief.[8] The most important justification given for public health legislation was therefore its economic rationality. The Poor Law Commissioners themselves expressed this in the following terms in 1838,

> All epidemics and all infectious diseases are attended with charges immediate and ultimate on the poor rates. Labourers are suddenly thrown by infectious disease into a state of destitution, for which immediate relief must be given. In the case of death, the widows and children are thrown as paupers on the parish. The amount of burdens thus provided is frequently so great, as to render it good economy on the part of the administrator of the Poor Laws to incur the charge for preventing the evils which are assignable to physical causes, which there are no other means of removing.[9]

It was on these grounds then, that supporters justified sanitary measures such as the 1848 act as well as the assumption by the Poor Law Commissioners of the responsibility for providing medical care for those who were dependent on the Poor Law.[10]

By the 1840s, changes were also beginning to occur in the nature of industrial production - changes which involved a shift away from the extreme labour intensiveness of the early part of the century, towards more capital-intensive production. However, levels of morbidity and mortality remained so high that it was difficult to exploit these new technologies to the full. A relatively small labour force was required, but one with more skills, improved physical health, and hence, greater reliability. At the same time, the first half of the nineteenth century was marked by a dramatic rise in working-class consciousness and levels of organisation.

> Although, as it now seems, the danger of a popular uprising on any considerable scale in the England of the first few decades of the nineteenth century was never very substantial there was a continual undercurrent of seditious talk, which did not fail to become known to the government, and which seemed to be illustrated by spasmodic little attempts at rebellion. From the food riots of 1795-1801 . . . right down to the impulsive *jacquerie* of the south-eastern counties in 1830, and the tension of the struggle over the Reform Bill, there was, it seems clear, what was regarded as a very ugly spirit among the mass of the people.[11]

Chartism in particular was seen as a threat to social order. There was always a danger that, as Chadwick put it,

> the sullen resentment of the neglected workers might organise itself behind the trade union leaders and the Six Points men . . . and thence, if a Chartist millenium were to be averted, the governing classes must free the governed from the sharp spur of their misery by improving the physical conditions of their lives.[12]

Thus, a combination of the need to improve the quality of the labour force, as well as a fear of working-class unrest, lay at the heart both of the 1848 Public Health Act and also the Factory Acts of the same period. During the early stages of the Industrial Revolution, working hours were extremely long and the demand for a ten-hour day became an important political rallying point in the first half of the nineteenth century.[13] Certain of the more paternalistic members of the aristocracy joined with the working class in attempting to force the manufacturers to improve factory conditions. Naturally employers initially resisted these demands since the unlimited exploitation of cheap labour was the basis of their competitive power. However, as working-class pressure mounted, a series of acts was passed between 1833-64 which regulated the length of the working day and the employment of women and children.[14] But the history of these acts illustrates a fundamental contradiction which is to be found in all subsequent British health legislation. The Factory Acts were undoubtedly an important goal of working-class struggle and did lead to an improvement in the health and well-being of workers. Nevertheless, they simultaneously reflected the interests of employers as the need for a fitter labour force became increasingly apparent. The passing of the 1848 Public Health Act must be seen as part of this same process. The social and economic costs of ill health and premature death were becoming all too obvious and the intention of the act was to limit these by reducing the burden of infectious disease.

The 1848 act was, however, a very limited piece of legislation.[15] It did not *compel* any town to carry out public health measures except in very extreme circumstances. Either ten per cent of rate-payers had to have asked for an enquiry by the General Board of Health, which had discretionary powers to enforce the act, or, alternatively, in really unhealthy areas (i.e. where the death rate had exceeded 23 per 1,000 over the previous seven years) the Board could enforce implementation of the act on its own initiative. The act was thus permissive rather than mandatory, and the powers of the Board of Health were very limited. The weakness of the act was due in part to opposition which had been widespread in various quarters. At an ideological level, this came particularly from sections of the aristocracy and the gentry who were fighting a rearguard action against the development of new 'centralising tendencies'. More significantly, however, opposition also came from those who had a more material interest in maintaining the existing situation. The private water companies, slum landlords, sewage commissioners and commercial sewage dealers, for example, were particularly threatened, and obstructed the movement of the bill through parliament. As Meredeth Turshen points out,

In the matter of sewerage, profits were made out of the vast dumps of ashes, night-soil, rotting vegetables, straw, dung, the sweepings of the street, the offal of the slaughter houses, and the contents of public latrines - refuse of all kinds in thousands of tons, occupying hundreds of cubic metres. If the privy were replaced by the water closet, dealers who retailed the sewage by the cart-load and barge-load to farmers, would lose a source of revenue.[16]

Opposition from these various quarters continued during the years following the passing of the act onto the statute books, thus weakening it still further. Nevertheless, attempts to organise public health schemes flourished, particularly between 1850-75. By the time Chadwick left the Board of Health in 1854, 182 towns had adopted such measures, and another 600 provided schemes between 1854-68. By the early 1870s, there was a rapidly expanding public health service which engaged medical officers in sanitary areas covering the whole country.[17] Hence, despite opposition from less enlightened sections of the bourgeoisie, the 1848 act, and subsequently the more comprehensive Public Health Act of 1875, did form the basis for a gradual improvement in the physical conditions of British towns, and as we shall see, made possible a substantial improvement in the health of the working class.

Medicine, social control and the sexual division of labour

Throughout the nineteenth century, medicine developed rapidly as a new and powerful science. Its therapeutic effectiveness however was very limited and it was in any case available only to a small proportion of the population. Nonetheless, medical ideas, and the activities and pronouncements of doctors, were a very powerful social force, particularly during the latter half of the century. This power arose from the ideological importance of medicine in defining and justifying new modes of social and economic organisation as well as from the growing significance of medical practice itself as a mechanism of social control. This is not of course to imply a conscious conspiracy on the part of doctors. As Ehrenreich and Ehrenreich have pointed out,

> to analyse something as a system of social control - as a mechan-
> ism for creating or reinforcing acquiescence to the given order
> of society - is not to view it as a conspiracy. The social control
> functions . . . grow out of the social structure of medical care
> and the organisation of the medical system, and not in our
> analysis out of the conscious motivations of men. Moreover,
> social control in itself is not necessarily bad. Any society must
> exercise social control if it is to survive. The question is: control
> for what? What is the impact and ideological content of a given
> system of social control?[18]

The nineteenth century was a period of rapid social and
economic change in which pre-industrial modes of legitimation -
religion in particular - were giving way to a new and secular
definition of the world. Science was becoming the metaphor within
which the existing social and sexual division of labour was justified
and reinforced.

> The tremendous vogue of Darwinism provided both a ration-
> alisation of competitive struggle and a general warrant for
> using scientific - and especially biological - concepts for
> explaining and justifying particular forms of social and
> economic relationships.[19]

The ideas developed within medicine and biology played a central
part in this process as scientists began increasingly to take over from
priests the task of defining and upholding the moral order. 'For
many doctors, playing churchman merely required translation of
ecclesiastical into medical language. What had been sin became
physically injurious.'[20] This enterprise was enthusiastically undertaken by doctors at a time when they were fighting very hard to
establish medicine as a profession worthy of middle-class status and
rewards. As Karl Figlio has pointed out, the nineteenth century
physician was a 'marginal member of the middle class' and this fact
of marginality had an important effect on the nature of medical
practice.[21]

The organisation of medical care reflected very clearly the class
divisions in Victorian society.[22] The wealthy were able to buy the
services of elite physicians and surgeons who usually attended them

in their own homes. The wealthier members of the middle classes were also able to buy medical care, usually at home or in the out-patients departments of the voluntary hospitals. For the lower middle class, and those sections of the working class who were in regular and reasonably paid employment, medical care was available through a variety of unofficial insurance schemes - provident societies, doctors' 'clubs' organised by individual doctors who undertook to provide care on receipt of an annual fee, and 'contract practice' under which doctors were hired to care for members of particular organisations. The doctors who organised these schemes were, of course, the less affluent and less prestigious members of the medical profession. For the poor, medical care was available only from the much-detested Poor Law, and they were often forced to take pauper status before such care could be obtained. The high cost and inferior quality of most medical care had particularly serious conse-quences for working-class women, who often had to make extreme sacrifices to pay for a doctor or midwife to help them in childbirth. The wife of one unemployed man, writing at the beginning of the nineteenth century, described her first two pregnancies in graphic terms.

> The first confinement I managed to get through very well, having some money left from what I had saved before marriage. But how I managed to get through my second con-finement I cannot tell anyone. I had to work at laundry work from morning to night, nurse a sick husband, and take care of my child three-and-a-half years old. In addition I had to provide for my coming confinement, which meant that I had to do without common necessaries to pay for doctors' fees, which so undermined my health that when my baby was born I nearly lost my life, the doctor said through want of nourishment.[23]

Many women were not so fortunate even as this, and Poor Law hospitals frequently seem to have been used for maternity cases.[24] The social divisions of Victorian society were, therefore, reflected in and reinforced by the mode of organisation of medical care. More generally, however, nineteenth century medical and biological thought were used to justify the very different lives (and deaths) of rich and poor. The working classes were blamed for their own unhealthiness since bad habits and lack of attention to hygiene, rather than appalling living and working conditions, were said to be at the root of much of the ill health experienced by the urban working class.[25] It is, however, in the example of the sexual division of labour and its articulation with the class structure that the wider social significance of nineteenth-century medical ideology becomes clearest. These relationships will, therefore, be examined here in more detail.

The late eighteenth and early nineteenth centuries witnessed a major transformation in the pattern of women's labour. Before the Industrial Revolution, women undertook a wide range of productive activities, usually within the context of the family unit. With the emergence of capitalism, they became increasingly involved in wage labour and in the production of goods directly for exchange.[26] The most dramatic change, however, came with the Industrial Revolution. Many of the rural poor were forced to move into the towns, and the rate of female participation in the labour force rose very markedly. Most importantly, work in the home and work outside it became separated. As Zaretsky has put it, 'with the rise of industry, capitalism "split" material production between its socialised forms (the sphere of commodity production) and the private labour performed predominantly by women within the home'.[27]

The consequence of this split was that the work done by women at home was denied social recognition. It was seen as unimportant because it was not in itself considered productive or remunerative, in the same way as waged work. The division between home and work also had the effect of strongly reinforcing old ideas of female domesticity - the belief that 'a woman's place is in the home'. This idea remained extremely powerful throughout the nineteenth century (as indeed it does today) despite the fact that working-class women continued to form a substantial proportion of the labour force. Moreover, the belief in the essential domesticity of women meant that when they did enter the labour force they were unable to do so on equal terms with men - the 'real' workers.

In Britain over the period of the nineteenth century women were employed in garment making, domestic service and textiles. In 1896, 19 per cent were employed in domestic service, 26 per cent in garment making and 14 per cent in the textile factories. And even within these occupations their tasks were subordinate, low paid and of low status. Even in a period of rapid technical change, urbanisation and population growth, a patriarchal tradition dominated the work process, reflected in a division of labour which defined women's work as unskilled and thus low paid and subordinate.[28]

The processes of urbanisation and industrialisation had a very different effect on the lives of bourgeois women. For them the division between public life and the private world of the home was absolute, and most became mere symbols by which their husband's financial and social status was evaluated. They were embodiments of conspicuous consumption and remained in their homes to provide their husbands and children with the tenderness, sensitivity and devotion to the arts which were so conspicuously lacking in the factories and mines of Victorian industry. As Linda Gordon has commented, 'The theory that women's moral influence would temper the savagery of capitalist competition was used by the whole bourgeois class to assuage its guilt and soothe its tensions.'[29]

The sexual divisions which had been characteristic of the pre-industrial and pre-capitalist period were therefore accentuated by the new organisation of labour demanded by industrial capitalism. Women worked inside the home and men outside it, and this strict differentiation between the spheres of men and women lay at the heart of Victorian society. This division of labour was not, however, easily achieved, and the question of the natural status and duties of women was a matter of much concern throughout the nineteenth century. The means by which the patriarchal authority of father and priest had traditionally been justified was being rapidly undermined by changing circumstances, and the task of defining the position of women increasingly fell to the proponents of the new science, and to doctors and biologists in particular. 'For centuries, the mode of Eve's creation and her greater guilt for the fall from grace had been credited as the cause of women's imperfect nature, but this was not an adequate explanation in a scientific age.'[30]

The dominant medical ideology emphasised the differences

between men and women by arguing that the status and capacities of women were entirely pre-determined by the nature of their reproductive organs. This was not, of course, a new idea - such views had been familiar for many hundreds of years. However, because of their slowly increasing knowledge of female physiology, as well as their own enhanced social status, doctors were able to provide more elaborate and apparently more scientific explanations of the nature of femininity, and thereby a rationale for woman's exclusive role as wife and mother. A woman's whole mental and physical existence was assumed to be at the mercy of her reproductive system, over which she herself could have very little control. The peculiarly menacing nature of medical patriarchy is evident in this melodramatic pronouncement from one Victorian doctor.

> Many a young life is battered and forever crippled in the breakers of puberty; if it crosses these unharmed and is not dashed to pieces on the rock of childbirth it may still ground on the ever-recurring shallows of menstruation, and lastly, upon the final bar of the menopause ere protection is found in the unruffled waters of the harbour beyond the reach of sexual storms.[31]

It was suggested that women had to tread very carefully if they were to avoid the crises produced by the natural functioning of their reproductive systems. Those who stepped outside the bounds set by their own physiology risked physical illness, insanity or even death. Women were encouraged to rest at all important times in their reproductive cycle - that is, during puberty, menstruation, pregnancy, lactation and the menopause. For the majority of Victorian women, this of course meant their entire lives. A malfunctioning uterus or ovary was said to spread disease elsewhere in the body. Doctors could provide no evidence to show exactly how this morbid process occurred, but it was assumed that the uterus, the ovaries and the nervous system were somehow connected, so that the nervous system transmitted pathological impulses to the rest of the body.[32] The role of the nervous system in the transmission of these impulses was particularly significant because it was the more 'irritable' nature of her nervous system which was supposed specifically to distinguish the nineteenth century woman from her male counterpart. In the man, intellectual abilities were assumed to be dominant; in the woman it was her nervous system and emotions.[33] It was argued that each human body possessed only a fixed reserve of energy, and that in a woman the normal functioning of the uterus and ovaries consumed a disproportionate amount of this energy.[34] Any additional exertion was therefore likely to be dangerous - particularly sexual 'over-indulgence'. Masturbation, for example, was regarded as particularly repellent in women, and Barker Benfield argues that it was sometimes a pretext for sexual surgery such as clitorodectomy.[35] While the frequency of sexual surgery of this kind should not be overestimated, female masturbation was regarded as both highly immoral and a drain on vital energies and, as such, was strongly condemned. Too much interest in 'normal' sexual activity was not to be encouraged either, and at the menopause this was seen as particularly reprehensible.

> my experience teaches me that a marked increase of sexual impulse at the change of life is a morbid impulse - Edward Tilt wrote in his widely read study of menopause - Whenever sexual impulse is first felt at the change of life, some morbid ovario-uterine condition will be found to explain it . . . It therefore is most imprudent for women to marry at this epoch without having obtained the sanction of a medical man.[36]

The danger of voluntary over-indulgence would not, however, seem to have been very great since it was widely believed that women had no sexual feelings. The dominant medical view expressed by writers such as William Acton was that women did not need or enjoy sexual activity - to have intercourse with their husband was an act of duty rather than one of pleasure. According to Acton himself, 'the majority of women (happily for them) are not very much troubled with sexual feelings of any kind'.[37]

The belief in female sexual anaesthesia was closely connected with the 'cult of motherhood', since it was assumed that the sexual instinct in men was paralleled by a maternal instinct in women. The glory of woman, her *raison d'etre* and her most sacred duty, was seen to lie in motherhood, and throughout the Victorian period and beyond, the 'cult of motherhood' exerted an extremely powerful influence on the lives of women of all classes:

> Nineteenth century ideologists offered the view that the two sexes were not only different in all things but nearly opposite. It became unfashionable among the educated to say outright that women were inferior... Victorian ideology about women included the pretence that the spheres of men and women were separate but equal. This belief, in turn, was part of a larger ideological system in which women, although considered inferior in intellectual, artistic and physical potential, were told that they were morally superior and that their greater holiness came from their innate capacity for motherliness.[38]

These two ideologies, the belief in female sexual anaesthesia and the glorification of motherhood, reinforced traditional sexual morality during a period of rapid social and economic change. Martha Verbrugge has summarised the social significance of the nineteenth century medical model of women.

> Generally these ideas rationalised the subordination of all women, and the prevailing norms about their duties and qualities. Idealising women as domestic and maternal beings, medical ideologues reinforced the character and implicit values of institutions such as the family which helped glue together the socio-economic system. Furthermore, they provided a gauge for judging women as either 'respectable' or 'deviant' and a rationale for treating them as such.[39]

Despite their common biological inheritance, women in different social classes did of course lead very different lives and this was reflected in medical ideology. It was bourgeois women with whom the nineteenth century medical establishment came into contact most frequently and who conformed most closely to the image of the ideal woman. For doctors, such women represented a source of income, as well as an important means by which to enhance their professional status. But medicine was still very limited in its effectiveness.

> Medical practice found itself in the painful position of having advanced far enough to discard ancient methods of therapy

without being able to offer anything new in their place. The patient and his or her inept but well meaning physician were left to fend for themselves.[40]

As a consequence, doctors were led towards the use of 'heroic methods' which would, by their very severity, convince patients of their effectiveness. Moreover, they were encouraged to define their professional role in moral rather than technical terms and to draw the boundaries of their functions very broadly. An exhortation made by Dr Charles Meigs to his fellow physicians provides a striking example of this:

> woman's intellectual and moral perceptivity and forces... are feminine as her organs are. Beyond all these, you shall have to explore the history of those functions and destinies which her sexual nature enables her to fulfil, and the strange and secret influences which her organs, by their nervous constitution, and the functions, by their relation to her whole life-force, whether in sickness or in health are capable of exerting, not on the body alone, but on the heart, the mind and the very soul of woman. The medical practitioner has, then, much to study as to the female, that is not purely medical - but, psychological and moral rather. Such researches will be a future obligation lying heavily on you.[41]

The impact of medical precepts on the lives of middle-class women came most clearly into perspective at the very time when women were beginning to press for birth control and for entry into higher education. By the 1860s middle-class women were beginning to take up various activities outside the home, and by the 1870s the question of higher education for women had become a much debated issue.[42] Women were already attending courses in London and Cambridge and were demanding to be allowed to enter all areas of higher education, including medicine. The old anthropological arguments about innate differences in brain capacity between men and women were beginning to look rather dubious and those who opposed women's entry into higher education were forced to articulate their objections more clearly. Medical pronouncements were therefore cited to back up the claim that, because their reproductive systems differed, men and women needed entirely different types of education. Menstruation in particular was presented as a serious obstacle to higher education for women, as one physician, John Thorburn, warned in 1884.

> There are few physicians who have not seen bright careers of mental work and usefulness cut short, never to be resumed, after a few days of hard, mental strain during a menstrual period. It cannot therefore be too strongly insisted upon that, with the young and the delicate, at any rate, and to some extent with all women, the period of menstruation should be a period of comparative repose, mental and bodily, but especially mental.[43]

It was suggested that women who entered higher education did so at the risk of ruining their health. Moreover, a woman who developed 'masculine' intellectual qualities would necessarily underdevelop her 'female' qualities both mental and physical. As a result, she was likely to become sterile, or at the very least to produce weakly children. This was emphasised by Herbert Spencer, the founding father of British sociology, who regarded education for women as disastrous for human evolution.

> Diminution of reproductive power is not shown only by the greater frequency of absolute sterility; nor is it only in the earlier cessation of childbearing, but it is also shown in the very frequent inability of such women to suckle their infants. In its full sense, the reproductive power means the power to bear a well-developed infant, and to supply that infant with the natural food for the natural period. Most of the flat-chested girls who survive their high-pressure education are incompetent to do this.[44]

During the nineteenth century, then, bourgeois women played supportive rather than directly or indirectly productive roles in society, and medicine was an important means by which these roles were reinforced. As Martha Verbrugge has commented,

> The biomedical portrait of women as inherently sensitive, dependent and maternal, legitimized this sheltered life-style; similarly the accusation that sickness originated in wilful

deviance was a means of reaffirming the boundaries of women's capacities and propriety. Thus, medical ideology about women slid easily between the realms of biological 'nature', social propriety and economic order.[45]

The position of working-class women was of course very different. The ideological emphasis on motherhood was common to women of all classes, and indeed was very important in sustaining and controlling the working-class family, often under conditions of extreme poverty. It was, however, impossible to define working-class women as physically weak and dependent like their middle-class sisters, and this contradiction was reflected in several different ways in medical ideology.

Most of the doctors who wrote about working-class women had very little contact with them. Their information was usually obtained at a distance and reflected wider social beliefs about the nature of the working class, and of working-class women in particular. Despite the nature of their material conditions and their obvious ill health, it was assumed that by and large working-class women were unusually *healthy*, especially by comparison with their middle-class counterparts. Moreover, their very 'healthiness' was often attributed precisely to those extremely hard physical labours which in reality contributed to their ill health. It was conveniently assumed that while the 'idleness' of many middle-class women contributed to their sickliness,[46] it was the hard work of proletarian women which kept them healthy. Working-class women were assumed to be naturally susceptible to the same diseases as other women but to be able to avoid them through 'health-giving' labour in the factory, over the scrubbing board or at the treadle of a sewing machine.

The idea of work being healthy for working-class women was, of course, in sharp contrast to the campaign against middle-class women entering higher education on the grounds that it would damage their health. This apparent contradiction appears to have been resolved in a variety of different ways. First, there was a general but loosely formulated assumption that working-class women were somehow of a different stock and were therefore able to work without risking their health. They were not expected to be regularly incapacitated by 'monthly problems' as the wives of their employers were and it was assumed that even pregnancy and childbirth could be taken in their stride.[47] Second, it was argued that the nature of the work itself had to be taken into account. Dr Edward Clarke, who was a major opponent of higher education for women, expressed his solution to this apparent dilemma quite clearly, as reported by Bullough and Vogt.

> It was also of some concern to Dr Clarke that young women of the lower classes were expected during puberty to take jobs in domestic service or in factories. In his practice he had seen evidence of ill health among such women which he blamed upon their work. Yet, he concluded that labour in a factory or at a loom was far less damaging to a woman, because it worked on the body, not the brain. It was primarily brainwork which destroyed feminine capabilities.[48]

This view that women were destroyed by brain work rather than manual labour reinforced the ancient view of the intellectual inferiority of all women, while at the same time justifying the very different life styles of bourgeois and working-class women.

Finally, it is important to recognise that some working-class women sold not only their labour but also their bodies.[49] As a result, they were greatly feared since they could spread venereal disease to the men who purchased their services and, through them, to innocent wives and possibly even to unborn children.

> The prostitute as human residue comfortably fitted the conventional image of the utterly degraded and downcast woman. And it legitimised the kind of sanitary and penal measures by which the community might purge itself of a 'material nuisance'. In a society where 'pollution' was the governing metaphor for the perils of social intercourse between the 'Two Nations', the prostitute threatened morally and physically to contaminate society.[50]

Middle-class women were frequently pregnant or nursing and hence assumed to be sexually unavailable. Men whose wives were prevented from sexual activity by their 'sickness' or by their very 'femininity' were compelled to seek their pleasure with working-class women who fortunately laboured under no such medical misapprehensions. In addition, a variety of social and economic pressures forced men to marry late in life, while men in the armed forces were not allowed to marry at all. Under such circumstances, prostitution became an inevitable part of Victorian society and was overwhelmingly a working-class occupation.[51]

Underlying the whole phenomenon of Victorian prostitution was a belief in the unrestrained sexuality of working-class women. Similar assumptions lay behind the continual fear that the working class were breeding too fast and would swamp their betters. Beliefs of this kind were clearly at odds with scientific pronouncements that women had *no* sexual feelings at all, but this contradiction seems to have been resolved through the concept of the 'fallen woman'. It was thought that all women were born innocent and with the capacity to subdue their (rather weak) sexual drive, given the right circumstances. However, they could also be led astray, either through seduction by a man, or simply by exposure to immorality in their early lives. It was for this reason that middle-class mothers were so anxious to protect their daughters from anything that could possibly defile their purity, (not least the purity of their minds). Domestic servants were of course feared as a particular source of moral contagion. The sexuality of working-class women themselves, was explained by the fact that from a very early age they would be exposed to immorality, living in cramped, overcrowded conditions, and witnessing all the many vices and degradations of the urban slums. In addition, they were assumed to be particularly at risk when they were employed in domestic service - the cultural image of the rich son seducing the servant girl was a very common one. Once her chastity was destroyed the woman in question became another type of being entirely - a corrupt and sensual creature.

> Exposed to the knowledge of the world, the daughters of the poor, 'like their mother Eve' were not contented with a little knowledge, but probed as deeply as possible and ate of the fruit of knowledge. Once innocence was lost, the daughter's chastity became vulnerable.[52]

Thus medical ideology and medical practice played an extremely important part in reinforcing both the class and sexual division of labour in Victorian society. As Ozonoff and Ozonoff have put it,

> The medical image was but a reflex of a social situation. On the one hand it justified and explained a life of leisure and privilege and on the other it reflected the true position of the working woman as a machine to be used (the seller of labour power) though a dangerous machine that could break loose from its moorings and turn on its masters and mistresses.[53]

Imperialism and the problem of proletarian health and welfare

Precisely because of their apparent success, funds were beginning to be withdrawn from public health schemes from the 1880s onwards.[54] On the one hand, it appeared that the environmental basis for a healthier population had now been constructed, while at the same time strong forces were pushing towards an extension of the role of the state in the provision of medical care for individuals. As a result, the split between preventive and curative approaches to health care widened, and the social policies of the early twentieth century formed the basis for the ultimate dominance of curative medicine.[55]

The late nineteenth century marked the development of working class organisations as an important force in British life. Membership of trades unions expanded enormously with an explosion in growth from one-and-a-half million members in 1890 to nearly four million by 1913.[56] The 1880s and 1890s also saw the emergence of working-class political organisations, several of them coming together with the trade unions to form the Labour Party in the early 1900s. In the first decade of the twentieth century, the Labour Party and the TUC were vociferous in demanding specific social reforms, and their programmes included free education for all, the introduction of old age pensions and, in the case of the Labour Party, the provision of a health service.[57] This increased level of working-class organisation formed the background to the social legislation enacted by Lloyd George's Liberal government in the period from 1906 onwards. It is important, however, to see these reforms as more than either a benevolent gift from the liberal, caring state or, alternatively, a mere ploy to buy off working-class radicalism. They were also an important element in the attempt to restructure British capitalism.[58]

While Britain had been the 'workshop of the world' in the 1850s, the last quarter of the nineteenth century was a period of relative stagnation which was to destroy this predominance forever. British capitalism faced intensified economic competition, particularly from the USA and Germany. Moreover, as international capitalism entered its imperialist phase, the need for strong military backing became more and more apparent.

It was also increasingly apparent, however, that Britain was ill-equipped for this struggle. During this same period, numerous investigations were being made into the condition of the British working class, using the techniques and concepts of the new 'social science'. The results provided no encouragement to those who wished to retain British predominance in the world, since they demonstrated with indisputable clarity the extremely low level of physical fitness of the British working class.[59] These findings were confirmed in a particularly dramatic way by the high percentage of recruits rejected as unfit during the Boer war. Poor physique was the main reason for rejection; although the minimum height for entry into the infantry was lowered from 5ft 6in to 5ft 3in in 1883, a further reduction to 5ft was necessary in 1902.[60] Though contradictory, the effects of the Boer war on demands for social reform were very important. At first it seemed that the war presented an obstacle to reform. It diverted resources away from possible welfare spending, while directing the attention of working people towards the glories of imperialism and away from demands for social reform.[61] However, as the war progressed, the physical state of the population was starkly revealed, so that, as Bentley Gilbert has put it,

> It seemed the time had come to re-examine the old assumptions about the inevitable superiority of the British social system and the British race. Were English ways of doing things any longer invariably the best? Were the ancient Anglo-Saxon people who had painted the map red now decaying? Did a nation forced to spend three years and £250 million to defeat a

handful of unorganised farmers have the right to call itself the greatest power on earth? The menace implicit in these unhappy reflections was that of armed, organised, vigorous Imperial Germany. [62]

Working-class demands for social reform, therefore, began to be echoed by enlightened sections of the ruling class. In particular, a new attitude began to develop towards the problems of poverty and disease. It was becoming increasingly clear that it was no longer possible simply to blame individuals for their 'pauperism' and for failing to make the most of what the economic system had to offer them. It was evident from Rowntree's study, for example, that for approximately one third of families in York, earnings were not sufficient to maintain even a minimum level of physical efficiency. [63] Thus, the purely coercive policies of the Poor Law which had been geared to the early needs of capitalism for a huge labour force of indiscriminate quality could no longer be effective. Similarly, it was believed that while earlier public health measures had been a prerequisite for the elimination of infectious diseases, they were a necessary but not a sufficient condition for producing healthier workers. It appeared that the sufficient condition for the creation of a more effective labour force was the extended involvement of the state in the provision of a broader range of health and social services. The attention of reformers during this period was therefore focussed mainly on the expansion of health measures directed towards *individuals*, and on the introduction of a minimum level of social security provision. The debate about social reform centred around the question of how to ensure a national minimum income and national minimum standard of health for each individual. These were assumed to be essential for the establishment of 'national efficiency' - for raising the capacity of the working class to service British economic and military competition.

The quest for national efficiency therefore gave social reform what it had not had before - the status of a respectable political question . . . The white man's burden had to be carried on strong backs. [64]

As Titmuss put it:

> Society was beginning to count and reassess the health costs of industrial progress in terms of the life chances of its next generation of workers, mothers and soldiers . . . Society was giving insufficient thought to investment in the next generation. Material thrift was not enough.[65]

It was now clear that the quality of human labour was a very crucial factor in capitalist development. Capitalists must, therefore, 'invest' in it, in the same way as they invested in other factors of production.

1911: Health insurance, scientific medicine and the reproduction of labour power

In the first decade of the twentieth century, a series of measures was introduced in an attempt to improve the health of the working class, the emphasis in this early legislation being on children and on male workers. The infant mortality rate was a matter of major concern, having risen as high as 163 per 1,000 in 1899.[66] Anxiety was focussed, however, not on the individual suffering entailed by such a large number of infant deaths, but on the implications they had for society.

> The birth rate then was a matter of national importance: population was power. Children it was said belonged 'not merely to the parents but to the community as a whole'; they were a 'national asset', 'the capital of a country'; on them depended 'the future of the country and the Empire': they were 'the citizens of tomorrow'.[67]

Attempts were therefore made to break the cycle of poverty and ill health through investing in the health of children at an early age. In 1906 and 1907 the Education (Provision of Meals) Act and the Education (Administrative Provisions) Act introduced free school meals for needy children and medical inspections for all. These measures were not universally welcomed. The debate over school meals in particular demonstrated the sharp conflict between nineteenth century values, which upheld the moral worth of individual effort, and the emerging emphasis on the social import-ance of investment in future generations. Indeed, it was even suggested that parents whose children ate school meals should be deprived of the vote, since they were evidently unable to live up to their responsibilities as citizens if they were failing to care for their own children.[68] As a result of widespread opposition, the provision of school meals was not made compulsory until 1914. Yet most supporters of school meals and medical inspections saw them not as mere acts of benevolence but primarily as an important means of promoting both physical and psychological growth in a debilitated population. At the same time, they prevented the waste of national investment in education. In fact, as Sir George Newman - a Chief Medical Advisor to the Ministry of Health - later wrote, it was increas-ingly doubted whether universal education was worthwhile at all if school meals and medical inspections were not also provided. He argued that the primary purpose of the legislation,

> . . . was not to create a healthy people but to enable every school child to take full advantage of the education provided him by the state. It was this common sense foundation which com-mended it alike to the MPs, to their constituents and to payers of rates and taxes. Thousands of children were compulsorily sitting in schools in 1906 . . . who could not by reason of lack of food receive proper advantage from the education provided. Likewise tens of thousands of other children were failing to gain advantage from their education by the state for their lack of health.[69]

Clearly these measures - meals in particular - were of consider-able value in improving the health of school children. The main concern, however, was to reduce infant mortality, the major cause of which was said to lie not in poor socio-economic conditions but in inadequate or ignorant mothering. Policies were therefore designed to educate working-class women to look after their children more efficiently. 'Schools for mothers', welfare clinics and numerous societies were set up to promote maternal education, while health visitors were appointed to visit mothers in their homes. They were able to offer little in the way of material support, but were designed to teach the 'skills of motherhood'. As Anna Davin points out,

> Doctors, district nurses, health visitors were all asserting their
> superior knowledge and authority, establishing moral sanc-
> tions on grounds of health and the national interest, and
> denigrating traditional methods of child care - in particular
> care by anyone except the mother: neighbours, grandmothers,
> and older children looking after babies were automatically
> assumed to be dirty, incompetent and irresponsible. The
> authority of state over individual, of professional over amateur,
> of science over tradition, of male over female, of ruling class
> over working class, were all involved in the redefining of
> motherhood in this period, and in ensuring that the mothers of
> the race would be carefully guided, not carried away by self-
> importance.[70]

Thus women were blamed for bringing ill health on their own
children through having unsanitary habits, going out to work,
dressing them in unsuitable clothing, or feeding them inappro-
priately. As a result, the significance of inadequate and overcrowded
housing, wages beneath subsistence level, and the need for women
to work in order to survive, were all obscured. Infant mortality was
blamed on the ignorance or selfishness of individual mothers rather
than on the material conditions generated by a capitalist economic
system. It is significant that the health of the women themselves was
given serious consideration only in so far as it directly affected their
role as mothers. A Midwives Act at the beginning of the century, and
the Maternity and Child Welfare Act of 1918 assured more medical
attention for women during pregnancy and childbirth, but despite
the chronic ill health that was so widespread among working-class
women, no organised system of primary care was available to them.
Indeed, apart from a small maternity grant, married women who
were not waged workers were entirely excluded from the provisions of
the 1911 National Health Insurance Act. Medical or midwife
attendance were not included in the act.

By the beginning of the twentieth century, it had become
evident that Victorian self-help organisations were materially unable
to provide a national minimum for all sections of the working class.
While the Victorian friendly societies and mutual benefit associations

had been of great value to the relatively secure, their solvency depended on the exclusion of significant sections of the working class. The idea of self-help was nevertheless clung to. It encouraged the work ethic and prevented individuals from acquiring the expectation that they should get something for nothing - an idea entirely antithetical to the capitalist spirit of competitive individualism. Supporters of the 'new liberalism' therefore campaigned for the replacement of the disintegrating Poor Law with a new system of social insurance based on individual contributions - a form of state-sponsored self-help. The ideological significance of any social insurance scheme of this kind is clear. Members have to contribute in order to receive benefits, and these contributions can only be paid when the member is working. At the same time, since it is the state (or its agents) which administer the benefits, such a scheme is also a powerful means of showing the benevolence of the state, and demonstrating its concern for its citizens. This is particularly true of the provision of medical care, as Keir Hardie pointed out in a speech to his constituents in 1911,

> What was the answer received when a minimum wage of thirty shillings for all and eight shillings per day was demanded for those who worked underground in unhealthy conditions? No, say the liberals but we will give you an Insurance Bill. We shall not uproot the cause of poverty but we will give you a porous plaster to cover the disease that poverty causes.[71]

The 1911 National Health Insurance Act was designed both to assuage working-class demands and also to improve 'national efficiency'. It provided first a basic income during sickness (and for certain workers during unemployment), and, secondly, a national scheme of primary medical care. The new scheme was to cover all workers earning below £160 per year (the limit for exemption from income tax), and all manual workers, irrespective of their level of earnings. It required a contribution of fourpence a week from the male worker (threepence from women workers) and threepence from the employer, to which a further twopence was added by the Treasury. Worker, employer and state were therefore bound together to provide security for the worker should sickness ever cause him to be unable to earn his own living. The male pronoun is rightly used here since the scheme was conceived primarily in terms of a male breadwinner. As the first report of the actuaries clearly stated, 'married women living with their husbands need not be included (in the insurance scheme) since where the unit is the family, it is the husband's and not the wife's health which it is important to insure'.[72] Lloyd George, the architect of the act, was still primarily interested (as Chadwick before him had been) in preventing poverty, rather than in providing medical care. He was initially concerned with reducing the numbers who were forced to depend upon the Poor Law, preferring them to draw sickness benefit towards which they had themselves contributed. Only later was it decided to incorporate basic medical care from a general practitioner into the scheme.

Any attempt to explain why the state became involved in the organisation of medical services in 1911 must take into account not only these wider social, economic and political considerations, but also developments within medicine itself. It was only after about 1880 that the general scientific advances of the nineteenth century began to be assimilated into clinical practice. By 1900, the discovery of x-rays and of blood groups, and above all the development of antiseptic techniques, meant that diagnosis and treatment began to be more successful, particularly in the field of surgery. New developments in bio-chemistry were making possible the beginnings of drug therapy, while ether, chloroform and nitrous oxide were increasingly used for the relief of pain and for anaesthesia. The availability of these new medical developments to the mass of the population was severely restricted, however, by two very important factors: cost and the existing organisation of medical practice. The cost of medical care had risen to a level at which basic medical care (such as it was) was beyond the means of much of the population. Hence the state had to become involved in medical care if the apparently limitless potential of these new medical developments was to be realised. Although there was broad agreement that some form of state-financed health service was desirable, this apparent consensus masked a range of widely different interests. A considerable struggle therefore ensued over the precise form that this new service should take, and the final structure of the 1911 National Health Insurance scheme represented a compromise between the interests of the state, the medical profession and all those organisations already providing medical schemes of various kinds.

The majority of doctors were dissatisfied both with their pay and their conditions of work. During the nineteenth century, the financial position of general practitioners in working-class areas had become increasingly insecure.[73] They were competing for patients, many of whom were unable to pay for the services they received. Those doctors who were full-time salaried employees in Poor Law or municipal institutions received a steady, but very low, income. Only specialists were well paid through the fees they received from wealthy patients. Moreover, many Poor Law doctors and general practitioners abhorred the loss of autonomy necessitated by working on a contract basis. Hence there was a great deal of resentment among doctors, and the newly-formed British Medical Association was split by the antagonism between the wealthy specialists and the great mass of their poorer colleagues. Despite this internal disunity Lloyd George was ultimately forced to concede most of the doctors' demands concerning the organisation of the new health insurance scheme.

It was agreed that the control of sickness benefits and medical care should be in the hands of 'insurance committees' rather than friendly societies or local authorities - the doctors were totally opposed to a state-salaried service. The doctors were given freedom of choice to join the scheme or not as they wished, and were also allowed the right to refuse to treat any particular patient. They achieved security of tenure, and also a higher capitation fee than Lloyd George had initially offered. Finally, they were also able to ensure that the maximum income level for participation in the scheme was fixed low enough to exclude all patients who could remotely afford to pay for care. This exclusion was regarded as extremely important by the doctors, because it meant that many patients would be forced to continue to obtain their medical care on a fee-paying basis, thus constituting an important source of additional revenue. One of their major complaints against the old 'contract practice' schemes had been that the more affluent were allowed to belong and pay the same capitation fee as less prosperous working-class patients, whilst often demanding a better standard of service. The doctors, then, were well pleased with the 1911 National Health Insurance Act. For most of them, it offered more freedom to practice medicine as they chose, and there was general agreement that it probably doubled the pay of the average doctor.

The doctors, however, were not the only people concerned to influence the structure of the new scheme. All those organisations which had previously been involved in providing medical care were anxious to protect their own interests and the industrial insurance companies were especially active in this struggle. Industrial insurance policies provided 'death benefits' which were basically designed to enable working-class people to cover their funeral expenses. Despite the limited scope of their activities, the volume of industrial insurance company business was enormous. During the first decade of the twentieth century, roughly ten million new policies were taken out annually, so that by the end of 1910 the companies had almost thirty million policies outstanding. These companies employed approximately a hundred thousand men, of whom seventy thousand were full-time door-to-door agents. Ninety per cent of industrial insurance business was monopolised by the largest twelve companies, of which the Prudential was the most wealthy.

> The Pru was the largest private owner of freehold properties in the UK. It was the largest shareholder of Bank of England stocks, and of Indian and colonial government bonds and stocks. It was a major source for local authority borrowing. Each month its investment committee had to find a profitable situation for about half a million more pounds; its premium income was about one third of the £20,000,000 per year enjoyed by the twelve largest companies together.[74]

As a consequence of this immense wealth, the 'Pru' (and its fellow companies) wielded very great economic and political influence. This was augmented by the fact that they had entry into so many working-class homes. Their opportunity to persuade working-class voters was used by the companies to ensure that their interests would be recognised in the National Health Insurance Act. By the early twentieth century, burial benefit had become the principal source of profit for the industrial insurance companies. They were, therefore, very disturbed when it was initially suggested that burial benefit be included in the new scheme, and this was dropped after sustained pressure from the companies. It was also agreed that the scheme would not be administered directly by the state but by 'approved societies', so that the existing providers of medical care (trade unions, friendly societies, and above all insurance companies) retained a crucial role in the new system. This compromise with specific financial and professional interests weakened still further the limited potential of the original plans, and led to the creation of an irrational and ultimately ineffective system for the provision of sickness benefit and medical care. Sheila Rowbotham has described the contradictory nature of these developments.

> By the end of the nineteenth century, the 'free' market economy was being increasingly influenced by state intervention. While the short-term interest of the individual capitalist was to extract as much surplus value from workers regardless of age, sex, or physical strength, the long-term interest of capital demanded some protection and guarding of future capacity. Thus not only protective legislation against the exhaustion of human body and mind at work, but public health measures, national education and various efforts to protect small children from neglect were introduced. Contemporaries often confused these changes with socialism and indeed it was often trade unionists, radicals and socialists who forced them through. They were obviously important defences against the expansion of capital at the expense of human physical and mental capacity. Changes in education, public health, and later in the beginnings of welfare also made possible the emergence of a working class which bargained with a new scale of expectations. But they brought also a new extension of state power and a direct relationship between the centralised bourgeois state and everyday life, and represented a newly assumed responsibility by capitalism for preserving capacity and skills for a more 'rational' exploitation.[75]

The act nevertheless stood as an important first stage in the process by which the state began increasingly to take a measure of responsibility for the physical condition of the working class. At the same time, it contributed to a growing belief in the existence of a 'benevolent' state presiding over a 'new' phase of capitalism - an image which was to culminate in the 'welfare state' of the 1940s.

The crisis of capitalist medicine during the inter-war period

After the allied 'victory' in the first world war, the expected resurgence in economic growth did not take place. Instead of expansion, came the depression. By the beginning of 1933 unemployment had reached an all time record of just under three million, and 23 per cent of all insured workers were out of work. The government responded to this situation by reducing levels of unemployment benefit, while employers simultaneously reduced wages. These social and economic conditions were reflected in deteriorating health for large sections of the working class - a deterioration exacerbated by the limitations of the National Health Insurance scheme.[76]

Even workers who were covered by the 1911 act were often unable to obtain satisfactory medical care. They were able to get basic medical attention from their 'panel' doctor but often little else. The 1911 act had included some provision for what were called 'additional benefits' (dental and ophthalmic treatment for example) but these were made entirely contingent on the financial status of the 'approved society'. In practice, such services were rarely available - a fact which can largely be explained by the irrational structure created to administer medical benefits. Although the national insurance scheme was to be in a formal sense non-profit making, those organisations which became 'approved societies' were able to use their new status to their own advantage. So far as the trade unions were concerned, the scheme benefited individual unions as well as their members. They were able, for example, to keep more of their funds for general union purposes, rather than paying them out in sickness benefit. Moreover, since the scheme brought them into contact with many potential members, national insurance became an important means by which new union members were recruited.

In the case of the commercial insurance companies, however, the significance of the scheme was quite different. Although they were supposed to administer the national insurance part of the business quite separately from their commercial insurance, certain undoubted advantages accrued to these companies from their role in the administration of national health insurance. Most importantly, they gained automatic entry to many more working-class homes. As Eckstein aptly comments,

> It is not pleasant, from any standpoint but the canvasser's, to picture the insurance agent invading a home in which serious illness had occurred and, after expressing the society's anxiety for the recovery of the patient, suggesting that it might perhaps be foresighted to provide for a decent burial. But that is precisely the sort of thing that happened in thousands of instances. [77]

Their national insurance activities also meant that the insurance companies were able to provide a steady income for an ever-increasing number of collectors who could call on working-class homes selling private insurance as well as giving out public benefits. As a result, the running of the scheme became a profitable activity for the companies concerned.

Naturally, it was working-class patients who suffered from the Liberal government's decision to compromise with companies who were concerned ultimately with making a profit rather than organising effective health care for their subscribers. The use of a multiplicity of approved societies instead of some form of unified state control also made the administration of the scheme more inefficient. Indeed, by 1939 there were over 7,000 different societies involved. This inefficiency meant that the scheme was extremely expensive to administer and the more the basic cost of the scheme rose, the less money was available for additional benefits. Moreover, such extra benefits as were available were not distributed according to need. Since the societies in the poorest areas obviously had more call on their funds for normal benefits, they inevitably had less money left over for those who needed additional help.

Women and children were the worst provided for, since they were excluded even from the limited system created by the 1911 act. While the emphasis on the importance of motherhood continued throughout the inter-war period, very little material support was provided for mothers. Certain limited additions were made to maternal and child health services, but the restrictions on local authority spending between the wars were a serious obstacle to any real improvement. As a result, the investment of the state in curative medical care was still confined basically to the labour force - despite a new anxiety about the threat of 'underpopulation'. Women were therefore forced to rely on a disorganised patchwork of arrangements if they could afford medical care at all. Various schemes involving voluntary weekly payments remained from the pre-war period, and local midwives continued to attend the births of most working-class women on a fee-paying basis.[78]

The general deficiency of medical services was reflected in the continuing lack of contraceptive provision for working-class women. Birth control had been opposed throughout the nineteenth century by the church, by doctors, by many socialists who saw it as an attempt to reduce the size and therefore the power of the working class, and even by nascent feminists concerned to protect the sanctity of motherhood.[79] By the end of the century, however, it was becoming evident that middle-class couples had been practising birth control for some time, and various groups, of very different political complexions, were campaigning for the spread of birth control information to the working class. The Malthusian League, for example, started open-air meetings for this purpose in 1913 - to send the information by post was still illegal.[80] Many churchmen and doctors remained implacably opposed to these attempts and expressed their views with peculiar ferocity. Dr Henry Corby for example, professor of obstetrics and gynaecology at University College, Cork, writing in *The Practitioner* as late as July 1925, warned that if birth control became widespread,

> the land will be cumbered by a weakly, degenerated race of neurasthenics and hypochondriacs, not a small percentage of whom will drift into lunatic asylums where, poor creatures, they will be in the midst of their fellow masturbators.[81]

Despite the warnings of men such as Dr Corby, a gradual change in attitude took place as more women began to realise that it was possible to limit the size of their families. Despite the dire warnings issued for so long by the medical profession, it became increasingly evident that birth control as practised at that time was not injurious to health - but rather that a reduction in family size was likely to improve women's health. Doctors themselves were also revising their views, but generally seemed more concerned with the moral issues underlying birth control than with organising concrete provisions. Hence, it remained extremely difficult for working-class women to obtain contraceptive information and supplies. This was reflected in the continuing high rates of maternal mortality. According to Dora Russell, an activist in the birth control movement of that period, 'We had a slogan then, that it was four times as dangerous to bear a child as to work in a coal mine, and mining was held to be man's most dangerous trade.'[22] Throughout the 1920s organisations like the Society for the Provision of Birth Control, the Women's Co-operative Guild, and the Workers' Birth Control Group, fought to increase the number of clinics providing contraceptive advice. Eventually the Minister of Health conceded, and in 1930 issued the famous memorandum 153/M.C.W. which *permitted* local authority maternity and child welfare clinics to provide contraceptive advice to married women on medical grounds. This made possible a gradual increase in the availability of birth control, although facilites remained fragmented and patchy. Despite its limitations, this new policy marked an important change in official attitudes towards birth control, reflecting as it did a limited acceptance by the state of the necessity to provide women with the means to control their own fertility.

Throughout the inter-war period, there were therefore serious limitations on the primary medical care available both to those covered by the 1911 act and those outside it. In the case of hospital care, arrangements were even more unsatisfactory - even those who were insured were not entitled to free hospital treatment, except for tuberculosis. Hospital care was provided on the one hand by the voluntary hospitals and on the other by the municipal institutions, many of which had been taken over from the Poor Law Administration under the Local Government Act of 1929.[83] The conditions in most public assistance and municipal hospitals remained very bad throughout the period. Any potential improvement was hampered by their role in caring for large numbers of the aged and chronic sick, as well as by the general shortage of local government funds during the depression. The voluntary hospitals continued to provide the focus for developments in scientific medicine, and to train both doctors and nurses. During this period they also began to acquire a dual character with the introduction of pay beds. New developments in medicine therefore became available to middle-class patients through the payment of fees, while working-class patients continued to get hospital care on a charitable, though means-tested, basis. Ultimately, however, payment from wealthier patients was insufficient to support the voluntary hospitals and throughout the interwar period government subsidies to these institutions rose continuously. This system of municipal and voluntary hospitals was therefore administratively chaotic, and quite inadequate to meet the medical needs of the British population. Above all, the hospitals were becoming financially unreliable, and increasingly dependent on state finance.

Throughout the 1920s and 30s there were demands from various quarters for the reform of this inefficient method of organising medical care. [84] Most importantly, there was continuous pressure from the Labour movement for a unified system of free medical care covering the whole population. Far-reaching plans were drawn up by the State Medical Services Association (later the Socialist Medical Association) among others. These would have entailed very significant changes in the health sector, including a much greater emphasis on preventive medicine, and total integration between the different levels of care. Plans of this kind were, however, perceived as a threat by other interest groups (particularly the majority of the medical profession) who accepted the need for reform but wanted a more limited scheme.

Although the vast majority of doctors had benefited greatly from the 1911 act, those who had urban, working-class practices still felt their conditions of service to be unacceptable and their salaries to be much too low. Thus they accepted the need for the extension of health insurance to the whole population but rejected any suggestion of an integration between preventive and curative services or the expectation that doctors should be engaged full time in a state-salaried service. Limited schemes for the reorganisation of medical care also received widespread middle-class support. Although they could rely on a better standard of service than working-class patients, most middle-class patients increasingly felt the cost of medical care to be too high. In particular medical care could be very costly for those who came just above the income limit for the national health insurance scheme, and could not qualify as charity patients in the voluntary hospitals. Moreover, the methods used to finance the voluntary hospitals were viewed by many middle-class patients as particularly invidious, since the free care provided for charity patients was dependent on fees paid by the better off.

It was against this background that plans for a state-organised medical service were formulated during the inter-war period. But it is important to note the wider social and economic significance of these schemes. Harold Macmillan's later reflections sum up the mood of the period well:

> Up to 1931 there was no reason to suppose that [changes] would not or could not follow the same evolutionary pattern which had resulted from the increased creation and distribution of wealth during the nineteenth century . . . Now after 1931 many of us felt that the disease was more deep rooted. It had become evident that the structure of capitalist society in its old form had broken down, not only in Britain but all over Europe and even in the United States. The whole system had to be reassessed. Perhaps it could not survive at all; it certainly could not survive without radical change . . . Something like a revolutionary situation had developed, not only at home but overseas.[84]

As a result, increased state intervention of various kinds (including the organisation of medical care), came to be seen as crucial in the struggle to avert the possible collapse of capitalism itself.

5: The National Health Service in Britain

The welfare state and the NHS

Throughout the second world war, plans were being drawn up for the creation of a 'new' Britain, based on the economic precepts of John Maynard Keynes and the complementary social policies recommended by William Beveridge. The creation of a welfare state, as conceived by Beveridge in his famous plan of 1942, was a central part of this strategy. The ineffectiveness of health and welfare policies during the inter-war period had made their extension and rationalisation a matter of immediate practical concern. Moreover, it had become apparent that British capitalism faced not only a crisis of profitability but also problems concerning political stability. As Gordon Forsyth comments,

> Rightly or wrongly the British government at the outbreak of war could not be sure that large sections of the working class were entirely satisfied about the reasons for fighting the war . . . For the sake of public morale the government tried to make it clear that after the war things were going to be very different from the heartbreak conditions of the thirties.[1]

The war itself temporarily deflected attention away from potentially dangerous political issues towards a national concern to defeat Germany. However, as in the first world war, the rhetoric of war-time propaganda encouraged the idea of 'fighting for a new Britain' - hence the publication of the Beveridge Report during the course of the war. The impact of the report was dramatic, as Kincaid has described.

For millions of people the report was taken as a major expression of the social ideals for which the nation had gone to war - the more so since its proposals were definite and concrete, more meaningful than the empty phrases about freedom and democracy written into official definitions of war aims such as the Atlantic Charter. On publication day a queue a mile long formed outside the government bookshop in central London and 70,000 copies were sold within three hours. Three weeks after publication, the Gallup Poll found that nineteen out of twenty adults had heard of the report and most of them approved of its recommendations. The Education Service of the Armed Forces was overwhelmed with requests for lectures on the subject. The newspapers were enthusiastic. The Archbishop of Canterbury pronounced that this was the first time that anyone had set out to embody the whole spirit of the Christian ethic in an Act of Parliament. [2]

The Beveridge Report was principally concerned with the provision of a minimum income for all through an effective system of social security. Beveridge described his scheme as follows:

The Plan for social security is put forward as part of a general programme of social policy. It is one part only of an attack upon five giant evils: upon the physical Want with which it is directly concerned, upon Disease which often causes that Want and brings many other troubles in its train, upon Ignorance which no democracy can afford among its citizens, upon the Squalor which arises mainly through haphazard distribution of industry and population, and upon the Idleness which destroys wealth and corrupts men, whether they are well fed or not, when they are idle. [3]

But the social security system was to be only part of a wider plan which would include economic policies designed to ensure the maintenance of full employment, family allowances, and a national health service. The welfare state was not, however, a revolutionary innovation designed to transform British society.

In his plan Beveridge gave expression to a broad section of hardheaded opinion in the ruling class of his period. He was for social reform, so long as the existing structure of society remained fundamentally the same. In fact he was for social reform precisely *because* it would allow the existing order to continue essentially unchanged. It is not as a visionary that Beveridge deserves to be remembered. Rather his particular distinction lay in an ability to translate the general objectives of ruling class reformism into detailed and technically workable proposals.[4]

The significance of social reforms of this kind in ensuring the stability of British capitalism in the post-war period can be demonstrated with particular clarity by the history of the NHS.

Who controls the NHS?

There can be no doubt that the National Health Service has been, from its inception, a more humane and also more cost-effective method of organising medical care than a system based on private practice. The creation of the NHS provided a much improved system of medical care for the British population and women and children in particular gained from its introduction.[5] However, as we shall see, this does not make it in any real sense a socialist health service. It is important, therefore, that a recognition of the undoubted advantages of the NHS and a concern to defend it, should not mean that its fundamental deficiencies are ignored nor that its relationship with the wider social and economic structure of British capitalism should go unexplored.

The creation of the NHS represented an important part of the post-war settlement between capital and labour, but the labour movement was unable to determine the precise form that this service would take.

> After the second world war there was an enormous amount of class pressure for the starting up of a health service that would meet the needs of the population. From the result of the 1945 election, from the feeling within the whole labour movement, Aneurin Bevan drew enormous strength in his struggles to set up a truly accountable service. Yet the organisation of the class politically and *ideologically* was insufficient for it to force itself upon the way in which the NHS was created.[6]

As a result, there was very little discussion about the basic philosophy underlying the new scheme, and the final structure of the NHS was determined by the outcome of negotiations between the state and various establishment groups - the voluntary hospitals, the former approved societies, and most importantly the leaders of the medical profession. There was a prolonged dispute between Bevan, the Minister of Health, and the BMA, which centred around three main issues. First, the doctors were concerned to maintain what they called their 'clinical freedom' - that is, they wished to prevent either local or central government from exercising any control over their medical practice. Second, they were concerned that the state should provide them with economic security without obliging them to become salaried state employees. Third, the consultants in particular demanded the retention of the private sector. They fought very hard for an NHS structure which would enable them to divide their time most profitably between public and private medicine and would also allow them maximum influence in running the NHS. As a result, the NHS which was created in 1948 was very different from that which had been originally proposed in 1943.[7]

The new NHS was to be organised into a 'tripartite system' (see Diagram 1) rather than being administered by local authorities as originally intended.

It was divided into three entirely separate parts - the hospital sector, the executive council sector, and the local health authorities. The general practitioners (GPs) as well as the dentists, pharmacists and opticians favoured the scheme since they avoided the status of salaried employees through having contracts with the 'executive councils' who replaced the old insurance committees. Thus they were able (on paper at least) to keep their status as independent contractors. They were also able to continue the tradition of panel practice by demanding and obtaining payment based on a 'capitation fee' - i.e. a yearly payment per patient - rather than a fixed annual salary. Overall, however, the GPs gained little more than a modestly increased and more reliable income. It was the specialists who dominated the negotiations and who gained the most. The consultants were prepared in the final analysis to accept the scheme and to become salaried hospital employees because of all the concessions

Diagram 1: The NHS 1948-74

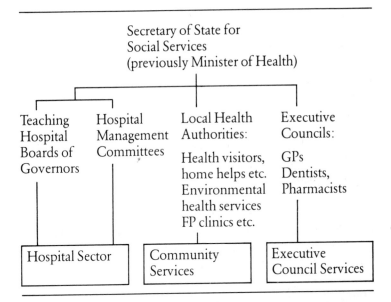

they were able to obtain.[8] Hospitals were to be removed entirely from local authority control, and put under regional hospital boards and hospital management committees on which consultants were granted a high level of representation. In addition, the teaching hospitals were able to retain their independent status whilst obtaining NHS funds since control over them was allowed to remain with the individual boards of governors. This was crucial for the maintenance of the medical hierarchy. The teaching hospitals were not only very wealthy, but also played a major role in determining the nature and priorities of medical research and medical education. Therefore, in maintaining their hold over the teaching hospitals, the consultants *as a group* were able to maximise their control over the practice of medicine.

The consultants - the elite of the profession - were also able to maximise their individual freedom since they obtained the right to work either full-time or part-time for the NHS. Thus all consultants were now to be paid on a regular basis (some for the first time) and those who wished also to retain the very considerable advantages of private practice were able to choose a *part-time* contract with the NHS with access to NHS facilities - 'pay beds' - for their private medicine.

In terms of power and resources, the hospital sector was dominant in the new NHS, followed by the executive council sector which provided primary medical care. The local authorities were left with a residual collection of environmental health services, mid-wives, health visitors, home helps and district nurses. The lack of resources awarded to the local authority sector, combined with the failure to provide an industrial health service, was the final nail in the coffin of preventive medicine. It was a clear illustration of the declining prestige of public health in the twentieth century, and reflected the fact that these caring and background services offered the least scope for tangible profitability, either to capitalist industry or to the medical profession. The health care provided by the NHS was therefore to be curative and hospital-based. The specialists, the medical equipment manufacturers and the pharmaceutical industry gained from this decision, while the public health sector, and ultimately of course the users of the health service, were the losers.

The NHS is usually referred to as a system of 'socialised medicine', but, for a variety of reasons, the term 'nationalised medicine' is more appropriate.[9] The British state took over responsibility for the organisation of medical care in the same way that it took over the mines, the railways or the steel industry - it was seen as a necessary part of the infrastructure for industrial production. Few additional resources were invested in medical care and power remained firmly in the hands of those who had always been in control - the doctors and administrators. The users of the health service were enabled to finance their own medical care more effectively, and indeed received all the benefits of a more rational and cost-effective system. They were not, however, given the power to determine the structure or priorities of their health service - a fact which was to become increasingly significant as the NHS developed.

Within a few years of its euphoric inception, the increasing cost of the health service began to cause anxiety in government circles.

There appears to have been a naive assumption that, although costs might rise in the early stages, ultimately they would be stabilised through an improvement in the general health of the population. Instead, NHS expenditure continued to rise. By the mid 1960s, the performance of the British economy was giving cause for serious concern, and this was reflected in attempts to rationalise government spending through the reorganisation of various sectors of the welfare state. The rising cost of the NHS made it an important target in this campaign and policies were designed both to increase 'patient throughput' and also to make the NHS managerially more efficient.[10] This general trend towards more centralisation and managerialism was also considered to be an expedient response to changing demographic and disease patterns. The growing proportion of old people in the population meant constantly increasing demands on the social services in general, and on the NHS in particular. At the same time, the pattern of disease had shifted away from acute illness towards chronic problems requiring caring rather than curing. It was argued that more effective utilisation of existing resources could be achieved through a reorganisation of the administrative structure of the NHS and that in this way, treatment for the increasing number of the old and the chronically sick could be provided without necessitating an unacceptable rise in public expenditure.

It was against this background that discussions took place about the precise form which such a reorganisation should take. Again, negotiations were long and protracted, with the doctors anxious to maintain what they had gained in 1948 and the governments concerned - both Tory and Labour - anxious to cut costs and increase managerial efficiency and control. But despite the ritual public battle between the medical profession and the state over questions concerning the status, power and working conditions of doctors, as in 1946, there was no basic disagreement between them over the underlying philosophy and overall mode of organisation of the health service. It was accepted without question that the NHS should remain predominantly curative, that the division of labour within the NHS should remain a hierarchical one, and above all that medical care was the business of experts - whether medical or managerial - rather than the concern of either the mass of health workers or the recipients of medical care - the patients. This basic agreement was reflected in the NHS structure created by the 1974 reorganisation. (See Diagram 2.)[11]

Diagram 2: The post-1974 NHS

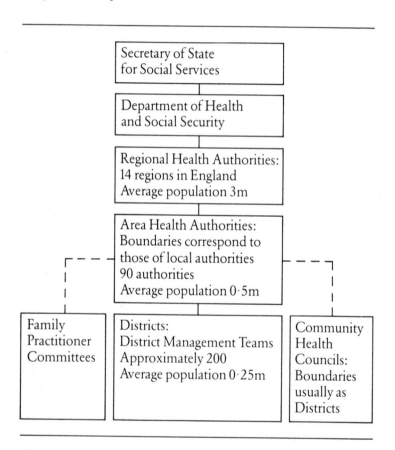

The tripartite structure was rationalised, bringing the administration of the NHS together into a unified structure. The fifteen regional hospital boards, numerous hospital management committees, local health authorities and executive councils were replaced by a hierarchy of 14 Regional Health Authorities (RHAs), 90 Area Health Authorities (AHAs), and 205 Districts. The new organisational structure was based on professional advice from private management consultants (the McKinsey Corporation in particular) and was designed to maximise managerial control in order to administer increasingly scarce resources more efficiently. At the same time, the interests of the doctors were given very careful consideration - sometimes at the expense of strict managerial efficiency - and they achieved a high degree of representation at the different levels of the NHS management structure.[12]

This professional and managerial domination was, however, accompanied by an apparent democratisation of the NHS, in that consumers were for the first time given a say in the running of the health service. During the 1960s there had been a gradual acceptance of the idea of 'participatory democracy' in the welfare state. In the case of the NHS, this resulted in the creation of Community Health Councils (CHCs) in the 1974 reorganisation. The political and ideological significance of this much-vaunted 'participation' has been widely discussed[13] and the experience of participation in the NHS conforms with that of other sectors of the welfare state. That is to say, the CHCs have been of symbolic rather than real significance. Officially, their role is to represent 'the local community's interests in the health services to those responsible for managing them'. However, none of the CHC members are directly elected - one third are nominated by the local voluntary organisations, one sixth by the RHA, and the remainder by the relevant local authority. As a result, there is little chance of the CHC members being representative of their local community. Recent surveys have shown, for example, that only a very small proportion of members are manual workers.[14] Most importantly, the CHCs are purely advisory, so that their effect on policy can only be extremely limited. Although some CHCs have done important work in investigating and publicising particular local deficiencies in medical provision, the CHCs have been denied any executive power. After 1974, patients (and of course most health workers) therefore continued, despite the CHCs, to have almost no say in the running of the health service.

The priorities of the NHS have tended, throughout its history, to be defined in terms of the wider interests of capital rather than reflecting the real needs of patients. It is, however, clearly impossible for the state to operate in an autonomous and coherent way to control the organisation of medicine in the interests of capital as a whole.[15] Even within the state apparatus there are conflicting demands for resources from semi-autonomous sectors. Thus there will be competition, for example, between the welfare sector and the demands of private industry for greater subsidies. There will also of course be competition within the welfare sector, so that, for example, health and education will be competing for resources - both claims having their own logic within the terms of capitalist rationality.[16] Moreover, those resources ultimately allocated to the health sector will be the object of negotiation and struggle among a wide range of groups over how they should be spent. It is important therefore that we identify some of these conflicting forces and assess their influence on the type of medical care provided by the NHS.

The majority of patients, as we have seen, have little formal power in the NHS. Nevertheless, those groups and individuals with access to more resources in general (income, education, etc.) do obtain better quality medical care. In the context of a generally low standard of provision, those most able to articulate and fight for their own interests are able to obtain a higher standard of care. This applies in the case of individuals fighting to obtain better quality care for themselves and their families, and also at the level of whole districts. More knowledge, more belief in their own intrinsic right to obtain the best, along with more confidence to make demands, ensures that middle-class patients are able to use the system to their best advantage. This tendency towards class-based inequality in the allocation of medical resources is obviously exacerbated by the fact that, despite their numbers, groups like the old or the chronically sick lack any economic power or effective organisation.

However, the major source of pressure on the state as the provider of medical care is not patients but the medical establishment, with the BMA and the Royal Colleges wielding particular power. We have already seen that they were able to exert considerable influence on the administrative structure of the NHS,[17] but their most significant impact has come from their commitment to high-technology medicine. Doctors are trained to see themselves as scientists, and, for the majority, job satisfaction is largely derived from the scientific and technological aspects of their work.[18] However, scientific medicine ultimately generates its own momentum and its own resource demands - demands which often bear little relationship to the real needs of patients.[19] This tendency is exacerbated both by the domination of hospital doctors (usually consultants) over medical decision making, and also by the fact that it is the doctors in ultra-scientific specialities who have the most power and prestige.[20]

The technological emphasis is, of course, reinforced and indeed often initiated by particular sections of capital - notably those involved in the production of medical equipment and drugs - who are concerned to maximise their sales to the NHS. But the extent of national and international corporate influence on medical policies is much wider than this. As we have seen in chapter two, there is a limit to the preventive strategies which can be undertaken in any health programme, without fundamental social and economic change which would directly impede the accumulation of capital. As a result, most attempts to move in the direction of prevention are likely to meet with considerable opposition from industrial interests. Indeed, as Navarro has pointed out,

> . . . the primary controllers and managers of medicine are not the professionals, but rather the controllers and managers of Capital . . . the concept of health and even the nature of medical practice has continuously changed and has been redefined according to the needs of the capitalist modes and relations of production. The medical profession intervenes in that redefinition, but *a posteriori*, i.e. they administer and influence but do not create the nature of medicine.[21]

The history of the NHS therefore reveals with particular clarity the contradictions inherent in a state-controlled medical care system in a capitalist society. As Navarro has rightly stated,

> there is no clearcut dichotomy between the social needs of capital and the social demands of labour. Any given policy can serve both. Indeed, social policies that serve the interests of the working class can be subsequently adapted to benefit the interests of the dominant class.[22]

Hence patients have undoubtedly gained from the introduction of the NHS, but the absence of any sustained working-class pressure to improve it and to make it more relevant to the needs of the majority of patients has meant that the NHS has increasingly become a means by which the interests of capital are served.

Who profits from the NHS?

The essentially capitalist nature of the NHS is clearly revealed first in the continued existence of a private market in medical care, and secondly in the fact that the NHS is supplied with drugs and equipment from the commercial sector. Moreover, hospitals and other health service premises are built and supplied by private contractors. This economic relationship with the commercial sector exerts a very considerable influence on the cost and the running of the NHS.

When the NHS was set up, the consultants were particularly insistent that a private market in medicine should be maintained. Accordingly, it was agreed that consultants should be allowed to choose whether to work full-time or part-time for the NHS. If they chose the latter, then it was assumed that they would supplement their income from private practice. In addition, it was agreed that a certain number of beds within the NHS (about 3,300 in 1978) should be available for the use of private patients.[23] The current options chosen by consultants show that these arrangements have proved to be particularly advantageous. Forty-three per cent of consultants work full-time for the NHS, 47 per cent work part-time (nine-elevenths of the commitment required by a full-timer), and 10 per cent work less than nine-elevenths, of whom only about three hundred (approximately 3 per cent of the total number of consultants) work wholly in private medicine.[24] Thus, almost half have chosen the part-time option, while very few indeed find it possible to work outside the NHS altogether.

Maintaining the private sector was a means by which consultants could be persuaded to accept the NHS. It provided the opportunity for them to supplement their income above the level at which the state could be expected to pay them. However, the continued existence of a private sector was not merely a concession to the consultants. It has also provided an option for those patients with sufficient resources to escape the worst rigours of the NHS, thus reinforcing the social differences between those who can afford to pay for greater comfort and flexibility and those who cannot. In fact, few private patients now pay for their medical care out of their own resources - about four per cent of the population are subscribers to private insurance schemes such as BUPA.[25] In recent years, however, there has been a decline in the number of individual subscribers to such schemes, and most new members have joined through schemes organised by their employers.[26] This represents a response by private capital to the problems created by an increasingly inefficient and undercapitalised health service. On the one hand, it maximises flexibility and choice when more senior employees have to undergo medical treatment, thus minimising possible inconvenience to firms. On the other hand, medical fringe benefits are seen as an important means of increasing incentives and rewards for white-collar, managerial workers during a period when wages are being held down.

The recent debate over pay beds has raised the question of the precise relationship between private practice and the NHS. It is evident that private practice in its present form could not exist without the NHS. It is dependent to a very considerable extent on the hospitals, the back-up services, the equipment and the highly-trained staff of the state sector, as well as on the ability of consultants to work on a part-time contract and to use NHS facilities for their private patients.[27] Moreover, it seems clear that patients obtaining treatment in the private sector of the NHS do not pay the full cost of their treatment.[28] Nevertheless, pay beds represent fewer than one per cent of all beds in the NHS (less than two per cent if long-stay beds are excluded) and hence the direct financial effect of private practice on the NHS is not enormous. It does, however, have other major disadvantages both for patients and for the majority of health workers.[29] The existence of private medicine has made it possible for queue-jumping to extend the already very lengthy waiting lists for 'non-essential' surgery.

Although joint waiting lists for NHS and private patients have

Table 1: Waiting Times for Operations

Operation	*Length of waiting time*	
	Private	*NHS*
Hysterectomy	2 weeks	4 months
Vasectomy	2 weeks	2 years
Gynaecology ops	1 week	1 year
Cataract	2 weeks	over 1 month
Tonsillectomy	2 weeks	18 months

Source: *NHS Facilities for Private Patients*. Fourth Report
of the House of Commons Expenditure Committee, Session 1971-72.
London, HMSO 1972

now been agreed by the Health Services Board, it remains to be seen how effective they will be. The presence of private patients also lowers the standard of care for some NHS patients, because consultants will give them proportionately more time and more ready access to medical resources. Moreover, other health workers are also expected to give more attentive care to private patients though they do not receive a share of the rewards going to the consultants. It is for all these reasons that pay beds have been an important focus of recent struggles within the NHS, and it was the actions of the health service unions which forced the Labour government in 1975 to order the phased withdrawal of pay beds from the NHS. Opposition to the original scheme mounted by the BMA and the private insurance companies under the slogan 'Patients Before Politics' was such that the scope of the plan was considerably reduced, and pay beds will be retained until alternative facilities are available.[30]

The provision of private medicine *within* NHS hospitals therefore has enormous symbolic and political significance. It contradicts the basic rhetoric of the NHS which claims to provide effective health care for the entire population regardless of financial means. Moreover, the continuation of private medicine *outside* the NHS remains an important (and increasing) source of profit for private capital and of additional income for the wealthiest doctors. In 1973 private insurance companies or provident associations paid out £8.4 million to doctors. Of this 90 per cent (£7.5 million) went to surgeons and ten per cent to physicians.[31] Finally, and very importantly, the continued existence of private practice makes it possible for overall standards in the NHS to be reduced without affecting the health care of the decision makers themselves.

In direct financial terms the most significant penetration of private capital into the NHS has been achieved by the pharmaceutical and medical equipment manufacturers. This process throws into sharp relief some of the most basic contradictions in the functioning of a state-controlled health sector in a capitalist society. On the one hand, the NHS is concerned with reproducing labour power at the least possible cost to capital. In order to do this, goods (in this case drugs) must be purchased from a sector of capitalist industry which demands a reasonable return on its investment. Clearly the most rational policy for the state in its role of managing the reproduction of labour power would be to nationalise the drug industry, thereby relieving itself of the need to finance their profits. However, this would conflict with its other role as a direct facilitator of capitalist accumulation. Hence, the high price paid by the NHS for drugs and equipment,[32] and the relative failure of attempts to control the drug industry, reflect the contradictions inherent in the role of the state as both the representative of manufacturing interests as a whole and also the purchaser of many of their products.

In 1977 the NHS drug bill amounted to £596 million,[33] so that the activities of the drug industry are very important for the NHS in strictly economic terms. However, they are also very significant in their effects on the nature and quality of medical practice itself. In order to understand the reasons for this more fully, it is necessary to make some general comments on the structure of the pharmaceutical industry. The most important characteristic of the industry is that it is primarily multinational, with a small number of firms dominating the world market.[34] In the case of Britain, for example, the Report of the Committee of Enquiry into the Relationship of the Pharmaceutical

Industry with the NHS in 1965-67 (the Sainsbury Report), pointed out that British firms supplied 27 per cent of the value of drugs prescribed in 1966, US firms 49 per cent, Swiss firms 14 per cent, and other European firms 10 per cent.[35] Furthermore, there is often a high degree of concentration *within* a particular sector of the drug market. For example, Roche's two main products, Librium and Valium account for about seventy per cent of the value of NHS prescriptions for tranquillisers, and are said to hold over one-third of the entire world tranquilliser market.

A second important characteristic of the drug industry is that it is highly research-intensive - most drug companies spend approximately one-tenth of their turnover on research and development. The companies have traditionally used this high level of research expenditure to justify their high rate of profit. However, most of the drugs produced as a result of this expenditure, rather than being fundamentally new are of the 'molecule manipulation' or 'me-too' type, designed to avoid the patent protection of drugs belonging to other companies. That is to say, drugs are produced which are very like existing products. They add little or nothing to the therapeutic armoury, but are intended simply to obtain a share of the market. They are not, therefore, socially useful products but are developed entirely for profit.[36] Representatives of the drug industry usually justify their great concern with patent laws in terms of protecting their research efforts, but in fact the use by pharmaceutical companies of patent legislation to make 'excessive' profits has been widely documented. As Vaitsos has commented,

> Once monopoly privileges leave the world of the individual inventor (a romantic memory of the past which, however, still influences government policy) and enter the real world of multiple patent ownership by large corporations, the main function of patents is not to encourage inventive activity but to aid profit maximisation through minimisation of competitive forces.[37]

But it is not just the existence of patent laws which enables the drug companies to make such a high rate of profit. The fact that the NHS exercises almost no control over doctors' prescribing habits is successfully exploited through the marketing techniques of the drug companies, whose sales and promotion effort in Britain in 1976 cost £48 million.[38] They employ approximately three thousand representatives to visit doctors, spending in the process approximately eight hundred pounds per doctor per year. As a result, the profits earned by drug companies are extremely high, making the pharmaceutical industry one of the most profitable in the world. It is difficult to get precise figures because of the noted ease with which multinational companies can mask their true profits by devices such as transfer pricing. It is known, however, that in the USA the average return on capital employed in the pharmaceutical industry in the years 1960-73 was around eighteen per cent, compared with only eleven per cent for manufacturing industry as a whole.[39] Similarly, a study in the UK showed a return on capital of 26 per cent for the years 1967-69, compared with a return of 12.6 per cent for manufacturing industry as a whole.[40]

Thus, it is clear that the drug companies make large profits and that drugs cost the NHS a great deal more than they need to, because they are commodities produced and marketed largely by multinational companies. In addition, the activities of the pharmaceutical industry affect the NHS in more subtle ways, actually influencing the type of health care which is provided. Since curative medicine is more amenable to pharmaceutical intervention than are preventive health measures, drug companies promote the former at the expense of the latter. They attempt to maximise the use of drug therapy, presenting it as the best resource for dealing with most of the problems presented to doctors, and this is reflected in the continuing rise in the volume of drugs of all kinds prescribed in the postwar period. The number of prescriptions written by GPs has risen from 4.96 to 6.88 per person in the period 1949-74.[41] This increase has of course been especially significant in the prescribing of psychotropic drugs for women.[22] Moreover, each drug manufacturer is concerned not simply to sell drugs, but rather to sell its own particular drugs. Since there are a very wide range of drugs available for a given disease or set of symptoms, they are often attempting to sell a drug which is either more expensive or less effective (or both) than some alternative drug. It is for this reason that drug companies promote the selling and prescribing of drugs by brand rather than by generic name, thus rendering it even more difficult than it would otherwise be for the doctor to make a rational choice. Doctors themselves are extremely vulnerable to this type of persuasion. By and large, they learn very little clinical pharmacology at medical school, and older doctors in particular may have scant knowledge of modern therapeutics. Once doctors have qualified, their major source of information about new drugs is usually the material distributed by the drug companies, which clearly does not provide the most objective account of the efficacy or safety of a given drug. Thus prescribing (especially in general practice) is neither the most cost-effective nor the most therapeutically efficacious. In 1965, a panel of British experts evaluating 2,241 of the pharmaceutical products then available estimated 35 per cent of them to be ineffective, obsolete or irrational combinations.[43] Moreover, there is now a growing volume of evidence that many drugs may actually be harmful. Adverse reactions to drugs are said to occur in ten per cent to twenty-five per cent of hospital admissions and to account for one in forty consultations in general practice.[44] In 1975, 576 people in England and Wales were said to have died as a result of accidental poisoning by drugs of various kinds.[45]

The problems created by the existence of a private drug industry have been widely acknowledged since the mid-1960s, particularly in Britain and the USA. The autonomy of the drug industry costs the NHS a great deal, and a recognition of this has led to attempts by the state to regulate the industry. Attempts such as voluntary price regulation and the restriction of promotional costs have, however, been very limited in their scope.[46] The ineffectiveness of these measures, and above all the refusal of the state to take over the pharmaceutical industry, illustrate with particular clarity the contradictory nature of socialised medicine as well as the nature of the relationship between international capital and the national state.

Who benefits from the NHS?

When the NHS was created in 1948, one of its declared aims was 'to divorce the care of health from questions of personal means or other factors irrelevant to it'. Medical care was to be equally available to all those in need, regardless of income, age, sex, occupation or area of residence. There can be no doubt that the NHS has increased the accessibility of medical care and reduced certain of the notable inequalities which had existed in medical services during the inter-war period. General practitioners, for example, were more equally distributed throughout the country, and the proportion of the population living in under-doctored areas fell very substantially during the early years of the service. Moreover, the inclusion of women in the scheme removed one of the most fundamental injustices which had existed in pre-war medical services. On the other hand, it is also indisputable that basic inequalities and distortions in resource allocation and utilisation still remain, and that many are actually increasing. These inequalities and distortions mirror the social and economic divisions in British society, while at the same time reflecting the concentration of power in the NHS. We will examine three aspects of NHS resource allocation here: inequalities between different sectors of the NHS, geographical inequalities, and finally, class inequalities.

Since the inception of the NHS, the hospital sector has more than maintained its share of total expenditure. In 1948, hospital services accounted for about fifty-five per cent of total NHS expenditure, but by 1974 the figure had risen to over sixty-five per cent.[47] The hegemony of the hospitals is in fact even more dramatic than appears at first sight, since the teaching hospitals (especially those in London) are much better endowed than the ordinary acute hospitals. (See Table two.) These additional resources do not derive simply from their teaching role but reflect the greater prestige and influence of the specialists who work in these 'centres of excellence', as well as the allure of high-technology, state-of-the-art medicine.

Resource allocation between different medical specialities shows a very similar pattern. Those specialties dealing in acute intervention obtain more resources than those dealing with the chronic sick, either on a community basis or in institutions. Table three shows that in those institutions dealing with non-acute illness, the actual 'housekeeping' costs are much lower than those in acute hospitals - a difference which is extremely difficult to justify on the grounds of medical need. Various 'exposés' of conditions in

Table 2: Cost per In-Patient Week in Different
Types of Hospital 1973-74

Teaching hospitals	
in London	£154.22
outside London	£131.50
Non-teaching hospitals	
acute	£104.78
mental illness	£36.60
mental handicap	£33.68

Source: DHSS, *Health and Personal Social Services
Statistics,* London, HMSO 1976

Table 3: Cost per In-Patient Week of Different Services in
Different Types of Hospital
As percentage of cost in acute non-teaching hospitals

Type of service	*Long stay*	*Chronic*	*Mental illness*	*Mental handicap*
Medical	27	13	26	13
Nursing	65	66	45	40
Domestic	58	60	27	27
Catering	55	48	45	43
Cleaning	68	55	35	32
Total net costs	44	39	32	30

Source: DHSS, *Hospital Costing Returns*, London, HMSO 1974

institutions such as mental subnormality hospitals have shown that the result of this deprivation of resources is an extremely low standard of care - which is primarily custodial - and serious demoralisation among staff.[48] The low level of resources allocated to these sectors would appear to reflect not just their lack of medical prestige, but also the lack of economic power or productive potential of most of their patients.

Data concerning geographical differences in resource allocation are among the easiest to obtain, and it has long been recognised that in health expenditure, as in other areas of public spending, the north of England fares noticeably less well than the south. Although some of these differences have been reduced, there is still a very considerable discrepancy in per capita expenditure between the richest and poorest regions.[49] Gross per capita expenditure is, however, a very crude measurement of regional differences and does not compare the various dimensions of health spending. It might be expected, for example, that low spending on hospital provision in a particular region would be compensated for by higher spending on community care. In fact, the poorer regions appear to be uniformly deprived in all areas of spending. Moreover, it is important to compare per capita expenditure between different *areas within regions* as well as *between regions*. A recent study by Buxton and Klein has demonstrated that while regions have great variations in their expenditure, the variation in resource allocation between Area Health Authorities within the regions is even greater,[50] and these discrepancies are also very evident at District level.[51] It might, of course, be assumed that these variations are a reflection of different needs in different areas. In that case, high spending in an industrial area, or one with a high proportion of old people in the population, would represent an egalitarian distribution of resources. Available evidence, however, points to an inverse correlation between medical need and medical provision which Julian Tudor Hart has characterised as the 'inverse care law'.

> In areas with most sickness and death, general practitioners
> have more work, larger lists, less hospital support and inherit
> more clinically ineffective traditions of consultation than in the

healthiest areas; and hospital doctors shoulder heavier case loads with less staff and equipment, most obsolete buildings, and suffer recurrent crises in the availability of beds and replacement of staff. These trends can be summed up as the inverse care law: that the availability of good medical care tends to vary inversely with the need of the population served.[52]

The idea of the inverse care law was supported by a recent study by Noyce, Snaith and Trickey which showed that a positive correlation exists between the resources provided for medical services in a given region and the proportion of professional and managerial workers in that region.[53] Thus, the distribution of resources between different regions is not a historical accident and it is misleading to talk about geographical inequalities as though they existed independently of more basic inequalities in income, housing and education. In other words, spatial inequalities cannot be separated from class inequalities.

Since the inception of the NHS, there has been a continuing debate about whether middle-class patients manage to obtain relatively more NHS resources or whether it is 'over-utilised' by working-class patients.[54] Such an analysis involves very complex methodological problems, not least of which are the lack of comprehensive national data on either class differences in morbidity and mortality or class differences in the utilisation of medical services. However, a review of the available evidence suggests that while working-class patients make more use of most services on a quantitative basis, their qualitative experience of health care is likely to be inferior in a variety of ways.

So far as quantitative data on the use of the NHS is concerned, there is a strong negative correlation between social class and the use of both GPs and hospital inpatient and outpatient services. That is, for working-class patients there is a greater use of most services and use declines as one moves up the socio-economic scale. Clearly, this reflects the higher levels of working-class morbidity and mortality - greater need is reflected in a higher utilisation of services. However, the larger number of consultations and admissions does not seem to be proportionately as great as the excess morbidity and mortality suffered by social class V in particular.[55] The pattern of use is, moreover, quite different in the case of those services which are basically preventive, so that middle-class patients make more use of services such as mass miniature radiography, cervical cytology, conservative dentistry, antenatal and postnatal care and family planning.[56] It seems then that middle-class patients use a broader range of the services available, often on a preventive basis, while working-class patients tend to get *post hoc* treatment for an existing medical problem.

It is difficult to compare the quality of care received by different groups of patients, but evidence of various kinds suggests that working-class patients receive poorer quality medical care. In the case of general practice, lists are larger in the poorer industrial areas and, in the absence of health centres, the physical premises are often grossly inadequate. In middle-class areas, practices are usually smaller, better-equipped and have better-qualified doctors.[57] In the case of hospital treatment, it has often been suggested that middle-class patients receive better care because they are more likely to be able to secure a referral to a teaching hospital. Data on the social origins of patients in teaching hospitals is difficult to obtain, but one study by Howlett and Ashley compared the class composition of 932 patients admitted to teaching hospitals and regional board hospitals for treatment of benign enlargement of the prostate gland. The authors concluded that 'admission to teaching hospitals may - rather like selective schools - be subject to a kind of creaming process'.[58]

But medical care cannot be assessed on a purely technical basis. The quality of the social relationships involved is also of crucial importance. The inequalities in power, knowledge and status which usually exist between doctor and patient are at their greatest when the patients concerned are working class, and this will be likely to have deleterious effects on their subjective experiences of medical care. Ann Cartwright's work, for example, has shown that in hospital the working-class patient is less likely to receive any detailed explanation of his/her condition than the middle-class patient.[59] Moreover, her study of general practice showed that elderly middle-class patients had consistently longer consultations than their working-class counterparts, and were able to discuss more of their problems with their doctor.[60] Few studies of patients' own experiences of medical care have as yet been undertaken,[61] but findings such as these are confirmed by the everyday experiences of many patients - particularly working-class women. As one woman recently wrote to a popular newspaper, 'I seldom visit my doctor, but on the occasions that I do, he always asks two questions. How old I am and how many children I have . . . And whether I've got flu or backache, he says what do you expect. This happens every time I see him'.[62]

The health labour force: who runs the health service?

The NHS labour force is a highly stratified one, with workers having very different levels of pay, status and power over their work situation. This pattern of a fragmented and increasingly specialised labour force has of course become the norm, not just in the health sector but in most areas of capitalist production. This method of organising labour is usually defended on the grounds that it is an essential prerequisite for industrial methods of production and for the exploitation of new technologies. In recent years, however, this view has been strongly criticised, and it is now argued that this fragmentation of the labour process - what Braverman calls the capitalist division of labour - arises not from needs created by the process of industrialisation itself, but from the need to control the labour force.[63] As a result, the divisions within all sectors of the labour force both reflect and reinforce existing class divisions in society.

There has, as yet, been no detailed study of the NHS labour force; what evidence is available suggests that there is a very selective recruitment into different levels of the hierarchy and that the system perpetuates the privileges of particular social groups. At the top of the NHS hierarchy are the consultants and senior administrators, who receive the highest incomes and effectively control the running of the health service.[64] It is assumed that the substantial benefits they receive are earned as a reward for their particular knowledge and skills, but clearly the opportunity to acquire these skills depends almost entirely on an individual's social origins. Several recent studies have shown the importance of class origins, and particularly a medical background, in gaining entry to a medical school.[65] Evidence given to the Royal Commission on Medical Education showed that the proportion of medical students with medical fathers actually increased from 17 per cent in 1956 to over 21 per cent in 1966.[66] In 1961 more than one-third of medical students came from parents in the professional and executive class (three per cent of the economically active population) while less than one-third came from the families of skilled workers (50 per cent of the population). Only three per cent came from the families of semi-skilled and unskilled workers (32 per cent of the population). By 1966 the proportion with professional parents had risen to 40 per cent, and while 71 per cent of qualified school-leavers came from state schools, 54 per cent of medical students still came from independent fee-paying schools. Doctors, then, come predominantly from an 'upper middle-class' background and their power and prestige within the NHS is based as much on their class position as on the technical knowledge to which they have been given privileged access. Beneath the doctors and administrators are the nurses and other 'para-medical' workers - technicians, physiotherapists, occupational therapists and so on. They comprise approximately 39 per cent of the labour force and can be loosely described as the 'lower middle-class' sector. Finally, the lowest position in the NHS hierarchy is occupied by the largest group of workers - the unskilled or semi-skilled ancillary workers, who constitute approximately 54 per cent of the NHS labour force. Among those included in the 'ancillary' category are laundry workers, gardeners, catering staff, ward orderlies, drivers, porters and telephonists. It is illustrative of their more general social invisibility that the annual DHSS statistics provide almost no information about these workers. Indeed, there is only one table in the Health and Personal Social Services Statistics devoted to the approximately 210,000 ancillary workers, whereas seven tables give information on the 27,000 hospital doctors. We do know, however, that the ancillary workers are the lowest paid health workers, that they have almost no representation in the NHS decision making process, and that they generally work in very bad conditions.

The health labour force is not, however, divided only on the basis of class - the sexual division of labour is also very marked. About seventy-five per cent of workers in the NHS are women.[67] This should not be surprising since so much work in the health sector involves the 'female' task of 'caring', or traditionally domestic jobs such as cleaning, cooking and laundering. But although they form such a large proportion of NHS workers, women are not equally represented at all levels in the hierarchy. Barbara Ehrenreich has described the position of women health workers in the USA and her description could equally well be applied to Britain.

> Whether we measure status in terms of income, or in terms of more qualitative factors such as decision making, or societal prestige, we find the same thing: within the US health industry, women occupy jobs characterised by lower income and less power and prestige than those occupied by males in the health industry, and even within the same job category, women receive lower incomes than men.[68]

The only real exceptions to this pattern of systematic discrimination against women occurs with those males (often migrants) who perform low-paid and low-status jobs in the ancillary sector, and those few women who manage to become doctors.

Only about twenty per cent of doctors in Britain are women, and although the proportion of female medical students has been rising, it is still only about thirty-five per cent.[69] Medicine is assumed to be a rigorous and scientific profession and women continue to be defined as ill-equipped and unsuitable to undertake it. But, whatever the obstacles to their admission, female medical students do better on average than their male counterparts. They qualify with honours more often than men, and more often have no failures in their final examinations.[70] However, despite their better performance at 'A' levels and in medical examinations, women achieve significantly less than men once they have qualified.[71] They gain higher degrees less often (30 per cent of women compared with 42 per cent of men go on to add to their basic qualifications) and obtain fewer consultant and other senior posts.[72] This can be explained, in part, through straightforward discrimination against women and, in part, by the effects of the wider sexual division of labour in society. Given the patriarchal nature of society in general, and of the medical profession in particular, women doctors are usually at a disadvantage when competing with men. This problem is exacerbated by the fact that the medical career structure tends to rely on a system of informal sponsorship rather than formal bureaucratic criteria in the allocation of jobs. Above all however, in a society where it is assumed that women have the responsibility for caring for home and children, women doctors are put at a disadvantage by the inflexible organisation of hospital medicine, and like all women working in the NHS, by the lack of any provision for child care at their place of work.[73] In the past few years, the DHSS has been placing a great deal of emphasis on the importance of retaining the services of expensively-trained women doctors, and various schemes have been introduced to try and facilitate this.[74] However, their limited success indicates that the obstacles to women doctors are deep-rooted, both in the nature of medical practice itself, and in the wider society.[75]

In the intermediate sector of the health labour force, the sexual division of labour is of course very different. The great majority of workers in this sector are nurses, and 'femaleness' has traditionally been built into the very definition of nursing. In 1976, there were well over 350,000 nurses in the NHS, more than ninety per cent of whom were women. We can better understand the nature of nursing today if we examine its emergence as a specific occupational category in the latter half of the nineteenth century.[76] Changes in the nature of medical practice produced the demand for a new type of worker, while at the same time a gradual change both in the social definition and also in the expectations of women produced a new supply of labour. The practice of medicine expanded very rapidly during the nineteenth century, with a great increase in both the number of doctors and the number of hospital beds. As medical activity became more specialised, there was a growing need for a new type of sub-ordinate worker to whom the doctor could delegate certain responsibilities. As a result, female nursing care was moved from the home into the hospital. Nurses were employed to provide efficient patient care based on the 'sanitary idea', but at the same time were expected to inject domestic comforts and devotion into the clinical situation. For many middle-class women, this new career of nursing offered the possibility of escape from the enforced leisure of Victorian womanhood into an occupation suitable for their female talents.

> ... the Nightingale nurse was simply the ideal Lady, trans-
> planted from home to the hospital, and absolved of reproduc-
> tive responsibilities. To the doctor, she brought the wifely
> virtue of absolute obedience. To the patient she brought the
> selfless devotion of a mother. To the lower level hospital
> employees, she brought the firm but kindly discipline of a
> household manager accustomed to dealing with servants.[77]

A basic division was therefore created between what were
regarded as the hard-headed, diagnostic aspects of medicine - the
'curing' which male doctors did, and the 'caring' which was to be
done by women. It was assumed that women did not have the
intellectual or emotional capacities to deal with scientific healing,
and conversely, that it would be a waste of their undoubted organisational, mothering and nurturing capacities were they to be
employed in anything other than the nursing role. Doctor and nurse,
man and woman, thus emerged as complementary roles, with a
sexual division of labour built into the enduring stereotypes of what
it is to be a doctor and what it is to be a nurse. The nature of nursing
education and nursing practice reflect the importance of this basic
ideology in maintaining nursing (and women) in an inferior
position. A nurse is trained to obey the orders of superiors (particularly doctors), to do things the 'right way' (whatever the circumstances), and to be dedicated to her patients and her 'calling'. As a
result, nurses have traditionally put up with low pay and difficult
working conditions, continuing to accept nursing as a 'vocation'
rather than simply a job.

Although this traditional view of nurses is still widely held, it
increasingly conflicts with the contemporary experience of nursing.
Attempts to use the nursing labour force more efficiently in terms of
bureaucratic criteria have produced increasing fragmentation and
specialisation. Those aspects of caring for a growing number of
chronically sick patients which require fewer formal skills, are
increasingly allocated to less-qualified and lower-paid staff, while
many nurses are undertaking more clinical tasks as well as co-
ordinating a range of other health workers at ward level.[78] For many

nurses, these developments have meant that their conditions of work have worsened. The image of the 'Nightingale nurse' has become increasingly anachronistic, and particularly for those who are young or who come from abroad, the mystique of dedication and professionalism is no longer sufficient to make up for low pay, difficult work, and often excessive control over their private lives. Many factors continue to militate against effective organisation by nurses - their 'female' socialisation in particular - and the stratification within nursing itself. However, the traditional passivity of nurses is fast disappearing, and the rapid 'proletarianisation' of this sector of the health labour force has been a significant development in the NHS over the past decade.[79]

The most exploited group in the NHS labour force are the so-called 'ancillary' workers, of whom about seventy-five per cent are women, the majority working part time. In 1976 they included over 10,000 laundry workers, 34,000 catering workers and 92,000 workers providing basic 'domestic services'. Women in the health sector are, therefore, concentrated in the same kind of low-paid, low-status jobs which they occupy elsewhere in the economy, and the highly visible 'miracles' wrought by predominantly male doctors continue to rest on a pyramid of invisible and predominantly female labour.

Finally, we need to examine the significance of race and nationality in the organisation of the NHS labour force. It has been a characteristic of the British economy during the postwar period that migrant workers from the third world, from southern Europe, and from Ireland, have been used to fill jobs for which British labour was not available.[80] A large number of migrant workers (both male and female) are therefore employed in the NHS and they are concentrated in the ancillary sector. One of the few surveys of this group of workers showed a wide regional variation in the proportion of immigrants employed, but revealed that in London teaching hospitals in 1968 as many as 65.6 per cent of the domestic staff were immigrants.[81]

The NHS is unusual, however, in that not all migrants are to be found in the lowest-paid jobs. British immigration laws have been selectively used to allow particular types of skilled labour into the country, and doctors and nurses have been among the few categories of foreign worker able to obtain immigration vouchers in recent years.[82] Naturally, this has had serious consequences for the countries from which they come, and the effects of this loss of skilled medical labour are discussed in more detail in chapter seven. So far as the workers themselves are concerned, their status as 'aliens' and the influence of entrenched racism means that they are not treated on equal terms with British workers of equal levels of skill, and, as a result, tend to be concentrated in the least desirable jobs *within* medicine and nursing.

In 1975, 20.5 per cent of all student and pupil nurses in Britain were from overseas and about half of them had actually been recruited in their country of origin.[83] That same year, 4,332 work permits were issued to nurses, the majority of whom had come from the Caribbean, Mauritius or Malaysia.[84] Many of those who come to Britain to train are encouraged to qualify as state enrolled nurses (SEN) rather than state registered nurses (SRN), and, as a result, are unable to gain promotion. Moreover, the SEN qualification is not recognised in some countries, so that after training nurses are forced to remain in the lower-paid jobs in the NHS rather than returning home. Nurses born overseas are over-represented in hospitals dealing with mental illness, mental subnormality, mental handicap and geriatrics, and very few indeed are to be found in the 'prestige' teaching hospitals.[85] Overseas nurses are, therefore, clearly used to compensate for the shortage of British recruits into notoriously underpaid and often unpleasant work. Their role as a 'reserve army' has recently been demonstrated with particular clarity by the fact that because of high levels of unemployment among British nurses, overseas nurses are increasingly being refused a renewal of their work permits.[86]

Strict control over the number of medical school places, combined with the pyramid structure of the medical hierarchy have meant that throughout its history the NHS has suffered from a chronic shortage of junior hospital doctors. This has been alleviated by a high degree of reliance on overseas doctors, most of them from former British colonial territories (India, Pakistan and Sri Lanka in particular).[87] It has been estimated that the NHS now operates on the basis of an annual inflow and outflow of approximately 2,500 overseas doctors, and there are usually between 20,000 and 25,000 foreign doctors in Britain at any given time. In 1975, 35.2 per cent of hospital doctors and 18.3 per cent of GPs were born outside the British Isles.[88] However, within the hospital sector these doctors are very unevenly distributed between regions, specialties, and grades.

The fact that overseas doctors are so unevenly distributed in the medical hierarchy - and particularly that so few become consultants - is often justified on the grounds that they come to Britain to receive training and then return home to their own countries. Indeed, the training of foreign doctors in British hospitals is often defined as part of British 'aid' to the third world. The fact is, however, that the amount of training received in junior hospital posts varies widely, and the distribution of foreign doctors between hospitals and between specialities would appear to minimise their own opportunities for training, while maximising those of British doctors. They enable the NHS to continue functioning precisely because they do the jobs most unacceptable to indigenous doctors, and the little training they receive in the process is often irrelevant to conditions in their own countries.

The divisions within the health labour force, therefore, reflect the class, sexual and racial divisions in the wider society. The use of female and of migrant labour has proved to be important in keeping down costs in an extremely labour-intensive sector. At the same time, the increasing fragmentation and specialisation of the labour process have facilitated schemes for increased productivity while simultaneously ensuring a greater degree of control over the workforce and limiting the development of solidarity among different types and grades of health worker.

The crisis and the NHS

Britain experienced an unprecedented period of inflation, economic recession and high unemployment in the 1970s. While this has been an international phenomenon, spreading throughout the capitalist world, the British economy has suffered particularly badly. Interpretations of this crisis have differed widely,[89] but there has been general agreement on the significance of the dramatic increase in public spending during the postwar period which resulted in a continual rise in public sector borrowing. Most commentators, of course, have emphasised capitalist solutions to the crisis - the control of wages and prices and, above all, reductions in public spending which they see as a luxury that cannot be afforded. Hence, there have been continuing demands for public expenditure cuts and capitalist interests have been united in demanding a transfer of resources from the 'unproductive' to the 'productive' sectors of the economy. At the international level, foreign finance capital, acting mainly through the IMF, is able to influence British economic policy in the same direction. As a result, reductions in the rate of growth of public expenditure have become a major component in policies designed to 'put the British economy back on its feet'. Welfare spending has suffered most, and within that sector, education, housing, and to a lesser extent health, have been most seriously affected.

In 1976 the projected rate of growth of expenditure on the NHS was to be only 1.8 per cent per year in real terms until 1980 - a figure which must be compared with an average growth rate of 3 per cent between the fiscal years 1968/9 to 1974/5.[90] Moreover, capital expenditure on hospital and community services was to be reduced by 21 per cent. When these reductions are examined against the background of a continuing increase in the number of old people in the population, it becomes evident that even existing standards of medical care could not be maintained. Evidence is already accumulating that the cuts have adversely affected both patients and workers in the NHS. Hospitals are closing, jobs being lost, waiting lists becoming longer, physical conditions in hospitals are deteriorating and supposedly 'non-essential' services such as family planning are being cut back.[91] If we examine these developments in more detail, it becomes apparent that there are at least three dimensions to current NHS policy: attempts are being made to maximise the efficient use of dwindling resources in accordance with cost-benefit criteria; policies are being designed to obscure the reality of these reductions in expenditure through presenting their effects as improvements rather than deteriorations in services; and finally, attempts are being made to reduce demands on the NHS by publicising the notion that every individual is responsible for his/her own health.

Attempts to maximise the efficient use of resources were facilitated by the 1974 reorganisation and by the introduction of a new planning system for the NHS in 1976. In an attempt to achieve a rational reallocation of resources between geographical areas, the Resource Allocation Working Party (RAWP) constructed a complex formula for diverting resources from the 'over-provided' to the more under-financed regions.[92] This approach has been criticised from a variety of perspectives.[93] First, it is clear that the fourteen English regions cannot be taken as a basis for resource planning since regional equality (even if it were possible) would not ensure an egalitarian distribution of resources within regions. It soon became evident, for example, that the RAWP scheme was doing little for many of the unhealthy and decaying inner-city areas which continue to be deprived of adequate medical provision.[94] Above all, however, it cannot be too strongly emphasised that RAWP (and similar schemes for the reallocation of resources) were concerned with relative and not absolute over-provision. The fact that metropolitan regions may have relatively more resources than their provincial counterparts in no way implies that they are adequately provided for. RAWP was, therefore, an attempt to allocate resources more 'fairly' in a very limited sense, but, in setting the less well-provided regions against those which are 'over-provided', its main effect has been to detract attention from the decline of the NHS as a whole.

Attempts to keep down labour costs through increased productivity intensified in the 1970s. Increasingly, job vacancies were not being filled, making the workload greater for those already employed. Along with strategies to keep down wages and to increase productivity, there were attempts to use less expensive delivery systems for medical care. One example of this was the development of the 'nurse-practitioner' who could take some of the clinical load off the better-paid and more highly-qualified doctor. While it is clearly desirable in principle for knowledge and responsibility to be more widely shared, such schemes are carefully set up so as not to threaten the hierarchical structure of the NHS - particularly the gap between doctors and other health workers. Nurses have been getting more responsibility but little reward in either material or status terms, and only a few of them can aspire to a 'nurse-practitioner' position. The situation in nursing reflects a general trend throughout the NHS towards an increasing dependence on untrained or partly-trained staff.

This move towards less expensive health care delivery has tended to reinforce the growing criticisms of high-technology medicine. Ironically, it was in large part the need to reduce the costs of the NHS that forced DHSS and NHS administrators to recognise the increasing evidence concerning the serious limitations of modern curative medicine.[95] This was clearly reflected in the 1976 consultative document *Priorities for Health and Social Services in England*, which attempted to outline the basis upon which the reduced resources of the health sector were to be spent.[96] The document argued that the cost-effectiveness of high-technology medicine must be examined more carefully, and that resources must be directed towards the more economical primary care sector. This emphasis on primary care was extended to include community services of various kinds - home helps, meals on wheels, and both day-care and residential provision for the physically and mentally handicapped. Priorities of this kind may appear superficially progressive, and there can be no doubt that more resources are needed for primary care. In practice, however, the ultimate effectiveness of these proposals is likely to be extremely limited.[97] Local authorities are under as much financial pressure as the NHS, so that any health planning which is based on increased support from local authorities is likely to be a rhetorical rationalisation of central government cuts rather than a feasible local alternative. Moreover, the concept of 'the community' has been widely used to foster the illusion that outside institutions there is a network of caring relationships consisting of individuals with both the will and also the material resources to help those in need. In fact, as services are cut back in both the NHS and the local authority sector, it is individuals (usually women) without the necessary resources who are being forced to care for those with whom the system can no longer cope.[98] Discussions about 'the community' and 'community care' have become increasingly important in masking the reality of this situation.

Priorities for Health and Social Services in England argued not just for an emphasis on primary care, but for a greater proportion of resources to be allocated to the old and the physically and mentally handicapped. However, the great increase in the number of people over seventy-five which will occur over the next two decades means that even if these areas were to be made a priority, the resources available would not be sufficient to maintain the existing standard of services. The major objective of *Priorities for Health and Social Services in England* therefore seemed to be to redirect dwindling resources towards the fastest-growing sector of the population, while at the same time covering up the actual deterioration of the NHS and its inability to meet the growing need for health care.

Finally, an important part of the strategy for cutting costs in the NHS has been a new emphasis on the role of individuals in preserving their own health, and also in treating their own minor ailments. The critical reappraisal of high-technology medicine, combined with rhetoric about improved primary care facilities, have made possible a new (and economically convenient) emphasis on the importance of preventive medicine and health education. The official presentation of this new ideology is to be found in both *Priorities for Health and Social Services in England* and also in another consultative document from the DHSS - *Prevention and Health: Everybody's Business*.[99] The *Priorities* document defines its interest in prevention quite explicitly, 'Preventive medicine and health education are particularly important when resources are tightly limited, as they can often lead to savings in resources in other areas.'[100] Both documents stress the importance of health education in persuading individuals to adopt a healthier life-style. *Prevention and Health* emphasises the fact that most technological preventive measures (with the exception only of fluoridation and vaccination) are expensive yet yield little real benefit, and stresses instead the importance of health education as the major strategy in prevention. As the authors of the document themselves state,

> the prime responsibility for his own health falls on the individual. The role of the health professions and of government is limited to ensuring that the public have access to such knowledge as is available about the importance of personal habit on health and at the very least, no obstacles are placed in the way of those who decide to act on that knowledge.[101]

The message is clear - 'help yourself because no one else will' - or to put it another way, health is the responsibility of individuals, and the role of the state in helping those individuals is to be very limited. These limitations are shown most clearly in the discussion concerning the removal of obstacles to people's health. *Prevention and Health* discusses in some detail the health risks of smoking, alcohol, 'misuse' of drugs, over-eating, and what is euphemistically referred to as 'the sexual revolution'. These are assumed, however, to be due to the moral weakness of the individuals concerned, and there is no discussion of the social and economic context in which they occur. Only three short paragraphs are devoted to the dangers of the physical environment. One of these discusses ways in which the environment has improved, while another discusses road accidents. Even here the responsibility of individuals is stressed, since there is a great deal of emphasis on wearing seat-belts (quite reasonably), but none at all on the necessity for manufacturers to make safer cars or for a rational public transport policy. There are only passing references to industrial health and safety, and no evidence at all of any serious attempt to prevent ill health beyond increased fluoridation and moral exhortations for people to lead healthier lives. The recent official support of prevention must, therefore, be seen as another attempt to cut costs during a period of economic stringency. It legitimates a reduction in services through blaming individuals for their own misfortune, while at the same time distracting attention from the broader social and economic causes of ill health.

In attempting to reduce the cost of the NHS during a period of economic recession, the state can be seen as facilitating the interests of capital as a whole. Moreover, in a period of high unemployment there is no shortage of labour, so that even if sickness rates were to rise this would not threaten production. As we have already seen, however, the state does not act autonomously and the contradictions in the nature of the NHS once again become apparent when we examine the opposition which has developed to these policies designed to rationalise medical expenditure. Some sections of capital such as the pharmaceutical and medical equipment manufacturers have actually resisted attempts to reduce health service expenditure. There has also been, of course, a section of capital which actually profited from the deterioration of the NHS. Reductions in NHS standards, combined with an increase in foreign patients coming to Britain (especially from the Middle East), produced an increase in the demand for private medical care and this has been reflected in the expension of the commercial hospital sector.[102]

Naturally, resistance to attempts to divert resources away from high-technology medicine comes from members of the medical profession, the most powerful of whom are determined to resist the trend towards preventive medicine and primary care, as well as any significant redistribution of resources towards the old and the chronically sick. This was well illustrated in an editorial in the *British Medical Journal*. Under a heading 'Policy of Despair', the BMJ made the following comment on the government's choice of priorities: 'By putting "people before buildings" and by giving practical expression to public sympathy for the old and handicapped, Mrs Castle has perhaps allowed sentiment to overrule intellect.'[103] It then went on to argue for the expansion of acute services including kidney dialysis and transplantation, for the increased use of EMI scanners and, in particular, for more acute intervention in obstetrics. The defensive reaction of doctors in the London teaching hospitals to the RAWP proposals has been very similar, illustrating very clearly their strong commitment to maintaining technological 'centres of excellence'.[104] It remains to be seen, therefore, how far even the minor redistribution of resources suggested in the consultative documents can be implemented against medical opposition of this kind.

Finally, a different kind of resistance to the reduction in NHS spending has come from the mass of health workers. Junior hospital doctors took industrial action in 1975-76 to obtain improved conditions and overtime payments, and consultants and GPs fought hard to maintain or improve their financial position during a period of wage control and rapid inflation. More significantly, however, the state was also increasingly forced into open conflict with the rest of the health labour force.[105] Not surprisingly, the traditional passivity of many of these workers is being transformed in the struggle to resist increased unemployment or the transfer of jobs and to obtain a living wage. The industrial action of ancillary workers in 1972-73 over low pay, the nurses' strike of 1974, and above all the occupation of hospitals threatened with closure, are all evidence of this. This industrial action was accompanied by a very considerable increase in the level of unionisation of health workers and more co-ordination between public sector unions as a whole. Many of the actions by health service workers have been part of the broader struggle against wage restraint, but others, such as the campaigns against private medicine and against closures, are specific to the health sector.

The campaigns against hospital closures and reduced services have been an important catalyst in developing solidarity among health workers. For many, these struggles against the cuts mark a growing realisation that it is not just doctors and administrators who should make decisions about the NHS, but workers at all levels. Even more significantly, these campaigns have increasingly involved not just health workers but other local people who have been united around the demand to maintain local medical facilities. As yet, these struggles have been largely defensive, concentrating on the fight to retain existing standards. There is, however, a growing awareness of the need to move beyond the mere existence of a National Health Service towards the organisation of the sort of health care needed by the majority of patients.[106]

6: Women, Medicine and Social Control: The Case of the NHS

The creation of the NHS was extremely important for British women, giving them for the first time both primary and hospital care free at source. It was particularly valuable in ensuring that all women were able to obtain antenatal care and help during childbirth. Nevertheless, there has been growing criticism of the way in which women are treated within the NHS. Many of the more extreme ideas of nineteenth century medicine have now disappeared - or at least have taken on a new form - but modern medical ideology still contains within it the belief that women are essentially reproductive and ultimately inferior beings. These ideas are inevitably reflected in medical practice, exerting a powerful and deleterious influence on women's experiences of medical care. It is from these experiences that the feminist critique of the NHS has come.

Double burden: women's labour in the twentieth century

During the second half of the nineteenth century, the level of women's participation in wage labour fell, largely because an increase in the level of productivity meant that capital was less dependent on drawing women (and children) into the labour force. However, during the late nineteenth and early twentieth centuries structural changes in the economy were forming the basis for what was eventually to be a great increase in the number of women in the labour force. The labour shortage during the first world war meant that many women were drawn into wage labour for the first time, although most returned to their domestic role when the war was over. During the second world war, women again entered the labour force in large numbers, only to return home when the war had ended.

After the immediate postwar boom, however, many women began to take up paid employment on a more permanent basis, and the proportion of married women in the labour force increased particularly dramatically.[1]

By 1974, women accounted for 40 per cent of all employees in Britain, the overall activity rate for women was about 45 per cent, and mothers of dependent children formed a considerable proportion of women working either full-time or part-time outside the home.[2] Because women are still encouraged to view themselves primarily as wives and mothers, many continue to accept lower pay, worse conditions and more job insecurity than men, and are less likely to join unions. As a result, they have formed an increasingly useful 'reserve army' which can be moved in and out of work in accordance with the changing demand for labour. Their relatively lower cost, combined with their greater flexibility, have meant that women have been of particular significance to employers during the crisis years of the 1970s.[3]

Despite this long-term rise in women's waged labour, they have also continued to be responsible for most domestic labour. For the vast majority of women, working outside the home means a 'double shift' of wage labour and housework since there has been neither an increase in the socialisation of domestic labour (e.g. more nurseries, municipal canteens or laundries) nor any significant shift in the sexual division of labour in the home.[4] There have, however, been marked changes in the content, if not the organisation, of domestic labour during the twentieth century. The period of a woman's life spent in pregnancy and child rearing has gradually been compressed: the average woman now has fewer children than she did in the past and spends only about four years of her life either pregnant or looking after a child under one. Housework has, therefore, become increasingly distinct from child care, while the use of domestic appliances has made it physically easier for the majority of women. At the same time, however, an increasing emphasis on the *quality* of family life has placed new burdens on women.

Since the second world war, the formation of the welfare state has meant an increase in state intervention in the lives of individual families.[5] This has involved new standards of child rearing enforced by 'caring' professionals such as health visitors and social workers. Individual mothers are increasingly held to blame for any psychological problems experienced by their children, and 'maternal deprivation' is commonly invoked to explain a wide range of 'deviant' behaviour.[6] At the same time, as waged work has become less satisfying and more stressful, for many men, the role of the home (and therefore of the 'wife and mother') has become increasingly important as a form of compensation. During the postwar period, this process has been heightened by the growth of 'consumerism' which has been important both economically as a way of maintaining a high level of demand for consumer goods, and ideologically as a way of providing worker 'satisfaction'. It is the task of women to organise that consumption, and to maintain 'standards' even when the real value of a family income is falling. British capitalism has thus become increasingly dependent on both the wage labour and the domestic labour of women. This has led to the creation of significant contradictions in the material situation of most women - contradictions which are reflected in changing definitions of femininity and of motherhood.

The objective situation of most women today is further removed than ever it was from the traditional stereotype of the domesticated woman fulfilling her potential in motherhood. The entry of women into the labour force has not, however, abolished the patriarchal relationship between men and women. Instead a new form of oppressive ideology has emerged which is flexible enough to accommodate the changing role of women, while at the same time maintaining their ultimate inferiority.[7] Women are now accepted both as workers and as housewives/mothers, but they are assumed to be less effective mothers because their work interferes with their mothering, and less effective workers because their responsibilities as mothers interfere with their work.[8] This broadening of the range of acceptable female activities has legitimated the entry of an increasing number of women - both middle class and working class - into the labour market, whilst at the same time ensuring that they continue to perform their domestic duties in their 'spare time'. Definitions of femininity have, therefore, been liberalised - women are defined as workers and even as sexual beings, as well as mothers - but their essentially domestic, and therefore inferior, identity ensures their continued oppression and exploitation.

The process by which men and women come to define themselves and each other in terms of sex-role stereotypes is, of course, a very complex one.[9] It is clear, however, that in developed capitalist societies so-called welfare institutions have come to play an increasingly important part in bringing this about. It is now recognised, for example, that the education system plays a particularly important role in teaching boys and girls their respective gender roles.[10] It is also clear that the medical care system (in the case of Britain, the NHS) plays a similar role in the case of adults - and of adult women in particular. Thus, doctors are extremely important in defining the boundaries of what it is to be a woman (and to be a mother in particular) and in controlling those women who might attempt to cross these boundaries. As we shall see, this social control can be either material (refusing access to an abortion, for example) or ideological (as in the case of much psychiatry).

In recent years there has been growing criticism of what has been called the medicalisation of life - the process by which doctors have gradually been given jurisdiction over larger and larger areas of our everyday lives. This expansion of the medical sphere of influence has been especially significant for women for two reasons. First, women do, of course, have the capacity to become pregnant and give birth, and are usually responsible for subsequent child-care - all areas of human activity in which doctors are assumed to be 'expert'.[11] Moreover, most forms of reliable birth control involve formal contact with the medical care system. Their reproductive capacities therefore bring perfectly healthy women into frequent contact with their doctors, both if they become pregnant and if they wish to avoid doing so. Secondly, female 'deviance' usually consists of behaviour which is defined as 'sick' rather than criminal. Thus women come into contact with the police or go to prison relatively rarely compared with men. They do, however, consult their doctor more often about problems defined as neurotic or psychosomatic, and women are one and a half times as likely as men to enter a psychiatric hospital at some period in their lives.[12] For women, the processes of social control are therefore often less overt and frequently appear in the guise of benevolent help. This does not, however, make them any less important or less oppressive. Rather, as more conspicuous forms of sexual discrimination begin to disappear, it becomes even more important to uncover the subterranean and more subtle aspects of the social control of women, and a detailed analysis of the medical treatment of women is an important part of this task.

The medical view of women: the reproduction of inferiority

During the twentieth century, the Victorian belief in the *physical* weakness of women, and their subordination to the functioning of their reproductive systems, has been gradually transformed into an emphasis on the *psychological* inadequacies and weaknesses of women. Barbara Ehrenreich and Deirdre English have pointed out the significance of the work of Freud in this transition from physical to psychological justifications of female inferiority.[13] While few doctors could be said to hold a 'pure' Freudian position, there can be no doubt that aspects of Freudian thought are at the heart of much contemporary medical treatment of women. As capitalist production has become increasingly dependent on the labour of both middle-class and working-class women, a crude version of Freudian theory has formed the basis for a more unitary conception of women and a new way of legitimating the sexual division of labour. These beliefs are reflected both in the attitudes and actions of individual doctors (and other health workers) and also in the policies and priorities of the NHS itself.

It is difficult to articulate the medical model of women in any systematic way. It is not spelled out in textbooks, and must be constructed from an examination of the nature and content of medical education and medical practice. Two basic ideas seem to be central to contemporary medical definitions of women. The first is the tacit belief that men are 'normal' whereas women are 'abnormal'. That is to say, the intellectual, emotional and physical potential of women is measured against the male standard and women are found to be essentially defective. Secondly, this 'abnormality' is seen to derive from the fact that the 'natural' role of women is to reproduce, and that this is the central determining characteristic of a woman's being. The capacity to be a mother is no longer seen to make women physically ill - just intellectually and emotionally different and - by implication - inferior.

The basis of the medical view of women, therefore, remains the belief that their reproductive role is the pivotal point of their personality structure and hence of their psychological wellbeing. As Michèle Barrett and Helen Roberts have pointed out, men are seen basically as workers while women are defined as mothers.

> Working with GPs over some time, it became clear to us that our respondents made certain unspoken assumptions about the 'nature' of men and women. Men, it was clear, had a primary natural 'drive' to work to support their wife and family. Women had a similar 'drive' to nourish and cherish their husband and family.[14]

Hence motherhood and the maternal instinct are assumed by doctors to be central to women's lives. The equation of 'woman' with 'mother' in medical practice means that, so far as most doctors are concerned, it is *good* for women to become pregnant and have babies and *deviant* for them not to wish to do so. Indeed, as Elizabeth Wilson has commented, psychoanalysts have implied that, 'in motherhood - and in no other role or relationship - pleasure principle and reality principle coincide, and [. . .] the mother's *duty* of reproduction is simultaneously her highest pleasure and source of fulfilment'.[15] It may well be true that the majority of women want to have children at some time in their lives, but the idea of a maternal instinct raises this belief beyond the status of mere description. It implies that there is something wrong with a woman who does not wish to have a baby, and this belief is reflected in medical practice in a variety of ways.[16] The emphasis on motherhood, for example, means that infertility is often treated very much more sympathetically than an unwanted pregnancy.

Anecdotal evidence exists in abundance, to show that most doctors behave as though women were by nature abnormal and different from men in a perjorative sense. Indeed, the women's health movement has provided numerous testimonials of the distress and unhappiness which behaviour of this kind continues to produce. A recent American study attempted to provide more formal evidence of sexist attitudes of this kind through asking a sample of doctors which characteristics they regarded as being typical of a 'normal, healthy adult' (sex unspecified), those which they saw as typical of a 'normal healthy male', and those which they saw as typical of a 'normal healthy female'.[17] There were very few differences between the doctors' responses (they included both men and women), and for most of them the desirable traits for a 'normal healthy man' were the same as those for a 'normal healthy adult'. However, those for a 'normal healthy female' differed greatly from those for men and adults (sex unspecified). Typical traits for women (normal, healthy ones remember!) were that they were more submissive, less aggressive, less competitive, more excitable in minor crises, more easily hurt, more emotional, more conceited about their appearance, less objective and less interested in maths and science. Finally, what these doctors judged as healthy for adults (sex unspecified) and for adult males was, in general, very similar to what a cross-section of the lay population regarded as socially desirable. This study demonstrated very clearly a prevalent assumption among American doctors that women are not only different from men but inferior to them as well, and that even in their healthy state, are not 'normal healthy adults'. There seems little doubt that a comparable study undertaken in Britain would provide very similar results.

Women as the objects of modern medicine: sexism in the NHS

These basically sexist ideas about the nature of women and their place in society are abundantly clear both in the way in which medicine is taught, and in the content of the curriculum. Women are often used as a source of humour in the teaching situation, in a way that demeans and denigrates them. This is carried over into the content of lectures and seminars as Margaret Campbell, who was herself a medical student, has pointed out,

> Women are regarded here very much as they are stereotyped in any other role: as possessed by affect, incapable of rational or

analytic thought, scheming and opportunistic and not *worth* the time, energy and thought required for good patient care ... While it is true that medical trainees are taught, implicitly, that all patients are somewhat demanding, irrational, and of course less valuable than the wise doctors who make life-and-death decisions for them, it is clear that patients who are also women are doubly demeaned. Patient status plus female status makes one a very poor creature indeed, and one who is likely to provoke some annoyance or irritation from the physician.[18]

Little attention is paid in the medical curriculum to problems specifically concerning women, unless they relate directly to pregnancy and childbirth. This both reflects and ultimately perpetuates a notable lack of detailed information about certain aspects of female physiology. Problems which may be extremely distressing for women are not taken seriously - menstrual disorders or vaginal infections, for example.[19] Both medical education and the allocation of research priorities, therefore, tend to reflect the generally low status of women and their lack of social and economic power. We can illustrate this in more detail through looking first at medical accounts of female sexuality and secondly at the way in which, despite evidence to the contrary, most female reproductive disorders continue to be classified as 'psychosomatic'.

There can be no doubt that during the twentieth century the acceptance of women as sexual as well as reproductive beings has been of great importance, giving women new freedom after the severe repression of the Victorian period. However, that new freedom remains circumscribed, and female sexuality continues to be defined from a male perspective.[20] Recent evidence concerning the nature of female sexuality has made very little impact on medical ideology and medical practice, and for most doctors a crude and often distorted Freudian model remains the basic paradigm for understanding the sexual nature of women.

In sex, as in other aspects of life, a woman is thought to be dependent, passive and submissive, while a man is assumed to be more demanding and aggressive and to have an altogether stronger sex drive. These psychological and emotional attributes are believed to be rooted in more basic physiological differences in sexual functioning. Thus women are said to be inherently more slowly aroused than men and to find it less easy to achieve orgasm, while their sexual response is presumed to be very strongly conditioned by their emotional relationship with the man in question. These ideas are loosely derived from the work of Freud, who suggested that the primary erogenous zone for a girl was her clitoris. In order for her to make the successful transition into womanhood, she had to be able to transfer her erotic sensations from her clitoris to her vagina. Women who did not make this transition, and who had what Freud referred to as 'clitoral orgasms', were not mature women (and were therefore especially prone to neurosis and hysteria). This view of the superiority of the vaginal over the clitoral orgasm entered popular mythology and became the basis for both clinical and non-clinical attitudes towards female sexuality.

The first attempt to 'test' Freud's theory physiologically was carried out by Alfred Kinsey,[21] who published his results in 1953; but his work proved to have very little effect on entrenched quasi-Freudian opinion. He was followed in 1966 by Masters and Johnson whose massive study was based on actual observation, measurement, and testing of human sexual activity among both men and women.[22] They also did lengthy interviews with their subjects, emphasising for the first time the importance of the subjective accounts of women in understanding the nature of female sexual experience! Several important aspects of the physiology of female sexuality were clarified in this study. First, it was made clear that, despite Freud's claims, the dichotomy between vaginal and clitoral orgasms is entirely false, since *all* orgasms are centred on the clitoris, however the sexual stimulation has been achieved. Secondly, it was made clear that women are potentially multi-orgasmic; that is, if a woman is immediately stimulated following orgasm, she is likely to experience several orgasms in rapid succession. Thirdly, it was shown that the orgasms of women vary in intensity more than those of men, and that the most intense orgasms experienced by the research subjects were those obtained by masturbatory manual stimulation, followed by those involving manual stimulation by a partner. The least intense orgasms were those experienced during intercourse. Thus the female orgasm was shown to be as real and identifiable a physical entity as that of the male, and Masters and Johnson provided important evidence against the dominant Freudian-based ideas concerning the nature of female sexuality.

These ideas have, however, been very slow to change, and the role of doctors in their perpetuation has been very significant. In both Britain and the USA, the doctor is the acknowledged 'expert' on sexuality, and there are very few other sources of help and advice for men and women experiencing sexual problems. Nevertheless, an examination of medical school curricula indicates that students learn very little indeed about sexuality. Male sexuality is not usually perceived as a problem - men rarely seek medical help except in cases of premature ejaculation or impotence. Women, on the other hand, visit their doctors much more often with psycho-sexual problems. It is usually assumed, however, that these problems can be handled through the doctor's own common sense - they are rarely recommended for specialist advice, and indeed little specialist expertise on sexual problems is available within the NHS. The small amount of teaching which the more fortunate of medical students receive about female sexuality comes within the confines of their gynaecology course and tends to conform closely to a quasi-Freudian paradigm. Thus women are still seen as basically reproductive; 'real' sexuality continues to be defined in terms of vaginal orgasms and a woman's sexuality is still considered primarily in terms of her partner's sexual pleasure rather than her own.[23]

Diane Scully and Pauline Bart examined 27 general gynaecology textbooks published in the USA between 1943 and 1972.[24] Their intention was to assess how far the findings of Kinsey and Masters and Johnson were reflected in the discussions of female sexuality contained in medical textbooks. Both studies had been 'hard', 'scientific' projects, and even if they went against existing medical orthodoxy one would have expected them either to have been critically rejected, or to have been incorporated into the body of 'textbook' medical knowledge. Scully and Bart's conclusion was that the findings of Kinsey made no impact whatever on medical textbooks, while the only effect to be observed from the massive Masters and Johnson study was 'some changes in rhetoric'. For the period *after* the publication of the Masters and Johnson study (i.e. 1963-72), they summarise the textbooks as follows:

> Two-thirds of the books of that decade failed to discuss the issue of the clitoral versus vaginal orgasm. Eight continued to state, contrary to Masters and Johnson's findings, that the male sex drive was stronger, and half still maintained that procreation was the major function of sex for the female. Two said that most women were 'frigid' and another stated that one-third were sexually unresponsive. Two repeated that the vaginal orgasm was the only mature response. [25]

An examination of British gynaecology textbooks reveals a very similar pattern. It would seem then, that what passes for 'scientific evidence' in other fields does not do so where female sexuality is concerned. As Scully and Bart themselves comment, 'Gynaecologists, our society's official experts on women, think of themselves as the woman's friend; with friends like that, who needs enemies?' [26]

The medical belief in the inferiority of women is perhaps most clearly reflected in the widespread assumption that most women are basically 'neurotic'. This reflects much earlier ideas about the inherent sensitivity and irritability of women - ideas which have been reformulated in the light of recent developments in psychological and psycho-analytic theory. More specifically, women are assumed to be much more likely than men to suffer from illnesses which have no physical basis - which are not 'real'. Indeed, most of the common gynaecological problems experienced by women are usually assumed by doctors to fall into this category. Women have frequently described the reluctance of doctors to take seriously what they regard as 'minor' ailments. These observations were underlined in a recent article by Jean Lennane and John Lennane who examined a variety of 'female problems' usually assumed to be psychogenic, and showed the existence of perfectly acceptable clinical evidence concerning the *physiological* origins of all these problems. [27] As the Lennanes point out,

> Dysmenorrhea, nausea of pregnancy, pain in labour and infantile behavioural disturbances are conditions commonly considered to be caused or aggravated by psychogenic factors. Although such scientific evidence as exists clearly implicates

> organic causes, acceptance of a psychogenic origin has led to an
> irrational and ineffective approach to their management.[28]

Each of these problems occurs in a large proportion of women - nausea, for example, is experienced by over three-quarters of pregnant women. Each has a clearly identifiable physical cause. In childbirth, for example, pain is produced by strong contractions against a physical obstruction. Finally, symptom relief can often be obtained relatively easily *if* the problem is taken seriously. But despite such evidence, the medical belief in psychogenesis as the root of 'female problems' remains extraordinarily persistent. Moreover, problems associated with female reproductive functioning are often attributed (at least implicitly) to the refusal of the woman in question to accept her 'femininity' at particular stages in her life. In the case of primary dysmenorrhea, for example, the adolescent girl is often said to be neurotic, with the implied cause being her incapacity to accept the onset of womanhood. A woman experiencing pain in labour is assumed to be causing it through her own inability to relax. Finally, a woman whose baby cries and exhibits signs of 'infantile colic' in the first weeks after birth, is held to be responsible for the problem through behaving 'unnaturally' in her new role as a mother. (For those who find this last point far-fetched, it should be noted that 'infantile colic' is contained in many orthodox psychiatric textbooks, as an example of *maternal* mental health problems!)[29]

Clearly then, much of the illness and disability experienced by women is physical in origin and should be accepted and treated as such. This is not, of course, to suggest that women (or indeed men) do not have problems which could in medical terms be classified as psychosomatic - clearly they do. However, such problems are consistently denigrated and dismissed. The refusal to accept them as 'real' is a consequence of a medical ideology which emphasises the physical and the quantifiable at the expense of the psychological and phenomenological, and which treats women as of fundamentally less importance than men.

Most doctors are, therefore, encouraged by their own early upbringing as well as by their medical education to assume a 'neurotic' basis for many of the problems presented by their women patients. This is strongly reinforced by the sales techniques of drug companies, which use women as the most common subjects to advertise tranquillisers and anti-depressants. One recent study revealed, for example, that women were fifteen times more likely than men to appear in advertisements for mood-changing drugs.[30] The 'harassed housewife' and the 'neglected older woman' are common stereotypes of this kind. As Gerry Stimson has pointed out, these advertisements encourage 'at a glance' diagnosis by busy GPs who can prescribe a tranquilliser or anti-depressant for a wide range of symptoms.[31] More importantly perhaps, these advertisements also help to convince the doctor that s/he can offer the patient some real relief - no doctor likes to appear helpless. At the same time, patients themselves have come to believe that pills can help them, so will expect to have them prescribed. As a consequence, there has been a dramatic rise in recent years in the number of women who are being given tranquillisers to help them cope with the problems they experience in their daily lives. In 1972, tranquillisers, hypnotics and anti-depressants accounted for about 17 per cent of general practitioners' pharmaceutical expenditure,[32] and twice as many women as men were receiving prescriptions of this kind.[33]

This increasing use of tranquillisers has been widely criticised, and forms part of a broader feminist critique of the psychiatric treatment of women.[34] All doctors, whether psychiatrists or GPs, are working within the framework of certain ideas about what a 'well person' is like. These models reflect broader social attitudes and values, involving in the case of a woman patient, expectations about female emotionality and passivity and, above all, about the essentially 'mothering nature' of most women. In psychotherapy, women are therefore likely to find themselves manoeuvred (either implicitly or explicitly) towards what their doctor thinks they ought, as 'healthy women', to be like. It is increasingly obvious, however, that in many instances the nature of the female role as it is socially constructed is itself conducive to 'mental illness'.[35] As a result, a therapeutic process which attempts to 'resocialise' women is likely to be of very limited value - a fact which is reflected in the large number of women who are re-admitted to psychiatric hospital after courses of treatment. This growing criticism, both of the indiscriminate use of drugs and also of other aspects of orthodox psychiatric practice, should not be taken to imply that 'mental illness' does not involve suffering. It clearly does, and the immediate relief of symptoms by chemical or other means may be extremely valuable. But it is important to recognise that this relief does not imply a removal of the basic causes of the problem. Indeed, a very important area of activity within the contemporary women's movement is the experimentation with alternative forms of therapy which can help women to understand the nature of their own situation in more realistic ways, while avoiding the false consciousness embodied in orthodox psychiatric practice.[36]

It should by now be apparent that the practice of medicine within the NHS remains basically sexist, reflecting the nature of the wider society of which it is a part. Moreover, it functions as a mechanism of social control - a fact which can be most effectively illustrated through looking at the medical control exercised over aspects of sexual reproduction.

Women, the NHS, and the control of reproduction

The dramatic changes which have taken place in the lives of women during the twentieth century have been closely related to the development of various aspects of reproductive technology. It is now technically possible for all women to control their own fertility, either through contraception or abortion or more permanently through sterilisation. Moreover, when a woman does have a baby, giving birth is now safer than it has been at any other time in history, and the baby is less likely to die in infancy or childhood. It is often believed that we have modern medicine to thank for these developments, but serious reservations need to be expressed about any such assumption. Although medical intervention played some part in improving infant and maternal mortality rates in the late nineteenth and early twentieth centuries, it is now generally accepted that improved standards of housing and nutrition probably played the most significant role. Similarly, doctors had very little to do with the development of new methods of birth control, while few were in the vanguard of attempts to bring contraceptive knowledge to women who needed it.

Nevertheless, the medical profession (and through it the state) has increasingly taken control of reproductive technology, and this has had at least two important consequences. The first is that decisions relating to research and practice in this field have often failed to take the interests and feelings of women seriously into account. Thus, doctors have tended to glorify the contraceptive pill - the most 'scientific' method of birth control - while paying almost no attention to the development of a male contraceptive. They have consistently played down legitimate anxieties about the pill and its possible side-effects, whilst emphasising its ease and reliability. Secondly, the medical domination of reproductive technology has meant that the technical potential for women to control their own fertility has not been realised. Doctors - and through them the state, the church, and even particular sectors of industry - are able to influence issues such as whether or not a woman becomes pregnant, whether she continues an existing pregnancy, and even the conditions under which she will give birth. For women, the development of reproductive technology has therefore been a contradictory process. Technically, it has given women more control over their own bodies, but at the same time it has increased the capacity of others to exercise control over women's lives. We can explore these contradictions in more detail through looking at developments in contraception, in abortion and in childbirth.

The NHS has always been characterised by an ambivalent attitude towards the provision of contraceptive advice. Immediately after the war, the emphasis was on 'building-up' the population, so that birth control clinics were not made an integral part of the new NHS. Despite a growing emphasis during the postwar period on 'family planning' and on improving the quality of family life, the bulk of contraceptive advice has, until recently, been provided by the Family Planning Association (FPA) and other privately-run clinics such as the Brook Advisory Centres. As a result, working-class women in particular have often had difficulty in obtaining the advice they needed. In fact, it was not until 1976 that Area Health Authorities completed the takeover of the FPA clinics and integrated them into the NHS. Moreover, 'family planning' was until very recently available only to those who were already married. Sexuality outside marriage was not to be encouraged, and it was not until the late 1960s that clinics were prepared to offer birth-control advice to unmarried women. GPs were formally incorporated into the 'family planning' network in 1975,[37] but many problems still remain. Clinics are often extremely crowded, there are not enough of them, they are often not open at times which are suitable for working mothers, and the vast majority do not provide child-care facilities. Moreover there is increasing evidence that because of the particularly low priority given to services for women these shortages and inadequacies are being exacerbated as expenditure on the NHS is reduced.[38]

Problems in obtaining adequate contraception are not, however, limited to difficulties in physical access to advice and supplies. The knowledge gap between doctor and patient has widened so that it has become increasingly difficult for women to make an informed choice between different methods of contraception. The new techniques of birth control are much more complex than those of the past - the IUD needs to be inserted by trained personnel, while the pill, a chemical rather than a mechanical means of contraception, has far-reaching effects on body chemistry. Most women do not know the advantages and disadvantages of existing types of contraceptive device, and doctors themselves are often inadequately trained for their expanding role in family planning. Most spend very little time in discussion with women and provide very little information about possible alternatives. Indeed, with the encouragement of the drug companies, most doctors are themselves inclined to favour the oral contraceptive, despite recent research findings that on safety grounds the pill should be used much less frequently than it is at present.[39] Moreover, doctors are also inclined to choose a method which *they* believe to be most appropriate for the woman concerned, so that 'feckless' women may for example be given the injectable contraceptive Depo-Provera, without being adequately informed about the dangers involved.

The postwar period has, therefore, seen an expansion in the availability of contraception, as well as the introduction of new techniques. For women, these developments have brought significant advantages, but, as we have seen, they have also brought new problems. Hence, while contraception is a prerequisite for women's liberation, it has all too often created new forms of oppression through the way in which it has been provided. Moreover, it is important to recognise that the extension of 'family planning' was not just in the interests of individual women, but was at the same time in the interests of capitalism in a broader sense.[40] Women became more easily available for paid work; the nuclear family was strengthened, and 'problem families' which might have to be maintained by the state at great expense could be induced not to have any more children by the availability of free contraceptive supplies.

Attempts to liberalise the abortion laws have faced even greater opposition than attempts to extend the provision of contraception. The fight for the legalisation of abortion really gained strength in Britain in the 1920s, and many of the early pioneers were feminists and socialists - women like Stella Browne, Dora Russell and Janet Chance. The Abortion Law Reform Association (ALRA) was founded in 1936, but made little headway in the inter-war period, and the church, the state, and the medical profession remained united against abortion. ALRA took up the campaign again after the war, working mainly through parliamentary channels, and during the 1960s the cause of abortion reform became part of the more general reform movement of the period. The greater aura of social confidence meant that abortion was no longer perceived as a threat to the existing social order, and the eventual reform of the abortion law in 1967 must be understood as part of a wider process of social change. As Greenwood and Young have commented,

> The 1960s could be characterised as an era of social reform. Legislation in the areas of juvenile delinquency, poverty, divorce, capital punishment, drug use, homosexuality and criminal justice came in for a radical re-appraisal (e.g. Murder/ Abolition of the Death Penalty Act 1965, Sexual Reform Act 1967, Criminal Justice Act 1967, Divorce Reform Act 1969, Misuse of Drugs Act 1971). The political base for such a catalogue of reforms was the dominant bloc within the Labour Party which viewed a mixed economy as desirable and argued for state intervention backed by expert guidance. Problems abounded in society but these could be eliminated by selective social engineering and piecemeal reform.[41]

These general pressures for reform were strengthened by a growing awareness that the existing abortion law was being widely disregarded - it has been estimated that anything between fifteen thousand and one hundred thousand illegal abortions were being performed each year. Moreover, it was evident that many of the women who were deemed to need abortions most - particularly those with low incomes and large families - were not obtaining them. 'Problem families' of this kind were defined as a matter of serious concern by the new breed of social workers, and hence some of the support for the 1967 act had considerable eugenic undertones. The majority of doctors (GPs in particular) supported the proposed reforms, although they continued to express the fear that the 'social clause' in the bill would take away their 'clinical freedom', by making decisions about abortion a non-medical issue. However, other sections of the medical profession joined with the Roman Catholic church in forming part of a very vociferous opposition.[42]

Despite this opposition, the bill was passed and the new Abortion Act came into force in 1967. As a result, it was no longer illegal for a registered medical practitioner to perform an abortion if two doctors were of the opinion that to continue the pregnancy would be a greater risk to the life or health of the woman or her existing children than an abortion would be, or if there was a substantial risk that the child would be physically or mentally handicapped. After generations of repressive legislation, the effect of the act was to produce a sudden increase in the number of abortions. By 1973, the number of legal abortions performed on British residents had risen to nearly one hundred and twenty thousand, approximately half of them taking place within the National Health Service.[43] The 1967 act was, therefore, a very important step in widening the availability of abortion, but access still remains seriously limited. The difficulties faced by women seeking abortions reflect both the low level of resources allocated to abortion within the NHS, and also the control exercised by individual doctors over access to abortion.

When the 1967 act was passed, no extra resources were provided for abortion facilities. The legislation, therefore, represented an acceptance of the idea of more freely available abortion, but without the financial backing to implement this commitment. As a result, a form of implicit rationing has developed, and a large number of abortions continue to be performed outside the NHS.[44] This general lack of resources is exacerbated by the policies of individual consultants who are able to determine how many abortions will be performed in a given area. These various pressures have resulted in a situation where in 1973, for example, 79 per cent of women seeking an abortion in Oxford were able to obtain one from the NHS, while the corresponding figure in Leeds was 25 per cent and in Walsall only 10 per cent.[45] Moreover, individual consultants are also able to choose what type of abortion to provide, and as a result abortions are rarely available on an out-patient basis, as many women would prefer.[46]

At an individual level, doctors also make judgements about specific women, and whether or not they should be allowed to have an abortion. These judgements are an important illustration of orthodox medical ideas about the nature of female sexuality and reproduction, and particularly about the moral aspects of these questions. Other things being equal, it is more difficult, for example, for a married woman than for an unmarried woman to obtain an abortion, since doctors assume that having babies is a normal part of being married. Increasingly they are prepared to abort women who already have large families, and whose incomes are not adequate to support more, but few doctors will be prepared to recommend termination for a 'normal' married woman on the grounds of what the doctor may regard as 'mere convenience'. Similarly, Sally Macintyre has suggested that when doctors deal with abortion requests from *single* women, they classify them into three categories - 'normal as-if-married'; the 'nice girl who has made a mistake'; and the 'bad girl'.[47] The 'normal as-if-married' woman is someone who is in a stable relationship and who plans to get married - she has simply 'anticipated' the wedding. It is assumed that she will continue with the pregnancy as a married woman should, and that the pregnancy does not present a problem. The good girls and the bad girls are differentiated on the basis of their past sexual history and their present attitude towards the pregnancy. Doctors will ask their patients about their relationship to the father of the child (is it 'serious'?), their use of contraception, and any previous sexual experience. How the woman relates to the doctor, and how she makes her request, are also very significant. Jean Aitken-Swan came to the following conclusions from her study of the attitudes of a sample of Scottish doctors:

> Not unnaturally, the doctor does not like it if he and the help he can give seem to be taken for granted. The wording of her request, the wrong manner, too demanding or over-confident, even her way of walking ('she comes prancing in') may antago-nise him and lessen her chances of referral. On the other hand, too passive an approach can be misinterpreted. 'You get the impression with a lot of these lassies that you could push them one way or the other and in a situation like this I tend to say keep the baby...' The doctors respond best to a concerned approach and tears are never amiss.[48]

It seems then, that a woman needs to treat her doctor very carefully if she is to obtain an abortion. Good girls may be successful, because they just 'made a mistake' and are duly contrite, but bad girls are likely to be denied an abortion because their doctor believes it would encourage them in their 'promiscuity'.

Increasingly, doctors have come to control not just the means to *prevent* pregnancy but also the conditions under which children will be born. Reproduction is assumed to be the most 'natural' of female functions but giving birth has now become a medical event. As Ann Oakley has put it - 'it has lost its character as a taken-for-granted aspect of adult life'. Certainly, medical intervention has played some part in improving rates of infant and maternal mortality, but its importance is often greatly over-estimated.[49] Indeed, it is now being argued that, although certain obstetric techniques have clearly added to the comfort and safety of mothers and babies, the 'medicalisation' of childbirth and of antenatal care is now going beyond what is necessary or desirable.[50]

The history of childbirth in Britain has been characterised by a struggle between the male-dominated medical profession and female midwives for the control of care during pregnancy and child-birth.[51] The battle was, of course, won by the doctors and this is reflected in the fact that, in 1976 only about 2.5 per cent of births took place at home, compared with 33 per cent in 1961.[52] Although midwives still deliver about seventy-five per cent of all British babies, most of these births take place in hospital, and the role of midwives has been strictly circumscribed by their incorporation into the medical structure. The medical domination of the processes of pregnancy and childbirth has produced growing disquiet. On the one hand, there is a growing demand for women to be able to choose to have their babies at home where there are no medical indications of the necessity for a hospital delivery. On the other hand, there is growing criticism of the unnecessary and demeaning rituals which are involved in hospital deliveries - the shaving of pubic hair for example, and the giving of enemas at the onset of labour. Women have also protested about the routine use of anaesthetics and analgesics throughout labour, as well as the inflexible routines of maternity wards which create problems for breast-feeding. In recent years, these criticisms have concentrated to a considerable extent on what has been called the 'active management of labour', and particularly on the increase in the number of induced births.[53] While this debate is clearly of immediate practical importance for many women, it also provides important insights into the nature of medical ideology and practice.

Induction is the use of artificial means to start labour before it would have occurred naturally. This is usually achieved by surgical means (rupturing the membranes) followed by the use of an oxytocin or prostaglandin drip. The possibility of inducing labour may be of great therapeutic value where it is not advisable for the pregnancy to continue (e.g. in the case of post-maturity in the child, or hypertensive disease in the mother). However, evidence indicates that induction is now used on a much wider scale than this - in some hospitals as routine procedure for most women. Thus the number of surgical inductions rose from 13.7 per cent of all hospital deliveries in England and Wales in 1963 to 40.7 per cent in 1974, and it seems evident that these techniques are now frequently employed when there are no clinical indications of the need for immediate delivery. The increased 'management' of labour is usually justified either in terms of the increased comfort and convenience it affords the mother, or as a means of rationalising the workload of maternity units. Evidence shows, however, that routine induction is very difficult to justify on the grounds of either maternal[54] or administrative convenience.[55] More seriously, there is increasing evidence that induction and its associated techniques may have serious iatrogenic effects. Induction appears to be correlated with increased rates of neo-natal jaundice, an increased number of caesarian sections, increased use of forceps, a higher incidence of pre-term babies, and an increase in the general problems arising from the use of anaesthetics and analgesics.[56] While these potential problems would be regarded as an acceptable risk if the induction were clinically necessary, they take on quite different connotations when induction is spreading to the general population of mothers.

How then are we to explain this dramatic rise in 'active management' and in induced births in particular? It seems that part of the explanation must lie in the social organisation of obstetrics and its relationship to the wider structure of the medical profession. Obstetrics, like other branches of medicine, has evolved a practice which is based on a mechanistic model of the patient. Moreover, male obstetricians were eventually able to take control of childbirth from the midwives largely through their development of surgical techniques. Modern obstetrics, therefore, developed primarily within the hospital setting, and the physical aspects of labour and childbirth have come to be emphasised to the detriment of the social and the psychological. Childbirth has increasingly been transformed into a clinical 'crisis' and hence is regarded as a legitimate and important area for medical intervention.

This interventionist tendency has been exacerbated by the relationship between obstetrics as a speciality and the broader medical hierarchy. Power and prestige in medicine are allocated to a very considerable extent on the basis of scientific and technological innovation and on the extent to which particular specialists are able to exercise their instrumental skills. The sudden explosion in obstetric technology in the past few years has both enhanced obstetrics as a speciality and promoted the careers of individual obstetricians. Doctors are obviously anxious to acquire the latest equipment, and they are encouraged to do so by the medical equipment manufacturers for whom obstetrics has become a considerable growth area. Once new equipment has been purchased, it will inevitably tend to influence the pattern of clinical practice, particularly since, for most doctors, the use of technical equipment represents an important element in their job satisfaction. As a result, there is a very real sense in which doctors can often be said to expropriate the satisfaction of childbirth from the woman concerned. Women play almost no part either in planning the maternity services provided by the NHS or in managing their own labours, and, as a result, attempts to cut costs, to increase bureaucratic efficiency, or to develop increasingly sophisticated medical technology, have too often been allowed to override the interests of mothers and babies.[57] Thus, those elements of modern obstetrics which are potentially liberating remain largely distorted by the social relations involved in their production, and once again the undoubted gains which the NHS represented for women must be weighed against its very considerable deficiencies.

Conclusion

Women are both the major consumers and major producers of health care in the NHS, and medicine is therefore profoundly important to women's lives. However, health care is produced within the context of a set of social and economic relationships which reflect the sexism of the wider society. Indeed, that sexism is often more overt and apparent in medicine than elsewhere, and it is for this reason that a critique of medicine has been such an important element in the broader feminist critique of capitalist society.[58] As a result, women are playing an increasingly important part in the growing struggle to transform the ideology and practice of modern medicine. Many women health workers are beginning to reject the stereotyping which determines their position within the medical division of labour and are beginning to fight against their oppression, whatever their position in the hierarchy. More importantly, women as consumers are attempting to challenge the medical hegemony at several different levels. They are using self-help in order to increase their own knowledge and thereby to demystify medicine.[59] They are challenging existing medical attitudes and practices in obstetrics and gynaecology, through emphasising the right of women to participate fully in decisions about what should happen to them, whether in the case of childbirth or abortion.[60] Finally, they are providing an increasing challenge to the overall priorities of the NHS, in which the oppression and exploitation of women in the wider society are so clearly reflected. Women are not, therefore, concerned merely to defend what already exists nor even to demand more of the same. Feminists are challenging the very nature of contemporary medical ideology and medical practice, and hence their role in the struggle to obtain better health care is of paramount importance.[61]

7: Medicine and Imperialism

Disease was always a major obstacle to European expansion - a fact which became increasingly apparent during the seventeenth and eighteenth centuries as commercial activities intensified in many parts of the world. Long sea voyages had always been dangerous to health, and the growing necessity for the large trading monopolies to post permanent staffs overseas meant exposing their employees to even greater hazards. The resulting high rates of mortality and morbidity among Europeans led not only to the attachment of medical personnel to the merchant marine, but also to the gradual development of rudimentary hospital facilities at overseas trading posts by commercial organisations such as the East India Company. In fact, prevailing physical conditions and the crudity of medical techniques made the legendary barber-surgeons a rather dubious asset, as Captain Alexander Hamilton observed in 1708: 'The Company has a pretty good hospital at Calcutta, where many go in to undergo the Penance of Physic, but few come out to give an account of its operation.'[1] Nevertheless, these inauspicious beginnings were to form the basis of the Indian Medical Service (inaugurated in 1764) which ultimately became a model for the organisation of medicine throughout the British colonial system.

The Indian Medical Service was run by the East India Company until 1885, but throughout the nineteenth century the British government became increasingly concerned about the heavy toll of death and disease entailed in policing its commercial interests overseas. As a result, a series of statistical studies was undertaken in 1835 to discover the extent of mortality and sickness among British troops stationed abroad. The findings of these investigations were published shortly before the appearance of Chadwick's 1842 report on domestic health conditions, and they confirmed the gravity of the hazards facing army recruits in various parts of the world. Annual mortality among troops serving in Jamaica was found to be 15 per cent[2] (ten times higher than among soldiers stationed in Britain), while in the Gold Coast the figure rose to 67 per cent[3] - earning the Gold Coast its reputation as 'the white man's grave'.[4]

It was only in the latter part of the nineteenth century that a number of important developments coalesced to form the basis for a more concerted medical policy towards colonial health problems. Following the Indian Mutiny of 1857, the British government had assumed direct control over Indian affairs. The state was therefore given a strategic role - at that time unprecedented - in the determination of all aspects of social life. This made possible a gradual rationalisation of health policies in accordance with the changing requirements of an imperialist economy. The vast territorial expansion which occurred during the last decades of the nineteenth century obviously demanded the further deployment of white manpower overseas, with all the attendant risks of death and disease. Government concern was sharpened by the desire to maintain a healthy military capacity in the event of inter-imperialist conflict. Moreover, large-scale white settlement was considered necessary to ensure the security and profitability of the newly annexed African territories. The success of these ventures therefore came to be increasingly dependent on effective medical provision.

At the same time, developments in fields such as bacteriology and parasitology appeared to hold great promise for the eventual eradication of disease, and doctors concerned with colonial health problems began to redefine their objectives in light of the possibilities offered by laboratory research. Though this emphasis ultimately produced as many problems as it solved, it brought a new wave of optimism to the medical enterprise, earning doctors a scientific status and growing public esteem. Joseph Chamberlain, who became Secretary of State for the Colonies in 1895, was particularly receptive to these new developments. While consistently recommending a more active colonial policy to increase the productive capacity of what he termed Britain's 'underdeveloped estates', Chamberlain was well aware that disease seriously limited the scope of such plans. He therefore actively supported the establishment of the London and

Liverpool Schools of Tropical Medicine in 1899, affirming that 'the study of tropical disease is a means of promoting Imperial policies'.[5] The extent to which this claim was borne out by events can be assessed only through an analysis of the effects of these new colonial medical policies. The next section therefore examines these questions in more detail, using the early colonial period in East Africa as a specific case study.

Colonial health policies in East Africa

Initially, both British and German colonies were served by a handful of doctors who were directly employed by their respective trading companies and were required simply to attend to the immediate health problems of the small white community. By the turn of the century, commercial interests had in each case transferred responsibility for health to the imperial state, but for many years the scale of official medical provision was derisory. This was in keeping with the limited objectives of colonial health policy, which were set out in a directive to British medical administrators in 1903.[6] The East African medical department was instructed firstly, to 'preserve the health' of the European community, secondly to keep the African and Asian labour force in reasonable working condition, and lastly, to prevent the spread of epidemics. However, in 1903 the combined western medical personnel of Kenya and Uganda consisted of 26 doctors, six nurses and seven dispensers, so that even these limited objectives would appear to have been highly ambitious.[7] Moreover, when the practical implications of this policy are examined more carefully, it becomes clear that its limitations ran deeper than mere lack of resources.

The first task - preserving the health of Europeans - was simplified by the fact that expatriates in the colonial territories tended to be concentrated in particular favoured geographical areas (the Kenyan Highlands, for example). They also congregated in the towns - the commercial, military and administrative centres. As a result it was possible to direct a large proportion of the available funds towards health personnel and hospitals in areas of white settlement. Since these facilities were designated on a racial basis, even Africans and

Asians living nearby could not take advantage of them.[8] More important, however, was the standard of living enjoyed by Europeans, with low density accommodation, safe water supplies, provisions for sewage disposal, and an adequate diet. The nature and conditions of their work, too, were normally compatible with good health. Hence, whites enjoyed a hygienic environment, as well as being assured the use of any new medical treatment that became available.

The objective of keeping the African and Asian labour force in good working condition was very much a subsidiary one. Where particular economic importance was attached to a certain form of production, or a particular category of worker, some attempt was made to provide rudimentary first-aid. The building of the Uganda railway for example, in the early years of the century, was seen as a vital link in the imperialist economic chain, and labourers were specially imported from India to construct it. This obviously put a premium on their health, and they were accordingly provided with basic medical facilities.[9] Indeed, in all the East African countries, a preference for Asian workers meant that they received more medical attention and had greater access to hospital beds per head than the African population.[10] The African labour force was employed largely on plantations and in the mines, where there was very little attempt to prevent accidents or disease, and medical provision was usually limited to first-aid. At this time, however, the vast majority of Africans were not required as wage labourers at all, but remained in the countryside, receiving almost no western medical attention. Thus the health problems of the African masses (apart from a few crucial workers) were officially neglected unless Europeans were themselves threatened by contagion.

An additional aim of early colonial health policy - to prevent the spread of epidemics - was clearly envisaged as a necessary adjunct to the two already described. As in nineteenth century Britain, there was an overwhelming fear of contagion among the ruling class and in the colonial context the response was physically to exclude the supposed agents of infection by legally enforcing a system of racial segregation. This was the premise of all colonial planning in India and it was readily transferred to East Africa.[11] It imposed a physical separation of the various racial groups which in fact concretised prevailing social relations in environmental and spatial terms.[12] Africans, Indians and Europeans were each restricted to their own respective 'quarters' in designated geographical districts. Besides minimising social contacts, this arrangement lent itself to the selective introduction of amenities for whites - amenities which were all the more economical for being confined to such limited areas.

> Urban segregation in Africa has always been accompanied by differences in the provision of material facilities, such as water and electricity, drainage and sewage, roads, social services and housing itself.[13]

Indeed, British expatriates sometimes explicitly referred to their quarter as 'the sanitary district'.[14] By contrast, there was a systematic denial of public health provisions to the non-white population in the expanding urban areas - a policy which naturally resulted in a high incidence of disease. Ironically, this unhealthiness was itself often used as conclusive evidence of 'the insanitary habits of Asiatics and Africans'.[15] Thus for Europeans, concepts such as 'sanitary' and 'insanitary' had less to do with the quality of material life than with distinguishing the supposed moral superiority of the coloniser from the 'constitutional depravity' of the native.[16] So long as Africans and Asians could be berated for lacking the capacity for sanitary behaviour, the occupying power could consider itself absolved of responsibility for environmental health measures.

The practical implications of this self-fulfilling prophecy can be seen in British policy towards the recurring epidemics of plague which threatened Nairobi between 1902 and 1913. Plague, previously unknown in Kenya, is thought to have been imported together with consignments for the Uganda railway.[17] The disease became progressively more widespread and was soon a major killer among the Afro-Asian population. However, instead of acting to reduce the appalling overcrowding which perpetuated the infection, the Medical Department simply imposed a *cordon sanitaire* round the African and Indian communities to safeguard the health of the European quarter.[18] A government report later appeared, documenting the lamentable sanitary conditions in towns such as Nairobi and urging that racial segregation be further strengthened in response.[19]

Most of the diseases which were becoming endemic in east Africa were of little consequence to Europeans, because they were usually contracted directly through exposure to bad living conditions. There were, however, two important exceptions - malaria and sleeping sickness. Although it was deteriorating socio-economic and environmental conditions which encouraged the spread of these diseases among the population at large, their insect vectors showed little racial discrimination, and malaria, in particular, was regarded as the principal menace to British life and health in the colonial empire. Because these two diseases impinged so directly on metropolitan interests, attempts to control them provided the main focus for colonial medical activity and absorbed a large proportion of limited health resources in the region. This overriding concern with malaria and sleeping sickness was also reflected at the international level among the various precursors of the World Health Organisation - most notably the Office International d'Hygiène Publique and the Health Section of the League of Nations.[20]

Given the prevailing ideology of western medical science, it is not surprising that solutions to the health problems that appeared to threaten whites and 'natives' alike should have been sought in laboratory research and in the discovery of specific pathogenic microorganisms. In the case of both malaria and sleeping sickness, research was increasingly concentrated on the identification of the infecting parasite and on the description of the biological life cycle of the disease. In 1897, Ronald Ross finally succeeded in establishing that malaria was carried by the anopheles mosquito, and by 1903, Castellani and Bruce had uncovered the role of the tsetse fly in transmitting sleeping sickness. These findings made it possible to interrupt the transmission of the disease in question by destroying the vector. Further research therefore centred both on the chemical means by which this might be achieved, and also on the development of appropriate drug therapy. This latter strategy not only satisfied the medical predilection for biological intervention at the level of the individual, but also seemed appropriate to meet the immediate health needs of the small white population and of other colonial personnel. The focus on the welfare of the white community and the defence of its economic interests always militated against policies for mass prevention. Individual drug therapy, limited as it was, appeared to be both a necessary and effective line of defence in the absence of control of the disease vectors themselves.

Despite this dominant biochemical reductionism in medicine, there was nevertheless, a growing appreciation that some degree of intervention in the physical environment was required to safeguard even European health. In the case of malaria, for example, stagnant water was the favoured breeding place of the anopheles mosquito and it was necessary either to introduce drainage systems or to treat the water itself. With the tsetse fly, which thrived in areas of dense vegetation, bush clearance was regarded as the most appropriate means of physical control. In both cases, however, environmental responses were applied in a patchy and piecemeal way amidst much vacillation and discord. Interestingly, policy disagreements between the Colonial Office and local colonial administrations were often a reflection of conflicts between the 'scientific' ideology of laboratory medicine which predominated at the British schools of tropical medicine and the more practical concerns of colonial doctors over-whelmed by the magnitude of the public health problems confronting them. It is worth noting that while Ross, Castellani and Bruce all made their initial discoveries as medical workers in the colonies, subsequent research was placed firmly in the hands of more prestigious white-coated scientists, methodologically and physically detached in London. Researchers of this kind were able to obtain both financial resources and a considerable degree of influence over the direction of colonial medical policy while Ross, by contrast, was unable to secure funds even for public health campaigns made possible through his own research.[21] His own criticism of the prevailing scientism in malaria research was echoed by a medical officer of health in east Africa who attacked expenditure on what he called 'abstruse scientific research' when funds were not being released for the basic preventive work indicated by existing knowledge.[22] In reality, most colonial doctors were of course as deeply imbued with the ideology of laboratory medicine as their adversaries, but they were also exposed to some of its more glaring contradictions. As a result, they could, at the very least, appreciate the false economies involved in refining the clinical tools which might become available to a tiny minority of the population while the diseases which affected the masses grew increasingly out of control.

By the 1930s doctors and administrators were forced to acknow-ledge that attempts to control the spread of specific infections had been far from successful. Even the preventive policies adopted against malaria and sleeping sickness seemed doomed to failure in the absence of more fundamental public health provisions. Cam-paigns of this kind against individual diseases came increasingly to be seen as wasteful and ineffective, while more critical observers were coming to realise that the existing pattern of widespread ill health could only be altered by substantial economic development.[23] As Dr J.L. Gilks, director of the Kenya medical department asserted in 1929,

> Malaria is now being generally recognised as a 'social' disease which is dependent for its continuance in areas where it is endemic, on, among other factors, a low standard of living among the bulk of the population.[24]

Between 1928 and 1938 numerous reports elucidated the relationship between poverty and ill health in Africa, and it was increasingly accepted that adequate nutrition was essential to health. The implications of this new found social awareness were discussed at some length and there were countless suggestions about raising the level of health through improved diet, housing and sanitation. However, all such strategies were of course to take place within the existing framework of social relations - the structural constraints of colonialism were not challenged. In any case, despite this liberal rhetoric, the depression and the war which followed ensured that while a few specific diseases were still dealt with on a pragmatic, piecemeal basis, most of the 'diseases of poverty' continued to be neglected. Hence concern with the social determinants of ill health was to be short lived.

There was one element of colonial medical policy - dating from the early 1920s - which did claim to be bringing about important economic and social changes in the lives of the East African population. This was the chief measure employed throughout the colonial period to deal with sleeping sickness. It entailed the forcible uprooting of rural Africans thought to be in danger of tsetse infestation, and their resettlement under close supervision in concentrations.[25] While not providing a positive solution to the problem of sleeping sickness, this policy might have been expected to encourage a more holistic and socially-based interpretation of the disease. In practice, however, this massive intervention in the social and physical organisation of peasant life had singularly little impact on the narrowly conceived theory of the biological (as opposed to environmental) causation of the disease. Indeed, as Ford has observed,

> compulsory submission to medical examination and treatment, confinement of domicile to circumscribed areas, limitation of movement and the more or less compulsory turnouts of labour were regarded not as biological events but as conveniences to facilitate the work of the government technical services.[26]

Thus the supposed health benefits of the concentrations were very largely subordinated to a number of quite separate colonial objectives and by the 1940s the resettlements had become an important reservoir of migrant labour. Nevertheless, health considerations remained the principal justification for the dislocations and hardships which Africans had to endure. Although concentrations were increasingly planned explicitly to meet the needs of foreign capital for both labour and cheap food, the schemes continued to be administered by the director of medical services.[27]

The concentration policy originally associated with sleeping sickness was only one example of the way in which British colonialism established social and economic hegemony over the East African populations. In some senses it was atypical precisely because it sought to break up peasant communities, detaching them from their subsistence economy. As Brett comments,

> Colonial administration constantly operated within an unresolvable contradiction - on the one hand the demands of

the cash economy required that Africans be drawn out of their old routines and systems of social organisation; on the other, they could only be effectively kept in order provided traditional habits of deference were maintained. Change was both essential and dangerous.[28]

In the aftermath of the first world war these issues assumed critical importance in east Africa. Not only was the social and physical decline induced by colonialism becoming more apparent, but new forms of African resistance were beginning to emerge. The founding of the Young Kikuyu Association in Kenya in 1921 was soon followed in 1922 by the formation of the Tanganyika Territory African Civil Service Association.[29] Effective territorial control by British personnel was, however, out of the question since neither the human nor financial resources existed to implement it. A system of Indirect Rule was therefore introduced in 1926, vesting nominal authority in recognised local chiefs in the hope that this would effectively diffuse political discontent and strengthen traditional means of social control. The chiefs were accorded numerous privileges to encourage their co-operation, although in reality their close subordination to government requirements through the district commissioners gave them little room for manoeuvre.[30]

The establishment of these so-called native authorities meant that a basic administrative network now existed for implementing medical policy on a territorial scale - a situation which suited the changing priorities of colonial medicine. In the first place, it was increasingly accepted that attempts to control malaria and sleeping sickness would have little chance of success unless they were expanded into mass campaigns. Secondly, the new administrative network enabled the government to gain more direct control over production in a territory where so much agriculture was in the hands of independent peasant farmers. Thus, at the instigation of the central administration, native authorities issued numerous orders and rules - some relating to the control of animal and human disease - in order to regulate the labour process and increase productivity.[31] At the same time, other health directives were incorporated into law-and-order regulations. Cast in this authoritarian mould and narrowly concerned with limiting the spread of individual diseases, such policies appeared largely repressive to the Africans involved,[32] and it is certainly arguable whether they could be regarded as promoting public health at all. Highly fragmented approaches of this kind were, in reality, designed primarily as elements in the strategy to boost export production and effectively ignored basic needs such as sanitation and uncontaminated water. Hence they did very little indeed to improve health, contributing rather to the erosion of local food production and to increasing overcrowding in the rural villages.

British colonial medical departments were all formally divided into curative and preventive branches but the latter were always residual. For economic and ideological reasons the interests of public health services were always firmly subordinated to those of clinical medicine, as McDonald has noted with reference to India:

> Subordination is, unfortunately, the correct term, for there grew up a service custom . . . whereby there was allotted to officers on the clinical side, after careers as Civil Surgeons, positions such as Inspectors-General or Surgeons-General, which were much in advance of anything that could be achieved by the service exponents of public health. The former even came to be known as Administrative Officers, yet it was the latter who in practice possessed the only medical qualification. In 1912 the die was finally cast and from then onwards it was inevitable that work in the preventive field would continue to suffer from the poor prospects, lack of executive authority and generally poor conditions of recruitment and service, all of which were the subject of a special memorandum in 1913, and none of which has been tacked effectively to date.[33]

These observations (made in 1950) illustrate the contempt shown within the medical profession for those of their number interested in 'unheroic' issues such as water and food supplies. The Colonial Office, by and large, concurred with this assessment of medical priorities, and colonial health policies continued to be designed accordingly.

Throughout the period of British rule, it was the official view that the extension of medical services in any area should be conditioned by the capacity of the local population to foot the bill.[34]

Medical policy was thus used to reinforce market inequalities rather than to redress them. Moreover, it was recognised that Africans in the most advanced economic sectors were also the most politically volatile and the rural dispensary system set up under the native authorities was officially regarded as an important concession to the growing demands of the agricultural proletariat.[35] In fact, the dispensaries were acknowledged to be of negligible benefit to health:

> It was realised from the start that such a service could offer little of real value and could do scarcely more than pander to the popular desire for a quick and effortless cure. Economically and scientifically it could hardly justify its cost, and accordingly no attempt at elaborate training was made, and the drugs provided consisted of the minimum of harmless simples.[36]

Hence the real significance of the African dispensary system was ideological rather than material.[37] It was, after all, the only tangible benefit from taxation and for this reason alone, the British attempted to uphold the principle of free dispensary care even through the stringency of the depression.[38] Moreover, the personal treatment of sickness - however rudimentary - represented an antidote to the repressive strictures of public health (and other) regulations. But this did not mean that European curative medicine was universally popular or its claims uncritically received. Indeed the introduction of western medicine has met a strong degree of resistance in most underdeveloped countries, as is evident from the continued demand for indigenous medical care.[39]

In any assessment of colonial medicine, it is necessary to consider not just the role of the colonial administration itself, but also that of another feature of colonial penetration - the Christian mission. Missions are important in that their presence in East Africa both pre-dates colonial rule and has successfully outlived it. Indeed more than half of the church hospitals in modern Tanzania were founded *after* 1950.[40] Initially medical missionaries were concerned only with the health of their fellow-evangelists, but the proselytising potential of the 'signs and wonders' used to reinforce the gospel soon became clear - particularly their value in transcending language barriers. The 'kindly influence of medical work' was, as one missionary noted in 1899, considered most effective in preparing the ground for imperialist domination.

> The usefulness of the medical arm of the missionary service is indisputable. It breaks down opposition, dissipates prejudice, and wins its way to the hearts and homes of the high and low, the rich and poor. It receives the highest official recognition, and thus facilitates the employment of all other agencies. The foreign doctor is *persona grata* even in palaces and halls of state.[41]

In East Africa, as elsewhere, missions generally served rural areas remote from direct government control and, until the establishment of the native authority system in 1926, they were the sole purveyors of western medicine to the local population. Through the favourable contacts they developed with African communities their medical work 'was acknowledged to be most helpful to the government in their endeavour of opening up tropical Africa'.[42] Indeed, even after the new dispensaries began to appear, the continuing advantages offered by European medical missions gained official recognition in the form of government subsidies. In return, the colonial authorities saw the limited scope of existing facilities somewhat expanded, and far more cheaply than was possible by direct means. But at least as important as the provision of medical care itself was the fact that missions and state alike had an interest in undermining indigenous culture and institutions, while socialising Africans into European modes of behaviour. In pursuing that goal, the missionaries found that the formal conversion of large numbers to Christianity was insufficient in itself to transform existing patterns of life, and hence it was argued that,

> the missionary doctor must abandon his evangelistic itinerations, stay in his hospital and train African nurses and medical assistants to replace the sorcerer in village life. And equally, if the children of monogamous marriages were to survive in sufficient numbers to compensate for the renunciation of polygamy, then maternity work, child welfare and infant dietetics must all come within the missionary's sphere.[43]

Elementary medical training together with maternity and child health therefore became major concerns of the missions throughout the colonial period. Their increasing role in medical training reflected the government's view that both the need for low-level African medical staff as well as the demands of Africans themselves for skilled employment could be met most economically by modest state support for the existing work of the missions.[44] With regard to maternal and child health the missions were especially zealous. Their hospitals tended to favour female patients, making ample provision for childbirth so as to deliver as many new candidates as possible for baptism.[45] Given the existing labour shortages, high infant mortality rates were of particular concern and small grants-in-aid were therefore made to medical missions to encourage their work in this field.[46] The missions have always been overwhelmingly concerned with curative, hospital-based medicine. As Schulpen points out, it is only the concept of healing that carries religious potency, so the notion of prevention has always been distinctly unappealing to missionaries.[47] Besides, the social or community approach implicit in public health activities was unacceptable to missions because it allowed little opportunity for direct personal contact. Only leprosy work combined both aims to the satisfaction of the churches and - along with maternal and child health - this was one of the few areas of prevention in which they engaged.[48]

Although the colonial authorities saw medical missions as fulfilling a valuable role, there were also certain conflicts of interest between them. While the government upheld the professional status of doctors by demanding adherence to metropolitan criteria of service, medical missions often used less qualified staff. Apart from protecting the standing of the medical profession, the colonial authorities also seem to have been concerned about their own authority over the churches and, through them, their African converts. This antagonism was well expressed in the Annual Medical Report for Kenya in 1921.

> A government hospital is a tangible sign of government activities which is understood by every native, but it is doubtful whether a subsidised mission hospital is in any way connected in the minds of the majority of the patients as being anything

more than a token of benevolence of the missionaries who therefore reap the credit and resulting influence. It is a fact which cannot be gainsaid, that the provision of medical attendance, even of the crudest and most primitive description, is the best form of advertisement for any form of activity among the natives.[49]

Despite such conflicts, however, the missions and the colonial state succeeded in working together to reinforce their more fundamental common interests, and in so doing, laid the foundations for the expansion of western medical practice which was to occur in the era of political independence.

To conclude this analysis of medical provision under colonialism, it is necessary to consider briefly the question of British economic assistance under the Colonial Development and Welfare Acts. This assistance is often regarded as the major contribution of the British to the well-being of their colonised populations. It must, however, be seen primarily in the context of economic and political developments within Britain itself during the interwar years, when chronic unemployment and the possibility of serious social upheaval were regarded by the government as matters of major concern. One response to this situation was to further exploit the economic potential of the empire by increasing the supply of raw materials to British manufacturers while, at the same time, expanding colonial demand for British manufactured goods. In order to effect this, new investment was required to stimulate production within the Empire itself and this was the intention behind the Colonial Development Act of 1929. As Lord Passfield (Sidney Webb), then Secretary of State for the Colonies, publicly declared, 'the principle motive for the introduction of this measure is connected with the lamentable condition of employment in this country, and this is an attempt to stimulate the British export trade . . . '[50]

Financial support was therefore given to schemes which would provide immediate and substantial orders for British goods and materials. In addition, some funds were also made available for health-related projects because of the 'consequent improvement . . . in the productive capacity of the populations affected, resulting in increased purchasing power'.[51] The aims of the legislation seem, then, to have been rather less than altruistic. Moreover, the material significance of colonial assistance must be gauged in relation to the severe economic cutbacks which occurred in the colonies during the 1930s and the war which followed. Medical expenditure in Tanganyika, for instance, was reduced by approximately one-third between 1930 and 1936 (from £275,000 to £186,000).[52] Hence the Colonial Development Act was of dubious benefit in promoting the health of local populations. A combination of expediency, conceptual weakness and financial stringency prevented any notable practical achievements and - most importantly - many of the failings of the initial act were to be perpetuated throughout the remaining colonial period and beyond.

In the immediate postwar years of economic expansion and political realignment, the old doctrine of colonial self-sufficiency was relaxed in favour of a policy of 'assisted development'. Indeed, bilateral aid such as that provided through successive Colonial Development and Welfare Acts during the 1940s and 1950s can be seen as a counterpart to the growth of state intervention in the metropolitan economies. Thus British aid was given primarily for infrastructural projects designed to improve export production and meet the opportunities offered by the commodity boom. There were, in addition, strong political pressures on the British government to remedy its long neglect of medical and other social services. As a result, the welfare component of British colonial aid was increased, so that in Tanganyika, for example, the contribution of aid to the local medical budget rose from three per cent in 1947 to fourteen per cent in 1950.[53] The benefits, however, were negligible. For the vast majority of Africans, the rural dispensaries remained the only source of medical attention. These were grossly inadequate since they were still locally funded by impoverished native authorities, while central government revenues were allocated to hospitals and other curative facilities in the urban areas.

Colonial assistance therefore merely strengthened the existing bias in health policies. But this did not happen by default. Rather, it was the outcome of three official policy documents which appeared between 1947 and 1956, all stressing the appalling extent of health needs in the rural areas while simultaneously demanding the extension of hospital medicine which would do little to meet those needs.[54] Various attempts were made to resolve this paradox, particularly by arguing that Africans themselves favoured curative services. Thus Dr E. Pridie, chief medical advisor to the Colonial Office and author of one of the reports, suggested that,

> Although preventive and social medicine have more lasting beneficial effects it is essential to have a well-balanced medical service, giving due importance to curative medicine, as curative medicine is demanded by the people and its popularity makes preventive medicine acceptable to them.[55]

In the context of growing African resistance to colonial domination, curative medicine was certainly not the foremost popular demand but it was one of the most politically acceptable so far as the British were concerned. The repeated assertion that 'curative medicine is what people understand and what they want'[56] was thus taken as a convenient rationale for current policy rather than a relic of past policies which needed to be changed.

Neo-colonialism: the consolidation of western medical practice

During the postwar period, there has been a growing assumption by third-world governments that western scientific medicine provides the most appropriate means of coping with human disease. Most underdeveloped countries have - to a greater or lesser extent - reproduced a pattern of medical provision which is hospital-centred, highly technological and dispensed on an individual curative basis. In reality, however, there are a number of reasons why western medicine is inadequate to deal with the problems created by the underdevelopment of health. Bryant, for example, has remarked on the impotence of western techniques in combatting the childhood diseases which account for approximately half of all deaths in the third world,

> The great weapons of modern medicine are aimed at the patho-physiology of disease and its susceptibility to pharmaceutical,

immunological, or surgical attack. Health services are designed
to deliver these weapons mainly through the hands of doctors.
The dismal fact is that the great killers of children - diarrhoea,
pneumonia, malnutrition - are beyond the reach of these
weapons.[57]

There are, of course, many health problems for which western
medicine can offer either effective therapy or valuable symptomatic
relief. But it is important to appreciate that in the absence of the
fundamental social and environmental constituents of health, a predominantly curative policy has serious limitations. Thus, while the
application of western medical treatment under third world conditions may have extremely beneficial short-term consequences for the
individual patient, it cannot reduce the high incidence of disease,
nor raise the general level of health. Malcolm Segall has illustrated
this point very well.

For example, a man has hookworm anaemia (common in
Tanzania). He has been ill for years; eventually he has to stop
work altogether. He is admitted to hospital. He needs
laboratory tests, skilled medical and nursing attention, drug
treatment and a blood transfusion. After a time he improves,
and he eventually goes back to work. At home, he catches
hookworm again; the whole process is repeated. If his village
had used pit latrines none of this would have happened.[58]

It is important to realise, therefore, that while those aspects of
curative medicine which have been successful in the metropolitan
countries have been predicated on the prior implementation of basic
public health measures, in the third world, curative medicine has
become a *substitute* for public health and as a result is inevitably
much less effective. Moreover, the vast majority of people living in
underdeveloped countries are currently denied access even to those
curative services which would be of value to them. This arises because
the priority given to curative medicine, focussed on hospital facilities, has perpetuated the gross maldistribution of resources characteristic of the colonial period.

In Tanzania, barely seven per cent of the population live in the
urban areas where about half of all hospital beds and 60 per cent of

all doctors are to be found. Similarly, it has been estimated that in Ghana no more than twenty per cent of the population has reasonable access to health services. Nigeria has a rural population constituting about eighty per cent of the total, but despite the country's more favourable economic position only ten per cent of these people are thought to be served by medical facilities. In India, which has experienced a greater degree of economic development than most third world countries, the rural areas contain some eighty per cent of the population but estimates indicate that less than one-third of the country's doctors are located there.[59] Similar disparities can be found throughout the third world, though the distribution of medical services in some Latin American countries appears slightly more favourable. These countries, however, have a much larger proportion of urban dwellers than most African or Asian states, as well as a more highly developed private medical sector, and as a result statistics tend to obscure new sources of inequality within the urban areas themselves.[60]

Crude as these indices are, it is clear that the extreme maldistribution of services remains a striking feature of medical care systems in the third world. To some extent, of course, this can be explained as a straightforward material inheritance from the past. But it is the continuing links of dependence within the modern world economy which are crucial in perpetuating and even reinforcing earlier inequalities. These links have ensured that a large part of the economic surplus continues to be syphoned off, depleting the resources available to underdeveloped countries for building up their social infrastructure. However, it is not lack of resources alone which accounts for inadequate medical provision. Economic incorporation into the world system has also helped to create social structures within the periphery which are responsive to the dynamics of metropolitan capitalism. In particular, it is the role characteristically taken by the state and by the dominant class in third world countries which determines the nature of health policies.

Two points are evident in relation to the state in most underdeveloped countries. First, in comparison with advanced capitalist countries, the directly economic functions of the third world state have tended to predominate over intervention in the sphere of social reproduction. Secondly, there is often a high level of military and defence expenditure, with a tendency for repression rather than the generation of 'consensus' to be the basis of social order.[61] Thus, third world governments do not, as yet, use welfare measures on any significant scale either as a means of physically reproducing labour power or in order to maintain their own legitimacy - the only real exception being the provision of welfare services for the small pool of skilled urban labour. So far as health services are concerned, the state sector generally functions merely as an adjunct to the commercial sector, rather than representing the major source of medical care.

The emergent bourgeoisie in most underdeveloped countries has been characterised not so much by its economic power as by its privileged position as intermediary in the process of capital accumulation. Fanon's graphic description of this underdeveloped ruling class is still widely applicable.

> The university and merchant classes which make up the most enlightened section of the new state are in fact characterised by the smallness of their number and their being concentrated in the capital, and the type of activities in which they are engaged: business, agriculture and the liberal professions. Neither financiers nor industrial magnates are to be found within this national middle class. The national bourgeoisie of underdeveloped countries is not engaged in production, nor building, nor labour; it is completely canalised into activities of the intermediary type. Its innermost vocation seems to be to keep in the running and to be part of the racket. The psychology of the national bourgeoisie is that of the businessman, not that of a captain of industry; and it is only too true that the greed of the settlers and the system of embargoes set up by colonialism has hardly left them any other choice.[62]

Though lacking any extensive economic base, the bourgeoisie of underdeveloped countries shares with the metropolitan class which it emulates, a 'spirit of indulgence', and this is particularly significant in any attempt to understand third world medical policies. That is to say, there is an important sense in which western scientific medicine - with its associated apparatus - represents yet another item of luxury consumption for the few who can afford it, and in many third world countries the present mode of its organisation has allowed it to become very little else. Such a pattern of medical care does, of course, have advantages for a class which has the personal resources to pay for it, and which is protected from the life-threatening environmental conditions to which the bulk of the population is exposed. Thus the exclusive residential areas formerly occupied by the colonialists have now been taken over by the national bourgeoisie and, with them, the mentality of the *cordon sanitaire*. As the chief immediate beneficiary of scientific medicine, this dominant class has, therefore, worked to consolidate the development of western medical practice in the third world. One of the most important mechanisms for achieving this has been provided by a system of medical education whose structure and ideology are directly derived from the colonial era.

The rudiments of the western system of medical education were introduced into Africa very gradually during the colonial period, partly to offset shortages of white medical personnel and partly to create a subordinate but well trained medical labour force. Caste-like racial distinctions were enforced so that, in East Africa, for example, Europeans were 'doctors', Asians were 'sub-assistant surgeons' and Africans 'assistant medical officers' - yet towards the end of colonial rule, all received a similar training.[63] In Uganda in 1947 a black doctor was paid only a quarter of the salary of a white doctor, and half the salary of a white nurse.[64] However, the introduction of the National Health Service so improved conditions for doctors in Britain, that it became increasingly difficult for the colonial service to recruit them[65] and there was therefore a growing tendency for local medical training within the British empire to be granted official recognition (although the speed at which this occurred should not be overestimated). For example, by the time Tanganyika won political independence in 1961, only 12 out of a total of 403 doctors in the country were of local origin.[66]

Despite their subordination within the colonial system, African and Asian doctors tended on the whole to take a narrow view of the anti-colonial struggle, identifying themselves as professionals who would inherit their rightful role from the departing colonialists. As a result, even in the post-colonial period, colonial medical associations continued to be affiliated to the British Medical Association in

London. This emulation of metropolitan 'standards' helped to ensure reciprocal recognition of medical qualifications and hence the creation of an international market for doctors. Continued dependence of this kind has, of course, involved the adoption of medical curricula drawn from metropolitan medical schools[67] - a tendency which has often been defended on the grounds that it provides a necessary basis for the establishment of western medical systems in third world countries. However, it is becoming increasingly evident that these western skills and values learned by most doctors are, in reality, a major constraint on the development of effective health services in the third world.

In most underdeveloped countries, the acquisition of officially recognised medical skills takes place only within the context of the western medical model. There is therefore a strong emphasis on the study of basic science and on diagnostic and curative techniques within a clinical setting. Although a few countries are now attempting to rectify the neglect of social and preventive medicine, the academic framework within which these subjects are presented militates strongly against their potential effectiveness, and students are quick to resist what they see as attempts 'to make doctors into public health inspectors'. This rigid adherence of third world students to the western medical model is usually accompanied by a largely negative view of indigenous health systems - an attitude which is strongly reinforced by medical education which either gives no account at all of traditional medicine or actively seeks to discredit it.

Naturally, close adherence to the medical curricula used in Britain, France or the USA prepares students for patterns of illness and treatment which are often irrelevant to the health problems of underdevelopment. Moreover, the socio-economic determinants of these specifically third world problems are usually ignored. In so far as colonial medical training has taken any account at all of the conditions of local life, students have usually been expected to study their own 'customs and taboos' as interpreted by a largely racist anthropological tradition.[68] Consequently both poverty and ill health have tended to be explained in cultural terms, and the causal relationship between them obscured. Even in the postwar period, scientific legitimacy has continued to be granted to theories claiming that 'the native' is by definition pathological. In 1954, for instance, Dr James Carothers produced a report for UNESCO which likened the personality of the normal African to that of a 'lobotomized European'. 'The African makes very little use of his frontal lobes. All the peculiarities of African psychology can be put down to frontal laziness'.[69] Fanon described how in his own experience such theories found their way into the university syllabus.

> It is thus that Algerian doctors who are the graduates of the faculty of Algiers are obliged to hear and learn that the Algerian is a born criminal. Moreover, I remember certain among us who in all sincerity upheld and developed these theories that they had learned. They even added, 'It's a hard pill to swallow, but it's been scientifically established'.[70]

Extreme as such theories may appear, they do illustrate one aspect of the process by which, as bearers of western science and rationality, aspiring medical students of the colonial era have become the bourgeois doctors of the neo-colonial state.

A fundamental component in the process of western medical socialisation has been its reproduction of a division of labour based on class and sex. In the case of Tanzania, for example, there was a marked crystallisation of the medical hierarchy in the years immediately preceding independence.

> This hierarchy was based on pay and status differences between diagnosis and treatment workers, nursing and caring workers, and the unskilled category of cleaners, cooks and other hospital workers, and mimicked exactly the hierarchical ladder found in the British medical services.[71]

Little has, as yet, been written on the reproduction of sexual divisions within waged employment in the third world, but Alanagh Raikes has shown how a deliberate policy was in operation in Tanganyika during the 1950s which totally recast the sex ratios within nursing. Whereas in 1950 only 20 per cent of nursing graduates were women, ten years later, over three times as many women as men were being trained.[72] Although this has given women access to skills and employment previously denied to them, it has simultaneously built sex role stereotyping and differentials into the structure of the labour force. Indeed in many third world countries today, nursing is one of the few skilled occupations considered to be socially acceptable for women. Ironically, of course, countries in which the seclusion of women is most extreme sometimes provide wider opportunities for female health workers at all levels, since 'decency' is thought to necessitate this.[73]

However, it is the reproduction of class relations which is most evident in the social organisation of the medical labour force in underdeveloped countries. In the post-war period the division of labour in the health sector has been characterised by a rigid adherence to the hierarchies and distinctions created under colonial rule, with indigenous doctors concerned to maintain their own superiority over other health workers. Moreover, the new ruling elites - of which they are a part - have clearly attached great importance to being treated by 'real' doctors, and hence lend every encouragement to the medical profession in perpetuating the existing relations of production in health care. Those selected as medical students are invariably members of the urban elite. Already cut off economically, socially and culturally from the mass of the local population, students then undergo a process of western medical socialisation. This turns out doctors with what one writer has described as the 'trained incapacity for rural practice which is itself the product of the British system of medical training within large centralised hospitals'.[74] Thus, doctors are encouraged to develop intellectual preoccupations in specialised clinical fields. In India, for example, where opportunities for specialisation have expanded rapidly since the 1950s, there are now about one-third as many annual enrolments in post-graduate medicine as in undergraduate training.[75] Moves towards specialisation, however, are probably most advanced in Latin America, where only a minority of doctors work in general practice.[76] While these developments are obviously antithetical to the objective health needs of third world populations, they are strongly defended by doctors, who emphasise the overriding importance of 'intellectual stimulation' and 'professional satisfaction'. Indeed, notions of this kind are now so uncritically accepted that a recent World Bank report on medicine in the third world even alluded to 'the natural human urge to do clinical work'.[77]

It is clear, then, that the professional demands of doctors can generally be satisfied only in the main urban areas. However, state medical services even in the towns are often of a residual nature. In most cases only a minority of doctors are wholly employed by the state and remuneration is low in comparison with the rewards of commercial practice. On the other hand, although most third world countries have a lucrative private sector at the very centre of their health system, it is usually very small in relation to the number of doctors. Hence for many doctors, the only opportunity for achieving what they have come to regard as a satisfactory income and professional status lies outside their own country altogether.

> The very expensive training costs of medical doctors (which are so high because doctors are trained in keeping with private sector traditions) mean that the level of effective economic demand of most of the population cannot possibly meet the expectations and requirements of the medical graduates. Therefore, there is an 'overflow' of these graduates to those parts of the world where demand is greater than the current supply of doctors, most notably North America.[78]

Thus, control over medical education by the internationally organised medical profession, in conjunction with the economic command of the market by western countries, has added skilled labour to the flow of resources leaving the third world. The significance of these transfers was illustrated by a recent UNCTAD report which estimated that in 1970 the trained manpower resources transferred to the USA were worth $3,700 million - a figure in excess of the entire US non-military foreign aid budget for the same year.[79] More specifically, it has been suggested that the *annual* loss to Latin America caused by the flow of doctors to the US is equivalent in value to the total volume of medical aid from the US to Latin America during the decade 1960-70.[80] The most obvious consequence of these movements of skilled workers has been the exacerbation of existing international inequalities in the distribution of doctors, nurses and midwives. Thus the long-standing shortage of trained health workers in the third world is perpetuated, while shortages in Britain, West Germany or the USA are filled by men and women trained at the expense of some of the poorest people in the world. Those under-developed countries which produce a relatively large number of doctors lose a large proportion of them to the developed countries - Sri Lanka, for example, has lost over fifty per cent of its medical graduates each year for the past 25 years.[81] Even more seriously, those countries which do not produce enough of their own doctors then have to pay extremely high wages to attract doctors away from Britain and the USA - a strategy adopted in recent years by the oil producing countries. As a result, countries which cannot afford to compete in this way - many of those in Africa for example - are left with an extremely small number of trained workers to cope with massive health problems.

The advantages of this migration for the developed countries are obvious. In Britain, for instance, where it costs over £40,000 to train one doctor, the number of medical school places has long been insufficient to meet estimated staffing needs. However the fact that former colonies have been actively encouraged to maintain British 'standards' of medical education means that they can supply doctors to meet the shortfall, effectively subsidising high cost health care in Britain. Vast numbers of nurses, midwives and unskilled hospital workers are also exported from third world countries. During the 1960s, for example, only three out of every seven newly trained West Indian midwives were actually working in the Caribbean, while four were in Britain.[82]

In recent years some third world countries have attempted to control medical migration in order to conserve their supply of skilled labour. In Pakistan and Sri Lanka, for example, exit permits are denied to medical graduates until they have worked for a statutory period in their own country. However, such schemes are having little success. The regulations are widely evaded and many doctors simply emigrate later in their careers. Elsewhere in the third world, attempts are being made to compensate for medical migration and the general lack of doctors in the countryside, through the use of medical auxiliaries or medical assistants. These auxiliaries are less highly trained than doctors but take on a wide range of medical tasks. The use of auxiliaries has obvious advantages in that they can be paid much lower wages than doctors and can also be expected to remain in the rural areas. However, schemes of this kind have also met with very considerable difficulties. In reality, as Bryant has pointed out, the auxiliaries often do exactly the same work as doctors, though under much more difficult conditions. In addition, they tend to receive *less* supervision than 'real' doctors, who have in most cases shown little interest in working with them.[83] Moreover, many medical assistants have themselves been reluctant to remain in their subordinate position, often aspiring to full medical status. At an institutional level, this tends to produce what has been termed a 'process of creep', whereby auxiliaries acquire a training of ever increasing length, until they are almost as fully trained as the professionals. Fendall has described how this process occurred at the Dar-es-Salaam School of Medicine which was opened in 1963.

> The School could not persist in the face of the internationally recognised medical school at Makerere, Uganda, and the proposed new medical faculty of full professional standard for Kenya at Nairobi. Within five years it became a medical school of comparable standard within the University of East Africa.[84]

As a result of pressures such as these, most attempts to use medical assistants have met with very limited success - indeed recent evidence suggests that in some countries their numbers have actually fallen in recent years.[85]

It is true that certain of the advanced capitalist countries are themselves beginning to place controls on the entry of foreign doctors - Canada and the USA for example - but this does not spring from any desire to assist third world countries. Rather, it is a response to demands from the American and Canadian medical associations to restrict the number of doctors available. Moreover, such controls will in practice do little to alter the basic pattern of skilled labour migration, which will continue so long as third world countries go on producing large numbers of medical personnel who are eminently better suited to the structural requirements of the advanced capitalist countries than to the health needs of their own people.[86]

We have seen, then, that western medical practice - however

inappropriate - has become the basic model adopted for use in the third world. At the same time, the reproduction of the technical training apparatus of the metropolitan countries within the periphery has created a supply of migrant labour for the ailing medical systems of those countries. In addition, however, the transfer of western medical practice to the third world also provides an important nexus for capital accumulation since doctors are specifically trained to use a wide range of medical commodities produced in the metropolitan countries. The training of third world hospital staff is therefore of great commercial significance to the developed world, as the British Secretary of State for Social Services recently acknowledged.

> We have exporting potential which I am doing the best I can to help mobilise. One way of encouraging exports is to train people here, where they will become accustomed to using some of the best products which we are making and which can be used abroad.[87]

Neo-colonialism: medicine as a commodity

The most important - and best documented - example of medicine as a commodity is provided by the multinational pharmaceutical industry. Although overall medical expenditure in the third world is much less than it is in the developed world, expenditure on drugs is proportionately very much greater. Whereas in Britain, drugs account for about eleven per cent of NHS spending, they represent roughly twenty-five per cent of the health budget in most African countries;[88] and in some third world countries, they absorb as much as forty or fifty per cent of total health expenditure.[89] Underdeveloped countries sometimes pay considerably more than European countries for the pharmaceutical products themselves.[90] Moreover, the drug market is dominated to an even greater extent than in developed countries by the large corporations, which use the patent system as an important mechanism for maintaining their control - some 85 per cent of all drug patents in the third world are owned by foreign companies.[91] Once a patent is registered, no competitor - either foreign or national - can legally enter the market, whether or not the patent is being exploited by its holder. Since a large proportion of patents in fact remain unexploited by the companies concerned, this effectively impedes investment from other sources and restricts the flow of technology from the industrialised countries to the third world.[92] At the same time, individual patent holders - usually multinational companies - can secure captive export markets for pharmaceuticals produced in their existing plants, thereby consolidating their monopoly trading power.

Even where international corporations have been compelled by law to licence indigenous firms to manufacture a patented drug, the time lag involved in starting local production has often allowed the original producer to develop a new drug to supersede the first.[93] While this may not be a serious problem from a medical point of view, it does underline the marginal character of much economic development even in relatively industrialised countries such as India or Brazil, whose competitive weakness is further maintained by devices such as export restrictions which are commonly imposed by parent companies.[94] It is important to appreciate, however, that the bulk of drug production in the third world is controlled by multinational corporations and consists simply of the formulating and packaging of imported chemicals. Since these imports normally come from another subsidiary of the same corporation, internal accounting mechanisms are frequently used by firms to inflate the cost of the constituent chemicals, and hence the price of the finished product. This practice - known as transfer pricing - has been well documented in the drug industry, with the most notorious example coming from Colombia, where in 1968 the imported chemical constituent of valium was found to be overpriced by 6,584 per cent.[95]

The dominant role of the multinationals in the production of pharmaceuticals is, of course, carried over into their activities in advertising and promotion. In the third world, these efforts to manipulate consumption are more intensive, more calculated and very much more dangerous than they are in the developed countries. While in Britain there is roughly one drug company representative for every twenty doctors, and in the US one for every ten, in underdeveloped countries it is common to find one representative for only three to five doctors.[96] Although a country like Tanzania may spend only two per cent of the amount the British NHS spends on drugs, there are several reasons why the pharmaceutical industry attaches so much importance to such markets. In the first place, overall drug sales are increasing at a much faster rate in underdeveloped countries; secondly, the relative spending power of individual doctors is greater than in Britain; and thirdly, promotion is likely to be more effective, since the drug companies are able to maintain a monopoly on the supply of pharmaceutical information.[97] We have already noted that even in Britain the primary source of information about new drugs remains the manufacturers themselves and, in underdeveloped countries, an independent evaluation is even more difficult to obtain.[98] This corporate monopoly of information has led to widespread and well documented abuses in the promotion of pharmaceuticals in the third world. One recent study comparing descriptions of identical drugs issued in Latin America and in the USA concluded that,

> in nearly all of the products investigated in this study, the differences in the promotional or labelling material were striking. In the United States the listed indications for each product were usually few in number, while the contra-indications, warnings, and potential adverse reactions were often in extensive detail. In Latin America, the listed indications were far more numerous, while the hazards were minimised, glossed over, or totally ignored. In some cases, only trivial side effects were described, but potentially lethal hazards were not mentioned.[99]

The drug *dipyrone* for example is licensed in the US only for patients with terminal malignant disease whose fever cannot be reduced by safer measures. In Brazil, on the other hand, it is recommended for numerous mundane complaints from rheumatism to toothache. Yet this drug has a mortality rate as high as 1 in 200.[100] Some products are specifically promoted for conditions commonly found in the third world, for which they are not only fundamentally unsuited, but actually dangerous. Anabolic steroids for instance, which are considered too toxic in the developed countries 'for all but the narrowest use', are promoted in underdeveloped countries for the treatment of malnutrition.[101] Perhaps the most significant example of abuse concerns the antibiotic *chloramphenicol* which, in developed countries, is normally reserved specifically for the treatment of typhoid. In the third world it is promoted for a wide range of common infections, often without any warning about the serious or even fatal aplastic anaemia which it can induce.[102] Its intensive use in parts of the third world has resulted not only in an abnormally high incidence of aplastic anaemia but also - in Mexico and South East Asia - in the development of chloramphenicol-resistant strains of typhoid.[103] An important contributing factor in this situation has been the fact that dangerous drugs are widely available without prescription - it is estimated that in some underdeveloped countries 75 per cent of drugs are obtained in this way. Moreover the trend towards self-medication in the third world as a whole is growing - a fact which has of course been noted with considerable interest by the drug industry.[104]

It has often been observed that while people in the third world pay more than their share towards the massive research and development expenditure of the multinational drug industry, such research does little to meet their real health needs. There are, of course, important exceptions, such as the vaccines developed in the industrialised countries, which are of great value in the third world. Overall, however, the drugs currently available are of limited use in treating the diseases of underdevelopment. Moreover, the pharmaceutical industry has recently been *reducing* its investment in the development of drugs relevant to the third world[105] and innovations are now geared overwhelmingly to the industrialised countries. One recent report has suggested that within the US drug industry, attempts are now being made to diversify into potentially more profitable areas of research such as agrichemicals and veterinary products.[106] Meanwhile the WHO estimated in 1976 that total world expenditure on tropical disease research was about $30 million per year - a sum equivalent to just two per cent of the amount spent annually on cancer research alone.[107]

Although the pharmaceutical industry is a major source of economic and technological control over third world health policies, it represents only one sector of the expanding international medical industry. Other profitable fields include hospital construction, development and outfitting, the supply of medical, surgical and diagnostic equipment, and numerous ancillary goods and services. Apart from the vast capital outlay required for the initial construction, the recurrent costs of running a hospital are extremely high. This is particularly true in third world countries, where such costs are tied to technical installations which can be restocked only through imports. Hospital development can therefore distort the whole balance of third world health expenditure and it is not uncommon to find up to half of the recurrent budget consumed by one or two big city hospitals.[108] Moreover, budgetary limits tend to be set not at the point of purchase of costly capital intensive medical apparatus, but subsequently, so that it is characteristic for equipment to remain unused either because necessary parts cannot be obtained or because there are no trained staff to run it.

The medical industry has long been dominated by US corporations many of which, in addition to supplying capital goods, also market hospital management services and medical personnel on an international scale. Some have diversified their interests so broadly that they are able to process entire hospital projects from inception to long-term administration. In recent years British based firms, too, have become increasingly involved in the production of expensive medical 'export packages', and the profitability of these operations has been greatly increased by the widening markets in the oil producing states. The British medical supply industry increased its exports in value by 93 per cent from 1972-74, and by a further 300 per cent from 1974-77.[109] Not only is the medical industry growing more rapidly than any other, but it is expected by some to become Britain's major source of overseas earnings within the next decade. This export drive has been greatly aided by the newly created Industries and Exports Division of the DHSS, which has become the official sponsor of the British medical supplies industry - its role being to 'intensify in the national interest the export of British health systems and products'.[110] Among its diverse methods is the initiation of special arrangements,

> between the UK regional hospital authorities and overseas countries, whereby British health care management and

technical expertise might be transferred expeditiously to small nations with embryonic health services.[111]

Underdeveloped countries are therefore increasingly seen to provide lucrative opportunities for the medical supplies industry, even for the sale of such specialised technical devices as diagnostic body scanners, which cost vast sums of money but whose practical value is by no means established.

The problem facing metropolitan producers, however, is that most third world countries lack the foreign exchange needed to make significant purchases of these commodities. To mitigate this they look to programmes of economic assistance, sponsored by western governments and supranational development agencies, and it is in this sense that Robin Murray has described foreign aid as 'an overseas extension of state functions *vis a vis* private capital'.[112] As we shall see, during the postwar period the provision of aid has become an important mechanism for the expansion of international markets, both in the health sector and elsewhere.

In the first place, overseas aid lends support to national firms engaged in foreign competition, through lowering costs, while at the same time providing infrastructural developments to meet the needs of private investment. It also fosters dependence both on foreign capital and on manufactured goods, often initiating longer-term commercial flows. Finally, it acts as a lever to ensure the implementation of other policies in the third world which, while not directly economic, are important in creating conditions favourable to capitalist interests. In the health sector, for example, a growing concern in the metropolitan countries about the world 'population problem' has meant that a large proportion of medical aid is now either directly channelled into controlling fertility, or else is tied to an acceptance by the recipient country of some kind of population policy. Even more fundamentally perhaps, most medical aid either takes a technological form or is tied to technological inputs. Hence it encourages a form of health care which will ultimately be of little value to the mass of third world inhabitants, but which is extremely profitable to the donor countries and to multinational corporations.

The obvious commercialism of much metropolitan aid has led

to recent attempts to reformulate objectives in more acceptable terms. British policy, for instance, as outlined in the 1975 White Paper, *The Changing Emphasis in British Aid Policies: More Help for the Poorest*, stresses that aid should go to those countries most in need and should be used specifically for projects likely to benefit the poor.[113] At present, however, there seems little evidence of such priorities being realised. In recent years there has been a decline in the percentage of British GNP devoted to aid, from an average of 0.54 per cent during 1960-64 to 0.38 per cent during 1970-74. Only about four per cent of this total (approximately thirteen million pounds) is allocated to medical aid - £9 million in the form of bilateral aid and £4 million as multilateral aid.[114] Alastair White has analysed government aid to the health sector during the years immediately preceding 1974, in an attempt to determine 'whether the purposes served are related to the priority needs of the majority of the population in the recipient countries'.[115] He looked at the two major elements in aid programmes - technical assistance and project aid. Technical assistance which accounts for about forty per cent of all British health aid, consists largely of training foreign nationals in the UK, and is strongly biased towards tertiary care - i.e., the acute, high technology hospital sector.[116] As we have already seen, training of this kind is recognised to play an essential role in creating professional demand for technological commodities within the third world. Whether such training is conducted in the guise of aid or on market terms, the economic benefits are likely to be very similar for the country offering the training.

So far as project aid is concerned, a very similar pattern prevails. Only about three per cent of the total is allocated to primary care, while the proportion going to tertiary care is very high - roughly 40 per cent in recent years - and shows no sign of falling. Hence only about five per cent of all medical aid is related to primary care[117] - a figure which reflects the fact that the receipt of aid tends to be tied to British goods and services, and that commercial criteria are often applied in the selection of recipient countries. These considerations help to explain the particular pattern of health aid distribution which has been adopted in recent years. During the 1970s there has been a notable shift away from former British colonies towards increased involvement with Latin American countries - a trend which is clearly related to their growing industrial and commercial importance. In 1973 for example, an agreement was signed with Colombia for a £4 million loan to purchase British medical equipment, and this was followed by a £2 million loan to Brazil for three hospitals to be built and equipped by British firms.[118] Even where aid is not specifically tied, the fact that it is designed to cover only capital costs, has the effect of tying future expenditure by the recipient governments, who must meet the recurrent costs of capital installations, including the purchase of further equipment and spare parts from the donor country.[119] Thus while aid forms only a small proportion of health expenditure in most third world countries,[120] it nevertheless exercises a strong influence over the services provided, reinforcing a pattern of health care which is increasingly recognised as inappropriate to third world needs.[121] In the British case aid is important in promoting the export of British goods and services, in fostering dependence on British scientific expertise, and in reinforcing the general dominance of the western medical paradigm over potentially more effective alternatives.

Neo-colonialism: disease as an international problem

Since the second world war, and the unprecedented internationalisation of capital which followed, there has been a shift towards the provision of aid on a multilateral basis. As a result, medical policy in underdeveloped countries is now directly influenced not just by third world governments and the particular metropolitan countries with which they have historically been associated. Numerous agencies affiliated to the UN - including those specifically associated with the promotion of capitalist development such as the IMF and the World Bank - are also very important. As regards health, the major international agency is, of course, the World Health Organisation which was established in 1948.

The ideology which has sustained the activities of the WHO was strongly influenced by wartime advances in chemical disease controls, initially developed to reduce the high levels of sickness among troops in areas such as North Africa and the Pacific.

> During the second world war, there was considerable develop-
> ment of better drugs and artificial chemical insecticides. After
> the war, the use of these chemicals began to dominate the
> methodology of disease control just as the discovery of the life
> cycles of the parasites had dominated its theory and policy fifty
> years earlier. These developments were also reflected in the
> structure of the World Health Organisation where expert
> advisory panels, committees, study groups and scientific
> groups were set up to study specific health problems.[122]

A fragmented and primarily technical response to health problems
has dominated WHO policy ever since, and an early rhetorical
commitment to public health and rural development was never
translated into practical strategies. Instead, WHO preventive
policies have focussed on 'key' diseases - notably smallpox and
malaria - which were selected as realistic targets for eradication. As in
the case of colonial disease campaigns, these efforts have been
narrowly conceived, and undertaken largely in the absence of
measures to improve the conditions of everyday life in the third
world.

The virtual elimination of smallpox has undoubtedly been *the*
success story of the WHO (for reasons peculiar to the nature of the
disease as much as the concerted campaign to eradicate it). Its anti-
malarial strategy, on the other hand, represents a monumental
failure. In the years after the war it was increasingly recognised that
malaria not only killed a great many people, but also interfered
significantly with agricultural and industrial production.[123] With the
advent of the 'miracle' insecticide DDT, it seemed that the ideal
weapon existed for eliminating the anopheles mosquito, and as a
result the WHO launched its historic programme of malaria eradication in 1957. The very wide scope of this policy owed much to US
financial backing obtained following the recommendation of a
major report on the issue, whose special consultant was Dr Paul
Russell of the Rockefeller Foundation.

> Dr Russell pointed out that although malaria is no longer a
> problem in the US it is of tremendous importance to the
> American businessman, as 60 per cent of our imports come
> from and 40 per cent of our exports go to countries in which it is

a problem ... In concluding Dr Russell pointed out that a
malaria eradication program was a dramatic undertaking that
would penetrate into the homes of people and would benefit
the US politically and financially.[124]

The extent to which the resulting anti-malarial programme comple-
mented US corporate interests is indicated by the fact that, while
campaigns were strongly focussed on Asia and Latin America,
virtually nothing was attempted in sub-Saharan Africa which at that
time was becoming increasingly marginal within the international
economy.

By the mid-1960s remarkable progress appeared to have been
made in the main campaign areas. Indeed some observers attributed
a reduction in mortality rates in regions such as the Indian subcontinent almost entirely to the dramatic decline in the incidence of
malaria.[125] Moreover the apparent success of malaria eradication by
chemical means seemed to vindicate an approach to health problems
which eliminated the need either for active cooperation by the
affected population or for any significant alteration in existing social
and economic relations. A decade later, however, it is clear that the
anti-malarial programme has undergone a massive reversal in all the
areas of its previous success. In India, the anti-malaria programme
reduced the incidence of the disease from 75 million cases in 1952, to
just 60,000 by 1962. Since the late 1960s, however, malaria
incidence has surged upwards once more, reaching 6 million in 1976.
In Pakistan, the number of cases rose from 9,500 in 1968 to 10 million in 1974. Serious increases in Malaria incidence during the 1970s
have also been reported in countries such as Sri Lanka, Afghanistan,
Nepal, Bangladesh, Iran, Turkey, Burma, Thailand, Honduras,
Nicaragua and Costa Rica.[126]

The most usual explanations for this failure are technical ones
related either to deficiencies in the chemicals available or to inadequate financial resources. 'Technical' problems certainly do exist -
the rapid spread of insecticide resistance in mosquitoes has been well
documented, and is seriously aggravated by the large-scale use of
pesticides in cash crop production. No less than one-third of the

people in the malarious regions of the world now live in areas where vector resistance is a problem. Moreover, the most dangerous form of malaria, *plasmodium falciparum*, is now showing increasing resistance to chloroquine, the drug normally used against it.[127] It is also true that shortage of funds has been an important element in bringing about the resurgence of malaria. Harry Cleaver, for example, has argued that basic lack of funding is the most decisive problem, pointing out that international agencies such as USAID, UNICEF and PAHO, as well as national governments, have greatly reduced their support for anti-malarial programmes in the last few years.[128] However, an exclusive focus on technical and financial problems often leads to a neglect of the fundamental structural and conceptual limitations of the programmes themselves. In order to be successful, any campaigns against individual diseases need to be co-ordinated with, and reinforced by, more general environmental health policies - a strategy which has never been adopted in the anti-malaria campaigns. Indeed, as Fraser Brockington has suggested,

> . . . there was more emotion than reason in the malaria eradication scheme . . . Had a substantial fraction of the enormous sum spent on malaria been expended in establishing permanent public health services the world might be a healthier place today.[129]

Indications are that the WHO still adheres strongly to laboratory medicine and to the relatively cheap but ineffective 'search and destroy' tactics to which it leads. For a variety of reasons however the past decade has seen the development of a new interest by the WHO in more community based and less technological forms of medical care. This trend reflects the changes taking place both in the nature of imperialism (particularly in the mode of economic exploitation of the third world) and also in aspects of the social structures of underdeveloped countries themselves. Since these apparently progressive developments represent the most recent patterns of health policy found in underdeveloped countries, they are of considerable analytic and strategic importance, and therefore need to be examined in some detail.

Recent developments: the reproduction of the labour force

As we have already seen, medical services are very unequally distributed in third world countries and their use has tended to be confined to members of the ruling elites. Although international firms have often been willing to supply supplementary nutrients and subsidised dispensaries for their own workers, state involvement in the provision of medical services has usually been limited to its own employees - particularly strategic groups such as the military and the police. In recent years, however, as industrialisation has increased, third world governments have begun to organise medical services both for a wider range of state employees and also for an increasing number of workers in industrial employment. Various forms of pre-paid insurance and state-subsidised schemes have been adopted, with coverage varying from country to country - though rarely extending beyond the small urban proletariat. Some of the most advanced schemes of this kind are to be found in Latin America although they are now also being adopted in many Asian and African countries. By 1958 all 20 Latin American republics already had some sort of health insurance programme although they usually covered only the 5-15 per cent of the population engaged in steady, urban employment.[130]

The development of medical services has followed a broadly similar historical pattern in most third world countries. Initially, medical care is available only for the rich, who either pay for private medicine or go abroad to obtain treatment. With some degree of economic development, and a growth in the number of government officials and white collar workers, private practice is able to expand in response to an increasing market for medical care. At the same time, multinational firms make provisions for their own employees, and mutual benefit organisations are created by various groups to provide their own medical benefits. It is at this point that third world governments have usually attempted to organise health expenditure more rationally through the introduction of limited social insurance schemes - a process which we will now examine in more detail.

In countries where there is an almost infinite supply of cheap labour, there is little incentive for the state to undertake the task of providing curative medicine. Those workers who become ill can simply be replaced by others at little or no economic cost, as the WHO has acknowledged.[131] In recent years, however, the quality and stability of the labour force have become increasingly significant as small, capital-intensive sectors have developed in third world economies.[132] Once an industrial labour force is required and workers are no longer so easily interchangeable, the maintenance of those who have acquired skills, becomes a matter of some concern. It is at this point that the provision of medical services begins to be economically important - as the World Bank clearly recognises.

> Ill health affects the productivity of workers, since their strength, stamina and ability to concentrate suffer . . . A recent Bank study of construction and rubber plantation workers in Indonesia showed that the effects can be very important. The prevalence of hookworm infestation was 85 per cent and 45 per cent of the victims suffered from a resulting iron deficiency anemia. Treatment of the anemic workers with elemental iron for 60 days, at a total cost of 13 US cents per laborer, resulted in an increase in productivity of approximately 19 per cent. This implies a cost benefit ratio of 280 to 1.[133]

In their concern to quantify the economic rationality of medical expenditure for selected groups of workers, the World Bank point out that premature death is actually a preferable alternative to absenteeism.

> Both premature death and absenteeism due to illness reduce the availability of labor. However, the sizable unemployment and underemployment in developing countries implies that premature mortality may not impose an economic cost in itself . . . Morbidity in the labor force leading to absenteeism may have a greater economic impact. Absenteeism usually disrupts the production process, even under conditions of high unemployment, the temporary replacement of absent workers is likely to result in loss of output . . . A careful study of tuberculosis control in the Republic of Korea concluded that an optimal disease program resulting in increased worklife and decreased absenteeism would yield a return of $150 for each dollar spent.[134]

Urban workers are however not only more productive than peasants - their potential for political organisation is also greater. As a result, the provision of health care is becoming increasingly important as a means of maintaining support amongst the urban proletariat. Roemer makes this point in his discussion of the introduction of medical provisions in Latin America.

> It is the struggle to obtain or maintain power that, in my view, accounts mainly for the increasing movement of Latin American governments towards the central planning of health services . . . in the larger political struggles for power of Latin America, health service reorganisation is not too threatening to the power elite. Unlike agrarian reform, ownership of the means of production or foreign policy, health care is a sector in which concessions to the principle of equality are more readily made.[135]

Thus while the bourgeoisie continue to have by far the greatest access to medical resources, the skilled working class now also absorb a disproportionate amount of health expenditure, leaving both the rural and urban poor almost entirely unprovided for. In Colombia for example, about ten per cent of the population is covered by social security but consumes 50 per cent of all public sector health expenditure.[136] Moreover, in many third world countries the advantageous health facilities enjoyed by state employees and the skilled working class are financed not just by direct contributions but through general taxation levied on the entire population, most of whom are in fact excluded from the schemes.[137]

The growth of state-run insurance schemes for the skilled working class is, of course, entirely compatible with the continuing existence of a flourishing private sector in health care. Indeed, state services often contribute substantially to the profitability of private medicine.[138] In most third world countries, social insurance schemes and the private sector are inextricably intertwined, since insured workers usually receive care within the commercial sector, and are then reimbursed by the state. Even where separate government facilities do exist for the insured, doctors tend to use these as a basis for private practice, and very few work only for the state. The World Bank has drawn particular attention to this, claiming that a major advantage of social insurance schemes is precisely the fact that they enhance the private sector.

> . . . it would appear appropriate for governments to encourage the development of insurance schemes and prepayment mechanisms for the relatively affluent. While such a programme might be expected to enroll only a small part of the population, it would nevertheless foster the private alternative in health care and relieve the public sector health budget.[139]

Recent developments: population control

Over the past decade, international aid and development organisations have become increasingly concerned with the question of 'over-population' and how to control it. Indeed, according to what is often called 'the population lobby', the rapid growth of population in underdeveloped countries represents the major problem now facing the world. Control over the growth of population in the third world was first seriously advocated in the USA in the 1950s, with campaigns initiated by private organisations such as the Rockefeller Foundation, the International Planned Parent Foundation (IPPF) and the Ford Foundation. By the early 1960s, very considerable political support had been engendered, resulting in the active involvement of the United States government.

Indeed policies of this kind became a central pivot in US foreign policy particularly after the revolution in Cuba. It was considered important to control the size of third world populations both for political reasons - to stave off the threat of revolution among the 'starving millions' - and also to provide (particularly in Latin America) an economic climate as conducive as possible to American investment. Hence an Office of Population was opened in 1964, as part of the Alliance for Progress which the USA had concluded with the Latin American countries.

Throughout the 1960s the idea of a population crisis was being further elaborated and fertility control became a major priority in the funding of both research and aid. A great deal of money was invested in attempts to find the cheapest and easiest way of controlling the size of third world populations, and the giving of all kinds of aid became increasingly tied to the acceptance of an approved family planning programme. By the late 1960s however, the predominance of the USA in these efforts was gradually diminishing, as the Americans managed to shift a degree of responsibility to international agencies - the United Nations Fund for Population Activities (UNFPA) being set up as an autonomous body in 1969. Naturally the USA still retains a great deal of control over policy making (USAID now provides more than sixty per cent of all international assistance for population programmes)[140] but, as Bonnie Mass has pointed out, this multilateral approach helped to diffuse some of the hostility that was developing towards the US in parts of the third world.[141]

Since the early 1970s, population policies have become increasingly sophisticated and, on paper at least, are often presented as only one element in a wider development plan. In reality, however, measures to control fertility retain an extremely high priority, often being undertaken in preference to other health-related programmes and sometimes in the total absence of any effective medical facilities. In 1975-6 for example, population programmes were allocated no less than two-thirds of all US foreign assistance to the health sector.[142] Banerji has graphically described the effects of strategies of this kind in India.

> Policy planners side-tracked work on the country's basic problems of poverty, social injustice, ill health, unemployment and illiteracy and attempted instead to bring about a decline in the birth rate through a gigantic birth control programme. What is more, as a 'crash programme', the birth control programme *crashed into* other social and economic development programmes, causing them considerable damage.[143]

It cannot, and should not be denied that in the context of the *existing* social and economic structure of most underdeveloped countries, a rapidly expanding population cannot be adequately supported. However, that does not mean that all third world problems should be attributed to overpopulation, nor that they can be solved through the sort of population control measures currently being advocated.

Indeed the limitations of the very concept of overpopulation have been graphically pointed out by Saghir Ahmad, using the example of Pakistan.

> . . . only in a static sense does Pakistan have a problem of population. The overpopulation exists in terms of the *presently available* means of living and in relation to productive plants and equipment. Pakistan is not overpopulated in terms of natural resources and productive potential. In the words of Engels, 'the pressure of population is not upon the means of subsistence but upon the means of employment'.[144]

Nevertheless, it is population control - rather than economic development - which continues to be widely canvassed as the major solution to the problems posed by population growth in the context of poverty and underemployment. The proliferation of sprawling shantytowns inhabited by people with no material commitment to the economic system, represents a particular threat both to international capitalist interests and to the indigenous bourgeoisie - a threat which can be averted, it is argued only through the use of strong measures to control fertility. However, despite the vast resources expended on attempts to control population size, most schemes have so far had very limited success. Certain countries such as Puerto Rico, Taiwan and Singapore have been success stories for the population controllers[145] but overall, little reduction has been achieved in the rate of population growth. India, for example, first adopted birth control policies in 1952 at which time annual population growth was five million. Twenty years later, after a considerable intensification of effort, population growth was 13 million per annum.[146] Various reasons can be adduced for these apparent failures, and we need to examine them more closely.

Most attempts at population control have, until very recently, been of the 'technological fix' variety. That is to say, they have assumed that it is possible to convince people by rational argument that they should not have so many children, and that it then only remains to provide them with the means to control their fertility. It is evident, however, from any examination of the effectiveness of recent policies that this mechanistic approach runs up against very serious obstacles. In the first place, population programmes all put pressure of one kind or another on people to use birth control - pressures ranging from tax incentives and cash payments, to legally enforced compulsory sterilisation.[147] Too little attention has been paid either to the *subjective* aspects of contraceptive techniques or to their consequences for health. Thus the emphasis is on efficacy, low cost and ease of use and as a result, choice of method is more often determined by programme directors than by women themselves.

Women in the third world have frequently been used without their knowledge to test new contraceptive devices for possible side effects before attempts are made to market them in the developed countries; the most notable example being the clinical trials of oral contraceptives which were undertaken in Puerto Rico and Mexico during the 1950s and 60s.[148] A more recent instance concerns Depo-Provera, a contraceptive developed by the US drug company Upjohn, tested in Thailand, banned as unsafe in the USA, but still used extensively in underdeveloped countries. It is very attractive as a method of population control, since it is an injectable contraceptive which needs to be administered only at intervals of three to six months, does not demand the active and continuous support of the women using it, and avoids the sort of drug wastage which occurs with oral contraceptives. As far as women themselves are concerned, Depo-Provera does, however, have a number of undesirable side effects. A recent study in Bangladesh showed that among the 60 per cent of women who were still using Depo-Provera after one year, at least half were experiencing side effects described by the researchers as 'menstrual chaos'.[149] This phenomenon of intermittent bleeding is of course especially serious in cultures where women are excluded from important areas of social life so long as they show signs of menstrual bleeding. Moreover, 147 out of 1,020 women who received their first injection of Depo-Provera while they were breast feeding, experienced a reduction in milk supply.[150] Finally and most seriously, other studies have indicated that Depo-Provera may induce permanent sterility, while it is the suggested carcinogenicity of Depo-Provera that has caused it to be banned in many western countries.

An even more fundamental weakness underlying these mass

schemes for population control is their disregard for the cultural, social and economic significance of sexuality and reproduction. At the cultural level, family planning programmes have tended to take very little account of the motivations, customs and attitudes that structure reproductive behaviour. Thus there are built-in assumptions about the transferability of technology and of the methods for purveying it, which objectify the recipients and isolate their reproductive experience from the rest of their lives. The major goal is apparently to 'motivate' people to see the need for limiting their family size. But while arguments couched in terms of 'world food shortages' or 'social problems' may be rational in terms of international capitalist interests they are not necessarily rational for peasants in the third world. Indeed, the peasants themselves may well have an entirely different rationality so far as family size is concerned, and as Qadeer has pointed out, their apparent conservatism cannot be equated with irrationality.

> In fact, they act with a high degree of rationality, given their circumstances. Their reluctance to accept contraceptive practices indicates a shrewd understanding of their situation. With high infant mortality, the callous indifference of governments, and the absence of security for the future, having a large number of children is the best insurance against the helplessness and unemployment of old age.[151]

Similarly, Mahmood Mamdani concluded from a study of villagers in the Khanna area of India, that,

> an overwhelming majority of the people...have a large number of children not because they overestimate their infant mortality rates, but because they want *larger* families. More important, they want them because they *need* them.[152]

Since the economy of the villages is very labour-intensive, children make a vital contribution to the family's subsistence from an early age. They do agricultural tasks such as sowing, weeding and harvesting, bring in the family water supply, and do a wide range of household jobs. Without several children, it is difficult for a married couple to survive. Hence, so long as most peasants live on the land at subsistence level, they will wish to go on having large families.[153] An analysis such as this clearly illustrates the inextricable relationship between patterns of fertility and the structure of economic and social life. For most people in the third world, a large family is part of the traditional pattern by which they define the quality of their lives; an essential component in the struggle to survive, and a source of security in illness or old age. For all these reasons, they may well resist birth control programmes so long as their general economic and social circumstances remain unchanged.

In discussing the objective relation of biological reproduction to economic reproduction in the third world, Meillassoux has suggested that in subsistence agriculture it is control over the means of *reproduction* which is of primary importance.[154] This raises the question of how such control is exercised and by whom. Many accounts of biological reproduction and patterns of fertility leave the analysis at the level of 'the family', 'the peasants' or 'the class' without considering possible contradictions and conflicts within these categories. In particular, there has been a failure to appreciate the significance of women's oppression in relation to fertility. Nevertheless, population planners have often made extravagant claims about relieving women of their reproductive burdens, stressing in particular the benefits to women's health which would accrue from the prevention of continuous pregnancies. While improved physical health undoubtedly represents one of the most significant potential advantages for women of effective contraception, the humanitarian claims of the population lobby have a decidedly hollow ring. We have already seen how women have been physically exploited and their health put at risk in order to achieve both acceptable contraceptives for western women, and the more fundamental goal of population control in the third world. Similarly, while resources are lavished on free medical services for purposes of birth control, those same women who are provided with contraceptives are often unable to obtain skilled assistance in childbirth, or free advice in the event of serious illness. The overwhelming publicity surrounding population control has therefore obscured the broader health needs of women - a fact which is well illustrated by the fate of the large numbers of third world women who are infertile. It has been estimated, for example, that in large areas of both East and West Africa, approximately one-third of all women are sterile, and the social consequences for such women are devastating. As Gebbie has reported, 'suicide is not uncommon and rejection by the husband almost invariable'[155] - yet medical assistance is most unusual.

Recent developments: rural health or social control?

There has been a growing recognition within the WHO and other international agencies that as long as the number of infant deaths continues to remain so high, population control policies are doomed to failure. Thus, in an attempt both to improve childhood survival rates and to promote the use of contraceptives, maternal and child health provisions have in recent years been accorded a much greater priority. This development has played an important part in the general shift away from high technology medicine which has occurred recently in the health policies of international agencies, though these changes have, as yet, had little practical effect. Both the WHO and the World Bank are in agreement that,

> . . . the official system of health care at present is top heavy; too much is being spent on doctors and hospitals in urban areas, while coverage in the countryside is extremely limited. Future policy should correct this bias by (1) extending the coverage of the primary health care system; (2) increasing the responsiveness of existing health posts and district hospitals to the needs of the primary health worker; and (3) planning the extension of primary care with the aim of supplementing the role played by traditional healers in village society.[156]

Thus the idea of 'community' health services is becoming increasingly fashionable among health planners. However there are serious obstacles to the creation of such schemes while the social and economic relations in most third world countries remain so profoundly undemocratic.

Much of the rhetoric advocating more community-based and preventive medicine is based on somewhat grandiose ethical and philosophical justifications. However, a recent article by two WHO planners puts the dilemma of third world health planning into a more realistic context.

Health by the people is both a philosophical and a pragmatic idea. Philosophically one can believe that community organisations, using their powers of self-determination, *should* be the starting point of health care services. Practicably, since there is seldom enough money in most developing countries to consider any other course of action, community organisation has to be a starting point.[157]

There is then a growing recognition that third world economies are unlikely to generate increased resources for medical care - a fact of both practical and political significance.

International agencies are therefore attempting to influence the allocation of health resources in the direction of more cost-effective policies. Clearly it is not in the interests of international capital to waste resources in the third world either through counter-productive medical expenditures or through investment in economic projects which may be undermined by endemic disease. Again, the World Bank has summarised the issues involved:

Ill health is thought to impose economic costs by (1) reducing the availability of labor; (2) impairing the productivity of employed workers and capital goods; (3) wasting current resources, particularly nutrients; and (4) impeding the development of natural resources, animal wealth and tourism potential.[158]

Most of the arguments in favour of strengthening preventive and primary services therefore begin with a ritual obeisance to the value of 'community' projects, but stress the advantages in cost-benefit terms. In particular, they point out the proven effectiveness as well as cheapness of measures of this kind in other underdeveloped areas (notably China) and emphasise the greater return on investment that can be obtained from expenditure on preventive as compared with curative medicine.

Inevitably, any extension of primary health care for the poorest inhabitants of third world countries will have certain progressive effects, which should not be ignored. Nevertheless, it is also import-ant to recognise the serious limitations of such policies as they are currently conceived. The most common prototype used in the planning of health services (even by the WHO and the World Bank) is the People's Republic of China. Chinese 'barefoot doctors' are held up as an example of how local health workers should be recruited and trained, while the conspicuous success of the Chinese both in reducing population growth and in controlling disease are strongly emphasised.[159] However a closer examination of the organisation of health care in China illustrates that the achievements arising out of revolutionary change are not divisible - that health policies cannot simply be transferred from one social, economic and political context to another.

This point can be illustrated through looking at the work of Roneghy and Solter who compared barefoot doctors in China and in Iran. In China these local health workers have been democratically selected by their production team on the basis of a proven willingness to serve the people, with formal education (apart from literacy) playing no part in the selection process. Their training combines theory and practice, and takes place entirely in the rural areas. Once qualified, barefoot doctors continue their normal occupation, receiving no special payment. The medical care which they provide concentrates on disease prevention and on health education, varying according to the expressed needs of the local community. As Ronaghy and Solter have commented,

> The most remarked upon and the unique feature of the system is the ideological zeal shown by the barefoot doctor. Seemingly, total devotion to the health of his or her production team, without thought of personal material gain, has been observed frequently throughout China.[160]

However attempts to 'import' barefoot doctors to Iran (as to other areas of the third world) have not been conspicuously successful. This failure has arisen in part from the fact that wherever a western system of medicine predominates, any attempt to train auxiliary personnel to take responsibility for 'medical' tasks has met with very considerable resistance from the medical profession. Even where there is a severe shortage of doctors, the training of auxiliaries has been regarded as a threat to the profession. In Iran, this resistance has to some degree been circumvented by compelling all doctors who have completed their internship, to serve eighteen months in a rural area as part of their military service. Nevertheless, the recruitment and training of Iranian village health workers still presents formidable problems. As Ronaghy and Solter point out, the social structure of the villages is such that the democratic selection of local health workers is simply not possible in Iran. Either the headman himself, or one of his close relatives, are invariably put forward for what is perceived as a potentially important position in the village. Moreover, women are almost never selected to become health workers because the men will not allow them to leave the village to be trained. So far as the training itself is concerned, Iranian health workers continue to reflect more general social attitudes in defining the curative aspects of medical care as much more important than prevention. Thus, when their training is completed and they return to their villages, the majority of workers continue to define themselves in terms of their role in curative medicine, and are often more concerned with their own personal advancement, than with fulfilling their responsibility to the village.[161]

The Iranian case is by no means unique and other countries as diverse as India and Tanzania have introduced similar experiments in rural health development. In Tanzania the avowed commitment to a broad strategy of socialist development made the adoption of elements from the Chinese experience seem particularly appropriate. Yet in spite of the apparently favourable political environment, a recent assessment of rural health care in Tanzania reveals a number of problems not unlike those found in both Iran and India.[162] Rural health workers, for instance, exhibited distinctly negative attitudes towards the local people, whom they tended to regard as uncivilised, ignorant and stubborn. Instead, they identified strongly with the richer peasants and, despite their special training, sought their inspiration from the 'real' doctors at the top of the medical hierarchy. As a result, instead of facilitating perceptible improvements in health, rural medical schemes have tended once again to founder through their close reliance on the western model of medical practice. Further, by vesting knowledge and control in those already allying themselves with existing power groups in society, these schemes also provide new mechanisms of social control over the peasant population, who are expected to put their own resources and labour into health schemes over which they will have no real control.

This chapter has shown that the export of western medicine to the underdeveloped countries of the world is of very considerable social and economic importance for the metropolitan countries. However, when this is set against the background of the social and economic causes of ill health among third world populations, the incapacity of this commodity form of medicine to meet their health needs is glaringly obvious. Moreover, evidence suggests that in so far as western medicine has made any impact on ill health in the third world, it has tended to avert death without improving life.[163] That is to say, while medicine may in some instances have reduced mortality rates, in the absence of improved living standards it has produced large numbers of mere survivors, handicapped by constant illness and incomplete recovery. Indeed, it is probable that debilitation on the current scale is without historical precedent.[164] However, it is not only the ineffectiveness of western medicine itself that must be taken into account. It is also important to emphasise that in consuming such a high proportion of third world investment, curative medicine actually kills by diverting scarce resources away from other projects that would be more immediately beneficial to health. Finally and most fundamentally, in so far as western medicine is presented as a substitute for self-generating economic development, it helps to perpetuate the very conditions of underdevelopment which lie at the heart of third world health problems.

Postscript: The Struggle for a Healthier Society

We have argued that in order to understand the political economy of health under capitalism two distinct questions need to be considered - the relationship between health, illness and capitalism, and the relationship between capitalism and medical practice. Furthermore, while attention has traditionally been focused on the latter - on the organisation of medical practice - an understanding of *both* these issues is of the utmost importance if the political struggles for improved health are to succeed.

We began by arguing that the problems at present plaguing the medical care systems of most developed countries do not merely reflect an immediate 'fiscal crisis'; they cannot adequately be explained simply in terms of the worldwide economic recession of the 1970s. Rather they reflect, first the obvious and growing contradiction between health and the pursuit of profit under capitalism, and second the contradictions inherent in the particular forms of medical practice which have evolved within capitalist societies. Finally, we have shown that these considerations not only apply to the metropolitan countries, but must also serve as the starting point in any attempt to explain the enormous burden of disease and premature death still borne by the mass of the population in underdeveloped parts of the world. Our aim in this postscript is briefly to discuss the significance of these ideas in informing our struggle for a healthier society.

In the developed countries such as Britain and the USA most opposition to the current 'crisis' in medical care has been organised around a defence of working class interests through protecting the right to medical care. That is to say, there has been resistance to reductions in medical services, coupled with demands for increased state expenditure on health care and a more equal social distribution of medical resources. These defensive struggles are extremely important. In so far as modern health care *is* effective, the fight to save existing services, to ensure their availability to all, and to obtain a higher economic priority for them, is obviously vital. The British NHS, for all its limitations, has shown itself to be a genuinely progressive development as far as patients are concerned; and the struggle to save jobs is of paramount importance for workers in the health sector.

Nevertheless, a struggle which is centred around these issues alone - which merely demands 'more of the same' - has fundamental limitations. First, it tends to exclude debate about the value, or otherwise, of medicine in its present form. Thus there is an underlying assumption that all medical technologies and procedures are by definition beneficial and are, in themselves, devoid of wider social or political significance. It is assumed that more medicine can only be a good thing - the way in which it is delivered is rarely challenged. Second, and more important, struggles to obtain more medical care usually ignore the crucially important and logically prior question of the social production of health and illness - what makes us ill in the first place and how much of this illness is avoidable?

The belief that western medicine is a value-free science, the application of which is invariably beneficial, has been shown in various ways to be false. As we have already seen, medical techniques themselves are not merely the logical consequence of 'scientific progress', but rather the product of a particular conjunction of social, economic and political forces. Hence we have to understand the existence of any particular practice or technology not simply in terms of its proven utility in helping the sick - indeed it may be of very little therapeutic value - but in terms of the activities of powerful groups in society whose various interests are furthered by the initial development and continued use of such technologies. There is growing evidence that many medical products and techniques, including a variety of common surgical procedures and a considerable number of drugs, have little or no efficacy. More seriously, it is becoming increasingly clear that certain medical procedures are not merely ineffective but positively harmful and may themselves cause damage to health. In this respect, we have already examined the case of high technology obstetrics as well as considering the dangers of various drugs. It would, of course, be absurd to argue that adverse side effects could always be avoided, since the use of potent treatments inevitably involves some degree of risk if their potential benefits are to be realised. It is evident, however, that doctors continue to employ drugs and techniques whose use cannot be justified when their possible benefit is balanced against potential risks or distressing side effects.

Under these circumstances, then, it makes little sense merely to demand more medical care without recognising the need both for a critical evaluation of treatments currently in use, and for a greater awareness of the social and economic processes involved in their development and continued use. These considerations apply particularly dramatically in the third world, where the export of western medicine is growing rapidly despite the fact that most of it is of little value in alleviating the ill health of the majority of the people living there. Often medical commodities and techniques which *might* be of use in the industrialised countries are simply inappropriate when applied in a different context. However their continued export is encouraged by the ruling elites in underdeveloped countries, by the international medical profession, and by pharmaceutical and medical equipment manufacturers in the metropolitan countries. Conversely, commodities which *would* be of value in helping to meet third world health needs have not been developed because they would not be profitable.

But it is not just the physical hardware and medical technologies which must be regarded as problematic. As we have shown, the consequences of medical practice extend far beyond the physiological/biological domain, and the social relations involved in the production of medical care reflect other aspects of capitalist economic and social structures. Thus class divisions, sexual divisions and racial divisions in society are reinforced by the social organisation of medicine. To simply demand more medical care of the same kind is to ignore the fundamental ways in which our present health care system has been shaped and moulded by the particular character of capitalism. This failure to acknowledge the essentially capitalist nature of much modern medicine is perhaps most clearly demonstrated in the commonly-voiced demands for state control over the profit-seeking activities of doctors and the drug industry. In this view the avarice of these groups is sabotaging what would otherwise be a satisfactory system. Of course controls over specific interest groups may produce certain beneficial effects and hence should be fought for. In the same way, it may be possible to obtain changes in, for example, the admission policies of medical schools, the content of medical education or the control exercised by doctors within the health service. However reforms of this kind cannot in themselves fundamentally alter the nature of medicine under capitalism.

For all these reasons, then, the abolition of scarcity in medical provision is a necessary but not a sufficient condition for achieving effective health care. The struggle must therefore go beyond the immediate demand for more state-organised medicine, towards a critical re-evaluation of the more qualitative aspects of the current organisation of medicine and a redefinition of our health needs.

This is not, of course, to suggest that in a socialist society all existing medical knowledge and skills should simply be abandoned in favour of something called 'proletarian medicine'. Rather it is to imply that the underlying theoretical preconceptions of scientific medicine would need to be critically re-examined to see how far they are capable of providing the basis for an adequate understanding of both the organic and the more subjective dimensions of human health and illness. Further, it is to suggest that no technology would be used uncritically and without some assessment of its value according to criteria which had been democratically decided upon. Finally, it is to stress that the more technical aspects of medicine cannot be separated from the social relations involved in their production.

Hence a socialist health service would not only have to provide equal access to medical care but would also have to address itself seriously to such problems as how to demystify medical knowledge and how to break down barriers of authority and status both among health workers themselves and also between workers and consumers. Indeed the whole notion of 'treating patients' - of seeing them as passive recipients of medical expertise - would need to be rethought.

As Mick Carpenter has put it, 'a socialist health service will be one which seeks to devise social relations of health care which respect the personal autonomy of those who work for it and those who are unavoidably sick'.[2] Furthermore, as John Ehrenreich has rightly pointed out, such a health service would have to recognise not just autonomy but also the existence of human dependency, and to develop sympathetic and humane ways of meeting these needs.[3] Naturally changes such as these are not easily achieved and, indeed, can occur only as part of a much broader transformation of social and economic life. However, an awareness of these issues and, above all, an understanding of their complexity, is needed to inform our current campaigns for more effective and appropriate health care.

But however widely the struggle around medical care is defined, it can constitute only one part of the struggle for a healthier society. At least as important is the creation of an awareness of the aspects of economic and social life that make us unhealthy. In this way, the wider struggle to change society can incorporate strategies to improve health - strategies which will inevitably expose some of the most fundamental contradictions of life under capitalism.

As we have already seen, bourgeois ideology offers two basic explanations of the generation of ill health. The first is that it is somehow 'natural', resulting from a' timeless set of biochemical processes which can rarely be interfered with, except after the event with curative medicine or, at best, with specific preventive measures such as vaccines. Thus in the developed countries micro-organisms and inherent degenerative processes are seen as the major culprits, while in the third world climatic conditions are thought to create additional problems. In the industrialised countries, however, the old enemies such as infectious diseases have now largely disappeared, while new hazards such as cancer and heart disease increasingly appear resistant to medical intervention. As a result a second type of explanation - the 'life-style' approach - is becoming increasingly popular. Thus it is said that these 'new' diseases are not so much the result of random biological processes as the inevitable outcome of a particular way of living. Ironically, it is precisely the supposed achievement of widespread affluence in the developed countries which is said to be the problem. Capitalism, it is argued, has 'produced the goods'; people have higher incomes and greater longevity, but as a result they now *choose* to spend their money and increased leisure time on commodities and activities which are dangerous to their health. Thus it is said that individuals are to blame for their own health problems and it is up to them to adopt a healthier life-style. The Victorian notion of 'the undeserving poor' is being replaced by the equally inappropriate notion of 'the undeserving sick'. Even in the very different conditions found in underdeveloped countries such victim-blaming ideologies have emerged. Wilful failure to use birth control or maintain a balanced diet, for instance, are often cited to explain ill health in the third world.

How, then, are we in industrialised societies to deal with these widely-invoked explanations of the present increase in chronic and degenerative disease? It would be absurd to argue that individuals have *no* control over their lives - people make all kinds of real choices every day. What we do have to make clear however, is the nature of the social and economic context within which individual choices are made and the many limitations that are imposed on personal freedom. It is the detailed examination of how the power of capital structures the context in which personal choices are made that must lie at the heart of a marxist epidemiology.[4] Only in this way can we make sense of the impact of living and working conditions, and patterns of social and economic relationships, on the health of individuals and groups, while at the same time creating the possibility of collective action to transform those conditions.

The refutation of existing myths about health and illness is a very important political task and the clarification of the ways in which capitalism damages health is beginning to form the basis for new areas of struggle. A recognition of the fact that much ill health is not accidental but can be traced to specific aspects of capitalist production is a potentially unifying force, bringing together people who might not otherwise easily perceive their common interests. The women's health movement and the occupational health and safety movement are, for instance, beginning to take up similar issues from rather different contexts. The experiences associated with illness and death are in many ways universal ones, and the realisation that many apparently random and individual disasters fall into a broader pattern, provides powerful insights into the workings of capitalism.

Issues concerning health are not, however, merely consciousness-raising and unifying factors in the broader struggle, since the demand for a healthier society is, in itself, the demand for a radically different socio-economic order. Naturally we would not argue that a transformation of the mode of production would abolish illness - people will always become sick and die. But what we can show are the ways in which potentially avoidable illness has become prevalent under capitalism. Although certain health-damaging aspects of production can be removed in response to political pressure, reforms of this kind are inevitably limited. This is because it is an inherent feature of the capitalist mode of production that the imperatives of capital accumulation ultimately determine social and economic priorities. Consequently health itself has come to be defined in terms of the needs of accumulation and, as we have seen, health objectives will not be pursued if they conflict with profit - as ultimately they must. It follows from this that the demand for health is *in itself* a revolutionary demand and one which must be taken seriously in the broader struggle for socialism both in developed countries and in the third world.

References

The place of publication throughout is London unless otherwise stated.

1. Understanding Medicine and Health pp.11-46

1. Some of the contradictions between the goals of economic growth and improvements in health are discussed in P. Draper, G. Best and J. Dennis, *Health, Money and the National Health Service*, Unit for the Study of Health Policy, Dept. of Community Medicine, Guys Hospital Medical School 1976.

2. P. Corrigan, 'The welfare state as an arena of class struggle', *Marxism Today*, vol. 21 no. 3, March 1977, p.87.

3. This view of social policy is discussed in some detail in R. Pinker, *Social Theory and Social Policy*, Heinemann, 1971. It is criticised in I. Gough, 'Theories of the welfare state: a critique', *International Journal of Health Services*, vol. 8 no. 1, 1978, pp.27-40.

4. It is interesting, though, that this pattern is beginning to change, at least among some British sociologists of medicine. See, for example, the contributions to a recent British Sociological Association conference on medical sociology: M. Stacey, M. Reid, C. Heath and R. Dingwall (eds), *Health and the Division of Labour*, Croom Helm 1977.

5. T. Parsons, 'Definitions of health and illness in the light of American values and social structure', in E. Gartley Jaco (ed.), *Patients, Physicians and Illness: A Source Book in Behavioural Science and Health*, New York, Free Press 1972; also T. Parsons, *The Social System*, Routledge & Kegan Paul 1970, pp.428-79.

6. He does, however, also make the point that the 'patient' role is less dangerous than, for instance, the revolutionary role, and indeed stresses the importance of using medical (particularly psychiatric) categories to 'deal' with those who might pose a threat to the social order.

7. For critiques of Parsons see, G. Gordon, *Role Theory And Illness*, New Haven, College and University Press, 1966; H. Waitzkin and B. Waterman, *The Exploitation of Illness in Capitalist Society*, New York,

Bobbs-Merril 1974; R. Frankenberg 'Functionalism and after? Theory and developments in social science applied to the health field', *International Journal of Health Services*, vol. 4 no. 3, 1974, pp.411-27.

8. Parsons (1970), *op. cit.* p.313.

9. I. Illich, *Medical Nemesis: The Expropriation of Health*, Calder & Boyars, 1975. This was revised as *Limits to Medicine* in 1976, but references here are to the 1975 version.

10. J. Powles, 'On the limitations of modern medicine', in *Science, Medicine and Man*, vol. 1, 1973, pp.1-30; A.L.Cochrane, *Effectiveness and Efficiency: Random Reflections on Health Services*, Nuffield Provincial Hospitals Trust 1972; and Radical Statistics Health Group, *In Defence of the NHS*, 1977, pp.23-27, obtainable from B.S.S.R.S., 9 Poland St, London W.C.1. This latter includes a useful bibliography on the medical literature relating to the effectiveness of surgery.

11. E. Freidson, *Professions of Medicine*, New York, Dodd, Mead & Co. 1970; and I.K.Zola, 'Medicine as an institution of social control', *Sociological Review (New Series)*, vol. 20 no. 4, 1972, pp.487-504.

12. Illich, *op.cit.* p.73.

13. *Ibid.* pp.81-83.

14. *Ibid.* p.161.

15. There is an extremely good discussion of the problems with Illich's analysis in V. Navarro, 'The industrialization of fetishism or the fetishism of industrialization: a critique of Ivan Illich', *International Journal of Health Services*, vol. 5 no. 3, 1975, pp.351-71. pp.351-63; also in V. Navarro, *Medicine Under Capitalism*, Croom Helm 1976.

16. G. Ciccotti, M. Cini and M. de Maria, 'The production of science in advanced capitalist society', in H. Rose and S. Rose (eds.), *The Political Economy of Science*, Macmillan 1976, p.32.

17. Many of the philosophical roots of this approach lie in the work of Engels: F. Engels, *Dialectics of Nature*, Lawrence & Wishart, 1940; and F. Engels, *Anti-Dühring*, Lawrence & Wishart, 1969.

18. Ciccotti, Cini and de Maria, *op.cit.* p.33.

19. H.M. Enzensberger, 'A critique of political ecology', in H.M. Enzensberger, *Raids and Reconstructions: Essays in Politics, Crime and Culture*, Pluto Press 1976.

20. J. Eyer and P. Sterling, 'Stress related mortality and social organisation', *Review of Radical Political Economics*, vol. 9 no. 1, Spring 1977, p.2.

21. K. Figlio, 'The historiography of scientific medicine: an invitation to the human sciences', *Comparative Studies in Society and History*, vol. 19, 1977, p.265.

22. B. Ehrenreich and D. English, *Witches, Midwives and Nurses: A*

History of Women Healers, Writers and Readers Publishing
Cooperative 1976; M.J.Hughes, *Women Healers in Medieval Life and
Literature*, Freeport, New York, Books for Libraries Press 1943.

23. E.J.Dijksterhuis, *The Mechanisation of the World Picture*, Oxford
University Press 1961; T.S.Kuhn, *The Copernican Revolution*, New
York, Vintage Books 1959.

24. S.J. Reiser, *Medicine and the Reign of Technology*, Cambridge
University Press 1978; and R.H. Shryock, *The Development of Modern
Medicine*, New York, Hafner 1969.

25. R. Descartes, *The Philosophical Works* (translated by E.S.Haldane and
G.R.T.Ross), Cambridge University Press 1967, particularly
'Meditation VI'; G. Buchdahl, *Metaphysics and the Philosophy of
Science. The Classical Origins: Descartes to Kant*, Oxford, Basil
Blackwell 1969, pp.79-181.

26. T. McKeown, *The Role of Medicine: Dream, Mirage or Nemesis*,
Nuffield Provincial Hospitals Trust 1976; M. Rossdale, 'Health in a
sick society', *New Left Review*, no. 34, 1965, pp.82-90.

27. N. Jewson, 'The disappearance of the sick man from medical
cosmology, 1770-1870', *Sociology*, vol. 10 no. 2, 1976, pp.225-44.

28. N. Jewson, 'Medical knowledge and the patronage system in
eighteenth century England', *Sociology*, vol. 8 no. 3, 1974, pp.369-85.

29. Jewson (1976), *op.cit.*; I. Waddington, 'The role of the hospital in
the development of modern medicine: a sociological analysis',
Sociology, vol. 7 no. 2, 1973, pp.211-24; S.W.F.Holloway, 'Medical
education in England, 1830-58: a sociological analysis', *History*,
vol. 49, 1964, pp.299-324; M. Foucault, *The Birth of the Clinic*,
Tavistock 1973.

30. G. Rosen, *From Medical Police to Social Medicine: Essays on the
History of Health*, New York, N. Watson 1974.

31. N. Parry and J. Parry, *The Rise of the Medical Profession*, Croom Helm,
1976; and J.L.Berlant, *Profession And Monopoly: A Study of Medicine
in the United States and Great Britain*, Berkeley, University of
California Press, 1975.

32. Figlio, *op.cit.*

33. Illich, *op.cit.* p.111.

34. K. Helleiner, 'The vital revolution reconsidered', in D.V.Glass and
D.E.C.Eversley (eds.), *Population in History: Essays in Historical
Demography*, Edward Arnold 1965; also, E. Sigsworth, 'Gateways to
death? Medicine, hospitals and mortality, 1700-1850', in P. Mathias
(ed.), *Science and Society, 1600-1900*, Cambridge University Press
1972.

35. This is dealt with in more detail in chapter two.

36. Figlio, *op.cit*. pp.267-74.

37. S. Kelman, 'The social nature of the definition problem in health', *International Journal of Health Services*, vol. 5 no. 4, 1975, pp.625-42; H.S.Berliner, 'A larger perspective on the Flexner Report', *International Journal of Health Services*, vol. 5 no. 4, 1975, pp.573-92; M. Turshen, 'The political ecology of disease', *Review of Radical Political Economics*, vol. 9 no. 1, Spring 1977, pp.45-59.

38. E. Stark, 'Introduction' to the special issue on health, *Review of Radical Political Economics*, vol. 9 no. 1, Spring 1977, p.v.

39. H. Berliner, 'Emerging ideologies in medicine', *Review of Radical Political Economics*, vol. 9 no. 1, Spring 1977, pp.116-23; W. Ryan, *Blaming the Victim*, New York, Random House 1972. The impact of these ideas on recent British health policy is discussed in chapter five.

40. V. Navarro (1976), *op.cit*. p.126.

41. For an extremely good discussion see, B. Ehrenreich and J. Ehrenreich, *The American Health Empire: Power, Profits and Politics*, a Report from the Health Policy Advisory Centre, New York, Vintage Books 1971; L. Rodberg and G. Stevenson, 'The health care industry in advanced capitalism', *Review of Radical Political Economics*, vol. 9 no. 1, Spring 1977, pp.104-15.

42. L. Althusser, 'Ideology and ideological state apparatus', in *Lenin and Philosophy and Other Essays*, New Left Books 1971.

43. C. Cockburn, *The Local State: Management of Cities and People*, Pluto Press 1977, p.56.

44. K. Marx, *Capital*, vol. 1. Harmondsworth, Penguin 1976, p.275.

45. In Marx's analysis, the worker was assumed to be male.

46. Kelman, *op.cit*. p.634.

47. F. Edholm, O. Harris and K. Young, 'Conceptualising women', *Critique of Anthropology*, vol. 3 nos. 9 and 10, 1977, p.114.

48. The contradictory nature of these developments is discussed in more detail in chapter six.

49. B. Mass, *Population Target: The Political Economy of Population Control in Latin America*, Toronto, Women's Press 1976. This is discussed in more detail in chapter seven.

50. Figlio, *op.cit*. pp.285-86.

51. Rodberg and Stevenson, *op.cit*. p.113.

52. M. Renaud, 'On the structural constraints to state intervention in health', *International Journal of Health Services*, vol. 5 no. 4, 1975, pp.625-42.

2. Health, Illness and the Development of Capitalism in Britain pp.49-95

1. For the impact of early capitalist development on life in the country-side, see K. Marx, *Capital*, vol. 1, Harmondsworth, Penguin 1976, chapters 27 and 28.

2. W. Lazonick, 'Karl Marx and enclosures in England', *Review of Radical Political Economy*, vol. 6 no. 2, 1974, pp.1-33.

3. For a debate between the 'optimists' and the 'pessimists' about the effects of industrialisation on the urban working class see, E.J. Hobsbawm, *Labouring Men: Studies in the History of Labour*, Weidenfeld & Nicholson 1964, chapters 5 & 7; E.J. Hobsbawm and R.M.Hartwell, 'The standard of living during the industrial revolution: a discussion', *Economic History Review*, vol. 16 no. 1, 1963, pp.119-46. For a good bibliography see Hobsbawm, *op.cit*. chapter seven.

4. Population Census 1841, *Parliamentary Papers*, 1843, XVIII, 10.

5. E. Gauldie, *Cruel Habitations: A History of Working Class Housing, 1780-1918*, George, Allen & Unwin 1974; S.D.Chapman (ed.), *The History of Working Class Housing*, Newton Abbot, David & Charles 1971; J. Burnett, *A Social History of Housing, 1815-1970*, Newton Abbot, David & Charles 1978.

6. E.P.Thompson, *The Making of the English Working Class*, Harmondsworth, Pelican 1968, p.356.

7. This increase is discussed in W. Farr, *Vital Statistics* (N. Humphreys, ed.), Edward Stanford 1885, p.150. Part of Farr's pioneering work is reprinted in W. Farr and H. Ratcliffe, *Mortality in Nineteenth Century Britain*, Gregg International 1974.

8. M.W.Flinn, quoting the *Third Annual Report of the Registrar General, 1839-40,* pp.98-99, in his introduction to E. Chadwick, *The Sanitary Condition of the Labouring Population of Great Britain*, Edinburgh University Press 1965, p.13.

9. Marx, *op.cit*. p.795.

10. Thompson, *op.cit*. p.359.

11. Farr, *op.cit*. p.150.

12. Engels' *The Condition of the Working Class in England* dealt with the working class as a whole, rather than small sections of it or local areas, and attempted to put the analysis of health conditions into the context of 'a general analysis of the evolution of industrial capitalism, of the social impact of industrialisation, and its political and social conse-quences - including the rise of the labour movement' - E.J.Hobsbawm, 'Introduction' to F. Engels, *The Condition of the Working Class in England*, Panther 1969. Engels also provided an important survey of the existing literature on the health and living conditions of the

working class and the following comments on the health of the
industrial proletariat draw heavily on his account.

13. Engels, *op.cit.* pp.188-89.

14. For details, *ibid.* pp.163-301.

15. *Ibid.* p.191.

16. *Ibid.* p.271.

17. *Ibid.* p.192.

18. A.K.Chalmers, *The Health of Glasgow, 1818-1925*, Glasgow, 1930, p.3; quoted in Flinn, *op.cit.* p.9.

19. Any discussion of the effect of smallpox vaccine on mortality rates needs to take into account the recent work of Peter Razell: P.E.Razell, *The Conquest of Smallpox: The Impact of Innoculation on Smallpox Mortality in Eighteenth Century Britain*, Caliban 1977; P.E.Razell, *Edward Jenner's Cowpox Vaccine: The History of a Medical Myth*, Caliban 1977.

20. For interesting accounts of cholera in the nineteenth century see, R.J.Morris, *Cholera 1832*, Croom Helm 1976; A. Briggs, 'Cholera and society in the nineteenth century', *Past and Present*, no. 19, 1961, pp.76-96.

21. Flinn, *op.cit.* p.8.

22. In 1839, according to the first analysis by the Registrar General, identifiable consumption alone accounted for 17.6 per cent of all deaths. Needless to say, problems of diagnosis make it likely that the true figure was much higher. See Flinn, *op.cit.* p.11.
For a good discussion of the effects of TB on mortality rates, see T. McKeown and R.G.Record, 'Reasons for the decline in mortality in England and Wales during the nineteenth century', in M.W.Flinn and T.C.Smout (eds.), *Essays in Social History*, Oxford, Clarendon Press, 1974.

23. Although TB was more prevalent in the slums, it spread throughout society, as is evident from much nineteenth century literature. See G. Rosen, 'Disease, debility and death', in H.J.Dyos and M. Wolff (eds.), *The Victorian City: Images and Realities*, vol. 2, Routledge & Kegan Paul 1973, pp.625-67.

24. R. Dubos and J. Dubos, *The White Plague*, Gollancz 1953, p.207.

25. M. Hewitt, *Wives and Mothers in Victorian Industry*, Greenwood Press 1958.

26. For a useful collection of statistics on infant mortality due to infectious diseases in nineteenth-century cities, see Rosen, *op.cit.*

27. McKeown and Record, *op.cit.*; T. McKeown, *Medicine in Modern Society: Medical Planning Based on Evaluation of Medical Achievement*, Allen & Unwin, 1965; T. McKeown, R.G.Brown and

R.G.Record, 'An interpretation of the rise of population in Europe', *Population Studies*, vol. 26, 1972, pp.345-82; T. McKeown, *The Modern Rise of Population*, Edward Arnold 1976.

28. See chapter four.

29. E. Hobsbawm, *Industry and Empire: Economic History of Britain Since 1750*, Weidenfeld & Nicholson 1968, p.160.

30. McKeown and Record, *op.cit*. They discuss in particular the relationship between the decline in the mortality rate from TB and improvements in nutrition.

31. N. Branson and M. Heinemann, *Britain in the Nineteen Thirties*, Panther 1973.

32. L. Doyal, 'A matter of life and death: medicine, health and statistics' in J. Irvine, I. Miles and J.T.Evans (eds.), *Demystifying Social Statistics*, Pluto Press 1979; N. Hart, 'Health and inequality', an unpublished report prepared for members of the DHSS working party on inequalities and health, University of Essex 1978.

33. For details of all these statistics and their limitations see, Doyal, *op.cit*.

34. CSO, *Social Trends*, no. 8, HMSO 1977, p.134.

35. World Health Organisation, *WHO Chronicle*, no. 28, 1974, pp.529-38.

36. DHSS, *On the State of the Public Health for the Year 1975*, HMSO 1976, pp.12-13.

37. J. Powles, 'On the limitations of modern medicine', *Science, Medicine and Man*, vol. 1, 1973, pp.1-30; D. Burkitt, 'Some diseases characteristic of modern western civilisation', *British Medical Journal*, 3 February 1973, pp.274-78; M. Bookchin, *Our Synthetic Environment*, revised edition, New York, Harper & Row 1974; R. Dubos, 'The diseases of civilisation', *Milbank Memorial Fund Quarterly*, vol. 47 no. 3, 1969, pp.327-39.

38. Powles, *op.cit*.; Burkitt, *op.cit*.

39. Powles, *op.cit*.

40. Quoted in R. Lewin, 'Cancer hazards in the environment', *New Scientist*, 22 January 1976, pp.168-69. See also, J. Cairns, 'The cancer problem', *Scientific American*, vol. 233 no. 5, 1975.

41. The most detailed account of these data is contained in N. Hart, *op.cit*.; for a general discussion of inequalities in health see, J.N. Morris, 'Social inequalities undiminished', *Lancet*, vol. 1, 1979, pp. 87-90; C.O.Carter and J. Peel, *Equalities and Inequalities in Health*, London, Academic Press 1977.

42. OPCS, *Occupational Mortality 1970-72*, Decennial Supplement, HMSO, 1978. For a summary see: J. Fox, 'Occupational mortality, 1970-72', *Population Trends*, no. 9, 1977, pp.8-13.

43. OPCS, *Occupational Mortality 1970-72*, *op.cit.* p.157.
44. B. Preston, 'Statistics of inequality', *Sociological Review*, vol. 22 no. 2, 1974, pp.103-7. For a critique of this view see N. Hart, *op.cit.*
45. OPCS, *The General Household Survey, 1976*, HMSO 1978, pp.226-31.
46. Statistics on numbers of industrial accidents since 1880 are contained in: Department of Employment, *British Labour Statistics. Historical Abstract 1886-1968*, HMSO 1971, p.399.
47. Department of Employment, *Safety and Health at Work: Report of the Committee 1970-72* (Chairman: Lord Robens), HMSO, cmnd. 5034, 1972, p.1.
48. P. Kinnersly, *The Hazards of Work: How to Fight Them*, Pluto Press 1973.
49. CSO, *Social Trends No. 8*, HMSO 1977, p.110.
50. *Labour Research*, December 1976, p.264.
51. For more details see: Kinnersly, *op.cit.*; D. Hunter, *The Diseases of Occupations*, 5th edition, English Universities Press 1975.
52. D. Davies, 'Pneumoconiosis - the new scheme', *Labour Research*, May 1975, p.100. There is also growing evidence that miners have an increased incidence of lung cancer and arthritis (A. Tucker and A. Hartley, 'Cancer and arthritis: the price the miners pay', *The Guardian*, 7 February 1975) and coronary heart disease (D. Davies, 'Deaths from coronary artery disease and coalworkers' pneumoconiosis', *British Medical Journal*, 16 October 1976, pp.925-27).
53. The identification of occupational causes for non-specific respiratory disability is a particularly difficult problem. A recent study in the USA of the pulmonary capacity of firemen suggested that there was a clear correlation between loss of pulmonary function and exposure to fires. As the *Lancet* pointed out, 'there are a number of occupational groups in Britain that would lend themselves to similar studies': *Lancet*, vol. 1, 1975, p.439.
54. Reported in *The Guardian*, 13 September 1978.
55. P. O'Higgins, 'Factory legislation', in *The Origins of the Social Services*, New Society, 1968.
56. *Safety and Health at Work*, *op.cit.* p. 7.
57. *Ibid.* p.21.
58. For a very good critique of this view, which includes accounts of accidents by workers themselves see, T. Nichols and P. Armstrong, *Safety or Profit: Industrial Accidents and the Conventional Wisdom*, Bristol, Falling Wall Press, 1973.
59. *Labour Research*, April 1977, p.82.
60. D. Ball, 'Shop-floor health', *New Society*, 18 March 1971, p.440.

61. P. Taylor, 'Sickness absence: facts and misconceptions', *Journal of the Royal College of Physicians*, vol. 8 no. 4, 1974, pp.315-33. Also F.E.Whitehead, 'Trends in certificated sickness absence', CSO *Social Trends No. 2*, HMSO 1971, pp.13-21.

62. Taylor, *op.cit*. p.320.

63. OPCS, *The General Household Survey 1971*, HMSO 1975. For comparable data from the USA see, V. Navarro, 'The underdevelopment of health of working America: causes, consequences and possible solutions', *American Journal of Public Health*, vol. 66 no. 6, 1976, pp.538-47.

64. A book that deals particularly with the occupational hazards faced by women is J. Mager Stellman, *Women's Work Women's Health*, New York, Pantheon 1977.

65. M.H.Brenner, *Mental Illness and the Economy*, Cambridge, Mass., Harvard University Press 1973.

66. CSO, *Social Trends No. 4*, HMSO 1973, p.135.

67. See chapter six for more detailed references.

68. A. Oakley, *Housewife*, Harmondsworth, Penguin, 1976.

69. K. Marx, in *Karl Marx: Early Writings* (translated and edited by T.B.Bottomore), C. Watts & Co. 1963, pp.124-25.

70. H.M.Enzensberger, 'A critique of political ecology', in his *Raids and Reconstructions: Essays in Politics, Crime and Culture*, Pluto Press 1976, p.256.

71. *The Guardian*, 6 August 1975.

72. *New Scientist*, 3 October 1974.

73. J. Fabia and J. Dam Thuy, 'Occupation of father at time of birth of children dying of malignant diseases', *British Journal of Preventive and Social Medicine*, vol. 28 1974, pp.98-100.

74. However, it is difficult to escape the conclusion that the decisions as to which jobs should not be available to women are made on other than medical criteria. Thus, they have not been excluded from operating theatres where the effects of anaesthetic gases are well known, but where they are assumed to be 'needed'. For a useful summary of the reproductive hazards of work see, Stellman, *op.cit*. pp.158-59.

75. *Lancet*, vol. 1, 1976, p.945; D. Barker, 'Asbestosis - the 21 year old diary of disaster', *The Guardian*, 30 March 1976.

76. W.J.Blot and J.F.Fraumeni, Jr., 'Arsenical air pollution and lung cancer', *Lancet*, vol. 2, 1975, pp.142-44. Also V. Navarro, 'Crisis of the western system of medicine', *International Journal of Health Services*, vol. 8 no. 2, 1978, p.193.

77. **A**. Tucker, 'Sweets increase lead peril to children in big cities', *The Guardian*, 3 February 1975. Also Socialist Medical Association, *Lead Pollution in Birmingham*, SMA 1974; Department of the Environment, *First Report of the Joint Working Party on Lead Pollution Around Gravelly Hill*, HMSO 1974.

78. For an interesting discussion of TLVs and women see, 'Women at work at risk', *Science for People* 29, 1975, pp.18-20.

79. For a discussion of the politics of ecology see Enzensberger, *op.cit.*; J. Ridgeway, *The Politics of Ecology*, New York, Dutton 1971; E.E.Romøren and T.I.Romøren, 'Marx and ecology', *Ethics in Science and Medicine*, vol. 2, 1975, pp.97-104.

80. *Lancet*, vol. 2, 1977, p.260. This increase has, of course, been encouraged by the cigarette manufacturers who have aimed campaigns specifically at women - the creation of 'Virginia Slims' for example: *Financial Times*, 15 October 1976.

81. For good summaries of the evidence see, Royal College of Physicians, *Smoking and Health Now*, Pitman Medical 1971; World Health Organisation, *Smoking and its Effects on Health*, Technical Report Series 568, Geneva 1975.

82. *Smoking and Health Now*, *op.cit*. p.9.

83. G.E.Godber, 'Smoking disease: a self-inflicted injury', *American Journal of Public Health*, vol. 60, 1970, p.235.

84. *Smoking and Health Now*, *op.cit*. p.33.

85. *Ibid*. pp.95-96.

86. OPCS, *General Household Survey 1976*, HMSO 1978, p.239.

87. G.F.Todd, *Social Class Variations in Cigarette Smoking and in Mortality from Associated Diseases*, Occasional Paper 2, Tobacco Research Council 1976; see also J. Townsend, Smoking and Class, *New Society*, 30 March 1978, pp.709-10.

88. *New Scientist*, 17 April 1975, p.115.

89. P. Wilby, 'Smoked out by numbers', *New Society*, 11 December 1975, p.590.

90. This point is discussed in some detail in A.B.Atkinson and J.L. Townsend, 'Economic aspects of reduced smoking', *Lancet*, vol. 2, 1977, pp.492-95. They suggest that a 40 per cent reduction in smoking could be achieved without incurring any economic loss for the state.

91. M. Sherwood, 'Smoking goes scientific', *New Scientist,* 14 August 1975, p.369.

92. Wilby, *op.cit*. p.590.

93. *Ibid*.

94. The figure for state expenditure includes grants to Action on Smoking and Health (ASH) and to the Health Education Council.

95. H. Rothman and D. Radford, 'Bread advertising and scientific debate', *New Society*, 24 October 1974, p.266.

96. *Ibid*.

97. J. Burnett, *Plenty and Want: A Social History of Diet in England from 1815 to the Present Day*, Harmondsworth, Pelican 1968, p.99.

98. J. Boyd Orr, *Food, Health and Income*, Macmillan 1936.

99. *Ibid*.

100. National Food Survey Committee, *Household Food, Consumption and Expenditure: 1974*, Ministry of Agriculture, Fisheries and Food, HMSO 1976, pp.33-34.

101. Table taken from Morris, *op.cit*.

102. R.G.Wilkinson, 'Dear David Ennals', *New Society*, 16 December 1976.

103. D. Burkitt, 'Some diseases characteristic of modern western civilisation', *British Medical Journal*, 3 February 1973, p.276.

104. DHSS, *Prevention and Health: Eating for Health*, HMSO 1978, p.25.

105. Burkitt, *op.cit*. p.276.

106. National Food Survey, *op.cit*.

107. Burkitt, *op.cit*. p.276.

108. J.C.Drummond and A. Wilbraham, *The Englishman's Food, A History of Five Centuries of English Diet*, revised edition with a new chapter by D. Hollingsworth, Jonathan Cape 1957.

109. Little has yet been written on 'agri-business' in Britain, but see, C. Wardle, *Changing Food Habits in the UK: an Assessment of the Social, Technological, Economic and Political Factors Which Influence Dietary Patterns,* Friends of the Earth 1977; *Science for People*, no. 34, 'Food, Farming and Finance', Winter 1976/7; Agricapital Group, *Our Daily Bread - Who Makes the Dough?* BSSRS 1978.

110. See for instance the debate over the safety of nitrates: *The Guardian*, 11 February 1977; or about the advisability of using cyclamates and saccharine as sweeteners: G. Chedd, 'The search for sweetness', *New Scientist*, 9 May 1974, pp.299-302.

111. Food Additives and Contaminants Committee, *Report on the Review of Flavourings in Food*, HMSO 1976.

112. Royal College of Physicians of London and the British Cardiac Society, 'Prevention of coronary heart disease', *Journal of the Royal College of Physicians*, Vol. 10, 1976. However fat is only one of several dietary and other factors. Thus one recent article suggests that the relative increase in the amount of heart disease found in social classes IV and V since 1961, can largely be explained by their relatively high rates of smoking, combined with their high consumption of sugar and low consumption of wholemeal bread: M.G.Marmot, A.M.Adelstein,

N. Robinson and G.A.Rose, 'Changing social class distribution of heart disease', *British Medical Journal*, 21 October 1978, pp.1109-12. See also Wilkinson, *op.cit.*

113. Burkitt, *op.cit.*; D. Burkitt and H.C.Trowell, *Refined Carbohydrate Foods and Disease: Some Implications of Dietary Fibre*, Academic Press 1975. For a general discussion of some of the relationships said to exist between diet and cancer see, O. Gillie, 'Cancer and how to cut the risk', *Sunday Times*, 13 June 1976.

114. J. Yudkin, *Pure, White and Deadly: the Problem of Sugar*, Davis-Poynter 1972; T.L.Cleave, G.D.Campbell and N.S.Painter, *Diabetes, Coronary Thrombosis and Saccharine Disease*, 2nd edition, Bristol, Wright 1969. Dental decay is very widespread and its incidence shows a particularly steep social class gradient in childhood; R. Davies, N. Butler and H. Goldstein, *From Birth to Seven*, Longman, 1972.

115. S. Lock and T. Smith, *The Medical Risks of Life*, Harmondsworth, Penguin, 1976, p.36.

116. A.J.Stunkard, 'Obesity and the social environment', in A. Howard (ed.), *Recent Advances in Obesity Research, Proceedings of the First International Congress on Obesity*, 1975.

117. Lock and Smith, *op.cit.* p.38.

118. DHSS, *Present-Day Practice in Infant Feeding*, Report on Health and Social Subjects no. 9, HMSO 1974, p.3.

119. *Ibid*. See also D.P.Addy, 'Infant feeding: a current view', *British Medical Journal*, 22 May 1976, pp.1268-71, for a very useful review of recent research.

120. For a discussion of the serious consequences of this trend in the third world, see chapter three.

121. Of course, food is a political issue of a quite different kind in the underdeveloped world - again, see chapter three.

122. Agricapital Group, *op.cit.*; Technology Assessment Consumerism Centre, *Bread: an Assessment of the British Bread Industry*, Intermediate Publishing Ltd. 1974. The analysis of the bread industry which follows is largely based on these accounts.

123. As Michael Bateman recently pointed out, constipation is 'big business' and British consumers currently spend about £5 million per year on medicines to help them 'to do what should come naturally': *Sunday Times*, Business News, 9 March 1975. In 1976, the Monthly Index of Medical Specialities (MIMS) listed 45 proprietary preparations recommended for constipation: in the USA, over seven hundred such preparations are available. See K. Rutter and D. Maxwell, 'Diseases of the alimentary system: constipation and laxative abuse',

British Medical Journal, 23 October 1976, pp.997-1000.

124. D. Gould, 'Promises, promises: health for sale', *New Scientist*,
13 February 1975.

125. See for example, DHSS, *Prevention and Health: Eating For Health*,
op.cit.

126. Rothman and Radford, *op.cit.* p.266.

127. This point was well illustrated by the recent debate in the EEC about
the relative prices of butter and margarine. Despite the evident
desirability from a health viewpoint of a greater consumption of
margarine, it was argued that margarine prices should be raised simply
to clear the EEC 'butter mountain'.

128. Doyal, *op.cit.*; D.E.Smith, 'The statistics on mental illness (what they
will not tell us about women and why)', in D.E.Smith and S.J.David
(eds.), *Women Look at Psychiatry*, Vancouver, British Columbia,
Press Gang Publishers 1975, pp.73-120.

129. G.B.Hill, 'The expectations of being admitted to a mental hospital
or unit', in DHSS, *Psychiatric Hospitals in England and Wales. In-
Patient Statistics from the Mental Health Enquiry, 1970*, HMSO
1972.

130. S.C.Plog and R.B.Edgerton (eds.), *Changing Perspectives in Mental
Illness*, Holt, Rinehart & Winston, 1969; J. Coulter, *Approaches to
Insanity: A Philosophical and Sociological Study*, Martin Robertson
1973.

131. L.E.Hinkle, 'The concept of "stress" in the biological and social
sciences', *Science, Medicine and Man*, vol. 1, 1973, pp.31-48:
H. Selye, *The Stress of Life*, New York, McGraw Hill 1956; J. Cassel,
'The contribution of the social environment to host resistance',
American Journal of Epidemiology, vol. 104 no. 2, 1976, pp.107-23.

132. See the 'health packets' produced by the Health Movement Organisation. These can be obtained from HMO   c/o Health PAC.,
17 Murray Street, New York, NY 10007.

133. J. Eyer, 'Prosperity as a cause of death', *International Journal of
Health Services*, vol. 7 no. 1, 1977, pp.125-50; J. Eyer and P. Sterling,
'Stress related mortality and social organisation', *Review of Radical
Political Economy*, vol. 9 no. 1, 1977, pp.1-44; J. Eyer, 'Hypertension
as a disease of modern society', *International Journal of Health
Services*, vol. 5 no. 4, 1975, pp.539-58.

3. Health, Illness and Underdevelopment pp.96-137

1. The extent of these omissions is revealed only in rare comprehensive
surveys such as a major health study conducted in Colombia which

showed that, even among recorded deaths, 40 per cent lacked any medical certification: C. Agualimpia, 'Mortality and morbidity', in 'Social science and health planning: culture, disease and health services in Colombia', special issue of *Milbank Memorial Fund Quarterly*, vol. XLVI no. 2 part 2, 1968, pp.61-64; see also 'Childhood mortality in the Americas', *WHO Chronicle,* vol. 28, 1974, pp.277 and 280.

2. C. Elliott, discussion in G.E.W.Wolstenholme and K.M.Elliott (eds.), *Human Rights in Health*, Ciba Foundation Symposium 23, N. Holland, Elsevier-Excerpta Medica 1974, p.32.

3. J. Ford, 'African trypanosomiasis: an assessment of the tsetse fly problem today', in P. Richards (ed.), *African Environment: Problems and Perspectives*, International African Institute 1975, p.69.

4. Since any improvements in data collection are themselves likely to produce higher statistical rates of mortality and morbidity, historical comparisons and those between different countries are very problematic. See J. Bryant, *Health and the Developing World,* Ithaca and London, Cornell University Press 1969, p.33.

5. *Ibid.* p.35.

6. FAO , 'Population, food supply and agricultural development', in *The Population Debate: Dimensions and Perspectives*, Papers of the World Population Conference Bucharest 1974, vol. I, New York, United Nations 1975, p.487.

7. 'Childhood mortality in the Americas', *op.cit.* p.279. It has been claimed that a community is malnourished so long as its children die of measles: 'Measles in the tropics', *British Medical Journal*, 4 December 1976, p.1339. Similarly, many other common diseases such as pneumonia and gastro-enteritis can usually be attributed to malnutrition: see J.C.Escudero, 'The magnitude of malnutrition in Latin America', *International Journal of Health Services*, vol. 8 no. 3, 1978, pp.465-90.

8. R. Revelle, 'Food and population', *Scientific American*, vol. 231 no. 3, September 1974, p.162.

9. 'Foresight prevents blindness', *British Medical Journal*, 3 April 1976, pp.788-89. It is also noted that, in general, the world distribution of blindness approximates closely that of malnutrition.

10. Ministry of Overseas Development, *British Aid and the Relief of Malnutrition*, Overseas Development Paper No. 2, HMSO 1975, p.15.

11. M. Behar, 'Nutrition and the future of mankind', *International Journal of Health Services*, vol. 6 no. 2, 1976, p.316.

12. 'Nutrition and the brain', *British Medical Journal*, 17 June 1978, pp.1569-70; R. Lewin, 'The poverty of undernourished brains', *New Scientist*, 24 October 1974, pp.268-71.

13. 'Sowing the seeds of starvation', *The Guardian*, 6 January 1976.

14. WHO, *Fifth Report on the World Health Situation 1969-1972*, Geneva, WHO 1975, p.15.

15. 'Childhood mortality in the Americas', *op.cit.* p.280.

16. C. Wilcocks and P.E.Manson-Bahr, *Manson's Tropical Diseases*, 17th ed., Baltimore, Williams & Wilkins 1972, p.247.

17. R. Feachem, 'Appropriate sanitation', *New Scientist*, 8 January 1976, p.69.

18. 'The perils of poverty', *New Internationalist*, no. 50, April 1977, p.8.

19. A. Agarwal, 'Malaria makes a comeback', *New Scientist*, 2 February 1978, p.274.

20. *Ibid*. pp.274-77; 'Epitaph for global malaria eradication?', *The Lancet*, 5 July 1975, p.16. For a more detailed discussion, see chapter seven.

21. M. Muller, 'Schistosomiasis: next major health target?', *New Scientist*, 1 January 1976, p.18.

22. J. Ford, *op.cit.* pp.69-71; WHO, *op.cit.* p.11; 'Onchocerciasis - river blindness', *British Medical Journal*, 25 May 1974, p.401.

23. G.T.Stewart, 'Medicine and health: what connection?', *The Lancet*, 29 March 1975, p.705.

24. H.H.Scott, *A History of Tropical Medicine*, vol. I, Edward Arnold 1939, p.1.

25. *Ibid*. pp.88-89.

26. R. Dubos, *Mirage of Health*, New York, Doubleday Anchor 1959, p.74.

27. H.H.Scott, *op.cit.* pp.89-90. With the notable exception of venereal disease, the transmission of infections *from* the Americas does not appear to have been significant. But, as one writer has commented, 'truly the Old World paid back the New with interest for its gift of Syphilis'. G.T.Lescene, 'Brief historical retrospect of the medical profession in Jamaica', *West Indies Medical Journal*, vol. 4 no. 4, 1955, p.225.

28. R. Cornevin, 'The Germans in Africa before 1918', in L.H.Gann and P. Duignan (eds.), *Colonialism in Africa 1870-1960*, vol. 1, Cambridge University Press 1971, p.405.

29. *Ibid*. p.413.

30. See W.O. Henderson, 'German East Africa, 1884-1918', in V. Harlow and E.M.Chilver (eds.), *History of East Africa*, vol. 2, Oxford, Clarendon Press 1965, pp.141-42.

31. A. Beck, *A History of the British Medical Administration of East Africa 1900-1950*, Cambridge Mass., Harvard University Press 1970, p.77.

32. D.F.Clyde, *History of the British Medical Services of Tanganyika*, Dar es Salaam, Government Printer 1962, p.58.

33. *Ibid.*

34. H. Kjekshus, *Ecology Control and Economic Development in East African History*, Heinemann 1977, p.153.

35. A. Beck, *op.cit.* p.77.

36. P.D.Curtin, 'Epidemiology and the slave trade', *Political Science Quarterly*, vol. 83 no. 2, 1968, pp.195-99.

37. R.R.Kuczynski, *Demographic Survey of the British Colonial Empire*, vol. 2, Oxford University Press, 1949 pp.123 and 399.

38. A.E.Brett, *Colonialism and Underdevelopment in East Africa*, Heinemann 1973, pp.71-79.

39. R. Oliver and J.D.Fage, *A Short History of Africa*, 2nd ed. Harmondsworth, Penguin 1966, pp.196-200.

40. E. Berg, 'The development of a labour force in sub-Saharan Africa', *Economic Development and Cultural Change*, vol. 13 no. 4, 1965, pp.404-08.

41. Quoted in G. Omvedt, 'The political economy of starvation', *Race & Class*, vol. 17 no. 2, 1975, p.122.

42. N. Branson and M. Heinemann, *Britain in the Nineteen Thirties*, Panther 1973, p.239.

43. L. Cliffe, 'Rural class formation in East Africa', *Journal of Peasant Studies*, vol. 4 no. 2, 1977, pp.195-224.

44. H. Kjekshus, *op.cit.* p.47.

45. *Ibid.* pp.47-48.

46. E. Berg, *op.cit.* p.398. This is supported by numerous historical accounts of the process of underdevelopment which has occurred in different countries. See, for example, R. Palmer and N. Parsons (eds.) *The Roots of Rural Poverty in Central and Southern Africa*, Heinemann 1977; J. Suret-Canale, *French Colonialism in Tropical Africa 1900-1945*, New York, Pica Press 1971; J. de Castro, *The Geopolitics of Hunger*, Monthly Review Press 1977.

47. H. Kjekshus, *op.cit.* pp.51-68.

48. J. Ford, *The Role of the Trypanosomiases in African Ecology*, Oxford Clarendon Press 1971, pp.478-87.

49. H. Kjekshus, *op.cit.* p.161.

50. The rationale behind this policy will be examined in chapter seven.

51. H. Kjekshus, *op.cit.* pp.162-64; A. McKenzie, 'The native authority dispensary system in Tanganyika Territory', *East African Medical Journal*, vol. 7, 1948, p.273. The appearance of sleeping sickness as a major health problem in Uganda, Rhodesia, Nigeria, the Belgian Congo and French Equatorial Africa is likewise associated with the development of colonialism. See J. Ford, *op.cit.* and J. Suret-Canale, *op.cit.* p. 399.

52. C.C.Hughes and J.M.Hunter, 'Disease and "development" in Africa', in H.P.Dreitzel (ed.), *The Social Organisation of Health*, Collier-Macmillan 1971, p.169.

53. J. Iliffe, *Agricultural Change in Modern Tanganyika*, Nairobi, East African Publishing House 1971, p.30.

54. *Ibid.* p.31. There was, in fact, official recognition in Britain that colonial cash crops were produced at the expense of food crops. Reports cited cases of peasants improving their nutritional status by abandoning the market economy for subsistence farming, and of booming cash crop exports accompanied by desperate local food shortages. *First Report of the Committee on Nutrition in the Colonial Empire*, Part I, Cmnd. 6050, 1939, pp.42 and 47.

55. International Bank for Reconstruction and Development, *The Economic Development of Tanganyika*, Baltimore, Johns Hopkins Press 1961, pp.78-79.

56. M.C.Latham, 'A historical perspective', in A. Berg, N.S.Scrimshaw, and D.L.Call (eds.), *Nutrition, National Development and Planning*, Cambridge, Mass, MIT Press 1973, p.322.

57. International Bank for Reconstruction and Development, *op.cit.* p.27. For a more theoretical formulation, see C. Meillassoux, 'From reproduction to production', *Economy and Society*, vol. 1 no. 1, 1972, pp.101-103.

58. M. Turshen, 'The political economy of health', unpublished Ph.D. thesis, University of Sussex 1975, p.302.

59. E.B.Worthington, *Science in Africa*, Oxford University Press 1938, p.542; G. Edsall, 'The control of communicable disease: problems and prospects', in G.E.W.Wolstenholme and K.M.Elliott (eds.), *op.cit.* pp.180-81.

60. C. van Onselen, *Chibaro: African Mine Labour in Southern Rhodesia, 1900-1933*, Pluto Press 1976.

61. *Ibid.* pp.49-57. In fact, diseases such as pneumonia and scurvy - rare in the rural areas - were explicitly described as 'diseases of employment' by the Medical Director in Rhodesia.

62. J. de Castro, *op.cit.* pp.385-86.

63. C. van Onselen, *op.cit.* p.43.

64. *First Report of the Committee on Nutrition in the Colonial Empire, op.cit.* p.94. The government in fact urged employers to permit their workers to grow their own food. *Ibid.* p.100.

65. See for example, G. St.J. Orde-Browne, *Labour Conditions in East Africa*, Col. no. 193, 1946, pp.52-3.

66. M. Barratt Brown, *After Imperialism*, 2nd ed., Heinemann 1970, pp.168-69.

67. C. van Onselen, *op.cit.* p.125.
68. R. Elling, 'Industrialization and occupational health in under-developed countries', *International Journal of Health Services*, vol. 7 no. 2, 1977, p.219.
69. C. van Onselen, *op.cit.* pp.49-50.
70. *First Report of the Committee on Nutrition in the Colonial Empire*, *op.cit.* Part I, p.69.
72. C. van Onselen, 'Randlords and rotgut 1886-1903', *History Workshop Journal*, no. 2, Autumn 1976, pp.33-89.
73. E. Hobsbawm, *The Age of Revolution*, 2nd ed., Cardinal 1973, p.248.
74. R.R.Kuczynski, *op.cit.* see numerous entries.
75. A. Southall, 'The impact of imperialism upon urban development in Africa', in V. Turner (ed.), *Colonialism in Africa 1870-1960*, vol. 3, Cambridge University Press 1971, p.251.
76. C. van Onselen, *op.cit.* p.178. The only alternative for most women was to brew and sell beer for a living.
77. *First Report of the Committee on Nutrition in the Colonial Empire*, *op.cit.* p.98.
78. J. Berger and J. Mohr, *A Seventh Man*, Harmondsworth, Penguin 1975, p.147.
79. A. Kiev, *Transcultural Psychiatry*, Harmondsworth, Penguine 1972, p.160.
80. C.C.Hughes and J.M.Hunter, *op.cit.* pp.191-99.
81. F. Fanon, *The Wretched of the Earth*, MacGibbon & Kee 1965, pp.203-04.
82. 'Mental illness dogs South African blacks', *The Guardian*, 22 December 1977. The same WHO report attributes a high proportion of mental illness identified in the third world directly to the problems of migration and the splitting-up of families.
83. F. Fanon, *op.cit.* pp.248-50.
84. E. Boserup, *Woman's Role in Economic Development*, George Allen & Unwin 1970, pp.16-18.
85. In fact, the articulation between capitalist and non-capitalist modes of production is crucially based on a sexual division of labour: C.D.Deere, 'Rural women's subsistence production in the capitalist periphery', *Review of Radical Political Economy*, vol. 8 no. 1, 1976, pp.9-17.
86. P. Raikes, 'Rural differentiation and class formation in Tanzania', *Journal of Peasant Studies*, vol. 5 no. 3, 1978, p.309. The absence of men to help in bush clearance also encouraged the advance of the tsetse fly, making some labour reserve areas totally uninhabitable: J. Iliffe, *op.cit.* p.32.
87. In many countries today, 'cephalo-pelvic disproportion' is the greatest

obstetric problem. See, for example, D.A.M.Gebbie, 'Obstetrics and gynaecology', in L.C.Vogel, A.S.Muller, R.S.Odingo (eds.), *Health and Disease in Kenya*, Nairobi, East African Literature Bureau 1974, pp.486-87.

88. *Ibid.* pp.375 and 492.

89. H. Sibisi, 'How African women cope with migrant labor in South Africa', *Signs*, vol. 3 no. 1, 1977, pp.167-77.

90. M. Turshen, *op.cit.* p.308. Today these areas continue to be a major source of migrant labour and they remain the most poverty-striken parts of the country. P. Raikes, *op.cit.* p.292; for an account of the worsening situation of rural women in contemporary Africa, see M. Mueller, 'Women, men, power and powerlessness in Lesotho', *Signs*, vol. 3 no. 1, 1977, pp.155-65.

91. Quoted in E.B.Worthington, *op.cit.* p.543. See also O. Onoge, 'Capitalism and public health: a neglected theme in the medical anthropology of Africa', in S.R.Ingman and A.E.Thomas (eds.), *Topias and Utopias in Health*, The Hague, Mouton 1975, pp.219-32.

92. D. Feldman, 'The economics of ideology: some problems of achieving rural socialism in Tanzania', in C. Leys (ed.), *Politics and Change in Developing Countries*, Cambridge University Press 1967, p.93; S.R. Burstein, 'Public health and prevention of disease in primitive communities', *The Advancement of Science*, vol. 9 no. 5, 1952, p.79.

93. E.B.Worthington, *op.cit.* p.543.

94. U. Maclean, *Magical Medicine*, Harmondsworth, Penguin 1974, p.39.

95. R.R.Kuczynski, *op.cit.* pp.386-92. As in the first world war, the urgent need for African manpower from 1939-45 focussed attention on the appalling state of health of the population, with much disease directly attributed to malnutrition. Moreover, wartime conditions exacerbated all these problems greatly.

96. G. Arrighi and J.S.Saul, 'Nationalism and revolution in sub-Saharan Africa', in *Essays on the Political Economy of Africa*, Monthly Review Press 1973, pp.52-53.

97. F. Cardoso, 'Dependency and development in Latin America', *New Left Review*, 74, 1972, pp.91-95.

98. E. Boserup, *The Conditions of Agricultural Growth*, George Allen & Unwin 1965, pp.117-18. Population growth in the third world is discussed at greater length in chapter seven.

99. UN Department of Economic and Social Affairs, *Demographic Yearbook 1975*, New York, United Nations 1976, pp.142-47.

100. G. Omvedt, *op.cit.* p.118. In most third world countries, moreover, the ownership of productive land is highly inequitable. See K. Griffin, *Land Concentration and Rural Poverty*, Macmillan 1975.

101. Cited in G. Barraclough, 'The great world crisis', part I, *The New York Review of Books*, 23 January 1975, p.26.

102. *Ibid.* p.25.

103. A. de Janvry, 'Material determinants of the world food crisis', *Berkeley Journal of Sociology*, vol. 16, 1976-77, p.14.

104. G. Omvedt, *op.cit.* p.115.

105. L. Richards, 'The context of foreign aid: modern imperialism', *Review of Radical Political Economy*, vol. 9 no. 4, 1977, pp.66-68.

106. See E. Rothschild, 'Food Politics', *Foreign Affairs*, vol. 54 no. 2, 1976, pp.285-307.

107. A. de Janvry, *op.cit.* pp.14-15.

108. As a member of the US National Security Council staff commented in 1974, 'to give food aid to countries just because people are starving is a pretty weak reason'. Cited in L. Richards, *op.cit.* p.50.

109. This often entails the export of skimmed milk surpluses (left over from the manufacture of butter) to the third world. The detrimental effects of this particular form of aid - both economically and in terms of health - are examined below.

110. E. Rothschild, *op.cit.* p.303.

111. *The Guardian*, 8 June 1977.

112. G. Barraclough, *op.cit.* p.26.

113. FAO, *op.cit.* p.486.

114. R. Revelle, *op.cit.* p.163.

115. E. Rothschild, *op.cit.* p.286.

116. K. Bird and S. Goldmark, 'The food aid conspiracy', *New Internationalist*, no. 49, March 1977, p.20.

117. 'Paradox of hunger amid plenty', *The Times*, 2 May 1977.

118. D.B. Jelliffe, 'Commerciogenic malnutrition?', *Nutrition Reviews*, vol. 30 no. 9, 1972, pp.199-205. In addition to baby milk preparations, the author includes semi-solid 'weaning' foods and so-called 'tonic' foods. As will be seen below, many other western food products could be similarly categorised.

119. D.B. Jelliffe and E.F.P. Jelliffe, 'The infant food industry and international child health', *International Journal of Health Services*, vol. 7 no. 2, 1977, pp.249-50. For a more detailed account, see M. Muller, *The Baby Killer*, 2nd ed., War on Want 1975. Although this is the publication which recently attracted attention to the issue, it had already been the subject of barren professional observation for at least twenty years.

120. D.S.McLaren, 'The great protein fiasco', *The Lancet*, 13 July 1974, p.93; and J.P.Berlan, introduction to de Castro *op.cit.* pp.10-15.

121. G. Barraclough, *op.cit.* p.27.

122. North London Haslemere Group, *The Death of the Green Revolution*, Haslemere Group and Third World First 1973; J. Tinker, 'The Green Revolution is over', *New Scientist*, 7 November 1974, pp.388-93; Ministry of Overseas Development, *op.cit.* p.23.

123. D. Wilson, 'The economic analysis of malnutrition', in A. Berg, N.S.Scrimshaw and D.L.Call (eds.), *op.cit.* pp.129-144.

124. M. Anis Alam, 'Science and imperialism', *Race & Class*, vol. 19 no. 3, 1978, pp.249-50.

125. A. Southall, *op.cit.* p.247.

126. G. Arrighi, 'International corporations, labour aristocracies, and economic development in tropical Africa', in G. Arrighi and J.S.Saul, *op.cit.* p.140.

127. C.C.Hughes and J.M.Hunter, *op.cit.* pp.181-82.

128. D.J.Dwyer, *People and Housing in Third World Cities: Perspectives on the Problem of Spontaneous Settlements*, Longman 1975, p.16.

129. WHO, *Fifth Report on the World Health Situation 1969-1972*, *op.cit.* p.39; 'World health losing ground', *The Lancet*, 18 May 1974, 972. In rural parts of the third world, 86 per cent of the population are estimated to have no reasonable access to any form of piped water. R. Feachem, *op.cit.* p.69.

130. D.J.Bradley, 'Water supplies: the consequences of change', in G.E.W.Wolstenholme and K.M.Elliott (eds.), *op.cit.* p.86.

131. R. Feachem, *op.cit.* p.68; 'World health losing ground', *op.cit.* p.972. In India, improved water supplies have taken place without supporting drainage systems and, as a result, the population at risk from filaria (parasitic worms) has actually risen from about twenty million to over one hundred and twenty-five million in some fifteen years. T.R.Tewari, discussion in D.J.Bradley, *op.cit.* p.93.

132. R.F.Stock, *Cholera in Africa: Diffusion of the Disease 1970-1975*, International African Institute 1976.

133. C.C.Hughes and J.M.Hunter, *op.cit.* p.185.

134. K.V.Bailey, 'Malnutrition in the African region', *WHO Chronicle*, vol. 29, 1975, pp.357-58.

135. A. Berg, 'Increased income and improved nutrition: a shibboleth examined', *International Development Review*, vol. 12 no. 3, 1970.

136. R. Barnet and R. Muller, *Global Reach: The Power of the Multi-national Corporations*, Cape 1975, pp.181-82; K.V.Bailey, *op.cit.* p.359.

137. M. Muller, *Tobacco and the Third World: Tomorrow's Epidemic*,

War on Want 1978; *Business Week*, 26 March 1979, pp.39-40.

138. Many third world countries have already become 'pollution havens' for offending industries, notably the petrochemical industry. R. Barnet and R. Muller, *op.cit.* p.345.

139. Cited in H.M.Enzensberger, 'A critique of political ecology', in *Raids and Reconstructions: Essays in Politics, Crime and Culture*, Pluto Press 1976, p.271.

140. United Nations Industrial Development Organisation, *Industrial Development Survey*, New York, UN 1974, pp.288-89.

141. R. Elling, *op.cit.* p.221.

142. E. Eckholm and S.J.Scherr, 'Double standards and the pesticide trade', *New Scientist*, 16 February 1978, p.442. See also, 'Banned at home - but exported', *Business Week*, 12 June 1978, p.152.

143. T. Scudder, 'Ecological bottlenecks and the development of the Kariba Lake basin', in M.T.Farvar and J.P.Milton (eds.), *op.cit.* pp.206-35.

144. C.C.Hughes and J.M.Hunter, *op.cit.* p.169.

145. WHO, *Fifth Report on the World Health Situation 1969-1972*, *op.cit.* p.17.

146. World Bank, *Health Sector Policy Paper*, Washington, World Bank 1975, p.13.

147. M. Muller, 'Schistosomiasis: the next major health target?', *New Scientist*, 1 January 1976, p.20.

148. Capitalist agriculture has depleted soil and woodlands in many countries, causing desertification and making it difficult to conserve moisture. Hence natural sources of water have tended to disappear over the last few decades. T.D.V.Swinscow, 'Primary care: a look at Kenya', *British Medical Journal*, 21 May 1977, p.1337; C. Meillassoux, 'Development or exploitation: is the Sahel famine good business?', *Review of African Political Economy*, vol. 1, 1974, pp.27-33.

4. Public Health, Medicine and the Development of British Capitalism pp.141-76

1. The entire development of the 'welfare state' is often explained in these terms. For criticisms of this approach see D. Wedderburn, 'Facts and theories of the welfare state', in R. Miliband and J. Saville (eds.), *The Socialist Register 1965*, Merlin Press 1965; J.H.Goldthorpe, 'The development of social policy in England 1800-1914', in *Transactions of the 5th World Congress of Sociology*, Louvain, International Sociological Association 1964; V. George and P. Wilding, *Ideology and Social Welfare*, Routledge & Kegan Paul, 1976; P. Corrigan, 'The welfare state as an arena of class struggle', in *Marxism Today*,

vol. 21 no. 3, March 1977, and I. Gough, 'Theories of the welfare state: a critique', *International Journal of Health Services*, vol. 8 no. 1, 1978, pp.27-40.

2. For more information on early nineteenth century British philosophy see E. Halévy, *The Growth of Philosophic Radicalism*, Faber, 1972.

3. V. George, *Social Security and Society*, Routledge & Kegan Paul, 1973.

4. S.G. and E.O.A.Checkland (eds.), *The Poor Law Report of 1834*, Pelican 1974, p.335.

5. B.B.Gilbert, *The Evolution of National Insurance in Great Britain*, Michael Joseph 1966, p.15.

6. For an interesting discussion of the significance of this point see C. Rosenberg, *The Cholera Years: The United States in 1832, 1849 and 1866*, Chicago University Press 1962.

7. E. Chadwick, *Report on the Sanitary Condition of the Labouring Population of Great Britain, 1842*, Edinburgh University Press 1965. This edition has an extremely good introduction by M.W.Flinn.

8. In 1838, for example, Doctors Arnott, Kay and Southwood Smith were given the specific task of investigating the typhoid epidemic 'causing so much destitution throughout London'.

9. Quoted in R.G.Hodgkinson, *The Origins of the National Health Service*, Wellcome Historical Medical Library 1967, p.629.

10. For more details of the medical provisions of the Poor Law see Hodgkinson, *ibid*.

11. S. and B. Webb, *English Poor Law History: Part II: The Last Hundred Years*, vol. 1, Frank Cass 1963, p.32. Cited in M. Turshen, 'The political economy of health with a case study of Tanzania', unpublished Ph.D. thesis, University of Sussex.

12. R.A.Lewis, *Edwin Chadwick and the Public Health Movement*, Longman Green 1952; quoted in J. Robson, *Quality, Inequality and Health Care*, Marxists in Medicine 1977.

13. For a discussion of this struggle see, K. Marx, *Capital*, vol. 1, Harmondsworth, Penguin 1976, chapter ten.

14. For a brief account of these developments see P. O'Higgins, 'Factory legislation', in *The Origins of the Social Services*, New Society 1968.

15. For details of the genesis and content of the 1848 act see, S.E.Finer, *The Life and Times of Sir Edwin Chadwick*, Methuen 1970; A. Briggs, 'Public health: the sanitary idea', in *Origins of the Social Services*, *op.cit.*; and R.A.Lewis, *op.cit.*

16. Turshen, *op.cit.* p.107.

17. R.M.McLeod, 'The anatomy of state medicine: concept and application', in F.L.M.Poynter, *Medicine and Science in the 1860s*, Wellcome Institute of the History of Medicine 1969.

18. B. Ehrenreich and J. Ehrenreich, 'Medicine and social control', *Social Policy*, May/June 1974, pp.26-40. A longer version of the same article appears in J. Ehrenreich (ed.), *The Cultural Crisis of Modern Medicine*, Monthly Review Press 1978.

19. R.M. Young, 'Darwinism and the division of labour', unpublished paper, p.6. For general discussion of the significance of evolutionary theory in the nineteenth century see J.W. Burrow, *Evolution in Society: A Study in Victorian Social Theory*, Cambridge University Press 1966. Also J. Conway, 'Stereotypes of femininity in a theory of sexual evolution', in M. Vicinus (ed.), *Suffer and Be Still*, Bloomington, Indiana University Press 1972; E. Fee, 'The sexual politics of Victorian social anthropology', in M. Hartman and L.W. Banner (eds.), *Clio's Consciousness Raised: New Perspectives on the History of Women*, Harper & Row 1974.

20. L. Gordon, *Woman's Body, Woman's Right*, Harmondsworth, Penguin 1977, p.171.

21. K. Figlio, 'Chlorosis and chronic disease in nineteenth century Britain: the social constitution of somatic illness in a capitalist society', *Social History*, vol. 3 no. 2, 1978 pp.167-97. See also I. Inkster, 'Marginal men: aspects of the social role of the medical community in Sheffield, 1790-1850', in J. Woodward and D. Richards (eds.), *Health Care and Popular Medicine in Nineteenth Century England*, Croom Helm 1977.

22. For a discussion of the organisation of medical care in the nineteenth century see Hodgkinson, *op.cit.*; N. Parry and J. Parry, *The Rise of the Medical Profession: A Study of Collective Social Mobility*, Croom Helm 1977; R.M. Titmuss, 'Trends in social policy: health', in his *Commitment to Welfare*, George, Allen & Unwin 1968.

23. M. Llewelyn Davies (ed.), *Maternity: Letters From Working Women*, Virago 1978, p.24.

24. See Minority Report of the Royal Commission on the Poor Laws, 1909. On maternity provision during this period see also A. Oakley, 'Wisewoman and medicine man: changes in the management of childbirth', in J. Mitchell and A. Oakley (eds.), *The Rights And Wrongs of Women*, Harmondsworth, Penguin 1976; J. Donnison, *Midwives and Medical Men. A History of Inter-Professional Rivalries and Women's Rights*, Heinemann 1977.

25. Figlio, *op.cit.*

26. For discussions of the history of women's labour see, S. Rowbotham, *Hidden From History*, Pluto Press 1973; A. Clark, *The Working Life of Women in the Seventeenth Century*, Frank Cass 1968; I. Pinchbeck, *Women Workers and the Industrial Revolution, 1750-1850*, Frank Cass, 1969; N.J. Smelser, *Social Change in the Industrial Revolution*, Routledge & Kegan Paul 1959.

27. E. Zaretsky, *Capitalism, The Family and Personal Life*, Pluto Press 1976, p.29.

28. Political Economy of Women Study Group, 'Women: the family and industrialisation in Britain', unpublished paper, 1975, p.6.

29. L. Gordon, *op.cit.* p.21. But not all middle-class women lived a life of idle luxury - see, P. Branca, *Silent Sisterhood: Middle Class Women in the Victorian Home*, Croom Helm 1975. See also D. Crow, *The Victorian Woman*, George, Allen & Unwin 1971; F. Basch, *Relative Creatures: Victorian Women in Society and the Novel*, Allen Lane 1974.

30. S.A.Shields, 'Functionalism, Darwinism and the psychology of women: a study in social myth', *American Psychologist*, July 1975, p.740. See also E. Fee, 'Science and the woman problem: historical perspectives', in M.S.Teitelbaum (ed.), *Sex Differences: Social and Biological Perspectives*, New York, Doubleday 1976.

31. Quoted in C. Smith-Rosenberg, 'Puberty to menopause: the cycle of femininity in nineteenth-century America', in Hartman and Banner (eds.), *op.cit.* p.25. See also C. Smith-Rosenberg and C. Rosenberg, 'The female animal: medical and biological views of woman and her role in nineteenth century America', *Journal of American History*, vol. 60 no. 2, September 1973, pp.332-56.

32. This is discussed in more detail in C. Rosenberg, 'Sexuality, class and role in nineteenth century America', *The American Quarterly*, vol. 25 no. 2, 1973, pp.131-54.

33. A belief which of course continues today, see chapter six below.

34. See C. Rosenberg, *op.cit.* for a discussion of this idea.

35. Clitorodectomy was the surgical removal of the clitoris. B. Barker-Benfield, 'Sexual surgery in late nineteenth-century America', *International Journal of Health Services*, vol. 5 no. 2, 1975. But for reservations about the extent of such surgery see R. Morantz, 'The lady and her physician', in Hartman and Banner (eds.), *op.cit.* pp.38-54.

36. Quoted in Smith-Rosenberg, *op.cit.* p.31.

37. W. Acton, *The Functions and Disorders of the Reproductive Organs*, John Churchill 1857. Carl Degler has argued, however, that this view was not adopted by all doctors, and that in any case it is difficult to know what effect such ideas had on individual women: C. Degler, 'What ought to be and what was: women's sexuality in the nineteenth century', *American Historical Review*, vol. 79, 1974, pp.1467-90. For more detailed bibliography on sexuality see note 52.

38. Gordon, *op.cit.* pp.20-21.

39. M. Verbrugge, 'Historical complaints and political disorder. A review of Ehrenreich and English's study of medical ideas about women',

International Journal of Health Services, vol. 5 no. 2, pp.323-33.

40. Morantz, *op.cit*. p.45. See also A. Douglas Wood 'The fashionable diseases: women's complaints and their treatment in nineteenth century America', in Hartman and Banner, *op.cit*.

41. C. Meigs, *Woman: Her Diseases and Remedies*, second edition, Philadelphia, Blanchard & Lea 1851, p.54; quoted in Barker Benfield, *op.cit*. p.279.

42. The use of medical ideology to control women's demands for higher education is discussed in J.N.Burstyn, 'Education and sex: the medical case against higher education for women in England, 1870-1900', *Proceedings of the American Philosophical Association*, vol. 117 no. 2, April 1973, pp.79-84.

43. J. Thorburn, *Female Education from a Physiological Point of View*, London, 1884, p.7; quoted in Burstyn, *op.cit*.

44. H. Spencer, *The Principles of Biology 2*, London 1867, p.486; quoted in Burstyn, *op.cit*.

45. Verbrugge, *op.cit*. p.327.

46. Although, as we have seen, women were frequently warned to rest, there was also a growing belief, especially towards the end of the nineteenth century, that some women were *so* 'idle' that they made themselves ill! See Figlio, *op.cit*.

47. As Showalter and Showalter point out, the 'menstrual myth' did not apply to working-class women: E. Showalter and E. Showalter, 'Victorian women and menstruation', in Vicinus, *op.cit*. pp.38-45.

48. V. Bullough and M. Vogt, 'Women, menstruation and nineteenth century medicine', *Bulletin of the History of Medicine*, vol. 47 no. 1, 1973, pp.70-71.

49. For excellent discussions of the emergence of the 'professional' prostitute see J.R.Walkowitz and D.J.Walkowitz, ' "We are not beasts of the field" : prostitution and the poor in Plymouth under the Contagious Diseases Acts', in Hartman and Banner, *op.cit*.; also J.R.Walkowitz, 'The making of an outcast group: prostitutes and working women in nineteenth century Plymouth and Southampton', in M. Vicinus (ed.), *A Widening Sphere: Changing Roles of Victorian Women*, Bloomington, Indiana University Press 1977.

50. Walkowitz and Walkowitz, *op.cit*. p.192.

51. Prostitution in Victorian society is discussed in some detail in E.M. Sigsworth and T.J.Wyke, 'A study of Victorian prostitution and venereal disease', in Vicinus (ed.), 1973, *op.cit*.

52. P.T.Cominos, 'Innocent *femina sensualis* in unconscious conflict', in Vicinus (ed.), 1973, *op.cit*. p.157. Sexuality in Victorian society is discussed in more detail in E. Trudgill, *Madonnas and Magdalens:*

The Origins and Development of Victorian Sexual Attitudes,
Heinemann, 1976; G.J.Barker-Benfield, *Horrors of the Half-Known
Life: Male Attitudes Towards Women and Sexuality in Nineteenth
Century America*, New York, Harper & Row 1976; J.S.Haller and
R.M.Haller, *The Physician and Sexuality in Victorian America*,
Urbana: University of Illinois Press, 1974; B. Harrison, 'Underneath
the Victorians', *Victorian Studies*, 10, 1967, 239-262; S. Marcus, *The
Other Victorians: A Study of Sexuality and Pornography in Mid-
Nineteenth Century England*, Weidenfeld & Nicholson, 1967; F.B.
Smith, 'Sexuality in Britain 1800-1900: some suggested revisions', in
Vicinus (ed.), 1977, *op.cit.*

53. D. Ozonoff and V.W.Ozonoff, 'Steps towards a radical analysis of
health care - problems and prospects', *International Journal of Health
Services*, vol. 5 no. 2, 1975, pp.299-314.

54. McLeod, *op.cit.*

55. The historical origins and significance of this split are discussed in
more detail in chapter one.

56. A.H.Halsey, *Trends in British Society Since 1900*, Macmillan, 1972.

57. J.R.Hay, *The Origins of the Liberal Welfare Reforms 1906-14*,
Macmillan 1975, p.27.

58. *Ibid*. p.29.

59. C. Booth, *Life and Labour of the People in London*, Macmillan 1902;
S. Rowntree, *Poverty: A Study of Town Life*, Macmillan 1902;
Report of the Interdepartmental Committee on Physical Deterioration,
HMSO 1904, cmnd. 2175. There is a useful discussion of the 'condition
of the people' issue in Gilbert, *op.cit.* pp.59-101.

60. F.W.Clements, 'Some effects of different diets', in S.V.Boyden (ed.),
Impact of Civilisation on the Biology of Man, Toronto, University of
Toronto Press 1968. Arnold White was the first person to use the
famous illustration that three-fifths of the men attempting to enlist in
Manchester in 1899 had to be rejected as physically unfit, see Gilbert,
op.cit. pp.83-84.

61. B. Semmel, *Imperialism and Social Reform: English Social-Imperial
Thought 1895-1914*, George, Allen & Unwin 1960.

62. Gilbert, *op.cit.* p.60.

63. Rowntree, *op.cit.* especially chapter nine.

64. Gilbert, *op.cit.* p.61.

65. R.M.Titmuss, *Commitment to Welfare*, Allen & Unwin 1968, p.232.

66. A. Davin, 'Imperialism and motherhood', *History Workshop*, no. 5,
spring 1978, pp.9-65.

67. *Ibid*. p.10.

68. Social darwinism was still an important strand in early twentieth-

century philosophy. On opposition to school meals see Gilbert, *op.cit.* chapter three.

69. G. Newman, *The Building of a Nation's Health*, Macmillan 1939, pp.194-95.

70. Davin, *op.cit.* p.13.

71. E. Hughes, *Keir Hardie*, Allen & Unwin 1956, p.200.

72. *Report of the Actuaries in Relation to the Proposed Scheme of Insurance Against Sickness, Invalidity, etc.*, 21 March 1910, p.51; quoted in Gilbert, *op.cit.* p.315.

73. For details of the working conditions of doctors during this period see, Titmuss, *op.cit.*; S. and B. Webb, *The State and the Doctor*, Longman & Co. 1910. Shaw's description of Dr Blenkinsop in *The Doctor's Dilemma* provides an extremely graphic illustration of this type of sixpenny doctor: 'He is clearly not a prosperous man. He is flabby and shabby, cheaply fed and cheaply clothed', G.B.Shaw, *The Doctor's Dilemma*, Act I scene I.

74. Gilbert, *op.cit.* p.320. All the information given here on the industrial insurance companies derives from this source.

75. Rowbotham, *op.cit.* p.59.

76. See B.B.Gilbert, *British Social Policy 1914-19*, Batsford 1970. For detailed discussions of aspects of working-class life in Britain between the wars (including health) see N. Branson and M. Heinemann, *Britain in the 1930s*, Weidenfeld & Nicholson, 1971; J. Stevenson (ed.), *Social Conditions in Britain Between the Wars*, Harmondsworth, Penguin 1977; J. Stevenson and C. Cook, *The Slump; Society and Politics During the Depression*, Jonathan Cape 1977.

77. H. Eckstein, *The English Health Service: Its Origins, Structure and Achievements*, Boston, Harvard University Press 1958, p.24.

78. Very little has yet been written on the health of working-class women in the inter-war period, but see the reports on maternal morbidity and mortality by Dr Janet Campbell, issued by the Ministry of Health in 1924, 1927 and 1932. See also M. Spring Rice, *Working Class Wives, Their Health and Conditions*, Harmondsworth, Penguin 1939; and M. Balfour and J.C.Drury, *Motherhood in the Special Areas of Durham and Tyneside*, 1934.

79. For the history of birth control in the nineteenth and early twentieth centuries see, S. Rowbotham, *op.cit.*; L. Gordon, *op.cit.*; P. Fryer, *The Birth Controllers*, Secker & Warburg, 1965; A. McLaren, *Birth Control in the Nineteenth Century*, Croom Helm 1978; J.A.Banks, *Prosperity and Parenthood*, Routledge & Kegan Paul, 1954; J.A. and O. Banks, *Feminism and Family Planning in Victorian England*, Liverpool University Press, 1964.

80. Fryer, *op.cit.* p.236.
81. *Ibid.* p.248.
82. M. Simms, 'The compulsory pregnancy lobby, then and now', *Journal of the Royal College of General Practitioners*, 1975, vol. 25, p.710.
83. The history of British hospitals is dealt with in B. Abel Smith, *The Hospitals 1800-1948*, Heinemann 1964; J. Woodward, *To Do the Sick No Harm: A Study of the British Volunteer Hospital System to 1875*, Routledge & Kegan Paul 1974; and G.M. Ayers, *England's First State Hospitals and the Metropolitan Asylums Board, 1867-1930*, Wellcome Institute for the History of Medicine 1971.
84. Details of developments during this period are given in, Eckstein, *op. cit.*; V. Navarro, *Class Struggle, The State and Medicine. A Historical and Contemporary Analysis of the Medical Sector in Great Britain*, Martin Robertson 1978; and D.S. Murray, *Why A National Health Service? The Part Played by the Socialist Medical Association*, Pemberton Books 1971.
85. H. Macmillan, *Winds of Change*, Macmillan 1966, p.283; quoted in Branson and Heinemann, *op.cit.*

5. The National Health Service in Britain pp.177-214

1. G. Forsyth, *Doctors and State Medicine: A Study of the British Health Service*, Pitman Medical 1966, p.21.
2. J.C. Kincaid, *Poverty and Equality in Britain*, Harmondsworth, Penguin 1973, pp.45-46.
3. *Social Insurance and Allied Services* (Beveridge Report), HMSO, 1942, cmnd. 6404.
4. Kincaid, *op.cit.* p.48.
5. The government's *Surveys of Sickness* showed an increase in the use of GP services by lower income groups in 1945-52. W.P.D. Logan and E.M. Brook, *Survey of Sickness, 1943-1952*, London 1957.
6. P. Corrigan, 'The welfare state as an arena of class struggle', *Marxism Today*, vol. 21 no. 3, March 1977, p.91.
7. For a detailed discussion of these negotiations see, A.J. Willcocks, *The Creation of the National Health Service*, Routledge & Kegan Paul, 1967; H. Eckstein, *The English Health Service: Its Origins, Structure and Achievements*, Cambridge Mass, Harvard University Press 1958; V. Navarro, *Class Struggle, The State and Medicine: An Historical and Contemporary Analysis of the Medical Sector in Great Britain*, Martin Robertson 1978; Forsyth, *op.cit.*; M. Foot, *Aneurin Bevan: A Biography Vol II, 1945-60*, Davis-Poynter 1973.
8. Indeed Bevan is said to have stated that in order to win them over he

'choked their mouths with gold'. J.T.Hart, 'Bevan and the doctors', *Lancet*, vol. 2, 1973, p.1196.

9. M. Turshen, *The British National Health Service: Its Achievements and Lessons for the United States*, Washington DC, Health Service Action 1977, p.31.

10. By 1973, the NHS employed over 1,000 'efficiency experts' of various kinds at a total cost of about £6 million per year. P. Draper and T. Smart, 'Social science and health policy in the United Kingdom: some contributions of the social sciences to the bureaucratisation of the National Health Service', *International Journal of Health Services*, vol. 4 no. 3, summer 1974, pp.453-70.

11. R. Levitt, *The Reorganised National Health Service*, Croom Helm 1976; R.G.S.Brown, *The Changing National Health Service*, Routledge & Kegan Paul, 1973; T. Heller, *Restructuring the Health Service*, Croom Helm 1978. For a discussion of the lack of consumer participation in the debate about reorganisation see P. Draper, G. Grenholm and G. Best, 'The organisation of health care: a critical view of the 1974 reorganisation of the National Health Service', in D. Tuckett (ed.), *An Introduction to Medical Sociology*, Tavistock 1976.

12. Indeed it has been suggested that the doctors came nearer to achieving 'workers' control' than any other group of British workers!

13. H. Rose, 'Participation: the icing on the welfare cake', in K. Jones (ed.), *Year Book of Social Policy in Britain 1975*, Routledge & Kegan Paul 1976.

14. R. Klein and J. Lewis, *The Politics of Consumer Representation. A Study of Community Health Councils*, Centre for Studies in Social Policy 1976.

15. Questions concerning the nature and autonomy of the state are becoming an increasingly important issue in marxist political economy. For the most accessible introduction to the debate see, N. Poulantzas, 'The problem of the capitalist state', and R. Miliband, 'Reply to Nicos Poulantzas', both in R. Blackburn (ed.), *Ideology in Social Science: Readings in Critical Theory*, Fontana 1972. See also C. Offe, 'The theory of the capitalist state and the problem of policy formation', in L. Lindberg et al. (eds.), *Stress and Contradiction in Modern Capitalism*, Lexington Mass, Lexington Books/D.C.Heath 1975. The relevance of this debate for the health sector is discussed in V. Navarro, 'Social class, political power and the state; their implications in medicine' in his *Medicine Under Capitalism*, Croom Helm 1976.

16. I. Gough, 'State expenditure in advanced capitalism', *New Left Review*, 92, 1975, pp.53-92.

17. This should not, however, be taken to imply that they were necessarily *satisfied* with those arrangements. In the case of the 1974 reorganisation, for example, the doctors continued to complain bitterly about the added power given to administrators.

18. Thus it is the high technology specialities to which doctors aspire: C. McLaughlin, 'Career preferences', *Lancet*, vol. 1, 1974, p.870.

19. The most telling recent example of this is perhaps the EMI body scanner, which is eagerly sought by NHS consultants despite its very high cost and very limited usefulness. See B. Stocking and S.L. Morrison, *The Image and the Reality: A Case Study of the Impact of Medical Technology*, Oxford University Press for Nuffield Provincial Hospitals Trust, 1978.

20. For example, it is doctors in those specialities who receive the highest number of so-called 'distinction awards'. See supplement to DHSS Annual Report 1974; also P. Bruggen and S. Bourne, 'Further examination of the distinction awards system in England and Wales', *British Medical Journal*, 28 February 1976, p.536-7.

21. Navarro, 1978, *op.cit.* pp.86-7.

22. Navarro, 1976, *op.cit.* pp.220-21.

23. *Labour Research*, June 1978, p.135.

24. Radical Statistics Health Group, *In Defence of the NHS,* 1977, p.21.

25. Information about membership of private health insurance schemes is provided annually in Lee Donaldson Associates, *UK Private Medical Care, Provident Scheme Statistics*.

26. Radical Statistics Health Group, *op.cit.* p.20.

27. This dependence is, however, being somewhat reduced by the expansion of the private hospital sector: *Labour Research*, June 1978, p.135. For information on the number of beds in the private sector at any given time, the best source of information is the *Reference Book of Registered Nursing Homes*, published by the Registered Nursing Homes Association.

28. Evidence given by the DHSS suggests that in 1971-2 private patients were charged only £1 per week to cover the capital costs of their bed: Fourth Report from the House of Commons Expenditure Committee Session 1971-2, *National Health Service Facilities for Private Patients*, HMSO, 1972. See also Heller, *op.cit.* pp.40-41.

29. Evidence on this is difficult to obtain, but see Fourth Report from the House of Commons Expenditure Committee, *op.cit.*

30. DHSS, *Annual Report 1975*, pp.1-2.

31. Lee Donaldson Associates, *op.cit.* 1973.

32. It is important to realise, of course, that the NHS is able to purchase drugs at a *relatively* low cost compared with prices elsewhere in the

world, largely because of its position as a monopoly purchaser. In 1973, for example, valium cost twice as much in Australia and six times as much in Switzerland as it did in Britain.

33. *Lancet*, vol. 2, 1978, p.946.

34. For general discussion of the multinational drug industry see C. Levinson, *The Multinational Pharmaceutical Industry*, Geneva, International Federation of Chemical and General Workers 1974; Haslemere Group, War on Want and Third World First, *Who Needs the Drug Companies?*, 1976; M. Silverman and P.R.Lee, *Pills, Profits and Politics*, University of California Press 1974. For Britain see J. Robson, *Take A Pill! The Drug Industry - Private or Public?*, Marxists in Medicine, 1972; Labour Party, *The Pharmaceutical Industry - A Discussion Document for the Labour Movement*, 1976. The role of the multinationals in relation to the underdeveloped world is discussed in more detail in chapter seven.

35. *Report of the Committee of Enquiry into the Relationship of the Pharmaceutical Industry with the National Health Service 1965-7*, HMSO, cmnd. 3410, 1967, p.9.

36. It is this process above all, which explains the large numbers of drugs (approximately 7,500) available and prescribed by doctors in the NHS. It is increasingly argued that there is no medical justification for a drug list of this size.

37. C.V.Vaitsos, 'Patients revisited: their function in developing countries', in C. Cooper (ed.), *Science, Technology And Development*, Frank Cass 1973, pp.76-77. See also Monopolies Commission, *A Report on the Supply of Chlordiazepoxide and Diazepam*, HMSO 1973.

38. *Lancet*, vol. 2, 1976, p.680.

39. Silverman and Lee, *op.cit*. pp.30 and 328.

40. S. Lall, 'The international pharmaceutical industry and less developed countries with special reference to India', *Oxford Bulletin of Economics and Statistics*, vol. 36, August 1974, p.155.

41. DHSS, *Health and Personal Social Services Statistics for England 1975*.

42. See chapter six. In 1970, UK doctors wrote about five and a half million prescriptions for valium alone. See also I. Waldron, 'Increased prescribing of valium, librium and other drugs - an example of the influence of economic and social factors on the practice of medicine', *International Journal of Health Services*, vol. 7 no. 1, 1977, pp.37-61.

43. *Report of the Committee of Enquiry into the Relationship of the Pharmaceutical Industry with the National Health Service 1965-7* (the Sainsbury Report), *op.cit*. p.209. Few of these were removed from the market, and a recent estimate by the pharmaceutical industry itself,

suggested that the NHS now spends about £15 million per year on useless drugs: reported in *The Guardian*, 15 May 1975 under heading
'£15 million for useless drugs', and cited in *Who Needs the Drug
Companies?*, *op.cit.* p.13.

44. Radical Statistics Health Group, 'A critique of priorities for health and
personal social services in England', *International Journal of Health
Services*, vol. 8 no. 2, 1978, p.387. It includes a more detailed bibliography on this point.

45. OPCS Mortality Statistics: *Accidents and Violence, Review of the
Registrar General on Deaths Attributed to Accidental and Violent
Causes in England and Wales, 1974*, series DH4 no. 1, HMSO
1976.

46. See for example, DHSS, *Annual Report, 1975*, p.33, for the Roche
Case.

47. Navarro (1978), *op.cit.*, p.89.

48. DHSS, *Report of the Committee of Enquiry into Allegations of Ill-
treatment of Patients and Other Irregularities at the Ely Hospital
Cardiff*, HMSO, cmnd. 3975, 1969; P. Morris, *Put Away*, Routledge &
Kegan Paul 1969; B. Robb, *Sans Everything*, Nelson 1967.

49. Open University, Patterns of Inequality (D302), Unit 13, *Health and
Inequality*, Milton Keynes, Open University Press 1976: J.H.Rickard,
'Per capita expenditure of the English Area Health Authorities',
British Medical Journal, 31 January 1976, pp.299-30; G. Taylor and
N. Ayres, *Born And Bred Unequal*, Longmans 1969; B. Coates and
E. Rawstron, *Regional Variations in Britain*, Batsford, 1971.

50. M.J.Buxton and R. Klein, 'Distribution of hospital provision: policy
themes and resource variations', *British Medical Journal*, 8 February
1975, pp.345-49.

51. J.S.Yudkin, 'Changing patterns of resource allocation in a London
teaching district', *British Medical Journal*, 28 October 1978, pp.1212-
1215.

52. J.T.Hart, 'The inverse care law', *Lancet*, vol. 1, 1971, pp.405-12;
reprinted in C. Cox and A. Mead (eds.), *A Sociology of Medical
Practice*, Collier McMillan 1975.

53. J. Noyce, A.H.Snaith and A.J.Trickey, 'Regional variations in the
allocation of financial resources to the community health services',
Lancet, vol. 1, 1974, pp.554-57.

54. M. Rein, 'Social class and the utilisation of medical care services',
Journal of the American Hospital Association, 43:54, 1969; and M.
Rein, 'Social class and the Health Service', *New Society*, 20 November
1969. See also A. Cartwright and M. O'Brien, 'Social class variations
in health care and in the nature of general practice consultations', in

M. Stacey (ed.), *The Sociology of the National Health Service*, Sociological Review monograph no.22, Keele, University of Keele 1976; and P. Townsend, 'Inequality and the Health Service', *Lancet*, vol. 1, 1974, pp.1179-90.

55. J. le Grand, 'The distribution of public expenditure: the case of health care', *Economica*, vol. 45, May 1978, pp.125-42.

56. Cartwright and O'Brien, *op.cit.*; and A. Howlett and J. Ashley, 'Selective care', *New Society*, 2 November 1972, p.270.

57. A. Cartwright and R. Marshall, 'General practice in 1963: its conditions, contents and satisfactions', *Medical Care* vol. 3 no. 2, 1965, pp.69-87. See also J.R.Butler, J.M.Bevan and R.C.Taylor, *Family Doctors and Public Policy*, Routledge & Kegan Paul, 1973; and J.T. Hart, 1971, *op.cit.*

58. Howlett and Ashley, *op.cit.* p.271.

59. A. Cartwright, *Human Relations and Hospital Care*, Routledge & Kegan Paul, 1964.

60. Cartwright and O'Brien, *op.cit.*

61. But see G. Stimson and B. Webb, *Going to See the Doctor. The Consultation Process in General Practice*, Routledge & Kegan Paul, 1975; A. Cartwright, *Patients and Their Doctors*, Routledge & Kegan Paul, 1967; M. Barrett and H. Roberts, 'Women and their GPs' in B. Smart and C. Smart (eds.), *Women, Sexuality and Social Control*, Routledge & Kegan Paul, 1978.

62. A letter to *The Sun* quoted in H. Roberts, 'Women, medicine and men', a paper given to the British Association for the Advancement of Science Annual Meeting, Bath University, 4-8 September 1978.

63. H. Braverman, *Labour and Monopoly Capital*, Monthly Review Press 1974; and S.A.Margolin, 'What do bosses do? The origins and functions of hierarchy in capitalist production', *The Review of Radical Political Economics*, vol. 6 no. 2, 1974, pp.60-112. See also the special issue of *Monthly Review* devoted to Braverman's work, July/August 1976.

64. See table in Navarro, 1978, *op.cit.* p.74.

65. M.A.Simpson, *Medical Education: A Critical Approach*, Butterworth, 1972. J. Robson, 'The NHS Company Inc? The social consequence of the professional dominance in the National Health Service', *International Journal of Health Services*, vol. 3 no. 3, 1973, pp.413-25.

66. *Royal Commission on Medical Education* (Chairman Lord Todd), HMSO, cmnd. 3569, 1968.

67. An extremely useful and comprehensive account of women workers in the NHS is contained in M.A.Elston, 'Women, equal opportunity and the NHS', an unpublished draft prepared for the Equal Opportunities

332 *The Political Economy of Health*

Commission for evidence to the Royal Commission on the National Health Service, 1977.

68. B. Ehrenreich, 'The health care industry: a theory of industrial medicine', *Social Policy*, vol. 6 no. 3, November/December 1975, p.5. See also V. Navarro, 'Women in health care', *New England Journal of Medicine* 292, 20 February 1975, pp.398-402. In 1976, despite the Equal Pay Act, the average income of women workers in the NHS was still 60 per cent that of men: Elston, *op.cit.* p.21.

69. *British Medical Journal*, 28 February 1976.

70. G.R.Stanley and J.M.Last, 'Careers of young medical women', *British Journal of Medical Education* vol. 2, 1968, pp.204-09.

71. B.R.Bewley and T.H.Bewley, 'Hospital doctors' career structure and the misuse of medical womanpower', *Lancet*, vol. 2, 1975, pp.270-72.

72. *Ibid*. Evidence concerning the distribution of women doctors within the medical hierarchy can be obtained from the annual DHSS *Health and Personal Social Services Statistics*.

73. Berenice Beaumont, 'Training and careers of women doctors in the Thames regions', *British Medical Journal*, 21 January 1978, pp.191-93. Also Medical Women's Federation, *Evidence to the Royal Commission on the NHS*, 1976.

74. For details see DHSS, *The Women Doctors' Retainer Scheme*, HMSO, H.M. circular 72 (42), 1972. For limitations see Beaumont, *op.cit.*

75. Moreover, as Mary Ann Elston has pointed out, the basic intention of the schemes has been to use women to do the more unpopular, non-career jobs, thus reinforcing once again the sexual division of labour both inside medicine and outside it: M.A.Elston, 'Women doctors: whose problem?' in M. Stacey and others (eds.), *Health and the Division of Labour*, Croom Helm 1977.

76. B. Ehrenreich and D. English, *Witches, Midwives and Nurses: A History of Women Healers*, Writers and Readers Publishing Cooperative 1976; B. Abel Smith, *A History of the Nursing Profession*, Heinemann 1960; M. Carpenter, The new managerialism and professionalism in nursing', in Stacey and others, *op.cit.*; and C. Davies, 'Continuities in the development of hospital nursing', *Journal of Advanced Nursing* 2, 1977.

77. Ehrenreich and English, *op.cit.* pp.54-55.

78. Carpenter, *op.cit.* Ironically, one consequence of attempts to improve the 'career structure' of nurses has been greatly to increase the power of men in nursing. Despite their very small number, they have been able to obtain a disproportionate number of senior posts. R.G.S.Brown and R.W.H.Stones, *The Male Nurse*, G. Bell 1973; and R. Dingwall, 'Nursing: towards a male-dominated occupation?', *Nursing Times*, 12 October 1972.

79. S.S.Lewis, 'Nurses and trade unions in Britain', *International Journal of Health Services* vol. 6 no. 4, 1976; P. Bellaby and P. Oribabor, 'The growth of trade union consciousness among general hospital nurses, viewed as a response to 'proletarianisation', *Sociological Review*, vol. 25 no. 4, pp.801-22; and H. McKay, 'Membership patterns and attitudes of hospital nurses', *Nursing Times*, 3 October 1974.

80. A. Sivanandan, *Race, Class and the State: The Black Experience in Britain*, Race & Class Pamphlet no. 1, 1976; G. Hunt, 'A marxist analysis of migration to Britain since 1945', unpublished paper 1977; M. Castells, 'Immigrant workers and class struggles in advanced capitalism. The Western European experience', *Politics and Society*, vol. 5 no. 1, 1975, pp.33-66; S. Castles and G. Kosack, *Immigrant Workers and the Class Structure in Western Europe*, Oxford University Press for the Institute of Race Relations, 1973.

81. F.W.Mackeown, *Hospital Domestic Management Survey*, Association of Hospital Domestic Administrators, 1968. It is important to note, however, that in this survey the 'immigrant' category included black workers, foreign workers and Irish workers, not all of whom should be classified as 'immigrants'. Information on migrant workers in the NHS is very sparse, but much of the official data is available in: Department of Employment, *The Role of Immigrants in the Labour Market*, a project report by the Unit for Manpower Studies, HMSO 1976.

82. Sivanandan, *op.cit.* p.354.

83. For detailed information on this point, including the countries of origin of these nurses, see Department of Employment, *op.cit.* p.136. Also, M. Thomas and J. Morton Williams, *Overseas Nurses in Britain*, PEP Broadsheet 539, 1972.

84. *Department of Employment Gazette*, April 1975.

85. Department of Employment, 1976, *op.cit.* p.63. For a general account of the problems of overseas nurses see A. Wilson, 'Nursing and racism', *Spare Rib*, May 1978, pp.6-9.

86. Carpenter, *op.cit.* p.188. It is always difficult to assess levels of unemployment among women because many are not officially registered as unemployed, but 4,635 SRNs, SENs and certified midwives were so registered in December 1977: *British Medical Journal*, 15 April 1978, p.997.

87. About fifty per cent of overseas doctors in Britain come from the Indian subcontinent: Department of Employment, 1976, *op.cit.* p.58. See also Community Relations Commission, *Overseas Doctors: A Case for Consultation*, 1976.

88. Department of Employment, 1976, *op.cit.* p.58.

89. A. Gamble and P. Walton, *Capitalism in Crisis: Inflation and the State*, Macmillan 1976.

90. White Paper, *Public Expenditure to 1979-80*, HMSO, cmnd. 6393, 1976.

91. Information about these effects remains fragmented and patchy. They are, however, being monitored by the various organisations who are attempting to resist the cuts. See, for example, issues of *Fightback*, the newspaper of the Fightback organisation; also, Counter Information Services/CDP Special Report, *Cutting the Welfare State (Who Profits?)*, CIS Report no. 18, 1977.

92. DHSS, *Sharing Resources for Health in England*, Report of the Resource Allocation Working Party, HMSO 1976.

93. See, for example, Heller, *op.cit.* pp.102-05.

94. Yudkin, *op.cit.* discusses this with particular reference to City and East London Area Health Authority. See also A. Skrimshire, 'Health in Newham', *New Society*, 24 February 1977, p.396.

95. J. Powles, 'On the limitations of modern medicine, *Science, Medicine and Man*, vol. 1, 1973; A.L.Cochrane, *Effectiveness and Efficiency: Random Reflections on Health Services*, Nuffield Provincial Hospital Trust 1972; R. Dubos, *The Mirage of Health*, George, Allen & Unwin 1960; and T. McKeown, *The Role of Medicine: Dream, Mirage or Nemesis?*, Nuffield Provincial Hospitals Trust 1976.

96. DHSS, *Priorities for Health and Personal Social Services in England*, HMSO 1976; DHSS, *The Way Forward*, HMSO 1977.

97. See Radical Statistics Health Group, *op.cit.* 1978.

98. Counter Information Services, *Women Under Attack*, Crisis Report no. 15, 1976; and Elston, *op.cit.* pp.82-87.

99. DHSS, *Prevention and Health: Everybody's Business*, HMSO, 1976. This was followed by *First Report from the Expenditure Committee session 1976/77: Preventive Medicine*, vol. 1, HMSO, 1977; and White Paper, *Prevention and Health*, HMSO, cmnd. 7047, 1977.

100. DHSS, *Priorities for Health and Personal Social Services in England*, *op.cit.* p.22.

101. DHSS, *Prevention and Health: Everybody's Business*, *op.cit.* pp.62-63.

102. *Labour Research*, June 1978, p.136. The *Sunday Times* (4 December 1977) estimated that at least eighty per cent of the patients in the new Wellington Hospital in London are Arabs.

103. *British Medical Journal*, 3 April 1976, p.787.

104. See letter in Heller, *op.cit.* pp.103-4.

105. D. Widgery, 'Unions and strikes in the National Health Service in the United Kingdom', *International Journal of Health Services* vol. 6 no. 2, 1976, pp.301-308; also, T. Manson, 'Management, the professions and the unions: a social analysis of change in the National

Health Service' in Stacey and others, *op.cit.*; and N. Parry and J. Parry, 'Professionalism and unionism: aspects of class conflict in the National Health Service', *Sociological Review*, vol. 25 no. 4, pp.823-41.

106. What such health care would look like remains, of course, a big question. For a preliminary discussion of this issue, see the introduction to J. Ehrenreich (ed.), *The Cultural Crisis of Modern Medicine*, Monthly Review Press 1978.

6. Women, Medicine and Social Control: the Case of the NHS pp.215-38

1. For the recent history of women's participation in the labour force see E. Richards, 'Women in the British economy since about 1700: an interpretation', *History*, vol. 59 no. 197, 1974, pp.337-57; and K.E. Gales and P.H.Marks, 'Twentieth century trends in the work of women in England and Wales', *Journal of the Royal Statistical Society*, 137, part I, 1974, pp.60-74.

2. Department of Employment, *Women and Work: A Statistical Survey*, Manpower paper no. 9, HMSO 1974.

3. V. Beechey, 'Some notes on female wage labour in capitalist production', *Capital and Class*, no. 3, 1977; Revolutionary Communist Group, 'Women's oppression under capitalism', *Revolutionary Communist*, no. 5, 1976; Counter Information Services, *Women Under Attack*, CIS Special Report, 1976; and J. Gardiner, 'Women and unemployment', *Red Rag*, no. 10, 1975.

4. A. Oakley, *Housewife*, Harmondsworth, Pelican 1976; P. Mainardi, 'The politics of housework', in R. Morgan (ed.), *Sisterhood is Powerful*, New York, Vintage Books 1970.

5. E. Wilson, *Women and the Welfare State*, Tavistock, 1977; M. McIntosh, 'The state and the oppression of women', in A. Kuhn and A.M.Wolpe (eds.), *Feminism and Materialism*, Routledge & Kegan Paul 1978.

6. M. Rutter (ed.), *Maternal Deprivation Re-assessed*, Harmondsworth, Penguin 1972.

7. The literature dealing with the nature of that ideology and the processes by which it is inculcated is becoming very large. For a sample of recent British material see J. Chetwynd and O. Hartnett, *The Sex Role System: Psychological and Sociological Perspectives*, Routledge & Kegan Paul, 1978; C. Smart and B. Smart, *Women, Sexuality And Social Control*, Routledge & Kegan Paul, 1978; D.L. Barker and S. Allen (eds.), *Sexual Divisions and Society: Process and Change*, Tavistock, 1976; D.L.Barker and S. Allen (eds.), *Dependence and Exploitation in Work and Marriage*, Tavistock,

1976; S. Allen, L. Sanders and J. Wallis (eds.), *Conditions of Illusion*, Feminist Books, 1974; and S. Rowbotham, *Woman's Consciousness. Man's World*, Harmondsworth, Penguin, 1973.

8. Wilson, *op.cit.* p.151.

9. Chetwynd and Hartnett (eds.), *op.cit.*; P.C.Lee and R.S.Stewart (eds.), *Sex Differences: Cultural and Developmental Dimensions*, Urizen Books 1976; E.E.Maccoby and C.N.Jacklin, *The Psychology of Sex Differences*, Oxford University Press, 1975; S. Sharpe, *Just Like A Girl: How Girls Learn to be Women*, Harmondsworth, Penguin 1976.

10. Sharpe, *op.cit.*; G. Lobban, 'The influence of the school on sex-role stereotyping', in Chetwynd and Hartnett (eds.), *op.cit.*; J. Shaw, 'Finishing school: some implications of sex-segregated education', in Barker and Allen (eds.), *Sexual Divisions and Society: Process and Change, op.cit.*

11. The historical role of 'experts' in telling women what to do is discussed extremely well in B. Ehrenreich and D. English, *For Her Own Good: 150 Years of Experts' Advice to Women*, Pluto Press 1979.

12. G.B.Hill, 'The expectations of being admitted to a mental hospital or unit', in DHSS, *Psychiatric Hospitals in England and Wales. In-Patient Statistics from the Mental Health Enquiry 1970*, HMSO, 1972; S. Lipschitz, 'Women and psychiatry', in Chetwynd and Hartnett (eds.), *op.cit.*; W.R.Gove and J.F.Tudor, 'Adult sex roles and mental illness', *American Journal of Sociology*, vol. 4, 1972.

13. B. Ehrenreich and D. English, *Complaints and Disorders: The Sexual Politics of Sickness*, Writers & Readers Publishing Co-operative 1976; for an alternative feminist view on Freud see J. Mitchell *Psychoanalysis and Feminism*, Allen Lane 1974.

14. M. Barrett and H. Roberts, 'Doctors and their patients: the social control of women in general practice', in Smart and Smart, *op.cit.*

15. Wilson, *op.cit.* p.65.

16. This point is discussed in S. Macintyre, 'Who wants babies?: the social construction of instincts', in Barker and Allen (eds.), *Sexual Divisions and Society: Process and Change, op.cit.*

17. I.K.Broverman and others, 'Sex role stereotypes and clinical judgements of mental health', *Journal of Consulting Psychology*, 34 no. 1, 1970, pp.1-7; also, D. Miller, 'The influence of the patient's sex on clinical judgement', *Smith College Studies in Social Work*, vol. 64 no. 2, February 1974, pp.89-100.

18. M.A.Campbell, *Why Would A Girl Go Into Medicine?*, Old Westbury, New York, The Feminist Press 1974, p.72.

19. This general problem of medical priorities is discussed in N. MacKeith (ed.), *The New Women's Self-Health Handbook*, Virago 1978; and,

Boston Women's Health Book Collective, *Our Bodies Ourselves: A Health Book By And For Women*, British edition by A. Phillips and J. Rakusen, Penguin 1978.

20. A. Oakley, 'Cultural influences on female sexuality', in Allen, Sanders and Wallis (eds.), *op.cit.*; M. McIntosh, 'Who needs prostitutes? The ideology of male sexual needs', in Smart and Smart, *op.cit.*; S. Lydon, 'The politics of orgasm', in R. Morgan (ed.), *op.cit.*; L. Gordon, *Woman's Body Woman's Right. A Social History of Birth Control in America*, Harmondsworth, Penguin 1977, chapter eight; S. Hite, *The Hite Report*, New York, Dell 1977.

21. A.C.Kinsey, W.B.Pomeroy, C.E.Martin and P.H.Gebhard, *Sexual Behaviour in the Human Female*, Saunders 1953.

22. W.H.Masters and V.E.Johnson, *Human Sexual Response*, Boston, Little, Brown 1966.

23. B. James and D.J.Lord, 'Human sexuality and medical education', *Lancet*, vol. 2, 1976, pp.560-63.

24. D. Scully and P. Bart, 'A funny thing happened on the way to the orifice: women in gynaecology textbooks', *American Journal of Sociology*, vol. 78 no. 4, January 1973, pp.1045-50. An expanded version appears in J. Ehrenreich (ed.), *The Cultural Crisis of Modern Medicine*, Monthly Review Press 1978.

25. Scully and Bart, *op.cit.* p.1048.

26. *Ibid.* p.1049.

27. K.J.Lennane and R.J.Lennane, 'Alleged psychogenic disorders in women: a possible manifestation of sexual prejudice', *New England Journal of Medicine*, vol. 288, 1973, pp.288-92.

28. Lennane and Lennane, *op.cit.* p.288.

29. *Ibid.* p.290.

30. G. Stimson, 'Advertisements for drugs', unpublished paper, March 1975. Also M.C.Smith and L. Griffin, 'Rationality of appeals used in the promotion of psychotropic drugs. A comparison of male and female models', *Social Science and Medicine*, vol. 11 nos. 6 & 7, 1977, pp.409-14; J. Prather and L.S.Fidell, 'Sex differences in the content and style of medical advertisements', *Social Science and Medicine*, vol. 9 no. 1, 1975, pp.23-26.

31. Stimson, *op.cit.* pp.9-11.

32. W.H.Trethowan, 'Pills for personal problems', *British Medical Journal*, 27 September 1975, pp.749-751.

33. K. Dunnell and A. Cartwright, *Medicine Takers, Prescribers and Hoarders*. Routledge & Kegan Paul, 1972, pp.111-12; P.A.Parish, 'The prescribing of psychotropic drugs in general practice', *Journal of the Royal College of General Practitioners*, vol. 21, 1971, supplement no. 4.

34. P. Chesler, *Women and Madness*, Allen Lane 1974; S. Lipschitz, 'Women and psychiatry', in Chetwynd and Hartnett, (eds.), *op.cit.*; S.V.Levine and others, 'Sexism and psychiatry', *American Journal of Orthopsychiatry*, vol. 44 no. 3, pp.327-36; N. Weisstein, 'Kinde, Kuche, Kirche as scientific law. Psychology constructs the female', in Morgan (ed.), *op.cit.*; and D.E.Smith and S.J.David (eds.), *Women Look At Psychiatry*, Vancouver, British Colombia, Press Gang Publishers 1975.

35. For example, George Brown and others have shown that psychiatric symptoms in women are related to isolation in the home, to the stress produced by poverty, and to the *lack* of employment, as well as to individual life events such as bereavement: G.W.Brown and T. Harris, *Social Origins of Depression. A Study of Psychiatric Disorder in Women*, Tavistock 1978. Both J. Bernard, *The Future of Marriage*, New York, World Publishing Co. 1972, and Gove and Tudor, *op.cit.* deal with the relationship between marital status and psychiatric illness. See also M. Kimbell, 'Women, sex role stereotypes and mental health: catch 22', in Smith and David (eds.), *op.cit.* pp.121-43; and Chesler, *op.cit.*

36. F. Seton, 'Opening myself to change', *Spare Rib*, 44, 1976, pp.30-32; S. Orbach, *Fat is a Feminist Issue*, Paddington Press 1978; A. Griffith, 'Feminist counselling: A perspective'; R. McDonald and D. Smith, 'A feminist therapy session', and S. David, 'Becoming a non-sexist therapist' - all in Smith and David (eds.), *op.cit.*; and S. Young and L. Goodison, *Self-Help Therapy: A Feminist Perspective*, Women's Press (forthcoming) 1979.

37. They are, however, paid an additional fee for each item of service performed, indicating a continued reluctance to define contraceptive provision as a 'normal' part of the GP's job.

38. *The Guardian*, 6 April 1977; and *Women's Report*, vol. 4 nos. 4 & 5, 1976.

39. Royal College of General Practitioners, *Oral Contraceptives and Health*, Pitman Medical 1974; and 'Mortality among oral-contraceptive users', *Lancet*, vol. 2, 1977, pp.727-31.

40. The relationship between 'population control' and 'family planning' is discussed in L. Gordon, *op.cit.* chapter thirteen.

41. V. Greenwood and J. Young, *Abortion in Demand*, Pluto Press 1976, pp.15-16.

42. K. Hindell and M. Simms, *Abortion Law Reformed*, Peter Owen, 1971; S.J.Macintyre, 'The medical profession and the 1967 Abortion Act in Britain', *Social Science and Medicine*, vol. 7 no. 2, 1973, pp.121-34; and Greenwood and Young, *op.cit.*

43. 'Abortions - public and private facilities', *Labour Research*, May 1977.
44. *Ibid*.
45. OPCS *Registrar General's Supplement on Abortion in 1973*, HMSO 1974.
46. K. Hindell and H. Graham (eds.), *Outpatient Abortion*, Pregnancy Advisory Service, 1974.
47. S. Macintyre, *Single and Pregnant*, Croom Helm 1977.
48. J. Aitken-Swan, *Fertility Control and the Medical Profession*, Croom Helm 1977, p.65.
49. D. Baird, 'The interplay of changes in society, reproductive habits and obstetric practice in Scotland between 1922 and 1972'. *British Journal of Preventive and Social Medicine*, vol. 29, 1975, pp.135-146. Also DHSS, *Report on Confidential Enquiries into Maternal Deaths in England and Wales, 1970-72*, HMSO 1975, p.124; A. Oakley, 'Wise-woman and medicine man: changes in the management of childbirth', in J. Mitchell and A. Oakley (eds.), *The Rights and Wrongs of Women*, Harmondsworth, Penguin 1976.
50. D. Haire, 'The cultural warping of childbirth', in J. Ehrenreich (ed.), *op.cit.*; S. Arms, *Immaculate Deception: A New Look at Childbirth in America*, Boston, Houghton Mifflin 1975; N. Stoller Shaw, *Forced Labour: Maternity Care in the United States*, Pergamon Press 1974; and A. Rich, 'The theft of childbirth', *New York Review of Books*, 2 October 1975.
51. B. Ehrenreich and D. English, *Witches, Midwives and Nurses: A History of Women Healers*, Writers and Readers Publishing Cooperative 1976; J. Donnison, *Midwives and Medical Men: A History of Inter-Professional Rivalries and Women's Rights*, Heinemann 1977; and Oakley, *op.cit.*
52. CSO, *Social Trends*, no. 8, 1977, p.142.
53. M.P.M.Richards (ed.), *The Hazards of the New Obstetrics*, Pitman Medical 1978; 'A time to be born', *Lancet*, vol. 2, 1974, p.1183; M.P.M.Richards, 'Innovation in medical practice: obstetricians and the induction of labour in Britain', *Social Science and Medicine*, vol. 9 nos. 11 & 12, pp.595-602.
54. For women's experiences of induced births see: National Childbirth Trust, *Some Mothers' Experiences of Induced Labour*, London 1975.
55. For a summary of evidence see Richards (1975), *op.cit.*
56. *Ibid*. Also Richards, 1978, *op.cit.*
57. The present trend towards 'technological overkill' in NHS obstetrics co-exists uneasily with a policy of *reducing* expenditure on maternity services and concentrating them into larger units. DHSS, *Priorities for Health and Social Services in England*, HMSO 1976.

58. B. Ehrenreich, 'Gender and objectivity in medicine', *International Journal of Health Services*, vol. 4 no. 4, 1974, pp.617-23; E. Frankfort, *Vaginal Politics*, New York, Quadrangle Press 1972; B. Seaman, *Free and Female*, New York, Doubleday 1972; and C. Dreifus, *Seizing Our Bodies: The Politics of Women's Health*, New York, Vintage 1978.

59. N. MacKeith, *op.cit.*; and Boston Women's Health Book Collective, *op.cit.*

60. For an extremely good feminist guide to pregnancy and childbirth in the British context see C. Beales, *The Childbirth Book*, Turnstone 1978.

61. This is not, of course, to suggest that all women struggling around medical care are united. For an interesting discussion of varying feminist approaches, see E. Fee, 'Women and health care: a comparison of theories', *International Journal of Health Services*, vol. 5 no. 3, 1975.

7. Medicine and Imperialism pp.239-90

1. D. McDonald, *Surgeons Twoe and a Barber*, Heinemann 1950, p.85.

2. G.T.Lescene, 'Brief historical retrospect of the medical profession in Jamaica', *West Indies Medical Journal*, vol. 4 no. 4, 1955, pp.225-26.

3. P.D.Curtin, 'Epidemiology and the slave trade', *Political Science Quarterly*, vol. 83 no. 2, 1968, pp.202-03. In fact, up until the first world war, disease caused far more army casualties than did military combat.

4. H.H.Scott, *A History of Tropical Medicine*, vol. I, Edward Arnold 1939, p.44.

5. Cited in F.R.Sandbach, 'Preventing schistosomiasis: a critical assessment of present policy', *Social Science and Medicine*, vol. 9, 1975, p.102.

6. A. Beck, *A History of the British Medical Administration of East Africa 1900-1950*, Cambridge, Mass., Harvard University Press 1970, p.20.

7. *Ibid.* pp.15-16.

8. G. van Etten, *Rural Health Development in Tanzania: a case study of medical sociology in a developing country*, Assen, Van Gorcum 1976, p.25. Segregation of different racial groups within the medical system was maintained until political independence.

9. A. Beck, *op.cit.* p.14.

10. E.B.Worthington, *Science in Africa*, Oxford University Press 1938, pp.472-82.

11. A.D.King, *Colonial Urban Development*, Routledge & Kegan Paul 1976, p.118.

12. *Ibid.* p.39.
13. A. Southall, 'The impact of imperialism upon urban development in Africa', in V. Turner (ed.), *Colonialism in Africa 1870-1960*, vol. 3, Cambridge, Cambridge University Press 1971, p.242.
14. A. King, *op.cit.* p.71.
15. J.S.Mangat, *A History of the Asians in East Africa*, Oxford University Press 1969, p.100.
16. F. Fanon, *The Wretched of the Earth*, MacGibbon & Kee 1965, p.34.
17. A. Beck, *op.cit.* p.25.
18. *Ibid.*
19. J.S.Mangat, *op.cit.* p.112.
20. E.B.Worthington, *op.cit.* chapter fifteen.
21. A. Beck, *op.cit.* p.32.
22. *Ibid.* p.41.
23. F. Sandbach, *op.cit.*, p.523.
24. Quoted in A. Beck, *op.cit.* p.107.
25. H. Kjekshus, *Ecology Control and Economic Development in East African History*, Heinemann 1977, pp.168-76.
26. J. Ford, 'African trypanosomiasis: an assessment of the tsetse fly problem today', in P. Richards (ed.), *African Environment: Problems and Perspectives*, International African Institute 1975, p.70.
27. H. Kjekshus, *op.cit.* pp.175-76.
28. E.A.Brett, *Colonialism and Underdevelopment in East Africa*, Heinemann 1973, p.301.
29. J. Lonsdale, 'Some origins of nationalism in Tanzania', in L. Cliffe and J.S.Saul, *Socialism in Tanzania*, vol. I, Nairobi, East African Publishing House 1972, p.26.
30. E.A.Brett, *op.cit.* p.67.
31. L. Cliffe, 'Nationalism and the reaction to enforced agricultural change in Tanganyika during the colonial period', in L. Cliffe and J.S.Saul (eds.), *op.cit.* p.17.
32. G. van Etten, *op.cit.* p.20.
33. D. McDonald, *op.cit.* p.223.
34. G. van Etten, *op.cit.* p.28.
35. A. Beck, *op.cit.* p.203.
36. A. McKenzie, 'The native authority dispensary system in Tanganyika Territory', *East African Medical Journal*, vol. 7, 1948, pp.273-74.
37. *Ibid.*
38. A. Beck, *op.cit.* p.129.
39. Fanon has provided the most cogent account of the deep ambivalence experienced by a colonised people towards the encroachment of western medicine as part of a wider system of oppression. F. Fanon, 'Medicine

and colonialism', in J. Ehrenreich (ed.), *The Cultural Crisis of Modern Medicine*, Monthly Review Press 1978, pp.229-51. A related factor is the remarkable tenacity of traditional forms of medicine throughout the third world. The practices and concepts of traditional medicine continue to answer people's felt needs at least as adequately as modern medicine. See for instance, U. Maclean, *Magical Medicine*, Harmondsworth, Penguin Books 1971. Moreover, to put the uniquely 'scientific' claims of western medicine into some perspective in relation to other systems, see J.N.Riley, 'Western medicine's attempt to become more scientific: examples from the United States and Thailand', *Social Science and Medicine*, vol. 11, 1977, pp.549-60; also, C. Leslie (ed.), *Asian Medical Systems: A Comparative Study*, Berkeley, University of California Press 1976.

40. T.W.J.Schulpen, *Integration of Church and Government Medical Services in Tanzania*, Nairobi, African Medical and Research Foundation 1975, p.227.

41. Rev. J.S. Dennis, *Christian Missions and Social Progress*, vol. 2, Oliphant, Anderson and Ferrier 1899, p.406.

42. A. Beck, *op.cit.* p.55.

43. R. Oliver, *The Missionary Factor in East Africa*, Longman 1952, p.211.

44. T.W.J.Schulpen, *op.cit.* p.52.

45. *Ibid.* p.100.

46. *Ibid.* p.80.

47. T.W.J.Schulpen, *op.cit.* p.98.

48. *Ibid.* p.42.

49. Quoted in A. Beck *op.cit.* p.80.

50. Quoted in E.R.Wicker, 'Colonial development and welfare, 1929-1957', *Social and Economic Studies*, vol. 7 no. 4, 1958, p.174.

51. *Colonial Development Advisory Committee, 2nd Interim Report*, cmnd. 3876 of 1931, cited in E.A.Brett, *op.cit.* p.133.

52. O. Gish, *Planning the Health Sector*, Croom Helm 1975, p.16.

53. G. van Etten, *op.cit.* p.34.

54. W.K.Chagula and E. Tarimo, 'Meeting basic health needs in Tanzania', in K.W.Newell (ed.), *Health by the People*, Geneva, WHO 1975, pp.148-49.

55. Cited in O. Gish, *op.cit.* p.17.

56. G. van Etten, 'Towards research on health development in Tanzania', *Social Science and Medicine*, vol. 6, 1972, p.339.

57. J. Bryant, *Health and the Developing World*, Cornell University Press 1969, p.39.

58. M. Segall, 'The politics of health in Tanzania', *Development and Change*, vol. 4 no. 1, 1972, p.39.

59. G. van Etten, *op.cit.* p.51; F.T.Sai, 'Ghana', in I. Douglas-Wilson and G. McLachlan (eds.), *Health Service Prospects*, The Lancet and the Nuffield Provincial Hospitals Trust 1973, p.138; S. Scott Plummer, 'Widening the battle against disease', *The Times*, 22 July 1976; R. Jeffery, 'Allopathic medicine in India: a case of deprofessionalization?', *Social Science and Medicine*, vol. 11, 1977, pp.564-65.

60. D.K.Zschock, 'Economic aspects of health needs in Colombia', 'Social science and health planning: culture, disease and health services in Colombia', special issue of *The Milbank Memorial Fund Quarterly*, vol. 46 no. 2, part 2, April 1968, pp.223-24.

61. For a debate on the nature of the state in the capitalist periphery see, for example, H. Alavi, 'The state in post-colonial societies: Pakistan and Bangladesh', *New Left Review*, 74, 1972, pp.59-81; C. Leys, 'The "overdeveloped" post colonial state: a re-evaluation', *Review of African Political Economy*, no. 5, 1976, pp.39-48; W. Ziemann and M. Lanzendörfer, 'The state in peripheral societies', *The Socialist Register 1977*, (ed.), R. Miliband and J. Saville, Merlin Press 1977, pp.143-77.

62. F. Fanon, *op.cit.* p.122.

63. W.D.Foster, 'Makerere medical school: 50th anniversary', *British Medical Journal*, 14 September 1974, p.677. Similar distinctions continue to operate in some African countries today. See R. Frankenberg and J. Leeson, 'The sociology of health dilemmas in the post-colonial world', in E. de Kadt and G. Williams (eds.), *Sociology and Development*, Tavistock 1974, p.268.

64. W.D.Foster, *op.cit.*

65. A. Beck, *op.cit.* p.162. Whereas in earlier decades the colonial service had been an important safety valve for doctors facing the insecurities of medical practice in Britain. T.J.Johnson and M. Caygill, 'The BMA and its overseas branches: a short history', *Journal of Imperial and Commonwealth History*, vol. 1 no. 3, 1973, p.306.

66. O. Gish, *op.cit.* p.20.

67. Though we refer here to former British colonies, a similar process occurred in all underdeveloped countries, varying in detail according to the dominant imperialist power. See V. Navarro, 'The political and economic origins of the underdevelopment of health in Latin America' in *Medicine Under Capitalism*, Croom Helm 1976, p.10 and P.J.Donaldson, 'Foreign intervention in medical education: a case study of the Rockefeller Foundation's involvement in a Thai medical school', *International Journal of Health Services*, vol. 6 no. 2, 1976, pp.251-70.

68. A.M.Raikes, 'Medical education in transition: Tanzania', in

344 *The Political Economy of Health*

S.R.Ingman and A.E.Thomas (eds.), *Topias and Utopias in Health*, The Hague, Mouton 1975, p.166.

69. Cited in F. Fanon, *op.cit.* p.245.

70. *Ibid.* p.242.

71. A.M.Raikes, *op.cit.* pp.166-67.

72. *Ibid.* p.168.

73. E. Boserup, *Women's Role in Economic Development*, George Allen & Unwin 1970, pp.125-30.

74. T. Johnson, 'Imperialism and the professions', in P. Halmos (ed.), *Professionalization and Social Change*, Sociological Review Monograph no. 20, University of Keele 1973, p.297.

75. P. Ramalingaswami and V. Ramalingaswami, 'India' in I. Douglas-Wilson and G. McLachland (eds.), *op.cit.* pp.186-87.

76. V. Navarro, *op.cit.* p.20.

77. World Bank, *Health Sector Policy Paper*, Washington, World Bank 1975, p.45.

78. O. Gish, 'Medical brain drain revisited', *International Journal of Health Services*, vol. 6 no. 2, 1976, p.233.

79. O. Gish and M. Godfrey, 'Why did the doctor cross the road?', *New Society*, 17 March 1977, p.539.

80. V. Navarro, *op.cit.* p.14.

81. B. Senewiratne, 'Emigration of doctors: a problem for the developing and the developed countries', part I, *British Medical Journal*, 15 March 1975, p.619.

82. O. Gish, *Doctor Migration and World Health*, G. Bell & Sons 1971, p.139; see also, M. Manning, 'Problems of third world nurses', *Nursing Mirror*, 22 July 1976, p.40.

83. J. Bryant, *op.cit.* pp.157-58.

84. Quoted in M.J.Sharpston, 'Health and development', *Journal of Development Studies*, vol. 9 no. 3, 1973, p.459.

85. O. Gish, *Planning the Health Sector*, *op.cit.* p.74.

86. A. Portes, 'Migration and underdevelopment', *Politics and Society*, vol. 8 no. 1, 1978, pp.17-23.

87. David Ennals, in address to the Association of Nurse Administrators in London, 16 October 1976, quoted in *Nursing Times*, 4 November 1976, p.1698.

88. O. Gish, *Planning the Health Sector*, *op.cit.* p.172.

89. 'WHO in attack on drug firms', *The Guardian*, 30 January 1978. In spite of this there are still serious shortages of essential drugs in most countries and in India, for example, 80 per cent of the population have no access to drugs at all. S. Lall, 'Medicines and multinationals', *Monthly Review*, vol. 28 no. 10, 1977, p.28.

90. The Haslemere Group, *Who Needs the Drug Companies?*, Haslemere Group, War on Want and Third World First 1976, p.9.

91. 'WHO in attack on drug firms', *op.cit*. Many of the poorest countries, of course, have no drug manufacturing facilities at all.

92. C. Vaitsos, 'Patents revisited: their function in developing countries', in C. Cooper (ed.), *Science, Technology and Development*, Frank Cass 1973, p.78.

93. B.V.Rangarao, 'Foreign technology in the Indian pharmaceutical industry', paper at International Seminar on Technology Transfer, New Delhi, 11-13 December 1972, pp.6-7. See also, C. Barker, 'Pharmaceutical production in a less developed country', unpublished paper 1975, p.2.

94. C. Vaitsos, 'The process of commercialization of technology in the Andean Pact', in H. Radice (ed.), *International Firms and Modern Imperialism*, Harmondsworth, Penguin 1975, p.195.

95. C. Vaitsos, 'Patents revisited . . .' *op.cit*. p.86.

96. M. Silverman, 'The epidemiology of drug promotion', *International Journal of Health Services*, vol. 7 no. 2, 1977, p.162.

97. J.S.Yudkin, 'To plan is to choose', unpublished mimeo., University of Dar es Salaam 1977, p.9.

98. J.S.Yudkin, 'Provision of medicines in a developing country', *The Lancet*, 15 April 1978, pp.810-11. In addition to propaganda and 'normal' inducements to doctors, there have also been many reports from the third world of efforts by pharmaceutical firms to manipulate health policy at the highest levels through bribery of administrators and ministry officials: *ibid*. p.811. M. Muller, 'Selling health - or buying favour?', *New Scientist*, 3 February 1977, pp.266-68.

99. M. Silverman, *op.cit*. p.159. Similar observations have been made elsewhere in the third world, see J.S.Yudkin, 'Provision of medicines', *op.cit*. p.811.

100. J.S.Yudkin, 'Provision of medicines', *op.cit*.; 'Latin American drug sales criticised', *New York Times*, 17 August 1975.

101. *Ibid*.

102. M. Dunne, A. Herxheimer, M. Newman, and H. Ridley, 'Indications and warnings about chloramphenicol', *The Lancet*, 6 October 1973, pp.781-83; E.S.Anderson, 'Medicines to match the market?', *New Scientist*, 27 January 1977, pp.194-96.

103. M. Silverman, *op.cit*. p.163. 'Danger behind the modern cure-all', *The Guardian*, 16 June 1975.

104. M. Muller, 'Roche in the third world', *New Scientist*, 12 August 1976, p.327.

105. M. Muller, 'Drug companies and the third world', *New Scientist*, 29 April 1976, p.217.

106. *Ibid*. p.216. 'The drug industry's clouded future', *Business Week*, 23 November 1974, pp.66-67. Through the production of fertilisers, pesticides and feed additives, the pharmaceutical industry also impinges significantly on third world agriculture. See M. Turshen, 'An analysis of the medical supply industries', *International Journal of Health Services*, vol. 6 no. 2, 1976, pp.286-96. As noted in chapter three, however, improved output has benefited cash crops rather than food for local consumption, while the toxicity of the chemicals themselves is an important new health hazard for rural populations.

107. 'When sickness is a way of life', *Financial Times*, 1 July 1976.

108. M. Segall, 'Pharmaceuticals and health planning in developing countries', unpublished paper 1975, p.12.

109. Speech by S.J.Lloyd, reported in *News from The British Hospital Equipment Display Centre*, 27 October 1975; Medical Equipment Survey, *Financial Times*, 26 January 1978, p.35.

110. DHSS, *Annual Report 1975*, HMSO 1976, p.7.

111. Medical Equipment Survey, *op.cit.* p.33.

112. R. Murray, 'The internationalization of capital and the nation state', *New Left Review*, 67, 1971, p.92.

113. Ministry of Overseas Development, *The Changing Emphasis in British Aid Policies: More Help for the Poorest*, cmnd. 6270, HMSO 1975. This is in line with current accepted wisdom among international aid and development organisations. Its rationale and likely success are examined below.

114. A. White, *British Official Aid in the Health Sector*, IDS Discussion Paper no. 107, Brighton, University of Sussex 1977, pp.10-12. Multilateral aid is that allocated for dispersal by organisations such as WHO, UNICEF, the World Food Programme, the UN Fund for Population Activities, etc. In addition to official aid, voluntary agencies allocate a high proportion of their funds to the health field. Indeed, their annual contribution (about £8 million in 1973-74) is not much less than that of the government. S. Cole-King, *Health Sector Aid from Voluntary Agencies: the British case study*, IDS Discussion Paper no. 97, Brighton, University of Sussex 1976, p.18.

115. A. White, *op.cit.* p.1.

116. *Ibid*. p.26.

117. *Ibid*. p.33. This refers to British government aid. Voluntary agencies devote a higher proportion of their funds to primary care. On the other hand, almost half of their health aid takes the form of highly skilled expatriate medical personnel, tending to reinforce dependence

on the western clinical model. S. Cole-King, *op.cit.* pp.29-71.

118. A. White, *op.cit.* p.38.

119. Segall estimates that the annual running costs of a hospital amount to at least 25 per cent of the capital costs. M. Segall, 'The politics of health in Tanzania', *op.cit.* p.44.

120. In Colombia 1961-65, 'international assistance' averaged one per cent of all national health expenditure. 'Social science and health planning: culture, disease and health services in Colombia', *op.cit.* p.225. A notable exception, however, is Tanzania, where about 75 per cent of the capital budget for 1973-74 was expected to come from external sources. This appears to arise from an unusual coalescence of interests between 'progressive' donors (notably Sweden) and a 'progressive' but non-revolutionary recipient. O. Gish, *Planning the Health Sector, op.cit.* pp.189-93.

121. A. White, *op.cit.* p.45. Though a shift in emphasis may yet occur, the indications are not promising. See C. Whittemore, *The Doctor-Go-Round*, Oxfam Public Affairs Unit 1976, pp.13-14. Aid must be seen in relation to the commercial activities of the DHSS on behalf of the highly technological medical equipment industry. This is not only antithetical to the needs of the poor, but also requires the back-up of traditional forms of aid: 'Our ability to sell our products will often turn on our ability to arrange to provide the matching human resources. In this respect the UK is potentially particularly well placed. The NHS is much admired overseas and the health professions in this country have a long tradition of active participation in promoting the interchange of knowledge and skills between this country and others'. DHSS, *Health Circular*, HC(76)56, 1976. This form of 'assistance' is directly adjunct to the supply of capital goods and, indeed, Britain's own system of medical education is ill equipped to provide assistance of any other kind.

122. F. Sandbach, *op.cit.* p.523.

123. 'Epitaph for global malaria eradication?', *The Lancet,* 5 July 1975, p.15.

124. U.S. International Development Advisory Board, summary minutes, 13 April 1956, cited in H. Cleaver, 'Malaria, the politics of public health and the international crisis', *Review of Radical Political Economy*, vol. 9 no. 1, 1977, p.91.

125. K. Davis, 'The amazing decline of mortality in underdeveloped areas', *American Economic Review*, vol. 46, 1956, p.305; S.A. Meegama, 'Malaria eradication and its effects on mortality levels', *Population Studies*, vol. 21 no. 3, 1967.

126. H. Cleaver, *op.cit.* pp.82 and 101.

127. A. Agarwal, 'Malaria makes a comeback', *New Scientist*, 2 February 1978, p.274.

128. H. Cleaver, *op.cit.* p.83.

129. F. Brockington, *World Health*, 5th ed., Churchill Livingstone 1975, p.177.

130. M.I.Roemer, 'Organisational issues relating to medical priorities in Latin America', *Social Science and Medicine*, vol. 9, 1975, p.94.

131. WHO, *Fifth Report on the World Health Situation 1969-72*, Geneva, WHO 1975, p.19.

132. G. Arrighi and J.S.Saul, 'Nationalism and revolution in sub-Saharan Africa', in *Essays on the Political Economy of Africa*, Monthly Review Press 1973, p.50.

133. World Bank, *op.cit.* p.26.

134. *Ibid.* p.25.

135. M.I.Roemer, *op.cit.* pp.95-96.

136. 'Social science and health planning: culture, disease and health services in Colombia', *op.cit.* p.131.

137. F. Paukert, 'Social security and income redistribution: a comparative study', *International Labor Review*, vol. 98 no. 5, 1968, p.449.

138. The mechanisms by which this occurs are described in J. Segovia and O.J.Gomez, 'Implicit versus explicit goals: medical care in Argentina', in S.R.Ingman and A.E.Thomas (eds.), *op.cit.* pp.244-45.

139. World Bank, *op.cit.* p.31.

140. R.T.Ravenholt, 'USAID contributions to international population programs', *International Journal of Health Services*, vol. 3 no. 4, 1973, p.641.

141. B. Mass, *Population Target*, Toronto, Women's Press 1976, p.56.

142. *Ibid.* p.160. Approximately half of Britain's multilateral aid contributions are devoted to population control, in addition to a growing bilateral aid programme in this field. A. White, *op.cit.* p.12. Ministry of Overseas Development, *op.cit.* p.26.

143. D. Banerji, 'Population planning in India: national and foreign priorities', *International Journal of Health Services*, vol. 3 no. 4, 1973, p.774.

144. S. Ahmad, 'Population myths and realities', *Race & Class*, vol. 19 no. 1, 1977, p.25.

145. Such countries are usually strategic bastions of western capitalism and often in receipt of substantial U.S. aid as well as industrial investment.

146. M. Potts, P. Diggory, and J. Peel, *Abortion*, Cambridge, Cambridge University Press 1977, p.102.

147. *Ibid.* p.449.

148. P. Vaughan, *The Pill on Trial*, Harmondsworth, Penguin 1972.

149. L. Parveen, A.Q.Chowdhury, and Z. Chowdhury, 'Injectable contraception in rural Bangladesh', *The Lancet*, 5 November 1977, p.947.

150. *Ibid.* pp.947-48.

151. M.A.Qadeer, 'Why family planning is failing', *Social Policy*, vol. 6 no. 3, 1975, p.22.

152. M. Mamdani, *The Myth of Population Control*, Monthly Review Press 1972, p.43.

153. *Ibid.* pp.103-04.

154. C. Meillassoux, 'From reproduction to production', *Economy and Society*, vol. 1 no. 1, 1972, pp.99-101.

155. D.A.M.Gebbie, 'Obstetrics and gynaecology', in L.C.Vogel, A.S. Muller, and R.S.Odingo (eds.), *Health and Disease in Kenya*, Nairobi, East African Literature Bureau 1974, p.494.

156. World Bank, *op.cit.* p.42. See also K.W.Newell (ed.), *Health by The People*, Geneva, WHO 1975; and A. Agarwal, 'New strategy for world health', *New Scientist*, 22 June 1978, pp.821-23. 'Health services can bring tangible benefits to rural populations which cannot be as rapidly achieved in other sectors of development', B. Abel-Smith, *op.cit.* p.182. Health provision is increasingly being seen as a substitute for economic development.

157. A. Benyoussef and B. Christian, 'Health care in developing countries', *Social Science and Medicine*, vol. 11, 1977, p.401.

158. World Bank, *op.cit.* p.25.

159. In a single health symposium organised by the Ciba Foundation, at least half of the dozen contributors poured lavish praise on Chinese health policies. See G.E.W.Wolstenholme and K.M.Elliott, *op.cit.*

160. H.A.Ronaghy and S. Solter, 'Is the Chinese "barefoot doctor" exportable to Iran?', *The Lancet*, 29 June 1974, p.1331.

161. *Ibid.* pp.1331-33.

162. G. van Etten, *op.cit*: pp.114-36. See also, D. Banerji, 'Health behaviour of rural populations; impact of rural health services', *Economic and Political Weekly*, vol. 8, 22 December 1973, pp.2261-68; and P. Harrison, 'Basic health delivery in the third world', *New Scientist*, 17 February 1977, pp.411-13.

163. See for example, J.M.Bengoa, 'The significance of malnutrition and priorities for prevention', in A. Berg, N.S.Scrimshaw, D.L.Call (eds.), *Nutrition, National Development and Planning*, Cambridge Mass, MIT Press 1973, pp.110-25.

164. *Ibid.*

Postscript: The Struggle for a Healthier Society pp.291-7

1. The issues raised in this postscript owe a great deal to the discussions of the Politics of Health Group, and particularly to a summary of those discussions contained in Mick Carpenter's forthcoming paper, 'Left orthodoxy and the politics of health'.

2. M. Carpenter, *op.cit.* p.9.

3. J. Ehrenreich, Introduction to *The Cultural Crisis of Modern Medicine*, New York, Monthly Review Press 1978, p.27.

4. See M. Carpenter, *op.cit.* p.23.

Index

354 *The Political Economy of Health*